# The
# PLANTATION SOUTH

What was life really like on the great plantations of the ante-bellum South? The best answer, or answers, to this often asked question surely lies in the records left by those who knew that life at first hand; those Southerners who created and lived it; those Northerners and foreigners who traveled and visited in the South.

In her new anthology *The Plantation South* Katharine Jones has sought out just such accounts and records. She has selected from forty-seven different writers, more than half of them Southerners, the remainder visitors from the North or from abroad. She has combined them, with the skill that made her *Heroines of Dixie* so moving a characterization of the Southern woman during the War between the States, to form a fascinating, composite picture of a vanished way of life. Not one South, certainly not *the* South, emerges through the writings of Miss Jones's accomplished observers or unself-conscious historians. We see instead a startling and illuminating confirmation of this comment by a young Northerner who lived for a year in Mississippi. "I found that the South one reads and hears of is altogether different from the one that one sees and becomes acquainted with."

The anthology covers a vast range in both time and geography. The earliest account is dated 1799, the year in which the nation mourned the death of George Washington, and the last one was written in 1861 by a British journalist who had come to report for his newspaper on the new nation, the Confederate States of America.

# The Plantation South

1. *Topping Castle*, near Fredericksburg, Virginia
2. *Mantua*, King and Queen County, Virginia
3. *Bellevue*, King and Queen County
4. *Brandon*, on the James River, Virginia
5. *Monticello*, Charlottesville, Virginia
6. *Shirley*, near Petersburg, Virginia
7. *Cabell's Dale*, near Lexington, Kentucky
8. *The Hermitage and Overton Lodge*, Nashville, Tennessee
9. *Bellamy House*, near Wilmington, North Carolina
10. *Millwood*, near Columbia, South Carolina
11. *Sans Soucie*, near Greenville, South Carolina
12. *The White House*, near Georgetown, South Carolina
13. *Pimlico*, near Charleston, South Carolina
14. *Belmont*, near Augusta, Georgia
15. *The Hermitage*, near Savannah, Georgia
16. *Hopeton*, Darien, Georgia
17. *Hamilton*, St. Simon's Island, Georgia
18. *Pine Hill*, Leon County, Florida
19. *Ortega*, Lake Monroe, Florida
20. *Woodlands*, near Claiborne, Alabama
21. *Gaineswood*, Marengo County, Alabama
22. *Ridge House and Willow Dale*, Yazoo County, Mississippi
23. *Burleigh*, Hinds County, Mississippi
24. *Briarfield, Melrose and Dunleith*, Natchez, Mississippi
25. *Chateau de Clery*, near Baton Rouge, Louisiana
26. *Houmas House*, near Burnside, Louisiana
27. *The Shadows*, near New Iberia, Louisiana
28. *China Grove*, Brazoria County, Texas
    *And many others*

Tex.

La.

Gulf of

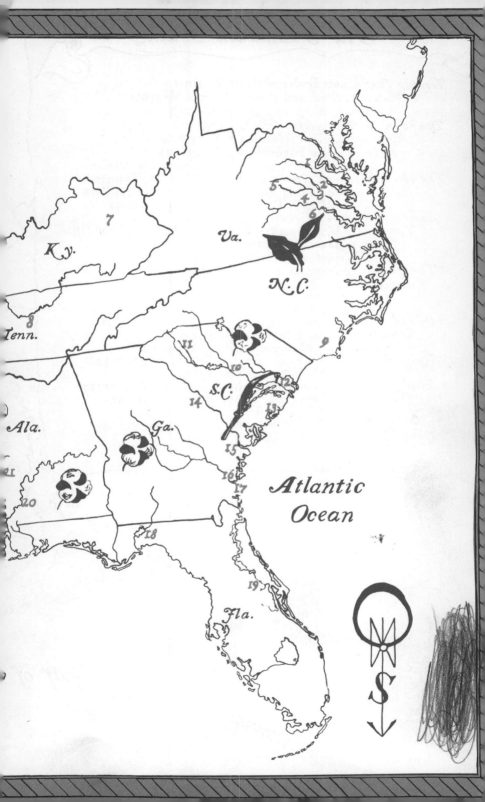

# THE PLANTATION SOUTH

# THE
# PLANTATION
# SOUTH

*By* KATHARINE M. JONES

**THE BOBBS-MERRILL COMPANY, INC.**

*Publishers*

INDIANAPOLIS • NEW YORK

*First Edition*

LIBRARY OF CONGRESS CATALOG CARD NUMBER: 57-9357

The following permissions are gratefully acknowledged:

Random House, Inc., for quotation from *Requiem for a Nun,* by William Faulkner (1951).

Rinehart & Company, Inc., for quotation from *The James: From Iron Gate to the Sea,* by Blair Niles (1945).

The University of North Carolina Press, for quotation from *Seed from Madagascar,* by Duncan Clinch Heyward (1937).

TO LULA GARRISON PATTON

# INTRODUCTION

"I found that the South one reads and hears of is altogether different from the one that one *sees* and becomes acquainted with."

So wrote young A. DePuy Van Buren of Battle Creek, Michigan, after a year in Yazoo County, Mississippi, where he taught the children of planters and unlearned some of the stereotyped notions of the South prevalent in his day and time.

At that, the contrast between what Mr. Van Buren expected and what he experienced was no greater than the differences between the diverse "Souths" that were to be found in the vast stretch of territory between the Potomac and the Rio Grande and in the half century of time covered by *The Plantation South.*

Miss Jones's book of that title is made up of pertinent and judiciously selected records of the observations of nearly half a hundred diarists, letter writers, journalists, natural scientists, inquisitive travelers and others—native, Northern and foreign—who lived on or visited Southern plantations. From these selections there emerges a composite picture of the institution, its people and its ways, as they appeared to contemporary observers of varying backgrounds and different attitudes.

The Southern plantation as here depicted was a protean institution of various and sometimes contradictory aspects. There was no agreement, even, as to what constituted a plantation, with President Madison insisting that his 3,000 acres at Montpelier was a "farm" while many a smaller place went by the more pretentious designation of "plantation." Those mentioned and to some extent described in this book varied in size from a few hundred acres, with an even smaller acreage under cultivation, to lordly estates measuring their acreage in the thousands. In geographical location they ranged from the Virginia Piedmont and the Kentucky Bluegrass to the bayous of Louisiana and the prairies of western Texas, where a Northern traveler found a "plantation that would have done no discredit to Virginia."

In their appointments and improvements they varied from the distinction of the famous places on the James River, or those in what Miss Jones refers to as "the rice kingdom" of the South Atlantic coastal country, to such simpler establishments as the one from which a young bride from the North wrote her mother that "things that

Northerners consider essential are of no importance here. The house and furniture is of little consequence." On the one hand, an English editor noted the "comfort and elegance" of the homes he visited, but a Northern visitor found planters whose "style of living was very farmer-like, and thoroughly Southern"—as he put it. There were white-pillared plantation mansions, but many a planter, especially in the newer regions of the old and the new Southwest, had only a "rough log dwelling for a home."

For the most part the accounts of travels through the South between 1800 and 1860—even those which might groan with descriptions of deplorable public accommodations when the writers were driven to seek them—glow with accounts of plantation hospitality. But even this characteristic of plantation life was not universal, for one traveler in Mississippi in the 1850s was told by his host that on the next stage of his journey he would not be able to find accommodations because the planters in that neighborhood were "all swell-heads" who would "never ask anybody but a regular swell-head to see them."

In one respect there was uniformity in the plantation scheme of things: they all depended on a labor force of slaves. But, judging from the observations quoted, in no feature of plantation life was there greater variety than in the conditions under which these bondsmen lived and worked. Captain Basil Hall noted slave quarters of "neat and comfortable" cottages. Another observer hailing originally from England, Frances Anne Kemble, saw those on other plantations as "the most miserable human habitations I ever beheld." Still another English observer found at John C. Calhoun's Fort Hill plantation "a great solicitude for the welfare of their slaves," but a fourth Englishman was told by a James River plantation overseer that "all attempts to make them work regularly by advice or kindness were unavailing" without "occasional hints from the cowhide." Of the general run of overseers it was said, however, that "their interest, as well as that of the planters, in the long run, is, unquestionably, to use the slaves well." It is unquestionable that there were occasions when interest was overborne by temper, passion or plain cruelty.

The planters, according to the same English visitor, "generally speaking, have a sincere desire to manage their estates with the least possible severity." To do so, however, the ruler of a plantation—as a Southern woman observed—"had need of a great store, not only of wisdom, but of tact and patience as well."

The demands on the mistress of a plantation were even more exacting, as more than one observer noted. The young bride from the North already quoted wrote that her mother-in-law "works harder than any Northern farmer's wife, I know." Young Rutherford B. Hayes, the future President of the United States, wrote home while visiting on a Texas plantation that his hostess, "instead of having the care of one family, is the nurse, physician, and spiritual adviser to a whole settlement of careless slaves."

No matter what the situation might be on individual plantations, it was the contention of Frances Anne Kemble that the South lived under a "habitual sense of danger" and that "every Southern *woman* to whom I have spoken on the subject has admitted to me that they live in terror of their slaves." While her writings are passionately subjective and are not representative of the situation as a whole, there was always the haunting recollection of the Nat Turner insurrection of 1831 in Southampton County, Virginia, dealt with in the present work by liberal extracts from the journal of Mrs. Mary Berkeley Minor Blackford.

To another Virginia lady, Mrs. Letitia M. Burwell, it seemed that "the negroes are the weight continually pulling us down. Will the time *ever* come for us to be free of them?" A young visitor from the North to the Georgia coastal plantations, the future Bishop Whipple, observed in similar vein that "the energies of the south are crippled by the incubus of slavery." In more measured language, a titled British traveler wrote that taking all factors into consideration, "slave labour is less cheap and profitable to the proprietor than it is sometimes assumed to be."

In a compilation of contemporary impressions such as this the point of view of the slave himself necessarily finds little direct representation. However, there are passages from the recollections of one former slave of his boyhood life on a Sumter County, South Carolina, plantation, whose forty or fifty slaves were "warmly clad, well fed and humanely treated." These are the recollections of a house servant. Field hands are described by the Swedish writer Fredrika Bremer as a "poor, black, enslaved, degraded people," but the most searing indictment of any feature of the institution of slavery quoted in this work is the description by John S. Wise of Virginia of the first slave auction which he witnessed in Richmond.

In compiling *The Plantation South* Miss Jones has ranged widely and well. Her selections are not brief snatches but are substantial segments of the writings of some forty-seven persons—twenty-two from the South, thirteen from the North, twelve from Europe. The materials from which quotations are drawn include letters and diaries in manuscript, periodical articles, and books, both well-known and rare, as set forth in the bibliography.

In the organization of the book, the selections have been grouped in three parts—"The Old Dominion and Its Neighbors," "In the Rice Kingdom" and "Cotton!" At a glance some of the assignments to these divisions may seem strained. For example, much cotton was raised on the rice coast. Yet, during the period covered, rice was a prime staple in the South Atlantic economy, so there is justification for grouping other activities of the region in the "kingdom" of rice.

In like fashion, the Nashville Basin of Middle Tennessee and the sugar regions of Louisiana are dealt with under the head of "Cotton!" although cotton was not raised to any notable extent in Middle Tennessee. Nevertheless, the outlet for the produce of the interior state of Tennessee was down the Mississippi into the "kingdom" of cotton, so perhaps the placing of an essentially noncotton section in the cotton category is warranted in consideration of commercial relationships.

These, however, are minor questions of arrangement. The solid merit of the book is in its selection of passages through which there may be glimpsed the way things were, or at least the way they appeared to be to contemporary observers, on numerous, different plantations of the ante-bellum South.

The labor system on which these plantations were based was overturned long years ago; the South of which these plantations were a part has profoundly changed. But still, as young Van Buren observed, the South of which one reads and hears is different from the South one sees and experiences. An essential part of that South is its history and its background, and part of that background is the plantation. *The Plantation South* should do its part in helping to bring about a better understanding of the South, replacing stereotypes with infinitely varied, intensely interesting vignettes of actuality.

ROBERT SELPH HENRY

Alexandria, Virginia

# ACKNOWLEDGMENTS

I want to express my gratitude to all those interesting persons of another century whose letters, diaries and travel accounts have furnished the material for this book. Every minute of their company was a pleasure and I leave them with regret.

I want also to express my appreciation and gratitude to the many kind individuals, librarians and archivists who have given suggestions and offered valuable assistance. I wish to thank them all and in particular the following:

Mr. Robert Tucker, Librarian, and Miss Alice Adams, Assistant Librarian, of the Furman University Library of Greenville, South Carolina.

Mr. Charles Stow of the Greenville, South Carolina, Public Library.

Mrs. Gale Despeaux of Greenville, South Carolina, whose grandmother, Ella Gertrude Clanton Thomas, appears in the pages of this book.

Mr. H. E. Littlejohn, Jr., Mr. John S. Taylor, and Mr. Robert Smeltzer of Greenville, South Carolina.

Mrs. Helen G. McCormack, Director of the Gibbes Art Gallery of Charleston, South Carolina.

Mrs. Harriet Hefner Cook of Clemson College, South Carolina.

Mrs. E. C. Threkeld of Atlanta, Georgia.

Miss Marcelle F. Schertz, Assistant and Reference Archivist, Louisiana State University.

Dr. J. H. Easterby, Director, South Carolina Archives Department.

Mrs. Louise Jones DuBose, Director, University of South Carolina Press.

Miss Mattie Russell, Curator of Manuscripts, and Miss Sarah Gray, assistant, Duke University Library.

Mrs. M. S. Buford of Greer, South Carolina.

Dr. Llerena Friend, Librarian, and Miss Winnie Allen, Archivist, of the Barker Texas History Center, University of Texas.

The staff of the Southern Historical Collection, University of North Carolina.

Miss Gladys Johnson of the North Carolina State Library, Raleigh, North Carolina.

Members of the staff of the Library of Congress.

Miss Cornelia Graham, Mr. John Goodman and members of the Clemson College Library staff, South Carolina.

Mr. Zack Spratt of Washington, D. C.

Finally, I wish to express my deep appreciation to Mr. D. Laurance Chambers, Mr. Herman Ziegner and Miss Anne McDonnell of The Bobbs-Merrill Company, whose help and guidance made this book possible.

# Table of Contents

PART III: Cotton!

Tennessee—Alabama—Mississippi—Louisiana—
Texas—Arkansas

*A portfolio of Southern plantations follows page 192.*

PART **I**

## The Old Dominion and
## Its Neighbors

### VIRGINIA—NORTH CAROLINA—KENTUCKY

"Tobacco was part of the Virginia landscape: the rising smoke in late
spring meant the burning of the plant patches; the patient figures in
the summer fields moved between rows of exotic green tobacco leaves;
tobacco barns stood forth gaunt and ill-proportioned. The very air was
scented by the life cycle of tobacco: by wood smoke, and the fragrance
of that sweet-scented tobacco. . . ."

BLAIR NILES, *The James: From Iron Gate to the Sea*

George Ticknor

# "THE HEARTIEST STYLE OF SOUTHERN HOSPITALITY"

*In 1815, two years after his admission to the bar in Massachusetts, a young Yankee, George Ticknor of Boston, accompanied by Francis Calley Grey, also of Boston, paid a visit to Thomas Jefferson at Monticello. The letters of the future Harvard professor of Modern Languages and Belle-Lettres to his father, Elisha Ticknor, describe Jefferson's way of life at Palladian Monticello with a certain condescension at once exasperating and amusing.*

*Grey's diary devotes an extended note to Jefferson's library.*

*During the visit it appears that the former President told him about the plans which eventually took form in the University of Virginia. Ticknor went abroad to study immediately after this visit, and during the three years of his sojourn Jefferson carried on a lively correspondence with him, in the course of which he offered him the professorship of Ideology, Ethics, Belle-Lettres and Fine Arts at the University of Virginia, which he declined. While abroad Ticknor collected many books for Jefferson, who said he was "the best bibliographer I have met."*

*With his wife, Anna Eliot Ticknor, and the Daniel Websters, he returned to Virginia in 1824 where he visited both Monticello and Montpelier, the home of James Madison. Mistress at Monticello was Martha, Jefferson's eldest daughter, who was born in 1772 and who had married Thomas Mann Randolph, Jr., at her father's house on February 22, 1790. When Jefferson was absent from Monticello as Secretary of State he left his affairs in the hands of Colonel Randolph, but in this same year, 1824, he entrusted them to his grandson, who was also his namesake.*

*Ticknor recorded his impressions of Montpelier (one was surprise at Mr. Madison's very evident good sense, which he had not expected from a man with whom he disagreed politically!) in a letter to his close friend William H. Prescott, the historian whose biography he was to write. At this time Dolley Madison, so long the queen of Washington society, was fifty-six years old.*

### GEORGE TICKNOR TO HIS FATHER, ELISHA TICKNOR

We left Charlottesville on Saturday, the 4th of February [1815], for Mr. Jefferson's. He lives on a mountain which he has named

3

Monticello, and which is a synonyme for Carter's mountain. The ascent of this steep, savage hill was as pensive and slow as Satan's ascent to Paradise. We were obliged to wind two thirds round its sides before we reached the artificial lawn on which the house stands; and, when we had arrived there, we were about six hundred feet, I understand, above the stream which flows at its foot. It is an abrupt mountain. The fine growth of ancient forest-trees conceals its sides and shades part of its summit. The prospect is admirable. . . . The lawn on the top, as I hinted, was artificially formed by cutting down the peak of the height. In its centre, and facing the southeast, Mr. Jefferson has placed his house, which is of brick, two stories high in the wings, with a piazza in front of a receding centre. It is built, I suppose, in the French style. You enter, by a glass folding-door, into a hall which reminds you of Fielding's "Man of the Mountain," by the strange furniture of its walls. On one side hang the head and horns of an elk, a deer, and a buffalo; another is covered with curiosities which Lewis and Clarke found in their wild and perilous expedition. On the third, among many other striking matters, was the head of a mammoth, or, as Cuvier calls it, a mastodon, containing the only *os frontis*, Mr. Jefferson tells me, that has yet been found. On the fourth side, in odd union with a fine painting of the Repentance of Saint Peter, is an Indian map on leather, of the southern waters of the Missouri, and an Indian representation of a bloody battle, handed down in their traditions.

Through this hall—or rather museum—we passed to the dining-room, and sent our letters to Mr. Jefferson, who was, of course, in his study. Here again we found ourselves surrounded with paintings that seemed good.

We had hardly time to glance at the pictures before Mr. Jefferson entered; . . . I was doubly astonished to find [him], whom I had always supposed to be a small man, more than six feet high, with dignity in his appearance, and ease and graciousness in his manner. He rang, and sent to Charlottesville for our luggage, and, as dinner approached, took us to the drawing-room,—a large and rather elegant room, twenty or thirty feet high,—which, with the hall I have described, composed the whole centre of the house, from top to bottom. The floor of this room is tessellated. It is formed of alternate diamonds of cherry and beech, and kept polished as highly as if it were of fine mahogany.

Here are the best pictures of the collection. Over the fireplace is the

Laughing and Weeping Philosophers, dividing the world between them; on its right, the earliest navigators to America,—Columbus, Americus Vespuccius, Magellan, etc.,—copied, Mr. Jefferson said, from originals in the Florence Gallery. Farther round, Mr. Madison in the plain, Quaker-like dress of his youth, Lafayette in his Revolutionary uniform, and Franklin in the dress in which we always see him. There were other pictures, and a copy of Raphael's Transfiguration.

We conversed on various subjects until dinner-time, and at dinner were introduced to the grown members of his family. These are his only remaining child, Mrs. Randolph, her husband, Colonel Randolph, and the two oldest of their unmarried children, Thomas Jefferson and Ellen; and I assure you I have seldom met a pleasanter party.

The evening passed away pleasantly in general conversation, of which Mr. Jefferson was necessarily the leader. . . . He seems equally fond of American antiquities, and especially the antiquities of his native State, and talks of them with freedom and, I suppose, accuracy. . . .

On Sunday morning, after breakfast, Mr. Jefferson asked me into his library, and there I spent the forenoon of that day as I had that of yesterday. This collection of books, now so much talked about, consists of about seven thousand volumes, contained in a suite of fine rooms, and is arranged in the catalogue, and on the shelves, according to the divisions and subdivisions of human learning by Lord Bacon. In so short a time I could not, of course, estimate its value, even if I had been competent to do so. . . .

On Monday morning I spent a couple of hours with him in his study. . . .

The afternoon and evening passed as on the two days previous; for everything is done with such regularity, that when you know how one day is filled, I suppose you know how it is with the others. At eight o'clock the first bell is rung in the great hall, and at nine the second summons you to the breakfast-room, where you find everything ready. After breakfast every one goes, as inclination leads him, to his chamber, the drawing-room, or the library. The children retire to their school-room with their mother, Mr. Jefferson rides to his mills on the Rivanna, and returns at about twelve. At half past three the great bell rings, and those who are disposed resort to the drawing-room, and the rest go to the dining-room at the second call of the bell, which is at four o'clock. The dinner was always choice, and served in the French style; but no wine was set on the table till the cloth was removed. The ladies sat until about six, then retired, but returned with the tea-tray a little before seven, and spent the evening with the gentlemen; which was always pleasant, for they are obviously accustomed to join in the conversation, however high the topic may be. At about half past ten, which seemed to be their usual hour of retiring, I went to my chamber, found there a fire, candle, and a servant in waiting to receive my orders for the morning, and in the morning was waked by his return to build the fire.

Today, Tuesday, we told Mr. Jefferson that we should leave Monticello in the afternoon. He seemed much surprised, and said as much as politeness would permit on the badness of the roads and the prospect of bad weather, to induce us to remain longer. It was evident, I thought, that they had calculated on our staying a week. At dinner, Mr. Jefferson again urged us to stay, not in an oppressive way, but with kind politeness; and when the horses were at the door, asked if he should not send them away; but, as he found us resolved on going, he bade us farewell in the heartiest style of Southern hospitality. . . .

Two little incidents which occurred while we were at Monticello should not be passed by. The night before we left, young Randolph came up late from Charlottesville, and brought the astounding news that the English had been defeated before New Orleans by General Jackson. Mr. Jefferson had made up his mind that the city would fall, and told me that the English would hold it permanently—or for some time—by a force of Sepoys from the East Indies. He had gone to bed, like the rest of us; but of course his grandson went to his chamber with the paper containing the news. But the old philosopher refused to open his door, saying he could wait till the morning; and when we met at breakfast I found he had not yet seen it.

One morning, when he came back from his ride, he told Mr. Randolph, very quietly, that the dam had been carried away the night before. From his manner, I supposed it an affair of small consequence, but at Charlottesville, on my way to Richmond, I found the country ringing with it. Mr. Jefferson's great dam was gone, and it would cost $30,000 to rebuild it.

There is a breathing of notional philosophy in Mr. Jefferson,—in his dress, his house, his conversation. His setness, for instance, in wearing very sharp toed shoes, corduroy small-clothes, and red plush waistcoat, which have been laughed at till he might perhaps wisely have dismissed them. . . .

### TO WILLIAM H. PRESCOTT

Monticello, December 16, 1824.

. . . We have had an extremely pleasant visit in Virginia. We left Washington just a week ago, and came seventy miles in a steamboat, to Potomac Creek, and afterwards nine miles by land, to Fredericksburg. . . .

On Saturday morning we reached Mr. Madison's, at Montpelier, on the west side of what is called the Southwest Mountain; a very fine, commanding situation, with the magnificent range of the Blue Ridge stretching along the whole horizon in front, at the distance of from twenty to thirty miles. . . .

We were received with a good deal of dignity and much cordiality, by Mr. and Mrs. Madison, in the portico, and immediately placed at ease; for they were apprised of our coming an hour or two before we arrived, and were therefore all in order, to show a little of that ceremony in which Mrs. Madison still delights.

Mr. Madison is a younger-looking man—he is now seventy-four—than he was when I saw him ten years ago, with an unsuccessful war grinding him to the earth; and he is one of the most pleasant men I have met, both from the variety and vivacity of his conversation. He lives, apparently, with great regularity. We breakfasted at nine, dined about four, drank tea at seven, and went to bed at ten; that is, we went to our rooms, where we were furnished with everything we wanted, and where Mrs. Madison sent us a nice supper every night and a nice luncheon every forenoon. From ten o'clock in the morning till three we rode, walked, or remained in our rooms, Mr. and Mrs. Madison being then occupied. The table is very ample and elegant, and somewhat luxurious; it is evidently a serious item in the account of Mr. M's, happiness, and it seems to be his habit to pass about an hour, after the cloth is removed, with a variety of wines of no mean quality.

On politics he is a little reserved, as he seems determined not to be again involved in them; but about everything else he talked with great freedom, and told an interminable series of capital stories, most of which have some historical value. His language, though not very rich or picturesque, was chosen with much skill, and combined into very elegant and finished sentences; and both Mr. Webster and myself were struck with a degree of good sense in his conversation which we had not anticipated from his school of politics and course of life. We

passed our time, therefore, very pleasantly, and feel indebted to him
for a hospitality which becomes one who has been at the head of
the nation.

On Sunday afternoon we took a ride of a dozen miles across different plantations, to see the country and the people. Mr. Madison's
farm—as he calls it—consists of about three thousand acres, with an
hundred and eighty slaves, and is among the best managed in Virginia.
We saw also one or two others that looked very well, but in general
things had a very squalid appearance. We stopped at the house of Mr.
Philip Barbour, one of the most active lawyers in the Commonwealth,
lately Speaker of the House of Representatives, and still one of its
prominent members. The house is of brick, and new, large enough,
and not inconvenient. Probably he lives with a sort of luxury which is
chiefly the result of abundance, and is not very refined; but certainly
there is little comfort in his establishment, and a good, honest New-
Englander, with a thousand dollars a year, would have more enjoyment of life than Mr. Barbour has with six or seven. . . .

Early on Tuesday we arrived at Monticello. Everything here is on
a larger scale than at Montpelier; the house, the grounds, and the
arrangements. There is, too, nothing that marks the residence of an
Ex-King. The family consists of Mr. Jefferson; Mrs. Randolph, his
daughter, about fifty-two years old; Mr. [Nicholas Philip] Trist, a
young Louisianian, who has married her fourth daughter; Miss Ellen;
two other daughters, of eighteen and twenty; Mrs. Trist; four sons
under sixteen; Mr. Harrison, a young lawyer of Harrisburg, who lately
studied at Cambridge; Mr. George Long, just from Cambridge, England, apparently an excellent scholar, and now a professor in the University at Charlottesville; Mr. Webster; and ourselves. . . .

Yesterday we formed a party, and, with Mr. Jefferson at our head,
went to the University. It is a very fine establishment . . . the whole
situated in the midst of two hundred and fifty acres of land, high,
healthy, and with noble prospects all around it. . . .

Mr. Jefferson is entirely absorbed in it, and its success would make
a *beau finale* indeed to his life. He is now eighty-two years old, very
little altered from what he was ten years ago, very active, lively, and
happy, riding from ten to fifteen miles every day, and talking without
the least restraint, very pleasantly, upon all subjects. In politics, his
interest seems nearly gone. He takes no newspapers but the Richmond
*Enquirer*, and reads that reluctantly; but on all matters of literature,

philosophy, and general interest, he is prompt and even eager. He reads much Greek and Saxon. I saw his Greek Lexicon; it was much worn with use, and contained many curious notes. . . .

Mr. Jefferson seems to enjoy life highly, and very rationally; but he said well of himself the other evening, "When I can neither read nor ride, I shall desire very much to make my bow." . . .

Timothy Flint

## "THE KENTUCKIANS ARE A HIGH-MINDED PEOPLE"

*A graduate of Harvard in the class of 1800, Timothy Flint of Salem, Massachusetts, taught for two years before he became minister of the Congregational Church at Luxemburg in his native state. He went to the Southwest in 1815 under the auspices of the Missionary Society of Connecticut.*

*Most of the time between 1815 and 1825 he traveled through the Mississippi Valley, though he paused for several years at Rapide, Louisiana, to be principal of a seminary. From 1827 to 1830 he edited the Western Monthly Review in Cincinnati, and in 1833 the Knickerbocker in New York. He was the author of a number of books, including* The Biographical Memoir of Daniel Boone, Indian Wars of the West *and* History and Geography of the Mississippi Valley. *Before his death in 1840 at the age of sixty he returned again to Louisiana for a brief interval.*

*The following account, from his* Recollections of the Last Ten Years, *describes his journey through Frankfort to Louisville, Kentucky, in the spring of 1816. Along the way he stopped to perform divine services.*

*His reference to the hatred of Yankees has to do with resentment of the anti-war feeling in New England before and during the War of 1812. Kentucky was a hotbed of pro-war sentiment. And already there was bitter division on the slavery question.*

At a small town at the mouth of Kentucky River, I crossed into that state. . . . As soon as you depart from the Ohio, and find yourself in the region of hills and springs, you will nowhere see fairer and fresher complexions, or fuller and finer forms, than you see in the young men and women, who are generally exempted from the necessity of labour.

They have a mild and temperate climate, a country producing the greatest abundance, and sufficiently old to have possessed itself of all the comforts of life. The people live easily and plentifully, and on the "finest of the wheat." The circumstances, under which they are born, tend to give them the most perfect development of person and form. It struck me, that the young native Kentuckians were, in general, the largest race that I had seen. There was obvious, at once, a considerable difference of manners between the people of this and the opposite states, that do not possess slaves. . . .

I felt grieved to see so many fine young men exempted from labour, having no liberal studies and pursuits to fill up their time, and falling, almost of course, into the prevailing vices of the West—gambling and intemperence. . . .

The ease and opulence, that are so visible in the appearance of the people, are equally so in the houses, their appendages, and furniture. Travelling through the village in this fertile region, where the roads are perfectly good, and where every elevation brings you in view of a noble farm-house, in the midst of its orchards, and sheltered by its fine groves of forest and sugar-maple trees, you would scarcely realize that the first settlers of the country, and they men of mature age when they settled it, were, some of them, still living. Every thing is young or old only by comparison. The inhabitants, who are more enthusiastic and national than the other Western people, and look with a proud disdain upon the younger states, designate their own state, with the veneration due to age, by the name of "Old Kentucky." To them it is the home of all that is good, fertile, happy, and great. As the English are said to go to battle with a song extolling their roast beef, instead of saying their prayers, so the Kentuckian, when about to encounter danger, rushes upon it, crying, "Hurra for old Kentucky." Every one in the western country has heard the anecdote, that a Methodist preacher from this state, in another state was preaching, and expatiating upon the happiness of heaven. Having gradually advanced towards the cap of his climax, "In short," said he, "my brethren, to say all in one word, heaven is a Kentuck of a place."

At this time the people were in the height of their sugar-making, a kind of Saturnalia, like the time of vintage in France. The cheerful fires in the groves, the respectable looking ladies, who were present with their servants, superintending the operations, especially when seen by the bright glare which their fires cast upon every object by night, rendered it a very interesting spectacle.

In advancing towards Frankfort, I generally performed divine services every night, and found it necessary only to give the usual half hour's notice, to assemble a large audience—a sufficient proof, that the people have abundance of leisure, and that they have the usual portion of curiosity. New England has every where at the south the reputation of being the land of troublesome inquisitiveness; but it strikes me, that this people possess the spirit at least in an equal degree. A stranger, if understood to be such, is exposed to being annoyed with questions by the country people, and especially to be invited to "swap horses," as the phrase is. Horse-trading, indeed, seems to be a favorite and universal amusement through the country.

I entered Frankfort in a violent shower of rain. . . . After two days' stay I took the road to Lexington. It is a fine road, and I remarked the same series of good houses, pleasant farms, and by night the bright fires of the sugar-camps. The aspect of the landscape is fertile and pleasant. The air is soft. I scarcely recollect to have had a more pleasant ride, than that from Frankfort to Lexington.

Lexington is situated in the centre of what the Kentuckians affirm to be the finest body of land in the world. I believe no country can show finer upland; and for a great distance from the town, plantation adjoins plantation, in all directions. The timber is of that class that denotes the richest soil. The wheat fields equal in beauty those of the far-famed county of Lancaster, in Pennsylvania. I am now in the region where the farmers designate their agriculture by the term, "raising a crop." They do this, when a planter, with a gang of negroes, turns his principal attention to the staples of the country—hemp, flour, and tobacco. The greater part of the boats from this state are loaded with these articles. . . .

It is well known, that a jealousy, almost a hatred of Yankees, prevailed among the mass of this people, during the late war. . . . There is but too much of this feeling yet existing. . . . A native of the North has no conception of the nature and extent of this feeling, until he finds himself in the South and West. I have felt grieved to see, that too many of our books of travels, and most of the accounts of the West, carried to the East, tend to foster this spirit towards these regions, on our parts. The manner in which the slave question is agitated, keeps the embers glowing under the ashes.

In my whole tour through this state, I experienced a frank and cordial hospitality. I entered it with a share of those prejudices, which I had probably fostered unconsciously. I was aware how strongly they

existed in the minds of the people, with regard to the inhabitants of the
North. The general kindness with which I was every where received,
impressed me so much the more forcibly, for being unexpected. The
Kentuckians, it must be admitted, are a high-minded people, and
possess the stamina of a noble character. They are generally of one descent, and are scions from a noble stock—the descendants from afflu-
ent and respectable planters from Virginia and North Carolina. There
is a distinct and striking moral physiognomy to this people; an enthusiasm, a vivacity, and ardour of character, courage, frankness, generosity, that have been developed with the peculiar circumstances
under which they have been placed. These are the incitements to all
that is noble in a people. Happy for them, if they learn to temper and
moderate their enthusiasm, by reflection and good sense. Happy for
them if they more strongly felt the necessity of training their numerous and ardent youth to virtue and industry. Possessed of such physical
and moral capabilities, and from their imperfect education, their
habits of idleness, extravagance, and gambling, but too likely to turn
their perverted and misapplied powers against themselves and their
country. . . . In individual cases this impression has doubtless been felt,
for great exertions are making by individuals to educate their children.
Private tutors are employed. New seminaries are started. . . .

The fathers of the young men, in many instances, had high standing and influence in the state from which they migrated. Not a few of
them obtained fame, in the war of the revolution. Their children inherit their fame, and that confident and uncontrolled spirit, which is
so often observed to belong to the Virginia character. They seem to
feel that they have an hereditary claim to command, place, and observance. This perfect repose of self-confidence is in fact their good
star. I have often seen one of these young men in the new states farther west, with no other qualifications than that ease and perfect
command of all that they knew, which result from self-satisfaction,
step down into the "moving water," before the tardy, bashful, and
self-criticising young man from the North had made up his mind to
attempt to avail himself of the opportunity. "Sua dextra" is the constant motto, self-repose the guardian genius of the Kentuckian, which
often stand him in stead of better talents and qualifications. . . .

The Kentucky planters assert, that whatever article Old Kentucky
turns her chief attention to raising, is sure to glut the market for that
year. It would be remarked, perhaps, that flour, hemp, or tobacco, were
low in the market. They immediately find a solution in the fact that

the Kentucky crop has arrived. In truth, the astonishing productiveness
of their good lands, and the great extent of their cultivation, almost
justify such conclusions.

Louisville is more frequented by steam-boats, than any other port
on the Ohio. In New Orleans more are up for that place than any
other. It is seldom that many days elapse in that city, without offering
a steam-boat conveyance to Louisville. This trip is now performed in
twelve days. Accustomed to see the steam-boat with its prodigious and
untiring power, breasting the heavy current of the Mississippi, the
Kentuckian draws his ideas of power from this source; and when the
warmth of whiskey in his stomach is added to his natural energy, he
becomes in succession, horse, alligator, and steam-boat. Much of his
language is figurative and drawn from the power of a steam-boat. To
get ardent and zealous, is to "raise the steam." To get angry, and give
vent and scope to one's feelings, is to "let off steam." To encounter
any disaster, or meet with a great catastrophe, is to "burst the boiler."
The slave cheers his oxen and horses by bidding them "go ahead." . . .

## Dolley Madison

### "THERE ARE FEW HOUSES IN VIRGINIA"

*When the Madisons left the White House they retired to Mont-*
*pelier, their plantation in Orange County, Virginia, where Mr. Madi-*
*son busied himself most profitably in the cultivation of tobacco.*

*An important member of the retired President's household was*
*Madison's mother, who was then ninety-eight years old. She lived in*
*the original part of the house built by her husband.*

*Visitors to Montpelier were many and often quite distinguished.*
*One appreciative guest commented, "There are few houses in Virginia*
*that gave a larger welcome or made it more agreeable, than that over*
*which 'Queen Dolley,' the most gracious and beloved of all our female*
*sovereigns, reigned. . . ."*

*The two Barbours were James and Philip Pendleton Barbour, sons*
*of Thomas Barbour, who was a member of the 1774-1775 Virginia*
*Convention. Colonel Monroe was James Monroe, the President.*
*Mrs. Madison's sister, Anna Payne Cutts, was the wife of Richard*
*Cutts of Maine and the mother of Dolly and Mary Cutts. "Old Mr.*
*Patterson" was Mr. William Patterson of Baltimore, father of Eliza-*

*beth Patterson, who was the wife of Jerome Bonaparte, young brother
of Napoleon. Payne Todd was Madison's stepson.*

*The offending novel appears to be* The Wept of Wish-ton-wish
*by James Fenimore Cooper.*

*"Insurrections in the city" refers to the short-lived but bloody raid
led by Nat Turner, a slave living near Southampton, Virginia. An
account of the uprising by Mary Berkeley Minor Blackford is given
on pages 17-21.*

FROM MRS. MADISON TO HER SISTER ANNA PAYNE CUTTS

Montpelier, July 5, 1820

I have just received yours, dearest Anna, and rejoice that you are
well and have your friends about you. Yesterday we had ninety persons
to dine with us at one table,—put up on the lawn, under a thick arbor.
The dinner was profuse and good, and the company very orderly.
Many of them were old acquaintance of yours, and among them the
two Barbours.

We had no ladies except mother Madison, Mrs. Macon, and Nelly
Willis; the day was cool and pleasant; half a dozen only stayed all
night with us, and they are now about to depart. Colonel Monroe's
letter this morning announces the advent of the French Minister, and
we shall expect him this evening, or perhaps sooner. I am less worried
here with an hundred visitors than with twenty-five in Washington,—
this summer especially. I wish, dearest, you had just such a country
home as this. I truly believe it is the happiest and most true life, and
would be so good for you and the dear children.

Always your devoted sister,

DOLLEY P. MADISON

TO HER NIECES, MARY AND DOLLY CUTTS

Montpelier, July 30, 1826

Your letter, my dearest niece, with the one before it, came quite
safely, for which I return many thanks and kisses. I rejoice too, dear
Dolly, to see how well you write and express yourself, and am as proud
of all your acquirements as if you were my own daughter. I trust you
will yet be with me this summer, when I shall see your improvement in
person also, and enjoy the sweet assurance of your affection. Mary Lee
and her husband have been indisposed, but are better. They say often
they hope you will come with your dear mother, as do all your relatives

and friends in this quarter. The old lady,—even the negroes, young and old, want to see you, dear.

We had old Mr. Patterson and his son Edward from Baltimore to stay with us several days, and they tell me that Madame Bonaparte is still in France, and her son gone to Rome to visit his father. Mr. Monroe left us yesterday, disappointed in his views of raising money from his land. Mr. B. continued on his way to the Springs, and I was disappointed at not sending a packet to you, inclosing the flounce which I wanted you to wear, worked by me long ago.

I received by the last post a letter from your cousin Payne, at New York; he writes in fine health and spirits, and says he will be detained only a few weeks longer in that city. I sincerely hope to see him soon, though it is impossible for him to prefer Virginia to the North. If I were in Washington with you I know I could not conform to the formal rules of visiting they now have, but would disgrace myself by rushing about among my friends at all hours. Here I find it most agreeable to stay at home, everything around me is so beautiful. Our garden promises grapes and figs in abundance, but I shall not enjoy them unless your mamma comes, and brings you to help us with them. . . .

Adieu, and believe me always your tender mother and aunt,

DOLLEY P. MADISON

P.S. We are very old-fashioned here. Can you send me a paper pattern of the present sleeve, and describe the width of dress and waist; also how turbans are pinned up, bonnets worn, as well as how to behave in the fashion?

### TO DOLLY CUTTS

Montpelier, March 10,1830

I am now seated, pen in hand, my sweet niece, to write you, though not in the humor for the success I desire in producing an amusing letter such as mine *should* be in answer to yours.

Imagine, if you can, a greater trial to the patience of us farmers than the destruction of a radiant patch of green peas by frost! It came last night on the skirts of a storm; and while I was lamenting that our dear midshipman, Walter, should ever be exposed to such winds, my young adventurers at home were completely wrecked off their moorings! But away with complaints, other patches equally radiant will arise, and I will mourn no longer over a mess of peas or pottage, but would rather meet you somewhere, or hear about your last party. I had, indeed, my *"quantum sufficit"* of gayety in Richmond, but what I enjoyed most was the quiet but thorough hospitality of the inhabitants among whom I should like to spend my winters. Washington, if my old friends were still there, would no doubt be my preference; but I confess I do not admire contention in any form, either political or civil. In my quiet retreat I like to hear of what is going on, and therefore hope, my dear, you will not be timid in telling me, though your statements shall be seen by no one else. By the bye, do you ever get hold of a clever novel, new or old, that you could send me? I bought Cooper's last, but did not care for it, because the story was so full of horrors.

Adieu, my dearest Dolly, think of me as your own friend as well as aunt, and write as often as you can to

Yours affectionately,

DOLLEY P. MADISON

TO DOLLY

Montpelier, November, 1830

Dearest Niece,—I have been so much engaged in the book you kindly sent by the last post, that I have scarcely left myself time to thank you for it by this. I will, however, take an early opportunity to show my gratitude by a longer letter.

If you can send me the "Romance of History" I will be very glad, and will make proper dispatch in the perusal of it. Governor Barbour is here and will stay some time. . . .

Ever your affectionate aunt,

DOLLEY P. MADISON

TO MARY

Montpelier, September 18, 1831

My Dearest Mary,—I hasten to answer your nice letter in order to obtain your forgiveness about the mislaid letter; I fear Beckey may have used it to kindle the fire she was so anxious about for her master, and as far as I can discover collected everything in the way of paper on my table this morning. . . . I hope the alarm of "insurrections" is over in the city, though every one should be on guard after this. I am quiet, hearing little about it, and quite helpless if in danger. Tell Mr. Trist I send him a few leaves, if not the whole flower, of his dear lady (Cape Jessamine), who is now blooming, when all her contemporaries have changed color and are passing away, emblematic of her good disposition and heart, whose fragrance will last until the end.

Your Uncle Madison still wears the bead ring you placed on his finger, and I see him look at it every now and then without saying anything.

My eyes are troubling me, still I write on a great deal of nonsense. To-morrow I expect a large party from Richmond and the lower country to stay with us. . . .

Adieu, dearest niece. Ever yours,

DOLLEY MADISON

TO MARY

Montpelier, December, 1831

My Own Dear Niece,—I have been the most disconsolate of persons these three or four days, and all because of a violent toothache. . . . In my last I informed you that Walter and Payne had been detained abroad by bad weather, but now they are safe and sound with us, and we have played chess and talked together all this time without the appearance of ennui. . . .

I hope you will soon be going to parties, and give me a detailed account of what is going forward amongst the various characters in Washington.

I have so long been confined by the side of my dear sick husband, never seeing or hearing outside of his room, that I make a dull correspondent.

Your uncle is better now than he was three days ago, and I trust will continue to mend, but his poor hands are still sore, and so swollen as to be almost useless, and so I lend him mine. The music-box is playing beside me, and seems well adapted to solitude, as I look out at our mountains, white with snow, and the winter's wind sounding loud and cold. . . .

Good night, my love. Your fond aunt,

DOLLEY MADISON

Mary Berkeley Minor Blackford

INSURRECTION IN SOUTHAMPTON

*Nat Turner was a slave owned by Joseph Travis of Southampton County, Virginia. Largely through the influence of his mother, a native African, he was early convinced that he possessed supernatural powers, that he could read signs and omens, that voices directed him, that he*

*could remember things that happened before he was born. He gained
considerable influence among the slaves on the Travis plantation, and
when he became a preacher his influence extended to neighboring
ones as well.*

*Though he was never ill treated, had been taught to read by his
master's son and had not been influenced by Abolitionist propaganda,
he admitted to his captors that he had long planned a revolt. He inter-
preted an eclipse of the sun in late August of 1831 as a sign that the
time for the uprising had come.*

*His band of followers began with his master's household and grew
as he swept from plantation to plantation, attacking isolated homes
and killing sixty-one whites, mostly women and children. Beginning
on August 22 the uprising continued for some forty-eight hours till it
was quelled by a hastily organized posse of planters. Military and ci-
vilian patrols scoured the countryside. In a very short time fifty-three
Negroes were arrested and tried, of whom twenty-one were acquitted,
twelve were transported out of Virginia, and twenty were hanged.
Turner himself remained at large for nearly two months, then at last
he was captured, tried and hanged.*

*An account of the incident was recorded in her journal by Mary
Berkeley Minor Blackford, wife of William Matthews Blackford, of
Topping Castle plantation near Fredericksburg, Virginia. She hated
slavery and, as early as 1826, had freed many of her own slaves and sent
them to Liberia. In 1861 she gave five sons to the Confederate Army.*

*Bishop William Meade, who lived from 1789 to 1862, was the third
bishop of the Protestant Episcopal Church in the Diocese of Virginia.*

In travelling in the summer of 1832, about a year after the Insurrection in Southampton, I met with some members of the Whitehead
family who suffered so much at that time. This was the son (& his
wife) of the old lady of that name whose family and herself were
nearly all butchered by Nat Turner and his gang of ruffians. This
Gentleman and his wife did not live with his Mother, but at some
distance, and so escaped. I was so much struck with some instances
she gave me of the fidelity of many of the slaves to their owners at that
time that I took down *from her words* the following incidents to show
that justice had not been done them generally in the recital of the
crimes committed by a comparatively small number.

A few minutes after the negroes were seen riding up the lane leading
to the house (in this lane they killed her son, a young Minister), they

were in the house and had commenced their work of slaughter. The Mother of the family, who had always enjoyed the affection of her negroes, was among the first killed. Her own servants had nothing to do with the insurrection; on the contrary (as will be seen), did all they could to protect the family at the risk of their own lives.

A little girl clung to her Mistress and begged for her life until her own was threatened. She then fled and hid under the bed. An old negro man named Wallace vainly entreated for the life of his Mistress. After murdering the good old lady, they threatened to kill him. He told them to do it as he cared not to live now she was dead.

The youngest of the daughters happened to be a little way from the house in some very high corn, which concealed her, and might have escaped, but losing all presence of mind (on hearing what was going on) screamed loudly in spite of the entreaties of a young negro girl who was with her; drawn by her screams, the murderers rushed upon her. Aggy, the girl with her, endeavored to shield her young mistress at the risk of her own life, but was torn from her with such force as to tear the strong Virginia cloth dress she had on from her shoulders and thrown to the ground where she expected to be killed herself, but they contented themselves with the murder of her young mistress.

A young negro named Tom was in the yard watering the horses preparatory to their going to work (for it was very early in the morning). As soon as he saw what the gang were after, he set off full speed to give the neighbors notice of their danger, flying from one plantation to another. At one place the Master gave him a hatchet to defend himself should the insurgents attack him. Feeling however they might get hold of it and use it against the whites, he hid it. He afterwards met companies of white men assembled for the purpose of putting down the insurrection and it was thought that, had they seen him with a hatchet, they would have killed him on the spot, for at that time the innocent were often confounded with the guilty. The poor things would frequently fasten white rags on the end of a stick in token of their peaceable intention, but the innocent sometimes suffered. Tom ran until noon of that day when he arrived at the Guard House. He was altogether spent, it was a year before he recovered; it was thought for some time he would not survive the effort so much beyond his strength. Many lives were saved by it. Much praise and a certificate testifying to his exertions in saving the lives of so many whites at such an expense was all his reward in the world.

Old Mrs. Whitehead and her four grown daughters, a son and a

grandson were all murdered by those deluded fanatics. The only one
of Mrs. Whitehead's family (who was at home) whose life was saved
was her daughter Harriet, who hid between the bed and the mattress;
her Sister was killed at the foot of the bed she was concealed in. After
the company of banditti had left the house some of their number who
were well acquainted with the family, remembering that there was
one more to destroy, sent two of their number back to find and kill
her. In the meantime, her own slaves had contrived to disguise her
and were actually carrying her out of the house to a place of conceal-
ment when they saw these men coming on foot to the back of the
house for the purpose of surprise. Some of the slaves went immediately
to meet them & contrived by some means to turn their course. The
young lady was then carried and concealed in a swamp near the house
until the pursuit was over.

Out of forty negroes on this plantation, only three joined in the Insurrection, and they not until they were intoxicated. It afterwards
happened that one of the negroes, Hubbard, an old man who had assisted in saving Miss Harriet, was brought out as one of the murderers
to be shot. His young mistress, who had been conveyed to the place
for safety, heard accidently of it and ran out and saved him by relating
the circumstances of his conduct in aiding to save her life.

In the same neighborhood with Mrs. Whitehead lived an extremely
amiable lady and gentleman of the name of Porter. A negro woman
ran from a distance to warn them just in time for them to escape to the
woods in sight of the house. By a point of the finger of any of the
slaves there, the family might all have been murdered, but so far were
they from betraying them they contrived to direct the steps of the
murderers in another direction. Strange to say, that three of those who
went along to divert their course joined the murderous crew after
having saved the lives of their Master and Mistress.

Another lady of the neighborhood (Mrs. Nicholson) who was too
weak to move, having just recovered from a bilious fever, was taken up
in the arms of her slaves and hidden in the woods.

Such instances of faithfulness 'twere pity should be lost. I here
record them hoping that some day they may appear in a better garb
for the honour of the poor negro, and to prove how much of goodness
and kindness there is in his nature, notwithstanding that *as a people*
they have so many wrongs, though many slave owners I know are
among the most excellent of the earth, and this turns aside the wrath
of Heaven when such things are committed as are recorded in the

preceding notes. Bishop Meade said truly, "They are the most amiable people on the earth." For though I have recorded fearful wickedness in this insurrection, we must remember how few those have been, and how ignorant and deluded the negroes who joined it were. I only know of one insurrection before this of Nat Turner's, and of none since. And I am sure that with an hundredth part of the wrongs they suffer we white people would have risen in arms fifty times. . . .

O thou Almighty King! Look down in pity on those forsaken ones, forsaken of almost all but Thee, and open a way for their deliverance. Thou governest the hearts of men. Grant that the approaching meeting of the legislature may be productive of good to them and fix some date to their misery. Shew the people their sin and let them not go on until Thy judgements overtake them. . . .

Henry Barnard

## "YOU WOULD DELIGHT TO VISIT THIS REGION"

*Twenty-two-year-old Henry Barnard, native of Hartford, Connecticut, and a recent graduate of Yale College, decided in the early days of 1833 to tour the South Atlantic states. On his way he spent two months in Washington during the time of the great and violent debates on nullification. President Andrew Jackson was asking for the passage of his Force Bill. John C. Calhoun was defending nullification. Henry Clay introduced his Compromise Tariff Bill.*

*Barnard left Washington in March, well supplied with letters of introduction. It was Charles Campbell, the distinguished author of the* History of the Colony and Ancient Dominion of Virginia, *who gave him a note to his father, John Wilson Campbell, a bookdealer. Shirley Plantation near Petersburg, to which Mrs. Campbell took him, was the home of Hill Carter, first cousin of General Robert E. Lee, whose mother was Anne Hill Carter.*

*In Salisbury, North Carolina, Barnard visited an old family friend, Dr. Ashbel Smith, who had been born at Hartford in 1805, was graduated in medicine from Yale, studied surgery in France and at this time was practicing in Salisbury. Later, in 1839, he went to live in Texas. He became surgeon-general and secretary of state of the Republic of Texas, and Minister to Texas and Great Britain and France. In the*

*War between the States he was colonel of a Texas regiment. The class-mate who called at Salisbury was Warren G. Huie.*

*To his brother Chauncy and his sister Betty, Barnard wrote the following letters about his Virginia visit.*

Petersburg March 14th 1833

My Dear Brother.

I left Richmond on the 9th for this place 22 miles distant. The letter which Campbell gave me to his father, gave me the most cordial, hospitable reception from his family. . . .

His father is a very strong minded, college educated man, and his mother is a woman of the finest talents highly cultivated by reading and travelling and is connected with the first families in Virginia. His sister Elizabeth Moore Campbell, is a beautiful girl of about 18 or 19—and is the belle of this region. . . .

Campbell's young brother Alexander, is a fine lad, with an eye as bright as a star, full of fun and spirit and a very promising scholar.

From this family thus described I received the most kind attention and am indebted for one of the pleasantest and most profitable weeks I ever spent. I expected to leave Petersburg the next morning, but Mrs. Campbell sent down for my trunk and lodged me immediately in her best chamber. She gave me an invitation to accompany her and Elizabeth to Shirley, where she was just agoing, and I assure you I accepted the proposal without hesitation. Shirley and the neighboring plantations on James river, are the richest and oldest estates in Virginia. So we started off the next morning, for Shirley about 15 miles from Petersburg and 25 miles from Richmond. The old house, large and commodious was built nearly 2 centuries since, by the progenitors of the present proprietor, Mr. Carter. It consists of about 900 acres improved land of the first quality and 100 slaves and yields an income of nearly 10,000 dollars. He has this year *a field of wheat, of only 320 acres*, and raises for market about 300 barrels of corn. He keeps 20 horses. With such an income you may imagine his splendid hospitality. His service is all of silver, and you drink your porter out of silver goblets. The table at dinner is always furnished with the finest Virginia ham, and saddle of mutton—Turkey, then canvas back duck—beef—oysters etc, etc, etc, etc,—the finest celery—then comes the sparkling champagne—after that the dessert, plum pudding—tarts—ice cream —peaches preserved in Brandy etc, etc—then the table is cleared, and on comes the figs, almonds and raisins, and the richest Madeira, the best Port and the softest Malmsey wine I ever tasted. . . .

While at Shirley, I visited, by invitation the ancient seat of West-over and Berkley, which with one or two exceptions, are the richest plantations in Virginia.

This excursion of a week gave me more insight into the manners and customs of the higher classes of this State, than I could have derived from any other source. We returned to Petersburg this evening. In crossing the James which is two miles wide, opposite Shirley to City Point, we had a tempestuous sea, and the Ladies were excessively frightened, and to tell the truth there was danger of being overset. . . .

Petersburg, March 15th 1833.

My Dear Betty

I think you would delight to visit this region, merely to observe the difference of manners and habits, from what you have been accustomed to, aye and to experience the princely hospitality of the *gentle* born families. For the last week I have had a succession of feasts. I accompanied Mrs. Campbell who is one of the most devoted mothers and well educated women I ever met with, and her daughter Miss Betty, a beautiful sprightly accomplished girl, to Shirley, the seat of the Carter family. Mrs. Carter, is of a high and wealthy family, and is one of the plainest most unassuming women, you will meet with any where. Now, that you may understand how we lived there, and how one of these large establishments are carried on, I will describe a single day there. . . .

When you wake in the morning, you are surprised to find that a servant has been in, and without disturbing you, built up a large fire—taken out your clothes and brushed them, and done the same with your boots—brought in hot water to shave, and indeed stands ready to do your bidding—as soon as you are dressed, you walk down into the dining room—At eight o'clock you take your seat at the breakfast table of rich mahogany—each plate standing separate on its own little cloth—Mr. Carter will sit at one end of the table and Mrs. Carter at the other—Mrs. C. will send you by two little black boys, as fine a cup of coffee as you ever tasted, or a cup of tea—it is fashionable here to drink a cup of tea after coffee—Mr. Carter has a fine cold ham before him of the real Virginia flavor—this is all the meat you will get in the morning, but the servant will bring you hot muffins and corn batter cakes every 2 minutes—you will find on the table also, loaf wheat bread, hot and cold—corn bread.

After breakfast visitors consult their pleasure—if they wish to ride, horses are ready at their command—read, there are books enough in the Library,—write, fire, and writing materials are ready in his room. The Master and Mistress of the House are not expected to entertain visitors till an hour or two before dinner, which is usually at 3. If company has been invited to the dinner they will begin to come about 1—Ladies in carriage and gentlemen horseback.—After making their toilet, the company amuse themselves in the parlor—about a half hour before dinner, the gentlemen are invited out to take grog. When dinner is ready (and by the way Mrs. Carter has nothing to do with setting the table, an old family servant, who for 50 years has superintended that matter, does all that) Mr. Carter politely takes a Lady by the hand and leads the way into the dining room, and is followed by the rest, each Lady led by a gentleman. Mrs. C. is at one end of the table with a large dish of rich soup, and Mr. C. at the other, with a saddle of fine mutton, scattered round the table, you may choose for yourself, ham—beef—turkey—ducks—eggs with greens—etc—etc— for vegetables, potatoes, beets—hominy.—This last you will find always at dinner, it is made of their white corn and beans and is a very fine dish—after you have dined, there circulates a bottle of sparkling champagne. After that off passes the things, and the *upper* table cloth, and upon that is placed the dessert, consisting of fine plum pudding, tarts, etc., etc.,—after this comes ice cream, West India preserves, peaches preserved in brandy, etc.,—When you have eaten this, off goes the second table cloth, and then upon the bare mahogany table is set, the figs, raisins, and almonds, and before Mr. Carter is set 2 or 3 bottles of wine—Madeira, Port, and a sweet wine for the Ladies—he fills his glass, and pushes them on, after the glasses are all filled, the gentlemen pledge their services to the Ladies, and down goes the wine, after the first and second glass the ladies retire, and the gentlemen begin to circulate the bottle pretty briskly. You are at liberty however to follow the Ladies as soon as you please, who after music and a little chit chat prepare for their ride home.

Salisbury, Saturday March 30.

Reached this place yesterday morning. . . . Doctor Smith was very anxious and well pleased to see me, if evidence can be trusted—found him well and George too. About 8 I lay down and slept till 10. Doctor went out to visit a patient 6 miles—was called on by Huie, an old classmate—called with him and Dr. Smith at his home—saw his two sisters, of whom Dr. Smith has spoken often and hugely of them and their beauty . . . Was introduced at tea to Mr. Alexander who invited me to call on him—he has been a bitter opponent of Smith. Smith told me of an affair of his, which redounded very much to his credit with three or four young fellows. He told him he would fight, if they dared challenge him. . . .

Sunday Evening—

Slept from 1 till 4—walked out with Dr.—George contrary to his orders had gone out to ride with Huie. This displeased him very much. He yesterday had involved him in a difficulty with Col. Lemby. George is too forward and too bold for his age, and bringing him into this region of slaves and being accustomed to be called Master, will I fear not have a happy effect upon him. . . .

Monday night April 1st.

After breakfast Dr. Smith spent some time in my room. . . . We conversed about my route—thought I had better go to Charlotte then to Berke Co.—so to Greenville to Pendleton, to Columbia or Augusta, and to Charleston, and will give me letters to some of the places mentioned. We talked about politics—State rights—etc. . . . Took a ride this afternoon in the Huie Coach out to Mccoys plantation—a tract of 4000 acres—a mill, cotton gin, 100 negroes—lives amidst his plantation—unmarried. Fished awhile but did not get a nibble—returned about 5. . . .

Wednesday—April 3.

. . . Rode out with Dr. to Mrs. Gen. S.—a lady who has once been gay and fashionable. Dr. touched her vein—a beautiful girl, granddaughter—fine forehead—finely chiseled nose—large black eyes—clear complexion and fine figure—will make a beautiful girl—miss Mary S.

Took tea there—muffins—biscuits—waffles—bread—peach, ginger and lemon preserves—fine coffee—invitation to come again before I went. . . .

Susan Dabney Smedes

## THOMAS DABNEY, VIRGINIAN

*In the course of his long life Thomas Dabney lived on three plantations. He was born at Bellevue in King and Queen County, Virginia.*

*After his first marriage, to Mary Adelaide Tyler, he lived at Elmington in Gloucester County, Virginia, and was a tobacco planter. In 1835 he moved to Hinds County, Mississippi, where he bought four thousand acres of land and turned to the cultivation of cotton. His new home was named Burleigh.*

*Thomas and his second wife, the very beautiful Sophia Hill, had sixteen children, nine sons and seven daughters. In addition to the family at Burleigh there was a succession of governesses and tutors for the children, an English gardener, and two young wards committed to Mr. Dabney's guardianship upon the death of their parents.*

*War and perfidy destroyed his immense wealth. Finding himself penniless he turned at once and with a truly astonishing cheerfulness to the most humble labors. At eighty-seven, near death, he told his family, "I have nothing to leave you but a fair name." The happy and tender memories of him that his children, Susan especially, preserved show clearly that they understood the value of his bequest.*

*Susan Dabney, born in 1840, married Mr. Lyell Smedes when she was twenty years old. In three months she was left a widow. She never married again.*

*President John Tyler's plantation on the James River was called Greenway. Watkins Leigh was a member of the General Assembly and later senator from Virginia. According to* Tidewater Virginia, *by Paul Wilstach, Ware Church was built in 1693.*

My father, Thomas Smith Gregory Dabney, was born at Bellevue, his father's country-seat on the Pamunkey River, in the county of King and Queen, Virginia, on the 4th day of January, 1798, and he used to tell us that he was two years in the world before General Washington left it. . . .

On the 6th of June, 1820, Thomas was married to Miss Mary Adelaide Tyler, daughter of Chancellor Samuel Tyler, of Williamsburg. This lady lived only three years. . . .

When Thomas Dabney had been a widower about three years, he met at the county ball at King and Queen Court-House Miss Sophia Hill, daughter of Mr. Charles Hill of that county. She was but sixteen years of age, and this was her first ball. All who saw her at that time say that she was one of the most beautiful creatures that the eye ever rested on. . . .

Thomas Dabney always said that he fell violently in love with her as soon as his eye fell on her across the ball-room. He lost no time in securing an introduction, and before the evening was over he was resolved on winning this lovely girl for his wife. He drove from his home in Gloucester to her father's home, Mantua, an the Mattapony River, in King and Queen County, every two weeks during the two months' engagement. He went in his gig, with his body-servant following on horseback. Each time he took a gift,—sometimes handsome jewelry, and at other times volumes of standard English authors.

On each alternate week he wrote a letter to her. None of these letters were answered. He looked for no acknowledgment,—his thought was that he was honored sufficiently by her receiving them.

The marriage took place at the Mantua house, on the 26th of June, 1826. The ceremony was performed by the Rev. John Coles, in the midst of a large company of relatives and friends. One who saw the bride the next day said that as she sat in her soft white gown, with her fair hands crossed in her lap and a smile on the beautiful face, she was like the vision of an angel.

On that day Thomas took her home to Elmington. Her beauty and gentleness and modesty won the hearts of his friends. She found Elmington full of her husband's servants, who had been accustomed to take care of him during his life as a widower. She felt shy about taking things into her own hands, fearing to excite their jealousy, and she took no voice in the housekeeping for two years.

The butler, George Orris, was quite equal to the trust committed to him. It was only necessary to say to him that a certain number of guests were looked for to dinner, and everything would be done in a style to suit the occasion. George himself was said to know by heart every recipe in Mrs. Randolph's cookery-book, having been trained by that lady herself. Virginia tradition says that Mrs. Randolph had spent three fortunes in cooking. At the appointed hour, in knee-breeches and silk stockings and silver buckles, George came to announce that dinner was served.

George was so formidable in his dignity of office that the timid young wife stood quite in awe of him, and before she learned to know the good, kind heart that beat under that imposing appearance, was actually afraid to ask for the keys to get a slice of bread and butter in her husband's house.

The lady's-maid, Abby, whom Sophia found at Elmington, was in her department as accomplished and as faithful as George Orris was in his. She took the new mistress at once all over the house, giving her an inventory of everything that had been left in her care.

On the 27th of March of the following year the first child was born. The happy parents gave him the name of Charles. But the child lived only nine months. On Christmas-day, 1828, a second son was given to them, whom they named Thomas. Then followed James, another Charles, and Virginius.

The life at Elmington was the ideal life of a Virginia gentleman. Elmington was situated on an arm of the Chesapeake Bay, the North River, in the county of Gloucester, that has so often been called the garden-spot of Virginia.

The house was of red brick, quaint and old-fashioned in design. It was built very near the water's edge. The lapping of the waves of the incoming tide was a sweet lullaby to the quiet scene, as the eye rested on the greensward of the lawn, or took in the bend of the river that made a broad sweep just below the Elmington garden. The North River is half a mile wide. On the other shore could be seen the groves and fields and gardens of the neighboring country-seats. The low grounds on the river-shore extend back a distance of a mile and three-quarters, and lie like a green carpet, dotted here and there with grand old forest-trees, and corn, wheat, rye, and tobacco fields. Far as the eye can reach stretches this fair view around Elmington. And far over, beyond field and grove and creek, rises the line of soft, round hills that mark the highlands of Gloucester.

On the land side, the Elmington house was approached through the fields by a lane a mile and three-quarters long. It was broad enough to admit of three carriage-drives. Many of the lanes in Gloucester lie between avenues of cedar-trees, and the fields in most of the estates are divided by cedar-hedges. It was so on the Elmington lands.

About four miles inland from the North River, in a quiet spot, surrounded by venerable oak and pine and walnut and other native trees, stands old Ware Church. It was built in colonial times, and its age is unknown. It is nearly square in form, and altogether unlike the present style of church architecture in this country. But its ancient walls are churchly, and the look of unchangeableness is soothing to the spirit in this world of unrest. This was the parish church attended by the North River people. The old pew-backs were so high that the occupants were invisible to each other. Many of them might read the names of their deceased ancestors on the tombstones that served as a floor for the chancel. The floor of Ware Church was made of flagstones. Stoves were not then in use in churches, nor was any attempt made to heat them. Delicate people stayed at home in the winter, or had warming-pans of coals carried in by their servants to put to their feet.

Gloucester County had been settled by the best class of English people who came to this country, the younger sons of noble houses, and other men of standing, who were induced to make their homes over here by an inherent love of change, or because they had not the means to live in the mother-country in the extravagant style required by their station. These brought to their homes in the New World the customs and manners of the Old. The tone of society has always been truly English in Lower Virginia, the "tide-water country," as the people love to call it. Everybody kept open house; entertaining was a matter of course, anything and everything was made the occasion of a dinner-party. The country-seats were strung along the banks of the North River in a way to favor this. A signal raised on one could be seen for several miles up and down the river. If one of the colored fishermen, whose sole occupation was to catch fish for the table at the Great House, as they called their master's residence, succeeded in catching a sheep's-head, his orders were to run up a signal-flag. This was an invitation to dinner to every gentleman in the neighborhood. If a rabbit was caught the same rule was observed. Rabbits were not common, which seemed to be the pretext for this, for they were not really esteemed as a dainty dish. A rabbit was served up rather as a trophy of the hunt than as a part of the feast intended to be eaten. But the sheep's-head in those waters were not uncommon, and one was taken by the fisherman of one house or another nearly every day. At five minutes before the time for dinner the gentlemen would ride up, or come by boat to the door of the house that had the signal flying. If any one was unable to attend, his servant rode up promptly with a note of regrets. Punctuality in the observance of all the rules of courtesy and good breeding seemed inherent in the men and women in Gloucester society....

At this time John Tyler, afterwards President of the United States, was among Thomas Dabney's intimate friends, and he wrote to ask if he could come to Elmington for a week of absolute rest and quiet. Upon the invitation being sent, he came, and his wishes were respected in the true Virginia manner of letting the guests of the house be happy and comfortable in their own way. He sat all day over his papers, no one being allowed to intrude on his privacy. Every evening, when he came down to dinner, he found a company invited to dine with him....

Thomas Dabney was interested in all that was going on in Virginia. He rode to Richmond frequently. When it was known that Watkins Leigh, or R. G. Scott, or the Stannards, or any other of the distinguished men of that day, were to engage in a debate, he was pretty sure

to be there to hear them. Thomas was present at the famous dinner at
Yorktown given in honor of the nation's guest, the Marquis de Lafayette. At the table he was placed next to George Washington Lafayette,
who occupied the seat next to his father. It was in the month of October [1824], and there was a small dish of red Antwerp raspberries sent
by Mrs. Tayloe of Mount Airy. They came from her hot-houses, and
were set before General Lafayette. The courteous gentleman leaned
across his son and offered the berries to Thomas. He took two. . . .

At the time when the negro rising known as the Southampton insurrection was threatened, Thomas received from Governor Floyd a commission of colonel of militia. He and his men kept their horses saddled
and bridled in the stable every night for three weeks, ready for any
alarm or emergency. He was an accomplished horseman, and sat his
mettlesome, blooded stallion like a part of himself. A boy in the neighborhood, whom his father asked if he would like to go to the court-
house to see Colonel Dabney's soldiers drill, said in reply that he would
rather see Colonel Dabney on his horse at the head of his regiment
than all the soldiers.

On the night when it was understood that the negro rising was to
take place he called his own negroes up, and put his wife under their
charge, as his duty called him away from her. His charge to them was
that not only was she to be protected by them, but she was not even to
be alarmed; and if harm befell a hair of her head, they should be held
accountable for it. The negroes were faithful, and guarded the house
all night long, and with so much tact and genuine affection that when
Thomas Dabney returned to his home the next day, his wife was
amazed to hear from his lips the story of the peril that she, along with
every white woman in Gloucester, had passed through during the night.

It is a singular circumstance that, with the exception of the negroes
on the Elmington place, not a negro man was to be found in Gloucester County on that night by the patrol. It was supposed that the daring
spirits had gone to join in the uprising, while the timid ones had hidden
themselves in the woods.

About the year 1835 a great many Virginians were induced to remove
with their families to the far South. For several reasons Thomas began
to consider the expediency of moving out to the new country. He was
considered one of the most successful wheat and tobacco farmers in
his part of the State. But the expensive style of living in Gloucester
began to be a source of serious anxiety. He knew that with a young
and growing family to educate and provide for the difficulty would be

greater each year. He felt also the increasing difficulty of giving to his negroes the amount of nourishing food that he considered necessary for laboring people. In view of these facts, he made up his mind that he must leave his home in Virginia for a new one in the cotton-planting States.

Many and great were the regrets when it became known that Thomas Dabney had determined to leave Gloucester.

The farewell dinner given to him at the court-house was perhaps the most notable ever given within the limits of the county. . . .

Mr. Dabney gave a farewell dinner to his friends at Elmington. As the concluding toast was drunk,—it had been proposed by the host to their meeting again,—he struck off the stem of the delicate wine-glass that he held in his hand, that no future toast should be drunk in it, he said. He requested that each guest present should break his wine-glass and keep it as a memento. . . .

Thomas went through a large part of Alabama, Louisiana, and Mississippi looking at the country before deciding on a body of land in Hinds County, Mississippi. He succeeded in purchasing four thousand acres from half a dozen small farmers. . . .

When the southern move was decided on, Thomas called his servants together and announced to them his intention to remove, with his family, to Mississippi. He further went on to say that he did not mean to take one unwilling servant with him. His plan was to offer to buy all husbands and wives, who were connected with his negroes, at the owners' prices, or he should, if his people preferred, sell those whom he owned to any master or mistress whom they might choose. No money difficulty should stand in the way. Everything should be made to yield to the important consideration of keeping families together.

Without an exception, the negroes determined to follow their beloved master and mistress. They chose rather to give up the kinspeople and friends of their own race than to leave them. . . .

The Honorable Charles Augustus Murray

## A TITLED VISITOR TO THE TIDEWATER

*Charles Augustus, second son of George Murray, fifth Earl of Dunmore, came to the United States in 1834 at the age of twenty-eight. After three years of travel on the North American continent*

*he returned to England and soon after published his impressions
of the country.*

*Sixty-odd years before his visit to Virginia in the spring of 1835, the
grandfather of this young traveler, Lord Dunmore, had served as governor of the province of Virginia.*

*For ten days Charles visited among the planters whose estates were
situated on the James River. Among these plantations were:*

*Shirley in Charles City County, some seventeen miles southeast of
Richmond. Shirley was first occupied in 1613 and was known as West-
and-Shirley. The place was inherited by Elizabeth Carter in 1720 from
her brother, Edward Hill. Here was born Anne Hill Carter, mother of
Robert E. Lee. The present house was built about 1740.*

*Brandon in Prince George County at Burrowsville, the seat of Na-
thaniel Harrison and his descendants since 1720. The house where Sir
Charles was a guest was built around 1770.*

*Berkeley in Charles City County some seven miles west of Charles
City. Benjamin Harrison, signer of the Declaration of Independence,
lived here, and here his son, William Henry Harrison, President of the
United States, was born in 1773. General McClellan used Berkeley as
his headquarters during the summer of 1862.*

On the 9th of April 1835 I left Richmond, and embarked on the
James river, the banks of which received the first settlers that Britain
sent across the Atlantic. The morning was fine, and the view of the
receding city extremely beautiful. The banks of the river are generally
well wooded and cultivated, and every now and then is seen a country-
house more resembling those in England than any which I had hitherto
observed.

I availed myself with much pleasure of the hospitable offer of one
or two gentlemen, whose acquaintance I had made in Richmond, of
paying them a visit. I disembarked accordingly about sixty miles down
the river, and received a kind welcome in the house of one of the
oldest families in the state. Here I remained four or five days; and if
the wishes of the friendly and excellent host, or of his guest, had been
alone to be consulted I might have remained there as many weeks, so
agreeable was the domestic circle in which I found myself, and so pressing were the invitations to prolong my stay. In Virginia as in England,
a country-house is a very hothouse of acquaintance, and ripens it much
earlier than the common garden of society; and the hospitality of Virginia is deservedly celebrated.

Proceeding down the river about fifteen miles, I paid another visit to two gentlemen, brothers, who were connections of my former host. Indeed, a great many of the residents on the James river are, from intermarriage and division of old estates, mutually connected; and the cousinship of the old families of the Birds, Carters, Randolphs, and Harrisons, are almost as widely extended as a similar relation in the highlands of Scotland. They seem upon the most friendly terms—are constantly interchanging visits, without ceremony or invitation; and their hospitality to strangers is not surpassed in any country that I have seen. Here, too, I saw again walls adorned with the powdered heads and laced coats of our common ancestors. I sat at dinner beneath the sweet smile of Pope's Miss Blount, from the pencil of Sir G. Kneller; while Lord Orrey, Lord Albermarle, and the Duke of Argyle, frowned from canvas of respectable antiquity. The illusion was carried yet farther by the Anglicism of the names of their residences—such as Shirley, Brandon, Berkeley, &c.

As these were the first plantations, or farms, which I had as yet seen cultivated on a large scale by slave-labour, I naturally paid much attention to the appearance of the land and its cultivators. . . . I shall confine myself to a simple record of the facts which came under my observation during this excursion, reserving to another occasion the discussion of a subject which is confessedly the most important, the most disagreeable, and the most difficult that can engage the attention either of the politician or the moralist in the United States.

From what I had already seen of the social qualities of the gentlemen at whose houses I was a visitor, I was rather gratified than surprised to witness the comparative comfort and good usage enjoyed by their slaves. The huts in which they reside are constructed of wood, and divided in the centre by a compartment, in which is fixed a chimney, to convey the smoke from each division; their food (consisting chiefly of fish, broth, maize cooked after various fashions, bacon, &c.) is wholesome and sufficient; their clothing, coarse, but suited to their necessities and to the climate; their labour compulsory and constant, but not beyond their power. During the days that I spent in the neighbourhood, I did not see any corporal punishment; but each overseer was armed with a cowhide; and one, with whom I held a long conversation regarding the detail of his occupation, informed me, that he was obliged constantly to use the lash, both to the men and women: that some he whipped four or five times a week, some only twice or thrice a-month: that all attempts to make them work regularly by advice or kindness were unavailing, for their general character was stubborn idleness; and that many who were cheerful, and even appeared attached to the family, would not work without occasional hints from the cowhide. He owned he was extremely sorry that the race existed in Virginia, destroying as they must the market for the white man's labour; adding his conviction that his employer's estate would produce more clear revenue if every negro were removed from the state, and the property divided into farms under lease. The grounds for this opinion were the heavy original outlay in the purchase of slaves (the price of an able-bodied male being, at an average, 150£),— the expense of their maintenance—the perpetual losses incurred by their dying, running away, falling sick, and other casualities, the weight of which in free countries falls upon the labourer.

It is doubtless true that all these causes, taken together, render slave-labour less cheap and profitable to the proprietor than it is sometimes assumed to be; but there is also a fact usually advanced by the slave-holders in this district which must not be passed over, and the truth of which cannot be altogether denied, namely, that the banks of the James river are extremely unhealthy during the harvest and hot months, and it is very doubtful whether white labourers (who suffer much more severely than negroes from bilious and other local fevers) could perform the work requisite during the summer; so that the choice must lie between slavery and free-black labour, of which last the Virginians speak as an impracticable theory. That, however, remains to be proved. . . .

The abject submission and ignorance necessary to the continuance of slavery may be easily gathered from the following statement:—The farms of two gentlemen whom I visited occupied the whole of a peninsula formed by the James river: they had each two overseers: thus (their families being young) the effective strength of white men on their estates amounted to six: the negroes were in number about two hundred and fifty: nor was there a village or place within many miles from which assistance could be summoned. Let the reader only imagine the scene that must have ensued, had some of these blacks, while smarting under the pain of the lash, been taught the first crude notions of natural right, or been awakened to the first consciousness of their power, or been excited to one feeling of indignation or revenge strong enough to overcome the habitual terror of the cowhide! Hence it is not difficult to understand how justly the slave-holders urge the necessity of keeping from their slaves all glimpses of knowledge or liberty upon the ground of self-preservation; and thus the best apology for slavery furnishes the best evidence of its inhuman unholy nature.

But to return to the plantations on James river. There is a wide difference between the respective conditions of the domestic and the farm-labouring slave; the former has, in many instances, been brought up under the same roof with his owner—perhaps they have been playmates in early boyhood; he has rarely, if ever, felt the lash; and his respectability of demeanour and attachment to the family are characteristics which it is easy and pleasant to observe; his punishment when idle is generally confined to a scolding, and, if that fails, a threat to sell him will almost always reduce the most obstinate to obedience. But the farm-labouring slave is little brought into contact with his master, whose habitual feelings of humanity are, therefore, seldom excited in his favour: he is one of a gang from which, as from a team of horses, a certain quantum of labour is expected; he is entirely at the mercy of the overseer; and the merit of that functionary in the eyes of his employer being to extract the maximum of profit from the exertions of the slaves, he is apt to spare neither threats nor blows in the discharge of his office, and an appeal against him to the master is worse than hopeless, as the negro evidence is unheeded. . . . These overseers are generally men of harsh and unfeeling character, which every day spent in their disagreeable vocation must have a natural tendency to harden; but I have never heard in the southeastern states of their being guilty of the licentious atrocities of which they have been sometimes accused in Louisiana.

The marriage of the slave is entirely at the option of the owner, by whom it is generally encouraged. If the wife belong to a gang on an adjoining property, the husband is usually allowed to visit her from Saturday night until Monday morning, and sometimes once again in the week from sunset until the following daybreak: the children resulting from the marriage belong to the owner of the mother. The sexual morality of the negroes (being unchecked by any notions of decency or propriety) would be even more lax than it is, were it not restrained by prohibitory regulations on the part of their owners, whose interest it is to prevent all irregularities which might interfere with the labour of the male, or the fecundity of the female slaves.

The religion of the negroes is such as might be expected from the brutal state of ignorance in which they are brought up; the dignity, the responsibility, the immortality of man being unknown to them, their religion is a compound of superstition and absurdity, inculcating no virtue, duty, or self-denial, and filling their heads with drivelling fruitless fancies; they always prefer their own preacher (some brother-slave, whose vanity and volubility have induced him to assume the office) to any white minister that can be offered to them; and the only definite article of belief that I could obtain from several whom I examined, was, that if adultery, theft, and murder were very bad, a few prayers soon expiated the offence, and the "man might start again as good as ever!"

The soil on both banks of James river is naturally very fertile; but it has been much exhausted by neglect and by over-cropping. A better system of agriculture is now introduced; a triennial rotation is observed, consisting usually of wheat, Indian corn, and clover; fine beds of marle have lately been discovered of great extent, and the use of this, with shells and a free admixture of animal and vegetable manure, is already producing evident and rapid improvements in the soil and in the crops. Most of the implements of husbandry are made on the farm; the draught cattle consist chiefly of small, lean, but hardy oxen, and stout mules, which are fed upon the coarsest refuse of the produce: thus (with the exception of the value of slave-labour) the outlay upon these farms is not by any means heavy in proportion to their return; and were it not for the subdivision to which, by the laws of the country, they are so frequently subjected, these estates would maintain a comfortable and independent gentry.

I suppose my American friends would call it British prejudice; but I confess it often made me sad, in my journey through Virginia, to see good substantial manor-houses, built while the law of primogeniture was in force, either untenanted or half inhabited, because none of the heirs of the sub-divided property could afford to live in them.

On the 19th of April, I bade adieu to my kind hosts, and embarked again on James River for Williamsburgh, the former colonial seat of government. The steamer in which I found myself was the *Patrick Henry*. The name of the extraordinary man, after whom it was so called, is familiar to all who are in any degree conversant with the history of the American revolution. How little could he imagine, when he was stirring up the Virginians to revolt, and fulminating his elo-quent denunciations against their governor, who had proclaimed him outlaw and traitor, that in fifty years his own country would be a mighty independent empire, and the grandson of that governor be received there as a traveller with kindness and hospitality. . . .

Edwin Hall

## "I AM IN THE VERY BEST OF VIRGINIA SOCIETY"

*Among the tutors employed at various times by Dr. Mann Page at his plantation home Keswick or, as it was sometimes called, Turkey Hill, in Albemarle County, Virginia, was a young New Englander, Edwin Hall. A graduate of Bowdoin College in Maine, Hall stayed a year at Keswick and earned enough money to finance his medical education. He was later graduated from Dartmouth Medical School. During his year in Virginia he wrote a number of letters to his friend Cyrus Woodman, the originals of which are in the keeping of the State Historical Society of Wisconsin.*

*The founder of the Page family, one of the most famous in Virginia, was John Page, who emigrated from England around 1650. The first Mann Page was his grandson who built, beginning in 1725, the celebrated Rosewell. Since his time there has been a Mann Page in every generation.*

*Dr. Page's wife was Jane Frances Walker, the eldest daughter of Francis Walker and Jane Byrd Nelson of Yorktown, Virginia.*

*Francis Walker Page, Dr. Page's eldest son, accompanied Hall on his mountain "excursion."*

*Dr. Page's eldest daughter Maria, of whose illness Hall writes, died June 15, 1837. She was twenty years old.*

*The "Hon. Mr. Rives" was William Cabell Rives of Castle Hill near Charlottesville. Twice Minister to France, first from 1829 to 1831 and again from 1849 to 1853, he distinguished himself both officially and personally. During his first appointment he conducted negotiations with the French government which resulted in the famous Indemnity Treaty. So warm were his relations with the French court that Queen Amélie stood godmother to his daughter, conferring her name on the child. His wife was Judith Page Walker of Belvoir.*

*Rives's experiences in Revolutionary France made a deep impression upon him, and he strongly opposed Secession. However, his loyalty to Virginia and the South induced him to serve briefly in the Confederate Congress before failing health forced his retirement to private life.*

Lindsay's Store, Albemarle County, Virginia,
March 24th '37

Dear Cyrus,

As self is always the most important personage with me, and as I always desire, when I hear from my friends, to know all the particulars respecting them, I will in this letter endeavor to give you some account of the various scenes I have witnessed since I saw you. . . .

The next day after leaving Washington I arrived at Dr. Page's where I now find myself very comfortably situated. The Doct. my employer, is a very rich planter. His plantation contains upward of three thousand acres and he has upon it one hundred slaves. He is a well bred gentleman, very familiar and agreeable—is a brother in law to the Hon. Mr. Rives, who by the way is his nearest neighbor being only one mile distant. His wife is a very fine woman indeed. They have ten children only. The two eldest are girls—one 20, the other 18. . . . The three next in order are boys, the only members of the family whom I instruct. The remainder are small fry. The Doct. lives in great style, keeps his carriage and horses, has his wine upon his table & with it almost every other luxury. We breakfast at ½ past 7, dine at 3 or half past, and take tea at 7. o'clock. I have a very neat chamber to myself in the most retired part of the house, where I pass all the time I am not in school. I never see the family except at meals as I never go in the drawing room and sit with the family though often invited to. The reason is the girls are so everlasting shy and modest I cannot get them into conversation on any subject—nothing more than "yes" and "no," and I can talk sufficient with the old man and woman at meal time. . . . Every night the servant comes in and gets my boots and cleans them. Every morning he comes before I am up, brings me water to wash, brushes my clothes, and builds a fire when one is necessary. At night when I am down to prayers the chambermaid comes in and turns down the bed clothes and puts things in order for me to go to bed. In fine everything is done for me, I have nothing to do and I find it really convenient to be waited upon. Every day about a couple of hours after dinner they either send me some fruit or a glass of wine and piece of cake.

My school room is in a building on the plantation about one mile from the house. I have nine scholars only, all boys. The boys and girls never attend the same school in Virginia I am told. My scholars are studying the languages principally. Have one class in Virgil, one in

Sallust, one in Cicero, one just commencing Greek. Three days in the week we devote to languages and two to English studies. On Saturday have no school, that day to myself. School hours from nine A.M. to 3 P.M. inclusive with half an hour recess at twelve, the remainder of the day to myself. Have a lesson in French every morning. . . . The present year will probably be worth more to me than any preceding one I ever spent in college or elsewhere. I believe, as near as I can ascertain the feeling of my employer that he is perfectly satisfied with me and from the foregoing you will perceive that I have no reason to be dissatisfied with him. I think myself very fortunate in obtaining my present situation and am perfectly contented. I am in the very best of Virginia society and see a good deal of company as the Doct. has a great many visitors.

. . . The common price of tuition here is $50, and if I can establish my reputation as a teacher I shall endeavor next year to get a private school of twenty or thirty boys, which will make good business for me, if not I shall return to Maine. I have no doubts that in many parts of Virginia, an individual might open a school and clear one or two thousand dollars a year.

This section of the country is really delightful, we have for a month past been enjoying spring weather, equal to any we have at the North in May. It is very healthy indeed I am told. Everything looks green and flourishing. The Doct. made his garden long ago, peas up, cabbage plants almost large enough to transplant. I have not yet given you my geographical location. The Doct.'s plantation lies on the South side, at the base of Peter's Mountain one of the highest peaks of the blue ridge, 120 miles south of Washington, 15 E.S:E. of Charlottesville, and 70 W.S:W. of Fredericksburg. . . .

Yours truly in good health and fine spirits,

EDWIN HALL

Lindsay's Store, Albemarle Co. Va.<br>June 13th, 1837

Bro. Cyrus,

. . . Since I last wrote to you I have taken considerable pains to become acquainted with the people in my immediate neighborhood. The result is that by so doing I have added much to my happiness, and not only to my happiness but to my limited stock of information respecting them. One of the Doct.'s daughters has been sick for some time past. All the young ladies of her acquaintance have been here to assist in taking care of her. They generally remain about a week at a time. Though sickness was in the house, and a general gloom upon the countenances of all yet I have been able to form many acquaintances, though I have not enjoyed myself so well as I should had things been otherwise. The weather has been remarkably fine, and the evenings exceedingly pleasant. . . .

Now you may prepare yourself for as faithful a picture of the Virginia ladies as I can give you. I don't think that generally speaking they have so fair and expressive countenances as the Yankee girls, though almost all of them have perfectly black hair and eyes. . . . They are more reserved in the presence of gentlemen than our ladies, expecting, as I suppose, to be entertained by them without their taking any pains to keep up an interest in the conversation. I don't much like that idea of theirs. I am always willing to do my part so far as I can towards keeping up conversation, but I have no notion of doing it all, as I wish to hear the views of others as well as express my own. They are not so well educated as the young ladies of good families of the North: and in fact how can they be when they do not commence their education till ten and close at 15. (It is not uncommon for them to get married when 16 or 17.) Many of them are educated at home, and the advantages which they enjoy are what I should call third rate at least, as good teachers are mighty scarce in this state. A finished education for a young lady, as near as I can ascertain, is a tolerable knowledge of French, English Grammar and Music. They never meddle with the higher English Studies, if I can judge from conversation which I think to be a mighty good index. Histories, novels, and other light trash are all the works you meet with. Scientific works are mighty scarce: and in fact I know of no one who takes any interest in natural science. I have endeavored to induce the young ladies to study Botany, but it is useless. . . . Show them a flower which has some interesting peculiarity, or two flowers external appearances of which, are very unlike but when closely examined precisely similar, "it is very beautiful," "I think it must be an interesting study," and there it all ends.

Nonsense, great characters, things to be seen in Washington, and at the Springs, their relations and acquaintances are the most interesting and almost the only topics of conversation. A good stock of information respecting the principal characters of the day and the most popular works, with a good selection of anecdotes make a person appear quite respectable in a drawing room here. Also a knowledge of

the politics of the day turns to a very good account as almost every
gentleman here is more or less a politician.

It is not customary here to walk arm in arm with the ladies, unless
on the most *intimate* terms with them, but simply by their sides. It is a
custom very well suited to a warm climate; but I must confess I like the
N.E. one best. The boys and girls are always educated separately here,
which I think to be one reason why the latter are so reserved, and again
they do not have the privilege of mingling in mixed company which
our ladies do. So I will wind up this topic by saying that if I *were* to
take a wife I should choose a Northern lady in preference to a Southern
one. . . .

. . . From what observations I have been able to make on the climate
of this region I should say it is vastly preferable to that of Maine, at
least it is much more agreeable to my feelings. But yet I don't think
it is so favorable to the growth of that spirit of enterprise so conspicuous
in the character of Northern men; for I am of opinion that the climate
has some effect in producing it, as well as the differences in our institutions, for I have been informed by persons on whom I can rely that
the people south of this state are less enterprising than those of this
section, who I am certain are far behind the Yankees.

Now for the management of a plantation so far as I understand it.
The houses of the slaves are distributed about the plantation in groups,
several being in each. Large plantations are divided into one or more
farms as I will call the divisions: and the slaves work on those divisions only in which they reside. There is an overseer on each farm
whose duty it is to look after the slaves—be with them when they
work & show them how. The planter gives his orders to the overseer,
which is all he has to do. The overseer is a white man. On every well
regulated plantation they have a code of laws, which are known by the
slaves. When they violate any of them they are punished. The usual
mode of punishment is, to deprive them of their meat for a certain
time, and I am told it is the most effectual as they are very fond of it.
I was told by the Doct.'s overseers that he seldom flogged any one,
or punished in any other way than the one I have mentioned. The
slaves by no means work hard: our Northern daily laborers do at least
treble the work in the course of a year, that the same number of slaves
do. The principal productions are tobacco, wheat, and corn. The tobacco is raised thus.

A piece of new land, which is rich, is prepared, somewhat as we prepare our gardens and sown in the fall of the year. In the spring it is

covered with brush to protect the young plants against the storms; for they are very tender. About the middle of June the plants are taken up and transplanted in ground previously prepared to receive them. The crop is then managed as any other till harvested, with this exception, that when the plants are quite large the plants send out suckers which are all pulled off, and only the original one stalk left. In harvesting, they cut the stocks, before the leaves begin to wither, a few inches from the ground & hang them up to dry. When sufficiently dry they are hung up in houses, prepared for the purpose. In the winter the leaves are stripped from the stalks & packed in hogsheads & sent to the manufacturer.

The wheat is sown in the fall & not in the spring as with us. There is no other difference in the management of the crop, that is to say, the crop is managed as we manage it. Doct. Page has about 365 acres of wheat & as many of corn. . . . We had green peas the 27th of last month & also strawberries. Berries of all kinds are very abundant in this vicinity. . . .

Truly yours

Edwin M. Hall

Lindsay's Store<br>Aug. 30, 1837

Friend Cyrus,

. . . Wednesday Aug. 2nd I left this place to take a month's excursion through the mountains as we say here. I will give you a short sketch of my tour which has been by far the most interesting one to me I ever took. . . . And first my companion was a son of the Doct. about 17 years of age who had never been from home before. And here let me remark what I believe to be a sober fact, viz. that the Southern boys at 20 are not so well qualified to enter upon the duties of life as the northern boys at 14 yrs of age. Mounted on two gray horses with a pair of saddle bags and valise in which was our clothing we set off shaping our course to the blue ridge. On the morn. of the 2nd day we crossed the blue ridge at Rock fish gap, at the top of this gap we had a splendid mountain view of the valley and of eastern Va. A few words respecting the Valley of Va. That portion of Va. just west of the blue ridge or rather between that and the range called the North Mts. is called the valley of Va. It commences in Penn. and extends in a S. Westerly direction into N.C. It is almost entirely a limestone formation and in a great many places the stone lays so near the surface as to render the land unfit for cultivation. A great many small streams take their rise in the mountains which border on the valley and flow through it. Most of the land in this valley is quite good. That laying in the bottoms as they are called, i.e. close upon the rivers is very good indeed.

Leaving the ridge we passed through Waynesboro, Greenville, Fairfield, Lexington to the Nat. Bridge, 3 days travel, 90 miles. We arrived at this great natural curiosity in the eve, and passed the night at a good hotel within 50 yards of the Bridge. As soon as Aurora lit up the morn, accompanied by our landlord we hastened to view this interesting object. . . . Our guide first carried us to the upper side of the bridge to the edge of the precipice from whence if your head is strong enough you may have a fine view of the abyss below which is only 250 ft. deep. . . . After you look into the dreadful abyss from the top with utter amazement and astonishment for some time you feel as if you wished to go below.

We will go down. Winding down a steep hill on the lower side, you suddenly emerge from the bushes into the bed of the creek. The moment you behold the magnificent arch sweeping gracefully across from one abutment to the other, high above your head, you involuntarily stop—awe seizes you. It is then that you fully feel the weakness of language to describe a scene so vast, so sublime, yes even a painter would drop his pencil and acknowledge his utter inability to transfer its grandeur and sublimity to the canvas. The height of the bridge is 250 ft., distance between the abutments 90 ft., thickness of the arch 45, width I should think about 60 or 70 ft. A road which is much traveled passes over it. . . .

Leaving the Bridge we passed through Pattensburg, Buchanan and Fincastle. 17 miles west of Fincastle we came to the nine mile mountain so called because it is nine miles after you begin to ascend before you come to the foot on the opposite side. Crossing over this we stopped a short time in the valley. If you are a sportsman stop here, and you will find good accommodations with a plenty of deer, bear and wild turkeys to shoot. Leaving this valley which is not more than ½ mile wide we crossed over the Sweet Spring Mt.—5 miles—and arrived at the Sweet Springs. The water of these Springs tastes just like a weak dose of Eps. Salts, is a good tonic and serviceable in many cases of disease. The proprietor can accommodate about 100 guests.

Leaving these Springs and crossing the Alleganies we arrived at the

White Sulphur Springs one of the most fashionable resorts in Va. We found about 600 people there. . . . There are no large buildings connected with the establishment. The ones occupied by the visitors are cabins as they term them here. They are arranged with considerable order and give the appearance of a neat little village. There are a great many large oak and locust trees standing about the buildings which add very much to the beauty of the spot. The scenery about is very fine. Chance for game very good. At this watering place you meet with men of every grade and from all parts of the country, more particularly from the Southern states, who come here with their families to spend the hot season—here you have a fine chance to see Southern beauty and mingle in Southern society. The greatest harmony and intercourse prevail throughout. Balls every night. . . .

Leaving here we went to the Hot Springs, thence to the Warm Springs, thence to Augusta Springs, thence to Mt. Sidney, thence to Weyer's Cave, the greatest natural curiosity now known in the world, thence to Harrisonburg, thence to New Market, thence to Woodstock, thence to Winchester, thence to Warrenton, thence Fauquier White Sulphur Springs, the most fashionable resort in Va. where we found 550 visitors—100 of them young ladies, some very beautiful, thence to Fairfax, thence to Orange Court House, thence home, we traveled upwards of 500 miles without going over an inch of the same ground twice. . . .

Truly yours

EDWIN M. HALL

Lindsay's Store    Albemarle Co. Va.<br>Nov. 2nd    1837

Friend Cyrus,

. . . Though situated in the country yet I have my amusement. We have an abundance of game such as wild turkies, pheasant, partridges, hares, etc. The partridges are most numerous. They are a different bird from what we call partridge, being smaller, living in coveys or flocks and in the open fields. Their plumage and appearance is very much like that of our partridge. The method of hunting them is as follows. The hunter goes into the field with dogs of the pointer species. He sings out to them "high on" pointing the direction which he wishes them to take. They immediately commence running through the field in all directions. This species of dogs possess the power or faculty of smell to a great degree. They can smell a flock of birds some 30 or 40 feet, a single bird not quite so far. As soon as they smell a flock they approach within a few feet of them, point towards them with their nose and stand perfectly still. The hunter comes up, cocks his gun, and says to dogs "high on." The dogs spring upon the birds and as they fly he shoots. It is good shooting to kill six at ten shots, flying. There was a man in this neighborhood who killed ninety six at one hundred shots, flying. The dogs are so tractable that they are very easily learned to watch all your motions, and to notice no other birds except partridges. I was out a few hours not long since with four others; we killed 18 partridges and 2 hares. . . .

To get along with the ladies here we must possess a little smattering of most everything and be able to talk all kinds of nonsense, for to speak the plain truth, I have not heard five words of what I call rational conversation from a lady either at a party or anywhere else since I have been here. A lamentable state of things! What pleasure in having nonsense eternally ringing in one's ears! A little turn at flattery does not come amiss, and no lady appears to resent it though of the grossest kind. These, in my opinion are the essentials in gaining popularity and combined with cultivated manners will render one agreeable not only in the drawing room but everywhere else. Today I dined at Senator Rives'. We had a very large dinner party, about 30 present mostly young persons. We had a large dinner party at our house yesterday. The people live so far apart and the roads are so abominably bad that it is out of the question to have evening parties. It would frighten a country Virginian half to death to be out till nine o'clock in the evening. . . .

Ever and truly yours

EDWIN HALL

Sara Hicks Williams

## A YANKEE GIRL IN NORTH CAROLINA

*Sara Hicks was an eighteen-year-old school girl attending the Albany Female Academy in Albany, New York, when in 1845 she met medical student Benjamin Franklin Williams. Benjamin fell in love with her and began a courtship that was to continue for eight years until they were married. The two were from vastly different backgrounds—Sara a thoroughgoing Yankee, Benjamin a well-to-do North Carolina planter. Sara, born in New Hartford, New York, was the daughter of*

Samuel Hicks, manager of the Eagle Mills near Clayville, New York. Her mother had been Sara Parmelee, of Durham, Connecticut, descendant of a long line of New England forebears. Benjamin, seven years older than Sara, owned 2,000 acres of land in the central coastal region of North Carolina, in the vicinity of Snow Hill, largely cultivated cotton land and tracts of pine which were worked for turpentine. Although he became a licensed physician in North Carolina, his practice of medicine was only casual. Most of his time was devoted to the management of the extensive landholdings he had inherited.

They were married in the old Hicks mansion in September 1853 and went to live with Benjamin's widowed mother, Mrs. Joseph Williams, at the family plantation, Clifton Grove, about five miles from Snow Hill. Sara had misgivings about her husband's owning slaves: "I cannot make it seem right," she had written to her parents several months before her marriage, "and yet, perhaps there will be my sphere of usefulness."

Though she found Southern ways very strange, Sara became in time an efficient mistress of her husband's plantation in North Carolina and later in southeastern Georgia, where Benjamin's turpentine business took them. She died at Waycross, Georgia, in 1917.

These letters to her parents mirror her very first and freshest impressions of the new surroundings she had chosen to enter when she became a Southern slaveholder's wife. The original letters belong to the estate of the late Colonel Warren Lott of Blackshear, Georgia. More than a hundred of them have been deposited in the Southern Historical Collection, University of North Carolina, Chapel Hill.

Clifton Grove, [N. C.] Oct. 10, 1853

My dear Parents:

I arrived safely at my new home on Friday last, but have had no time to write until now. . . . You may imagine I have seen many strange things. As for my opinions, in so short a time, it would not be fair to give them. I have seen no unkind treatment of servants. Indeed, I think they are treated with more familiarity than many Northern servants. They are in the parlor, in your room and all over. The first of the nights we spent in the Slave Holding States, we slept in a room without a lock. Twice before we were up a waiting girl came into the room, and while I was dressing, in she came to look at me. She seemed perfectly at home, took up the locket with your miniatures in it and wanted to know if it was a watch. I showed it to her. "Well," she said, "I should think your mother and father are mighty old folks." Just before we arrived home, one old Negro caught a glimpse of us and came tearing out of the pine woods to touch his hat to us. All along the road we met them and their salutation of "Howdy (meaning How do you) Massa Ben," and they seemed so glad to see him, that I felt assured that they were well treated. As we came to the house, I found Mother Williams ready to extend a mother's welcome. . . . I felt at home. At dinner we had everything very nice. It is customary when the waiting girl is not passing things at table, to keep a large broom of peacock feathers in motion over our heads to keep off flies, etc. I feel confused. Everything is so different that I do not know which way to stir for fear of making a blunder. I have determined to keep still and look on for a while, at any rate.

Yesterday I went to Church in a very handsome carriage, servants before and behind. I began to realize yesterday how much I had lost in the way of religious privileges. We went six miles to church, as they have preaching at Snow Hill only every one or two Sabbaths. On arriving I found a rough framed building in the midst of woods, with a large congregation, consisting of about equal numbers of white and black. . . . The singing is horrible. Prize your religious privileges. They are great and you would realize it by attending Church here once. I shall miss these much. Things that Northerners consider essential are of no importance here. The house and furniture is of little consequence. To all these differences I expect to become accustomed, in time. My husband is all kindness and loves me more than I am worthy. With him I could be happy anywhere. I have seen enough to convince me that the ill-treatment of the Slaves is exaggerated at the North but I have not seen enough to make me like the institution. I am quite the talk of the day, not only in the whole County, but on the plantation. Yesterday I was out in the yard and an old Negro woman came up to me, "Howdy, Miss Sara, are you the Lady that won my young Master? Well, I raised him." Her name was Chaney and she was the family nurse. Between you and me, my husband is better off than I ever dreamed of. I am glad I didn't know it before we were married. He owns 2000 acres of land in this vicinity, but you must bear in mind that land here is not as valuable as with you. But I'll leave these things to talk of when I see you. . . . Ever your

SARA

I wish you could see the cotton fields. The bolls are just opening. I cannot compare their appearance to anything but fields of white roses. As to the cotton picking, I should think it very light and pleasant work. Our house is very unassuming. . . .

Clifton Grove, Oct. 22, 1853

My dear Parents:

... Ambition is satisfied here by numbering its thousands of dollars, acres of land and hundreds of negroes. Houses, furniture, dress are nothing. For instance, the Dr.'s brother, a very wealthy man, lives in a brown wood house without lathing or plastering. To be sure, he has a handsome sofa, sideboard and chairs in his parlor, which contrast strangely with the unfinished state of the house. However, he purposes building soon. His, I might say, is the common style of house, and ours, which is finished, the exception. As to household arrangements, I have discovered no system. Wash, bake or iron, just as the fit takes. ... Baking is all done in bake kettles and cooking at a fire place. Chimneys are all built on the outside of the houses. The Negroes are certainly not overtasked on this plantation. One house girl at the North will accomplish more than two here. But I think the great fault lies in the want of system. Mother Williams works harder than any Northern farmer's wife, I know. She sees to everything. ...

Clifton Grove, Nov. 18, 1853

My dear Parents:

... There is but one closet in our house, so you can imagine that I find some difficulty in knowing where to put things. And Mother Williams' ways are so entirely different from anything I have ever been used to that I sometimes feel disheartened and discouraged. She is very kind to me & I intend making my will bend to hers in every respect, but I assure you I miss the order and neatness which pervades a Northern home. ... I do not pretend to know much of housekeeping, but I know I could improve on some things here in the way of order. ...

Clifton Grove, Dec. 10th, 1853

My dear Parents:

... At present there is sewing a plenty on hands for the servants. At this season the women have each a thick dress, chemise, shoes, & a blanket given them. The men pantaloons & jacket, shirt, blanket & shoes, besides caps & bonnets. The children, too, are clothed in the same materials. Now, many keep a seamstress to do this, but Mother Williams has always done it herself with the assistance of her daughters when they were home. Of course, I choose to do my part. One week we made seven dresses & a few jackets and pantaloons we sent to a poor white woman. ... The servants have three suits of clothes a year and as much more in clothes and money as they choose to earn. . . . We need quite as thick clothing as you do. The houses are not as tightly built as with us, and they use fireplaces altogether, and there is a chill in the air. . . . I have made pumpkin pies, or helped, twice & the last, which are best, I made all alone, crust & all. They never had had them before & Ben particularly liked them. So, of course, my success pleased me. Soda biscuits, I have made twice with good success and measure cake. Not until you come here can you imagine how entirely different is their mode of living from the North. They live more heartily. There must always be two or three different kinds of meats on Mrs. Williams' table for breakfast & dinner. Red pepper is much used to flavor meat with the famous "barbecue" of the South and which I believe they esteem above all dishes is roasted pig dressed with red pepper & vinegar. Their bread is corn bread, just meal wet with water & without yeast or saleratus, & biscuit with shortening and without anything to make them light and beaten like crackers. The bread and biscuit are always brought to the table hot. . . . I wish we could send you some of our beautiful sweet potatoes & yams. . . .

Frederick Law Olmsted

## A TOBACCO PLANTATION IN VIRGINIA

*In 1853 Frederick Law Olmsted, who was born in Hartford, Connecticut, in 1822, was commissioned by the editor of the New York Times to travel through the seaboard slave states and write his unbiased impressions of slavery and the economic and social conditions of the South.*

*His newspaper articles were later collected and published under the title* Journey in the Seaboard Slave States. *"The author had," explained Mr. Olmsted, "at the outset of his journey a determination to see things for himself, as far as possible, and to see them carefully and fairly, but cheerfully and kindly. It was his disposition, also, to search for the cause and extenuating circumstances, past and present, of those phenomena which are commonly reported to the prejudice of the slaveholding community. . . . As a democrat he went to study the South—its institutions, and its people; more than ever a democrat, he returned from this labor, and has written the pages which follow. . . ."*

*Olmsted's abundant gifts as observer and reporter are well evidenced in this vivid account of his visit to a tobacco plantation near Peters-burg, Virginia.*

Petersburg, Dec. 28 [1853]—It was early in a fine, mild, bright morning, like the pleasantest we ever have in March, that I alighted, from a train of cars, at a country station. Besides the shanty that stood for a station-house, there was a small, comfortable farm-house on the right, and a country store on the left, and around them, perhaps, fifty acres of cleared land, now much flooded with muddy waters;—all environed by thick woods.

A few negro children, staring fixedly and posed as lifelessly as if they were really figures "carved in ebony," stood, lay, and lounged on the sunny side of the ranks of locomotive-firewood; a white man, smoking a cigar, looked out of the door of the store, and another, chewing to-bacco, leaned against a gate-post in front of the farm-house; I advanced to the latter, and asked him if I could hire a horse in the neighborhood.

"How d'ye do, sir?" he replied; "I have some horses—none on 'em very good ones, though—rather hard riders; reckon, perhaps, they wouldn't suit you very well."

"Thank you; do you think I could find anything better about here?"

"Colonel Gillin, over here to the store's got a right nice saddle-horse, if he'll let you take her. I'll go over there with you, and see if he will. ... Mornin', Colonel;—here's a gentleman that wants to go to Thomas W.'s: couldn't you let him have your saddle horse?"

"How do you do, sir; I suppose you'd come back tonight?"

"That's my intention, but I might be detained till tomorrow, unless it would be inconvenient to you to spare your horse."

"Well, yes, sir, I reckon you can have her;—Tom!—Tom!—*Tom!* Now, has that devilish nigger gone again! Tom! *Oh*, Tom! saddle the filly for this gentleman. Have you ever been to Mr. W.'s, sir?"

"No, I have not."

"It isn't a very easy place for strangers to go to from here; but I reckon I can direct you, so you'll have no difficulty."

He accordingly began to direct me; but the way appeared so difficult to find, I asked him to let me make a written memorandum, and, from this memorandum, I now repeat the directions he gave me.

"You take this road here—you'll see where it's most traveled, and it's easy enough to keep on it for about a mile; then there's a fork, and you take the right; pretty soon, you'll cross a creek and turn to the right—the creek's been up a good deal lately, and there's some big

trees fallen along there, and, if they ha'n't got them out of the way,
you may have some difficulty in finding where the road is; but you
keep bearing off to the right, where it's the most open, and you'll see
it again pretty soon. Then you go on, keeping along in the road—
you'll see where folks have traveled before—for maybe quarter of a
mile, and you'll find a cross-road; you must take that to the left; pretty
soon you'll pass two cabins; one of 'em's old and all fallen in, the
other one's new, and there's a white man lives in it. About a hundred
yards beyond it, there's a fork, and you take the left—it turns square
off, and it's fenced for a good bit; keep along by the fence, and you
can't miss it. It's right straight beyond that till you come to a school-
house, there's a gate opposite to it, and off there there's a big house—
but I don't reckon you'll see it neither, for the woods. But somewhere,
about three hundred yards beyond the school-house, you'll find a little
road running off to the left through an old field; you take that and
keep along in it, and in less than half a mile you'll find a path going
square off to the right; you take that, and keep on it till you pass a little
cabin in the woods; aint nobody lives there now; then it turns to the
left, and when you come to a fence and gate, you'll see a house there,
that's Mr. George Rivers' plantation—it breaks in two, and you take
the right, and when you come to the end of the fence, turn the corner
—don't keep on, but turn there. Then it's straight, till you come to the
creek again—there's a bridge there; don't go over the bridge, but turn
to the left and keep along nigh the creek, and pretty soon you'll see a
meeting-house in the woods; you go to that, and you'll see a path bearing off to the right—it looks as if it was going right away from the
creek, but you take it, and pretty soon it'll bring you to a saw-mill on
the creek, up higher a piece; you just cross the creek there, and you'll
find some people at the mill, and they'll put you right straight on the
road to Mr. W.'s."

"How far is it all, sir?"

"I reckon it's about two hours' ride, when the roads are good, to the
saw-mill. Mr. W.'s gate is only a mile or so beyond that, and then
you've got another mile, or better, after you get to the gate, but you'll
see some nigger-quarters—the niggers belong to Mr. W., and I reckon
there'll be some of 'em round, and they'll show you just where to go."

After reading over my memorandum, and finding it correct, and
agreeing with him that I should pay two dollars a day for the mare,
we walked out, and found her saddled and waiting for me.

I remarked that she was very good-looking.

"Yes, sir; she a'nt a bad filly; out of a mare that came of Lady Rackett by old Lord-knows-who, the best horse we ever had in this part of the country; I expect you have heard of him."

The filly was just so pleasantly playful, and full of well-bred life, as to create a joyful, healthy, sympathetic, frolicsome heedlessness in her rider. . . .

About eleven o'clock I crossed a bridge and came to the meeting-house. It was in the midst of the woods, and the small clearing around it was still dotted with the stumps of the trees out of whose trunks it had been built; for it was a log structure. In one end there was a single square port, closed by a sliding shutter, in the other end were two doors, both standing open. In front of the doors, a rude scaffolding had been made of poles and saplings extending out twenty feet from the wall of the house, and this had been covered with boughs of trees, the leaves now withered; a few benches, made of split trunks of trees, slightly hewn with the axe, were arranged under this arbor, as if the religious service was sometimes conducted on the outside in prefer-ence to the interior of the edifice. Looking at it, I saw that a gallery or loft extended from over the doors, across about one-third the length of the house, access to which was had by a ladder. At the opposite end was a square, unpainted pulpit, and on the floor were rows of rude benches. The house was sufficiently lighted by crevices between the upper logs.

Half an hour after this I arrived at the negro-quarters—a little hamlet of ten or twelve small and dilapidated cabins. Just beyond them was a plain farm-gate, at which several negroes were standing; one of them, a well-made man, with an intelligent countenance and prompt manner, directed me how to find my way to his owner's house. It was still nearly a mile distant; and yet, until I arrived in its im-mediate vicinity, I saw no cultivated field, and but one clearing. In the edge of this clearing, a number of negroes, male and female, lay stretched out upon the ground near a small smoking charcoal pit. Their master afterwards informed me that they were burning charcoal for the plantation blacksmith, using the time allowed them for holidays —from Christmas to New Year's—to earn a little money for them-selves in this way. He paid them by the bushel for it. When I said that I supposed he allowed them to take what wood they chose for this purpose, he replied that he had five hundred acres covered with wood, which he would be very glad to have any one burn, or clear off in any way. . . .

Mr. W.'s house was an old family mansion, which he had himself remodeled in the Grecian style, and furnished with a large wooden portico. An oak forest had originally occupied the ground where it stood; but this having been cleared and the soil worn out in cultivation by the previous proprietors, pine woods now surrounded it in every direction, a square of a few acres only being kept clear immediately about it. A number of the old oaks still stood in the rear of the house, and, until Mr. W. commenced his improvements, there had been some in its front. These, however, he had cut away, as interfering with the symmetry of his grounds, and in place of them had planted ailanthus trees in parallel rows.

On three sides of the outer part of the cleared square there was a row of large and comfortable-looking negro quarters, stables, tobacco-houses, and other offices, built of logs.

Mr. W. was one of the few large planters, of his vicinity, who still made the culture of tobacco their principal business. He said there was a general prejudice against tobacco, in all the tide-water region of the State, because it was through the culture of tobacco that the once fertile soils had been impoverished; but he did not believe that, at the present value of negroes, their labor could be applied to the culture of grain, with any profit, except under peculiarly favorable circumstances. Possibly, the use of guano might make wheat a paying crop, but he still doubted it. He had not used it, himself. Tobacco required fresh land, and was rapidly exhausting, but it returned more money, for the labor used upon it, than anything else; enough more, in his opinion, to pay for the wearing out of the land. If he was well-paid for it, he did not know why he should not wear out his land.

His tobacco-fields were nearly all in a distant and lower part of his plantation; land which had been neglected before his time, in a great measure, because it had been sometimes flooded, and was, much of the year, too wet for cultivation. He was draining and clearing it, and it now brought good crops.

He had had an Irish gang draining for him, by contract. He thought a negro could do twice as much work, in a day, as an Irishman. He had not stood over them and seen them at work, but judged entirely from the amount they accomplished: he thought a good gang of negroes would have got on twice as fast. He was sure they must have "trifled"

a great deal, or they would have accomplished more than they had. . . .
I asked why he should employ Irishmen, in preference to doing the
work with his own hands. "It's a dangerous work (unhealthy), and a
negro's life is too valuable to be risked at it. If a negro dies, it's a considerable loss, you know."

He afterwards said that his negroes never worked so hard as to
tire themselves—always were lively, and ready to go off on a frolic at
night. He did not think they ever did half a fair day's work. They
could not be made to work hard: they never would lay out their
strength freely, and it was impossible to make them do it. . . .

Mr. W. also said that he cultivated only the coarser and lower-
priced sorts of tobacco, because the finer sorts required more pains-
taking and discretion than it was possible to make a large gang of
negroes use. "You can make a nigger work," he said, "*but you cannot
make him think.*"

Although Mr. W. was very wealthy (or, at least, would be considered so anywhere at the North), and was a gentleman of education,
his style of living was very farmer-like, and thoroughly Southern. On
their plantations, generally, the Virginia gentlemen seem to drop
their full-dress and constrained town-habits, and to love a free, rustic,
shooting-jacket life. We dined in a room that extended out, rear-
wardly, from the house, and which, in a Northern establishment,
would have been the kitchen. The cooking was done in a detached
log-cabin, and the dishes brought some distance, through the open air,
by the servants. The outer door was left constantly open, though there
was a fire in an enormous old fire-place, large enough, if it could have
been distributed sufficiently, to have lasted a New York seamstress
the best part of the winter. By the door, there was indiscriminate ad-
mittance to negro-children and fox-hounds, and, on an average, there
were four of these, grinning or licking their chops, on either side of my
chair, all the time I was at the table. A stout woman acted as head
waitress, employing two handsome little mulatto boys as her aids in
communicating with the kitchen, from which relays of hot corn-
bread, of an excellence quite new to me, was brought at frequent
intervals. There was no other bread, and but one vegetable served—
sweet potato, roasted in ashes, and this, I thought, was the best sweet
potato, also, that I ever had eaten; but there were four preparations
of swine's flesh, besides fried fowls, fried eggs, cold roast turkey, and
opossum, cooked, I know not how, but it somewhat resembled baked
suckling-pig. The only beverages on the table were milk and whiskey.

I was pressed to stay several days with Mr. W., and should have been glad to have accepted such hospitality, had not another engagement prevented. When I was about to leave, an old servant was directed to get a horse, and go with me, as guide, to the rail-road station at Col. Gillin's. . . .

Letitia M. Burwell

## "THE WORLD ONE VAST PLANTATION"

*"All plantation reminiscences,"* says the author, *"resemble a certain patch work, made when we were children, of bright pieces joined with black squares. The black squares were not pretty, but if left out the character of the quilt was lost. And so with the black faces—if left out of our home pictures of the past, the character of the picture is destroyed."*

Then, lest her own representation might seem deliberately one-sided, she adds:

*"The pictures are strictly true; and should it be thought by any that the brightest have alone been selected, I can only say I knew no others."*

*Letitia Burwell, who gives the glowing, artless and affectionate account of her early life in the Piedmont, was born about 1840. Nine generations before her had been Virginia planters. Thomas Jefferson and James Madison had been neighbors of her grandfather, William Armistead Burwell, who served as a member of the State House of Delegates, as private secretary to President Thomas Jefferson, and as a member of the United States Congress from 1806 until his death, February 16, 1821.*

*Oaklands was the home of General Watts.*

*The master of Buena Vista was George P. Tayloe, one of the signers of the Ordinance of Secession. Of his four sons who served in the Confederate Army two were killed.*

*Grove Hill was the original seat of the Breckinridge family in Botetourt County. At the time of Letitia's account Mrs. Cary Breckinridge was mistress of the plantation. All four of her sons enlisted in the Confederate Army. All four were killed. Only the youngest rests in the plantation cemetery. The rest were buried on the battlefields.*

*Greenfield in Botetourt County was the home of both Preston and Breckinridge ancestors.*

*Elkwood in Culpeper County was burned by the Northern army in 1862.*

*The distinguished visitors to the Burwell home in 1859 were Senator Robert Toombs and Secretary of War John B. Floyd.*

Confined exclusively to a Virginia plantation during my earliest childhood, I believed the world one vast plantation bounded by negro quarters. Rows of white cabins with gardens attached; negro men in the fields; negro women sewing, knitting, spinning, weaving, housekeeping in the cabins; with negro children dancing, romping, singing, jumping, playing around the doors,—these formed the only pictures familiar to my childhood.

The master's residence—as the negroes called it, "the great house"— occupied a central position and was handsome and attractive, the overseer's being a plainer house about a mile from this.

Each cabin had as much pine furniture as the occupant desired, pine and oak being abundant, and carpenters always at work for the comfort of the plantation.

Bread, meat, milk, vegetables, fruit, and fuel were as plentiful as water in the springs near the cabin doors.

Among the negroes—one hundred—on our plantation, many had been taught different trades; and there were blacksmiths, carpenters, masons, millers, shoemakers, weavers, spinners, all working for themselves. No article of their handicraft ever being sold from the place, their industry resulted in nothing beyond feeding and clothing themselves.

My sister and myself, when very small children, were often carried to visit these cabins, on which occasions no young princesses could have received from admiring subjects more adulation. Presents were laid at our feet—not glittering gems, but eggs, chestnuts, popcorn, walnuts, melons, apples, sweet potatoes—all their "cupboards" afforded,— with a generosity unbounded. This made us as happy as queens, and filled our hearts with kindness and gratitude to our dusky admirers.

All were merry-hearted, and among them I never saw a discontented face. Their amusements were dancing to the music of the banjo, quilting-parties, opossum-hunting, and sometimes weddings and parties.

Many could read, and in almost every cabin was a Bible. In one was a prayer-book, kept by one of the men, a preacher, from which he read the marriage ceremony at the weddings.

Our house servants were numerous, polite, and well trained. My mother selected those most obliging in disposition and quickest at learning, who were brought to the house at ten or twelve years of age, and instructed in the branches of household employment.

These small servants were always dressed in the cleanest, whitest, long-sleeved aprons, with white or red turbans on their heads. No establishment being considered complete without a multiplicity of these, they might be seen constantly darting about on errands from the house to the kitchen and the cabins, upstairs and downstairs, being, indeed, omnipresent and indispensable.

The atmosphere of our home was one of consideration and kindness. The mere recital of a tale of suffering would make my sister and myself weep with sorrow. And I believe the maltreatment of one of our servants—we had never heard the word "slave"—would have distressed us beyond endurance.

I remember that once, when my grandmother scolded nurse Kitty, saying: "Kitty, the butler tells me you disturb the breakfast cream every morning by dipping out milk to wash your face," I burst into tears, and thought it hard that, when there were so many cows, poor Kitty could not wash her face in milk. Kitty had been told that her dark skin would be improved by a milk bath, which she had not hesitated to dip every morning from the breakfast buckets.

At such establishments one easily acquired a habit of being waited upon, there being so many servants with so little to do. It was natural to ask for a drink of water when the water was right at hand, and to have things brought which you might easily have gotten yourself. A young lady would ask black Nancy or Dolly to fan her, whereupon Nancy or Dolly would laugh good-naturedly, produce a large palm-leaf, and fall to fanning her young mistress vigorously, after which she would be rewarded with a bow of ribbon, some candy, or sweet cakes.

The negroes made pocket-money by selling their own vegetables, poultry, eggs, etc.—produced at the master's expense, of course. I often saw my mother take out her purse and pay them liberally for fowls, eggs, melons, sweet potatoes, brooms, shuck mats, and split baskets. The men made small crops of tobacco or potatoes for themselves on any piece of ground they chose to select.

My mother and grandmother were almost always talking over the wants of the negroes—what medicine should be sent, whom they should visit, who needed new shoes, clothes, or blankets—the principal object of their lives seeming to be in providing these comforts. The carriage was often ordered for them to ride around to the cabins to distribute light-bread, tea, and other necessaries among the sick. And besides employing the best doctor, my grandmother always saw that they received the best nursing and attention.

In this little plantation world of ours was one being—and only one—who inspired awe in every heart, being a special terror to small children. This was the queen of the kitchen, Aunt Christian, who reigned supreme. She wore the whitest cotton cap with the broadest of ruffles; she was very black and very portly; and her scepter was a good-sized stick, kept to chastise small dogs and children who invaded her territory.

Her pride was great, "for," said she, "aint I bin—long fo' dis yer little marster whar is was born—bakin' de bes' loaf bread, an' bes' beat biscuit and rice waffles, all de time in my ole marster time? An' I bin manage my own affa'rs, an' I gwine manage my own affa'rs long is I got breff. All our black folks done belonks to de Burl fambly uver sence dey come fum Afiky. My Granmammy 'member dem times when black folks lan' here stark naked, an' white folks hab to show 'em how to war close. But we all done come fum all dat now, an' I gwine manage my own affa'rs."

It was a long time before it dawned upon my mind that there were places and people different from these. The plantations we visited seemed exactly like ours. The same hospitality was everywhere; the same kindliness existed between the white family and the blacks.

We often listened with pleasure to the recollections of an old blind man—the former faithful attendant of our grandfather—whose mind was filled with vivid pictures of the past. He repeated verbatim conversations and speeches heard sixty years before—from Mr. Madison, Mr. Jefferson, Mr. Clay, and other statesmen, his master's special friends.

"Yes," he used to say, "I stay wid your grandpa ten years in Congress, an' all de time he was secretary for President Jefferson. He nuver give me a cross word, an' I nuver saw your grandma de leas' out of temper nuther but once, an' dat was at a dinner party we give in Washington, when de French Minister said something disrespectful 'bout de United States."

The only negro on the place who did not evince an interest in the white family was a man ninety years old, who, forty years before, announced his intention of not working any longer,—although still strong and athletic,—because he said, "the estate had done come down so he hadn't no heart to work no longer." He remembered, he said, "when thar was three an' four hund'ed black folks, but sence de British debt had to be paid over by his old marster, an' de Macklenbu'g estate had to be sold, he hadn't had no heart to do nothin' sence." All his interest in life having expired with an anterior generation, we were in his eyes but a poor set, and he refused to have anything to do with us. Not being compelled to work, he passed his life principally in the woods, and wore a rabbit-skin cap and a leather apron. Having lost interest in and connection with the white family, he gradually relapsed into a state of barbarism, refusing toward the end of his life to sleep in his bed, preferring a hard bench in his cabin, upon which he died.

Another very old man remembered something of his father, who had come from Africa; and when we asked him to tell us what he remembered of his father's narratives, would say:

"My daddy tell we chillun how he mammy liv' in hole in de groun' in Afiky, an' when a Englishmun come to buy him, she sell him fur a string o' beads. An' 'twas monsus hard when he fus' come here to war close; ev'y chance he git he pull off he close an' go naked, kase folks don't war no close in he country. When daddy git mad wid we chillun, mammy hide us, kase he kill us. Sometimes he say he gwine sing he country, an' den he dance an' jump an' howl tell he skeer we chillun to deaf."

They spoke always of their forefathers as the "outlandish people."

As soon as my sister and myself had learned to read and cipher, we were inspired with a desire to teach the negroes who were about the house and kitchen; and my father promised to reward my sister with a handsome guitar if she would teach two boys—designed for mechanics-arithmetic.

Our regular system was every night to place chairs around the dining-table, ring a bell, and open school, she presiding at one end of the table and I at the other. Our school proved successful. The boys learned arithmetic, and the guitar was awarded.

We knew of but one instance of cruelty on our plantation, and that was when "Uncle Joe," the blacksmith, burned his nephew's face with a hot iron.

The extent of these estates precluding the possibility of near neighbors, their isolation would have been intolerable but for the custom of visiting which prevailed among us. Many houses were filled with visitors the greater part of the year, and these usually remained two or three weeks. Visiting tours were made in our private carriages, each family making at least one such tour a year. Nor was it necessary to announce these visits by message or letter, each house being considered always ready, and "entertaining company" being the occupation of the people. Sometimes two or three carriages might be descried in the evening coming up to the door through the Lombardy poplar avenue— the usual approach to many old houses; whereupon ensued a lively flutter among small servants, who, becoming generally excited, speedily got them into their clean aprons, and ran to open gates and to remove parcels from carriages. Lady visitors were always accompanied by colored maids, although sure of finding a superfluity of these at each establishment. The mistress of the house always received her guests in the front porch, with a sincere and cordial greeting.

These visiting friends at my own home made an impression upon me that no time can efface . . . those dear, gentle faces, my mother's early friends, and those delightful old ladies, in close bordered tarlatan caps, who used to come to see my grandmother. These last would sit round the fire, knitting and talking over their early memories: how they remembered the red coats of the British; how they had seen the Richmond theater burn down, with some of their family burned in it; how they used to wear such beautiful turbans of *crepe lisse* to the Cartersville balls, and how they used to dance the minuet. At mention of this my grandmother would lay off her spectacles, put aside her knitting, rise with dignity, and show us the step of the minuet, gliding slowly and majestically around the room.

My mother's friends belonged to a later generation. They combined intelligence with exquisite refinement. I enumerate some of their charms:

Entire absence of pretense made them always attractive. Having no "parlor" or "company" manners to assume, they preserved at all times a gentle, natural, easy demeanor and conversation. They had not dipped into the sciences; but the study of Latin and French, with general reading in their mother tongue, rendered them intelligent companions for cultivated men. They also possessed the rare gift of reading well aloud, and wrote letters unsurpassed in penmanship and style.

These women also managed their household affairs admirably, and were uniformly kind to, but never familiar with, their servants. They kept before them the Bible as their constant guide and rule in life, and were surely, as nearly as possible, holy in thought, word, and deed.

Although presenting an infinite variety of mind, manner, and temperament, all the gentlemen who visited us, young and old, possessed in common certain characteristics, one of which was a deference to ladies which made us feel that we had been put in the world especially to be waited upon by them. Their standard for woman was high. They seemed to regard her as some rare and costly statue set in a niche to be admired and never taken down.

Another peculiarity they had in common was a habit—which seemed irresistible—of tracing people back to the remotest generation, and appearing inconsolable if ever they failed to find out the pedigree of any given individual for at least four generations. This, however, was an innocent pastime, from which they seemed to derive much pleasure and satisfaction.

Every Virginia housewife knew how to compound all the various dishes in Mrs. Randolph's cookery book, and our tables were filled with every species of meat and vegetable to be found on a plantation, with every kind of cakes, jellies, and blanc-mange to be concocted out of eggs, butter, and cream, besides an endless catalogue of preserves, sweetmeats, pickles, and condiments.

The first specialty being good loaf bread there was always a hot loaf for breakfast, hot corn bread for dinner, and a hot loaf for supper. Every house was famed for its loaf bread, and said a gentleman once to me: "Although at each place it is superb, yet each loaf differs from another loaf preserving distinct characteristics which would enable me to distinguish, instantly, should there be a convention of loaves, the Oaklands loaf from the Greenfield loaf, and the Avenel loaf from the Rustic Lodge loaf."

Time would fail me to dwell upon the incomparable rice waffles, and beat biscuits, and muffins, and laplands, and marguerites, and flannel cakes, and French rolls, and velvet rolls, and lady's fingers constantly brought by relays of small servants, during breakfast, hot and hotter from the kitchen. Then the tea-waiters handed at night, with the beef tongue, the sliced ham, the grated cheese, the cold turkey, the dried venison, the loaf bread buttered hot, the batter-cakes, the crackers, the quince marmalade, the wafers. . . .

In due time we were provided—my sister and myself—with the best instructors—a lady all the way from Bordeaux to teach French, and a German professor for German and music.

After some years we were thought to have arrived at "sufficient age of discretion" for a trip to New York City. Dazzled with the gloss and glitter, we wondered why old Virginia couldn't join this march of progress, and have dumb-waiters, and elevators, and water-pipes, and gas-fixtures, and washing-machines.

We asked a gentleman who was with us why old Virginia had not all these, and he replied: "Because, while the people here have been busy working for themselves, old-fogy Virginia has been working for negroes. All the money Virginia makes is spent in feeding and clothing negroes. These people in the North were shrewd enough years ago to sell all theirs to the South."

Telling our mother of all the wonders and pleasures of New York, she said:

"You were so delighted I judge that you would like to sell out everything here and move there!"

"It would be delightful!" we exclaimed.

"It is not so easy to sell out and move," replied our mother, "when you remember all the negroes we have to take care of and support."

"Yes, the negroes," we said, "are the weight continually pulling us down! Will the time *ever* come for us to be free of them?" . . .


One of the most charming places to which we made a yearly visit was Oaklands, a lovely spot embowered in vines and shade-trees.

The attractions of this home and family brought so many visitors every summer, it was necessary to erect cottages about the grounds, although the house itself was quite large. And as the yard was usually filled with persons strolling about, or reading, or playing chess under the trees, it had every appearance, on first approach, of a small watering-place. The mistress of this establishment was a woman of rare attraction, possessing all the gentleness of her sex, with attributes of greatness enough for a hero. Tall and handsome, she looked a queen as she stood on the portico receiving her guests, and, by the first words of greeting, from her warm, true heart, charmed even strangers. . . . This lady inherited from her father, General Breckinridge, an executive talent which enabled her to order and arrange her domestic affairs perfectly; so that from the delicious viands upon her tables to the highly polished oak of the floors, all gave evidence of her superior management and the admirable training of her servants.

Oaklands was famous for many things: its fine light-bread, its cinnamon cakes, its beat biscuit, its fricasseed chicken, its butter and cream, its wine-sauces, its plum-puddings, its fine horses, its beautiful meadows, its sloping green hills, and its refined and agreeable society collected from every part of our own State, and often from others. For an epicure no better place could have been desired.

Like all old homes, Oaklands had its bright as well as its sorrowful days, its weddings and its funerals.

And, apropos of weddings, an old-fashioned Virginia wedding was an event to be remembered. The preparations usually commenced some time before, with saving eggs, butter, chickens, etc.; after which ensued the liveliest egg-beating, butter-creaming, raisin-stoning, sugar-pounding, cake-icing, salad-chopping, cocoanut-grating, lemon-squeezing, egg-frothing, waffle-making, pastry-baking, jelly-straining, silver-cleaning, floor-rubbing, dress-making, hair-curling, lace-washing, ruffle-crimping, tarlatan-smoothing, trunk-moving,—guests arriving, servants running, girls laughing!

The guests generally arrived in private carriages a day or two before, and stayed often for a week after the affair, being accompanied by quite an army of negro servants. . . .

Another charming residence, not far from Oaklands, which attracted visitors from various quarters, was Buena Vista.

This residence—large and handsome—was situated on an eminence overlooking pastures and sunny slopes, with forest and mountain views in the distance.

The interior of the house accorded with the outside, every article being elegant and substantial.

The owner, a gentleman of polished manners, kind and generous disposition, a sincere Christian and zealous churchman, was honored and beloved by all who knew him.

His daughters, a band of lovely young girls, presided over his house, dispensing its hospitality with grace and dignity. Their mother's death, which occurred when they were very young, had given them household cares which would have been considerable but for the assistance of Uncle Billy, the butler—an all-important character presiding with imposing dignity over domestic affairs.

His mission on earth seemed to be keeping the brightest silver urns, sugar-dishes, cream-jugs, and spoons; flavoring the best ice-creams; buttering the hottest rolls, muffins, and waffles; chopping the best salads; folding the whitest napkins; handing the best tea and cakes in the parlor in the evenings; and cooling the best wine for dinner.

Of all the plantation homes we loved and visited, the brightest, sweetest memories cluster around Grove Hill, a grand old place in the midst of scenery lovely and picturesque, to reach which we made a journey across the Blue Ridge—those giant mountains from whose winding roads and lofty heights we had glimpses of exquisite scenery in the valleys below.

Arrived at Grove Hill, how enthusiastic the welcome from each member of the family assembled in the front porch to meet us! How joyous the laugh! How deliciously cool the wide halls, the spacious parlor, the dark polished walnut floors! How bright the flowers! How gay the spirits of all assembled!

One was sure of meeting here pleasant people from Virginia, Baltimore, Florida, South Carolina, and Kentucky, with whom the house was filled from May till November.

How delightfully passed the days, the weeks! What merry excursions, fishing-parties, riding-parties to the Indian Spring, the Cave, the Natural Bridge! What pleasant music, and tableaux, and dancing, in the evenings!

The lady presiding over this establishment possessed a cultivated mind, bright conversational powers, and gentle temper, with a force of character which enabled her judiciously to direct the affairs of her household, as well as the training and education of her children.

She always employed an accomplished tutor, who added to the attractiveness of her home circle. She helped the boys with their Latin, and the girls with their compositions. In her quiet way she governed, controlled, suggested everything; so that her presence was required everywhere at once.

While in the parlor entertaining her guests with bright, agreeable conversation, she was sure to be wanted by the cooks (there were six) to "taste or flavor" something in the kitchen; or by the gardener, to direct the planting of certain seeds or roots,—and so with every department. Even the minister—there was always one living in her house— would call her out to consult over his text and sermon for the next Sunday, saying he would rely upon her judgment and discrimination.

Never thinking of herself, her heart overflowing with sympathy and interest for others, she entered into the pleasures of the young as well as the sorrow of the old.

If the boys came in from a fox or deer chase, their pleasure was incomplete until it had been described to her and enjoyed with her again.

The flower-vases were never entirely beautiful until her hand had helped to arrange the flowers. The girls' laces were never perfect until she had gathered and crimped them. Her sons were never so happy as when holding her hand and caressing her. And the summer twilight found her always in the vine-covered porch, seated by her husband,—a dear, kind old gentleman,—her hand resting on his, while he quietly and happily smoked his pipe after the day's riding over his plantation, interviewing overseers, millers, and blacksmiths, and settling up accounts.

Not far from Greenfield was a place called Rustic Lodge. This house, surrounded by a forest of grand old oaks, was not large or handsome. But its inmates were ladies and gentlemen of the old English style. The grandmother, Mrs. Burwell, about ninety years of age, had in her youth been one of the belles at the Williamsburg court in old colonial days. Her manners and conversation were dignified and attractive.

The son of this old lady, about sixty years of age, and the proprietor of the estate, was a true picture of the old English gentleman. His manners, conversations, thread-cambric shirt-frills, cuffs, and long queue tied with a black ribbon, made the picture complete. His two daughters, young ladies of refinement, had been brought up by their aunt and grandmother to observe strictly all the proprieties of life.

This establishment was proverbial for its order and method, the most systematic rules being in force everywhere. The meals were served punctually at the same instant every day. Old Aunt Nelly always dressed her mistress at the same hour. The cook's gentle "tapping at the chamber door" called the mistress to an interview with that functionary at the same moment every morning—an interview which, lasting half an hour, and never being repeated during the day, resulted in the choicest dinners, breakfasts, and suppers.

Exactly at the same hour every morning the old gentleman's horse was saddled, and he entered the neighboring village so promptly as to enable some of the inhabitants to set their clocks by him.

I must add a few words to my mention of Smithfield, in Montgomery County, the county which flows with healing waters.

Smithfield, like Greenfield, is owned by the descendants of the first white family who settled there after the Indians, and its verdant pastures, noble forests, and mountain streams and springs, form a prospect wondrously beautiful.

This splendid estate descended to three brothers of the Preston family, who equally divided it, the eldest keeping the homestead, and the others building attractive homes on their separate plantations.

The old homestead was quite antique in appearance. Inside, the high mantelpieces reaching nearly to the ceiling, which was also high, and the high wainscoting, together with the old furniture, made a picture of the olden time.

When I first visited this place, the old grandmother, then eighty years of age, was living. She, like the old lady at Rustic, had been a belle in eastern Virginia in her youth. When she married the owner of Smithfield sixty years before, she made the bridal jaunt from Norfolk to this place on horseback, two hundred miles.

"When I was married," said she, "and first came to Smithfield, my husband's sisters met me in the porch, and were shocked by my pale and delicate appearance. One of them, whispering to her brother, asked: 'Why did you bring that ghost up here?' And now," continued the old lady, "I have outlived all who were in the house that day, and all my own and my husband's family."

The houses of these three brothers were filled with company winter and summer, making themselves a delightful society. The visitors at one house were equally visitors at the others, and the succession of dinner and evening parties from one to the other made it difficult for a visitor to decide at whose particular house he was staying.

One of the brothers, Colonel Robert Preston, had married a lovely lady from South Carolina. The eldest was William Ballard Preston, once Secretary of the Navy in the cabinet of President Taylor.

The last place visited by my sister and myself before the war of 1861 was Elkwood, a fine estate in Culpeper County, four miles from the railroad station, the residence of Richard Cunningham.

It was the last of June. The country was a scene of enchantment as the carriage rolled us through dark, cool forests, green meadows, fields of waving grain; out of the forests into acres of broad-leaved corn; across pebble-bottomed streams, and along the margin of the Rapidan, which flowed at the base of the hill leading up to the house.

The house was square and white, and the blinds green as the grass lawn and trees in the yard. Inside the house the polished "dry-rubbed" floors, clean and cool, refreshed one on entering like a glass of iced lemonade on a midsummer's day. The old-fashioned furniture against the walls looked as if it thought too much of itself to be set about promiscuously over the floor, like modern fauteuils and divans.

About everything was an air of dignity and repose corresponding with the manners and appearance of the proprietors, who were called "Uncle Dick" and "Aunt Jenny"—the *a* in "Aunt" pronounced very broad.

Aunt Jenny and Uncle Dick had no children, but took care of numerous nieces and nephews, kept their house filled to overflowing with friends, relatives, and strangers, and were revered and beloved by all. They had no pleasure so great as taking care of other people. They lived for other people, and made everybody comfortable and happy around them. From the time Uncle Dick had prayers in the morning until family prayers at bedtime they were busy bestowing some kindness.

Uncle Dick had requested Aunt Jenny, when they were married, forty years before, to have on his table every day dinner enough for six more persons than were already in the house, "in case," he said, "he should meet friends or acquaintances, while riding over his plantation or in the neighborhood, whom he wished to ask home with him to dinner." This having been always a rule, Aunt Jenny never set her table without dinner enough for six more,—and hers were no commonplace dinners; no hasty-puddings, no saleratus bread, no soda cakes, no frozen-starch ice-cream, no modern short-hand recipes, but genuine old Virginia cooking. And all who want to know what that was can find out all about it in Aunt Jenny's book of copied recipes . . . their "sum and substance" may be given in a few words:

"Have no shams. Procure an abundance of the freshest, richest *real* cream, milk, eggs, butter, lard, best old Madeira wine, all the way from Madeira, and never use a particle of soda or saleratus about anything or under any pressure."

These were the ingredients Aunt Jenny used, for Uncle Dick had rare old wine in his cellar which he had brought from Europe thirty years before, and every day was a feast-day at Elkwood. And the wedding breakfasts Aunt Jenny used to get up when one of her nieces married at her house—as they sometimes did—were beyond description.

While at Elkwood, observing every day that the carriage went to the depot empty and returned empty, we inquired the reason, and were informed that Uncle Dick, ever since the cars had been passing near his plantation, ordered his coachman to have the carriage every day at the station, "in case some of his friends might be on the train, and might like to stop and see him!"

Another hospitable rule in Uncle Dick's house was that company must never be kept waiting in his parlor, and so anxious was his young niece to meet his approbation in this as in every particular that she had a habit of dressing herself carefully, arranging her hair beautifully before lying down for the afternoon siesta, "in case," she said, "someone might call, and Uncle Dick had a horror of visitors waiting." This process of reposing in a fresh muslin dress and fashionably arranged hair required a particular and uncomfortable position, which she seemed not to mind, but dozed in the most precise manner without rumpling her hair or her dress.

In 1859 we had a visit from two old friends of our family—a distinguished Southern Senator and the Secretary of War—both accustomed to swaying multitudes by the power of their eloquence—which lost none of its force and charm in our little home circle. We listened with admiration as they discussed the political issues of the day—no longer a subject uninteresting or unintelligible to us, for every word was of vital importance. Their theme was, *The best means of protecting our plantation homes and firesides.* Even the smallest children now comprehended the greatest politicians. . . .

John S. Wise

## A VIRGINIA BOY SEES A SLAVE AUCTION

*John S. Wise was born in 1846 in Brazil where his father, Henry A. Wise, an appointee of President Tyler, was serving as minister. His mother was Sarah Sergeant, daughter of John Sergeant of Philadelphia, a lawyer and for many years a member of Congress.*

*In 1847 the family returned to their Plantation "Only" on the Eastern Shore of Virginia. By the time he was eight years old, John Wise could shoot, ride, fish, swim and sail a boat. In company with the slaves he learned the catechism from his mother. From his father he learned to love the Union next to his Maker. His mother died in 1852, but annual visits to her family in Philadelphia continued.*

*His father became governor of Virginia in 1856 and the family moved to Richmond. There they were joined by his brother Jennings, recently returned from diplomatic service in London and in Paris. Jennings became the editor of the Richmond* Enquirer *and within two years fought eight duels.*

*The men of the Wise family were prominent in the War between the States. The governor was appointed a major general in the Confederate Army. Jennings and the boys' charming young uncle were killed in battle, fighting on opposite sides. John entered the Virginia Military Institute at Lexington and saw active service in 1864 when the commandant brought the cadets into the concentration against General Hunter. After Appomattox John joined General Johnston's army in North Carolina and was paroled when it surrendered. Later he practiced law with his father.*

During our next visit to Philadelphia, everybody was talking about a book and a play called "Uncle Tom's Cabin." I had heard mention of the book at home, as a very powerful but very "pernicious" book. More than once the subject had come up in conversation in my presence; and I had heard the work spoken of as a cruel travesty upon Southern life, disgusting in its sentimental sympathy with the negro. I was surprised to find that everybody in the North was reading "Uncle Tom's Cabin," and pronouncing it a remarkable production; and when it was proposed, on our next visit to Philadelphia, to take me to a theatre to see this wonderful play of "Uncle Tom's Cabin," I was delighted.

Never did theatrical performance open to any one more gratifyingly than that wonderful drama. In my heart I had a feeling that our Northern kinsfolk thought their homes were finer than those in our beloved South. I did not think so. When in the opening act, I saw the beautiful Southern home, with its flowers and bowers and sunshine, I said to myself, "Now they will see how we live, and will envy us." Yes, old Uncle Tom and all his family were just such darkeys as were in Virginia. And as for Eva, there she was looking like a hundred little girls I knew, and infinitely sweeter in voice and eye than the prim Northern girls surrounding me. And Eva's father! I knew a hundred charming young fellows just like him. Her mother? Well, there was no denying it that now and then we saw one like her, but she was not a common or attractive type. And Topsy? Yes, there were darkeys just like her, even within my limited knowledge. I laughed and enjoyed myself along with the others over Topsy's queer antics.

The play moved on. In time the slave auction came, and the negro-buyers, and the terrible domestic tragedy to Uncle Tom, and the fearful Mississippi River trip, and the whipping of Eliza's husband,— her flight, the blood-hounds, and all the ghastly story which thrilled a nation. I was too young to grasp the moral of that story, yet old enough to feel my heart rebel against things which I had never before seen laid at the door of the people I loved and among whom I lived. I believed that many of them were the mere creations of a malignant enemy, who had conjured them up out of her own imagination to prejudice the outside world against my kith and kin, and I indignantly denied, when questioned concerning the play, that such scenes were possible. I had never witnessed them, or heard of them, in the home of my father. . . .

But the play made a deep and lasting impression upon me. The sweet vision of little Eva, the inexpressible pathos of Uncle Tom, the freaks of Topsy, came back to me time and time again. Alas! They returned yoked in my memory with the wretched figure of Legree, the blood-hounds, and the misery of the other scenes, and the possibility that it all might be true revealed itself to me in a way that I little expected. I knew there was such a thing as a negro-buyer. On one or two occasions I had had such men pointed out to me. I had been taught to regard them as an inferior class of humanity; but this knowledge came principally from the negroes themselves, for the grown people of my own class seldom referred to them, and they received no sort of social recognition. I had, in fact, seen in the newspapers advertisements of the sale of negroes, side by side with little figures of a man with a pack on his back, and the offer of a reward for a runaway. But never until my return from the North was my curiosity sufficiently aroused to make me locate the place of selling negroes, or determine me to see a sale.

Among my Northern kinsfolk was a young uncle, a handsome, witty fellow, much younger than my mother. Notwithstanding her death, he had kept up his affection and intimacy with father. . . . It was he who had taken me to see "Uncle Tom's Cabin;" and it was he who had petted me, and taken me about the streets of Philadelphia, and spoiled me in many ways; and it was he who had taken me to visit President Buchanan; and now he had come to visit us, and spend a week of leisure with his favorite brother-in-law.

My oldest brother had recently returned from Paris. He had been absent as Secretary of Legation in Berlin and Paris for nearly six years. He and my uncle were nearly of the same age, and devoted friends. Father loved this oldest son as the apple of his eye, and the feeling of that son for his father was little short of adoration. Father had higher ambitions than he had yet realized. He was becoming prominent as a possible candidate for the presidency. Both from a natural inclination and a desire to promote his candidacy, my brother had become editor of the "Richmond Enquirer," the leading Democratic journal of Virginia; my uncle was heart and soul enlisted in securing support for father among his own constituency. It was believed that his well-known conservatism on the subject of slavery, and his intense devotion to the Union, would make his prospects very good for the nomination.

The occupations of my father and brother left their visitor to find his own amusements until the evening hour, and he diverted himself at such times by reading or sight-seeing, or in diversions with the children, of whom he was very fond.

One Saturday, thus left alone with me, the subject of "Uncle Tom's Cabin" came up. He asked if I had ever seen a slave sale. "No," said I, all alert, for since I saw the play I had resolved that I would some time see a slave auction; "but I know where they sell them. I saw the sign a few days ago. Let us go and see what it is like." So off we started. Out of the beautiful grounds and past the handsome residences we went, turning down Franklin Street towards the great Exchange Hotel. Beyond it we passed a church, still used as such, although the locality had been deserted by residences, and stables and little shops surrounded it. As we proceeded, the street became more and more squalid and repulsive, until at last we reached a low brick warehouse, with its end abutting on the street and running far back. Over the place was the sign, with the name of an owner and the words "Auction House" conspicuously painted. At the door hung a red flag, with an advertisement pasted on its side, and up and down the street a mulatto man walked with another flag, ringing a large bell, and shouting, "Oh, yea! Oh, yea! Walk up, gentlemen. The sale of a fine, likely lot of young niggers is now about to begin." To these he added, in tones which were really merry, and with an expansive smile, that they were "all sorts of niggers, belonging to the estate of the late——, sold for no fault, but to settle the estate;" and that the lot embraced all kinds, "old ones and young ones, men and women, gals and boys."

About the door, and on the inside, a few men were grouped, some in their shirt-sleeves. For the most part, they had the appearance of hostlers. The place itself looked like a livery stable within the building. For a long distance back from the street, there were no sidelights or skylights. In the rear only was it light, where the structure projected beyond those on either side of it, and there the light was ample, and the business in hand was to be transacted.

We moved cautiously through the dark front of the building, and

came at last to the rear, where a small platform occupied the centre
of the room, and chairs and benches were distributed about the walls.
Another large mulatto man appeared to act as usher, standing near a
door, through which from time to time he furnished a fresh supply
of slaves for sale. A large man, with full beard, not a bad-looking fellow
but for the "ratty" appearance of his quick, cold, small black eyes,
acted as auctioneer. A few negroes sat on the bench by the door, they
being the first "lot" to be disposed of. The purchasers stood or sat
about, smoking or chewing tobacco, while the auctioneer proceeded
to read the decree of a chancery court in the settlement of a decedent's
estate, under which this sale was made. The lawyers representing
different interests were there, as were also the creditors and distributees
having interests in the sale. Besides these were ordinary buyers in need
of servants, and slave-traders who made a living by buying cheap and
selling for a profit. We took seats, and watched and listened intently.

After reading the formal announcement authorizing the sale, the
auctioneer became eloquent. He proceeded to explain to his auditors
that this was "no ordinary sale of a damaged, no-'count lot of niggers,
whar a man buyin' a nigger mout or mout not git what he was lookin'
for, but one of those rar' opperchunities, which cum only once or
twice in a lifetime, when the buyer is sho' that for every dollar he
pays he's gittin' a full dollar's wuth of real genuine nigger, healthy,
well-raised, well-mannered, respectful, obejunt, and willin'. Why,"
said he, "gentlemen, you kin look over this whole gang of niggers, from
the oldest to the youngest, an' you won't find the mark of a whip on
one of 'em. Colonel ——, for whose estate they is sold, was known to
be one of the kindest marsters, and at the same time one of the best
bringers-up of niggers, in all Virginia. These here po' devils is sold
for no fault whatever, but simply and only because, owin' to the
Colonel's sudden death, his estate is left embarrassed, and it is necessary to sell his niggers to pay his debts, and for distributin' some reddy
monny amongst numrus 'aars. Of these facts I assure you upon the
honor of a gentleman."

Having thus paved the way for good prices, he announced that
among the slaves to be offered were good carriage-drivers, gardeners,
dining-room servants, farm hands, cooks, milkers, seamstresses, washer-
women, and "the most promisin', growin', sleek, and sassy lot of young
niggers he had ever had the pleasure of offerin'."

The sale was begun with some "bucks," as he facetiously called
them. They were young, unmarried fellows from eighteen to twenty-

five. Ordered to mount the auction-block, they stripped to the waist and bounced up, rather amused than otherwise, grinning at the lively bidding they excited. Cautious bidders drew near to them, examined their eyes, spoke with them to test their hearing and manners, made them open their mouths and show their teeth, ran their hands over the muscles of their backs and arms, caused them to draw up their trousers to display their legs, and, after fully satisfying themselves on these and other points, bid for them what they saw fit. Whenever a sale was concluded, the successful bidder was announced, and the announcement was greeted by the darkeys themselves with broad grins, and such expressions as "Thank Gord," or "Bless de Lord," if it went as they wished, or in uncomplaining silence if otherwise. It was surprising to see how thoroughly they all seemed to be informed concerning the men who were bidding for them.

The scenes accompanying the sales of young women were very similar to those with the young men, except that what was said to them and about them was astonishingly plain and shocking. One was recommended as a "rattlin' good breeder," because she had already given birth to two children at seventeen years of age. Another, a mulatto of very comely form, showed deep embarrassment when questioned about her condition.

They brought good prices, "Niggers is high" was the general comment. Who bought them, where they went, whether they were separated from father, mother, brother, or sister, God knows.

"I am now goin' to offer you a very likely young chile-barin' woman," said the auctioneer. "She is puffectly healthy, and without a blemish. Among the family, she is a universal favorite. I offer her with the privilidge of takin' her husban' and two chillen with her at a very rejuced price, because it is the wish of all concerned to keep 'em together, if possible. Get up here, Martha Ann." A large-framed, warm, comfortable-looking, motherly soul, with a fine, honest face, mounted the block. "Now, gentlemen," said he, continuing, "ef you'll cast yo' eyes into that corner, you will see Israel, Martha Ann's husband, and Cephas and Melindy, her two children. Israel is not what you may call a raal able-bodied man. He broke his leg some years ago handlin' one of the Colonel's colts, and he ain't able to do heavy work; but I am asshooed by everybody on the place that Israel is a most valuable servant about a house for all kind of light work, and he can be had mighty cheap."

"Yes, sir," spoke up Israel eagerly, "I kin do ez much ez ennybody;

and, marsters, ef you'll only buy me and de chillun with Martha Ann, Gord knows I'll wuk myself to deth fur you."

The poor little darkeys, Cephas and Melinda, sat there frightened and silent, their white eyes dancing like monkey-eyes, and gleaming in the shadows. As her husband's voice broke on her ear, Martha Ann, who had been looking sadly out of the window in a pose of quiet dignity, turned her face with an expression of exquisite love and gratitude towards Israel. She gazed for a moment at her husband and at her children, and then looked away once more, her eyes brimming with tears.

"How much am I offered for Martha Ann with the privilidge?" shouted the auctioneer. The bidding began. It was very sluggish. The hammer fell at last. The price was low. Perhaps, even in that crowd, nobody wanted them all, and few were willing to do the heartless act of taking her alone. So she sold low. When the name of her purchaser was announced, I knew him, He was an old, wizen, cheerless old fellow, who was a member of the Virginia legislature from one of the far-away southside counties adjoining North Carolina. Heaven be praised, he was not a supporter of father, but called himself an Old-line Whig, and ranked with the opposition. He seemed to have no associates among the members, and nobody knew where he lived in the city. He was notoriously penurious, and drew his pay as regularly as the week rolled around.

"Mr. —— buys Martha Ann," said the auctioneer. "I congratulate you, Mr. ——. You've bought the cheapes' nigger here to-day. Will you take Israel and the young uns with her?"

Deep silence fell upon the gathering. Even imperturbable Martha Ann showed her anxiety by the heaving of her bosom. Israel strained forward, where he sat, to hear the first word of hope or of despair. The old man who had bid for her shuffled forward, fumbling in his pockets for his money, delaying his reply so long that the question was repeated. "No-o," drawled he at last; "no-o, I'm sorry for 'em, but I railly can't. You see, I live a long way from here, and I ride my horse to the legislatur', and, when I get here, I sell my horse and live cheap, and aims to save up enough from my salary to buy another horse and a 'chile-barin' woman when the session's done; and then I takes her home, ridin' behind me on the horse. Thar ain't no way I could provide for gittin' the man and the young uns home, even if they was given to me. I think I'm doin' pretty well to save enough in a session to buy one nigger, much less a whole family." And the old beast looked up over his spectacles as he counted his money, and actually chuckled, as if he expected a round of applause for his clever business ability.

A deep groan, unaccompanied by any word of complaint, came from the dark corner where Israel sat. Martha Ann stepped down from the platform, walked to where he was, the tears streaming down her cheeks, and there, hugging her children and rocking herself back and forth, she sobbed as if her heart was breaking.

My companion and I looked at each other in disgust, but neither spoke a word. I was ready to burst into tears. The old creature who had bought the woman lugged out his hoarded money in sundry packages of coin and paper, and, as he counted it, said, "Martha Ann, cheer up; you'll find me a good marster, and I'll get you a new husband."

The silence was oppressive. The veriest savage on earth could not have witnessed it without being moved. "Let us go away," I whispered. At last the suspense was broken. A handsome, manly fellow, one of the lawyers in the case, exclaimed, "By —— ! I can't stand this. I knew Colonel —— well. I know how he felt towards Israel and Martha Ann and their children. This is enough to make him turn in his grave. I am unable to make this purchase; but sooner than see them separated, I'll bankrupt myself. Mr. ——, I will take Martha Ann off your hands, so as to buy her husband and children, and keep them together."

"Well, now, you see," drawled the old fellow, pausing in his work, with trembling hand, "if you feel that way, the time to speak was when the gal was up for sale." His eye glittered with the thought of turning the situation to advantage. "You see she's mine now, and I consider her a very desirable and very cheap purchase. Moreover, if you want her, I think you ought to be willin' to pay me something for the time and trouble I've wasted here a-tryin' to git her."

The proposition was sickening. But the old creature was so small himself that his demand of profit was likewise small, and the matter was soon arranged. Whether he remained and bought another "chilebarin' " woman is unknown; for, sick at heart at the sights we had witnessed, we withdrew, and walked slowly back in the glorious sunlight, past the neighboring church, and up to the happy abodes of Virginia's best civilization, little inclined to talk of the nightmare we had been through. The horrors we had witnessed came back and back again to me. I was very, very unhappy.

That night, the experiences of the morning were the subject of
a long and anxious and earnest conversation between father, my
brother, and my uncle. At its close, I felt much relieved and proud of
them, and better satisfied, because they were all agreed that a system
in which things like that were possible was monstrous; and that the
question was, not whether it should be abolished, and abolished quickly, but as to the manner of its abolition. . . .

PART **II**

## In the Rice Kingdom

### SOUTH CAROLINA—GEORGIA—FLORIDA

"I know of no crop which in beauty can be compared with a crop of rice. . . . Until the middle of July the color of the rice never looks the same. Some days it changed as constantly as the colors change on the surface of the sea. As its blades changed their direction with each shifting breeze, they changed their color also. Over the field a breeze often blew, coming inland from the ocean across the salt marshes and up the lower reaches of the river. Thus the crop was kept in constant motion, swaying in one direction and then in another. The result was that the whole field, as far as one could see, appeared to be alive, shifting with the wind, the sunshine, and the shadows of passing clouds.

"As season advanced, a decided change gradually took place in the color of the field, for its green began to be mingled with gold as the heads of rice appeared and its stalks began to be weighed down with the ripening grain. Yellow then predominated over the green until the whole field looked like a mass of gold, as it awaited the hook of the reaper. . . ."

DUNCAN CLINCH HEYWARD, *Seed from Madagascar*

John Davis

## TUTOR TO THE DRAYTONS OF SOUTH CAROLINA

*In 1798 John Davis, a young Englishman, arrived in Charleston, South Carolina, and through the help of friends obtained a position as tutor in the family of Thomas Drayton. He spent the winter months with the family at Ocean Plantation near Coosawhatchie, site of a Revolutionary War battle. In May they moved to Drayton Hall on the Ashley, which had been built shortly after the first Thomas Drayton came to South Carolina from Barbados in 1671. The famed magnolia gardens were a later development brought about by the Reverend John Grimke Drayton's imagination and energy.*

*Thomas Drayton was the son of the Honourable John Drayton and also half brother to William Henry Drayton, chief justice of South Carolina from 1776 to the time of his death from yellow fever in 1779. His mother was Margaret Glen, daughter of Governor James Glen. Mary Wilson, daughter of Algernon Wilson of St. Paul's Parish, South Carolina, was Thomas Drayton's wife.*

*Colonel James Postell, "a man to whom nothing indeed appeared difficult," was one of Francis Marion's men.*

*When Davis returned to England he wrote a book entitled* Personal Adventures and Travels of Four Years and a Half in the United States of America, *from which the following account is taken.*

About half-way on the road from Charleston to Savannah, is situated a little village called Coosawhatchie, consisting of a blacksmith's shop, a court-house, and a jail. A small river rolls its turbid water near the place, on whose dismal banks are to be found many vestiges of the Indians that once inhabited them; and in the immeasurable forests of the neighborhood are several scattered plantations of cotton and rice. It was on one of these plantations that I passed the winter of 1798, and the spring of the following year.

I lived in the family of Mr. Drayton, of whose children I had undertaken the tuition, and enjoyed every comfort that opulence could bestow.

To form an idea of Ocean Plantation, let the reader picture to his imagination an avenue of several miles, leading from the Savannah road, through a continued forest, to a wooden-house, encompassed by rice-grounds, corn and cotton fields. On the right, a kitchen and other

offices; on the left, a stable and coach-house; a little farther a row
of negro-huts, a barn and yard; the view of the eye bounded by lofty
woods of pine, oak, and hickory.

The solitude of the woods I found at first rather dreary; but the
polite attention of an elegant family, a sparkling fire in my room
every night, and a horse always at my command, reconciled me to
my situation; and my impulse to sacrifice to the muses, which had
been repressed by a wandering life, was once more awakened by the
scenery of the woods of Carolina. . . .

The country near Coosawhatchie exhibited with the coming spring
a new and enchanting prospect. The borders of the forest were
covered with the blossoms of the dog-wood, of which the white flowers
caught the eye from every part; and often was to be seen the red-bud
tree, which purpled the adjacent woods with its luxuriant branches;
while, not unfrequently, shrubs of jessamine, intermixed with the
woodbine, lined the road for several miles. The feathered choir began
to warble their strains and from every tree was heard the song of the
red-bird, of which the pauses were filled by the mocking-bird, who
either imitated the note with exquisite precision, or poured forth a
ravishing melody of its own.

I commonly devoted my Sundays to the pleasure of exploring the
country, and cheered by a serene sky, and smiling landscape, felt my
breast awakened to the most rapturous sensations. I lifted my heart
to that Supreme Being, whose agency is every where confessed; and
whom I traced in the verdure of the earth, the foliage of the trees,
and the water of the stream.

In my walk to Coosawhatchie I passed here and there a plantation,
but to have called on its owner without a previous introduction, would
have been a breach of that etiquette which has its source from the
depravity of great cities, but has not failed to find its way into the
woods of America. When I first beheld a fine lady drawn by four
horses through the woods of Carolina in her coach, and a train of
servants following the vehicle, clad in a magnificent livery, I looked
up with sorrow at that luxury and refinement, which are hastening
with rapid strides to change the pure and sylvan scenes of nature into
a theatre of pride and ostentation.

My pupils in the woods of Coosawhatchie, consisted of a boy and
two young ladies. William Henry was an interesting lad of fourteen,
ingenuous of disposition, and a stranger to fear. He was fond to excess
of the chase. His heart danced with joy at the mention of a deer; and

he blew his horn, called together his dogs, and hooped and hallooed in the woods, with an animation that would have done honour to a veteran sportsman. O! for the muse of an Ovid, to describe the dogs of this young Actaeon. There were Sweetlips, and Ringwood, and Music, and Smoker, whose barking was enough to frighten the wood nymphs to their caves. His eldest sister, Maria, though not a regular beauty, was remarkable for her dark eyes and white teeth, and, what was not less captivating, an amiable temper. She was grateful to me for my instruction, and imposed silence on her brother when I invoked the muse in school. But it was difficult to control her little sister Sally, whom in sport and wantonness they called Tibousa. This little girl was distinguished by the languish of her blue eyes, from which, however, she could dart fire when William offended her. Sally was a charming girl, whose beauty promised to equal that of her mother. That I passed many happy hours in watching and assisting the progress of the minds of these young people, I feel no repugnance to acknowledge. My long residence in a country where "honour and shame from no condition rise," has placed me above the ridiculous pride of disowning the situation of a tutor.

Though the plantation of Mr. Drayton was immense, his dwelling was only a log-house; a temporary fabric, built to reside in during the winter. But his table was sumptuous, and an elegance of manners presided at it that might have vied with the highest circles of polished Europe. I make the eulogium, or rather, exhibit the character of Mr. Drayton, in one word, by saying, he was a gentleman; for under that portraiture I comprehend whatever there is of honour. Nor can I refrain from speaking panegyric terms of his lady, whose beauty and elegance were her least qualities; for she was a tender mother, a sincere friend, and walked humbly with her God. She was indeed deserving the solicitude of her husband, who would "not suffer the winds of heaven to visit her face too roughly."

It is usual in Carolina to sit an hour at table after supper; at least, it was our custom in the woods of Coosawhatchie. It was then I related my adventures to Mr. and Mrs. Drayton, in the eastern section of the globe, who not only endured my tales, but were elated with my successes, and depressed by my misfortunes.

About ten I withdrew to my chamber and my books, where I found a sparkling fire of wood, and where I meditated, smoked segars, and was lost in my own musings. But I was not without company. A merry cricket in my chimney corner never failed to cheer me with his song.

The country in our neighborhood consisted of lofty forests of pine, oak, and hickory. The land was perfectly level. Not the smallest acclivity was visible.

The staple commodity of the state is rice, but cotton is now eagerly cultivated where the soil is adapted to the purpose. The culture of indigo is nearly relinquished. It is to the crop of cotton that the planter looks for the augmentation of his wealth. Of cotton there are two kinds; the sea-island, and inland. The first is the most valuable. The ground is hoed for planting the latter part of March; but as frosts are not unfrequent the beginning of April, it is judicious not to plant before that time. Cotton is of a very tender nature. A frost, or even a chilling wind, has power to destroy the rising plant, and compel the planter to begin anew his toil.

The winds in autumn are so tempestuous, that they tear up the largest trees by the roots.

Of the feathered race, the mocking-bird first claims my notice. It is perfectly domestic, and sings frequently for hours on the roof of a log-house. It is held sacred by the natives. Even children respect the bird whose imitative powers are so delightful. I heard the mocking-bird for the first time on the first day of March. It was warbling, close to my window, from a tree called by some the pride of India, and by others the poison-berry tree. Its song was faint, resembling that of birds hailing the rising-sun; but it became stronger as the spring advanced.

The humming-bird was often caught in the bells of flowers. It is remarkable for its variegated plumage of scarlet, green, and gold.

The whip-poor-will is heard after the last frost, when, towards night, it fills the woods with its melancholy cry of "Whip poor Will! Whip poor Will!"

The woods abound with deer, the hunting of which forms the chief diversion of the planters. I never failed to accompany my neighbors in their parties, but I cannot say that I derived much pleasure from standing several hours behind a tree.

This mode of hunting is, perhaps, not generally known. On riding to a convenient spot in the woods, the hunters dismount, take their stands at certain distances, hitch their horses to a tree, and prepare their guns,—while a couple of negroes lead the beagles into the thickest of the forest. The barking of the dogs announces that the deer are dislodged, and on whatever side they run, the sportsmen fire at them from their lurking places. The first day two bucks passed near

my tree. I had heard the cry of the dogs, and put my gun on a whole
cock. The first buck glided by me with the rapidity of lightning; but
the second I wounded with my fire, as was evident from his twitching
his tail between his legs in the agony of pain. I heard Colonel Postell
exclaim from the next tree, after discharging his piece, "By heaven,
that fellow is wounded, let us mount and follow him; he cannot run
far." I accompanied the venerable colonel through the woods, and in
a few minutes, directed by the scent of a beagle, we reached the spot
where the deer had fallen. It was a noble buck, and we dined on it like
kings.

After killing half a dozen deer, we assembled by appointment at
some planter's house, whither the mothers, and wives, and daughters
of the hunters had got before us in their carriages. A dinner of venison,
killed the preceding hunt, smoked before us, the richest Madeira
sparkled in the glass, and we forgot, in our hilarity, there was any
other habitation for man but that of the woods.

In this hunting party was always to be found my pupil, William
Henry, who galloped through the woods, however thick or intricate,
summoned his beagles, after the toil of the chase, with his horn;
caressed the dog that had been the most eager in pursuit of the deer,
and expressed his hope there would be good weather to hunt again
the following Saturday.

Wolves were sometimes heard on the plantation in the night; and,
when incited by hunger, would attack a calf and devour it. Wild cats
are very common and mischievous in the woods. When a sow is
ready to litter, she is always enclosed with a fence or rails, for, otherwise, the cats would devour the pigs.

I generally accompanied my pupil into the woods in his shooting
excursions, determined both to make havoc among birds and beasts
of every description. Sometimes we fired in volleys at the flocks of
doves that frequent the corn-fields; sometimes we discharged our
pieces at the wild geese, whose empty cackling betrayed them; and
once we brought down some paroquets, that were directing their
course over our heads to Georgia. Nor was it an undelightful task to
fire at the squirrels on the tops of the highest trees.

The affability and tenderness of this charming family in the bosom
of the woods, will be ever cherished in my breast. My wants were always anticipated. The family library was transported without entreaty into my chamber; paper, and the apparatus for writing, were
placed on my table; and once having lamented that my stock of segars

was nearly exhausted, a negro was dispatched seventy miles to Charleston, for a supply of the best Spanish.

I conclude my description of this elegant family, with an observation that will apply to every other that I have been domesticated in, on the western continent; that cheerfulness and quiet always predominated, and that I never saw a brow clouded, or a lip opened in anger.

One diminution to the happiness of an European in the woods of Carolina, is the reflection that every want is supplied him by slaves. The negroes on the plantation, including house-servants and children, amounted to a hundred; of whom the average price being respectively seventy pounds, made them aggregately worth seven thousand to their possessor.

Two families lived in one hut, and such was their unconquerable propensity to steal, that they pilfered from each other. I have heard masters lament this defect in their negroes. But what else can be expected from man in so degraded a condition, that among the ancients the same word implied both a slave and a thief.

Since the introduction of the culture of cotton in the state of South Carolina, the race of negroes has increased. Both men and women work in the field, and the labour of the rice plantation formerly prevented the pregnant negress from bringing forth a long-lived offspring. It may be established as a maxim, that, on a plantation where there are many children, the work has been moderate.

It may be incredible to some, that the children of the most distinguished families in Carolina, are suckled by negro-women. Each child has its momma, whose gestures and accent it will necessarily copy, for children we all know are imitative beings. It is not unusual to hear an elegant lady say, "Richard always grieves when Quasheebaw is whipped, because she suckled him!"

It appears to me that in Carolina, the simplicity of the first colonists is obliterated, and that the present inhabitants strive to exceed each other in the vanities of life. Slight circumstances often mark the manners of a people. In the opulent families, there is always a negro placed on the look-out, to announce the coming of any visitant; and the moment a carriage, or horseman, is descried, each negro changes his every day garb for a magnificent suit of livery. As the negroes wear no shirts, this is quickly effected; and in a few moments a ragged fellow is metamorphosed into a spruce footman. And woe to them should they neglect it; for their master would think himself disgraced, and Sambo and Cuffy incur a severe flogging.

In Carolina, the legislative and executive powers of the house belong to the mistress, the master has little or nothing to do with the administration; he is a monument of uxoriousness and passive endurance. The negroes are not without the discernment to perceive this; and when the husband resolves to flog them, they often throw themselves at the feet of the wife, and supplicate her mediation.

Cotton in Carolina, and horse-racing in Virginia, are the prevailing topics of conversation; these reduce every understanding to a level, and to these Americans return from the ebullitions of the humorist, as the eye weary of contemplating the sun, rejoices to behold the verdure.

It was in the month of May, 1799, that Mr. Drayton and his family exchanged the savage woods of Coosawhatchie, for the politer residence of their mansion on Ashley river. In our migration we formed quite a procession. Mr. Drayton occupied the coach with his lady and youngest daughter; and I advanced next with my fair pupil in a chair, followed by William Henry, on a prancing nag, and half a dozen negro fellows, indifferently mounted, but wearing the laced livery of an opulent master.

About three in the afternoon, our journey being suspended by the heat of the weather, we stopped to eat a cold dinner, in a kind of lodge that had been erected by some hunters on the roadside, and which now hospitably accommodated a family travelling through the woods.

Here we took possession of the benches round the table to enjoy our repast; turning the horses loose to seek the shade; and cooling our wine in a spring that murmured near the spot. William Henry, having snatched a morsel, got ready his fowling piece, to penetrate the woods in search of wild turkies; and while we were rallying him on his passion for shooting, the cry from a negro of a rattle-snake! disturbed our tranquillity. The snake was soon visible to every eye, dragging its slow length along the root of a large tree, and directing its attention to a bird, which chattered and fluttered from above, and seemed irresistibly disposed to fall into his distended jaws. London, a negro servant, had snatched up a log, and was advancing to strike the monster a blow on the head, when a black snake, hastening furiously to the spot, immediately gave battle to the rattle-snake, and suspended, by his unexpected appearance, the power of the negro's arm. We now thought we had got into a nest of snakes, and the girls were screaming with fright, when William Henry, taking an unerring aim with his gun, shot the rattle-snake, in the act of repulsing his enemy. The black snake returned into the woods, and profiting by his example, we all pursued our journey, except William Henry, who stopped with a negro to take out the rattles of the monster he had killed. My pupil presented me with these rattles, which I carried for three years in my pocket.

In the venerable mansion at Ashley river, I again directed the intellectual progress of my interesting pupils, and enlarged the imagination of William, by putting Pope's version of the Odyssey into his hands, which I found among other books that composed the family library. He had before read the Iliad.

The garden of Mr. Drayton's mansion led to the banks of Ashley river, which, after a rapid course of twenty miles, discharged itself into the Atlantic. . . .

An elder brother of Mr. Drayton was our neighbor on the river; he occupied, perhaps, the largest house and gardens in the United States of America. Indeed, I was now breathing the politest atmosphere in America; for our constant visitants were the highest people in the state, and possessed of more house servants, than there are inhabitants at Occoquan. These people never moved but in a carriage, lolled on sophas instead of sitting on chairs, and were always attended by their negroes to fan them with a peacock's feather.

From Ashley river, after a short residence, we removed to Charleston, which was full of visitors from the woods, and exhibited a motley scene. Here was to be perceived a coach, without a glass to exclude the dust, driven by a black fellow, not less proud of the livery of luxury, than the people within the vehicle were of a suit made in the fashion. Such is the pride of the people of Charleston, that no person is seen on foot unless it be a mechanic. He who is without horses and slaves, incurs always contempt.

To avoid the fever, which every summer commits its ravages at Charleston, Mr. Drayton removed with his family in July, to a convenient house on Sullivan's island. The front windows commanded a view of the Atlantic, whose waves broke with fury not a hundred yards from the door. Sullivan's island lies opposite to Charleston, at the distance of eight miles.

No families are more migratory than those of Carolina. From Sullivan's island we went again to the mansion on Ashley river, where I had invitations to hunt, to feast, and to dance. But nothing could soothe the despondency I felt on the approaching return of Mr.

Drayton to the woods of Coosawhatchie. He guessed the cause of my
woe-begone looks, and, rather than be deprived of my services, politely
offered to pass the winter on the banks of Ashley river; nay, he even
proposed to send his son, when the war terminated, to make with me
the tour of the continent of Europe. . . . but I dreaded the tainted
atmosphere that had dispatched so many of my countrymen to the
house appointed for all living; and, filled with apprehension, I left this
charming family in whose bosom I had been so kindly cherished, to
seek another climate, and brave again the rigours of adversity.


Aaron Burr

## A REFUGEE ON A GEORGIA PLANTATION

*Shortly after the duel in 1804 between Aaron Burr and Hamilton,
which resulted in the latter's death, Burr departed to the South. There
he spent some weeks at Hampton Plantation on St. Simon's Island
as the guest of Major Pierce Butler.*

*His distinguished host was born in Ireland in 1744, the third son of
Sir Richard Butler, a member of Parliament. He came to America as
a major in Her Majesty's army and married Mary, daughter of Thomas
Middleton of Prince William's Parish, South Carolina, in 1771. After
his marriage he resigned his commission and devoted himself to planting and politics. He was a member of the Continental Congress, of
the Constitutional Convention, and a United States Senator from
South Carolina. After leaving his South Carolina plantation he purchased lands on the Georgia sea islands and built the beautiful Hampton on St. Simon's Island.*

*From Hampton Aaron Burr wrote daily letters to his daughter
Theodosia, wife of Joseph Alston, whose home was near Georgetown,
South Carolina, on the Waccamaw River. On December 30, 1812,
Theodosia set out from Georgetown on the ship Patriot to visit her
father, who had returned to New York. The ship was never heard of
again.*

*Roswell King, mentioned by Burr, was Major Butler's overseer.*

*"Mr. Couper" was John Couper, proprietor of Hopeton Plantation
near Brunswick, Georgia, and also owner of Cannon's Point, a large
plantation on St. Simon's Island. Couper had only recently come to
the United States from Scotland in 1804. In partnership with a boy-*

*hood friend, James Hamilton, he had bought the two thousand acres*
*on the Altamaha that comprised Hopeton. His wife was the former*
*Rebecca Maxwell.*

Hampton, St. Simon's, August 28, 1804

We arrived on Saturday evening, all well. The mail, which arrives
but once a week, had just gone. An accidental opportunity enables
me to forward this to Savannah.

I am at the house of Major Butler, comfortably settled. A very
agreeable family within half a mile. My project is to go next week to
Florida, which may take up a fortnight or ten days, and soon after
my return to go northward, by Augusta and Columbia, if I can find
ways and means to get on; but I have no horse, nor does this country
furnish one. . . . Enclose to "Mr. R. King, Hampton, St. Simon's."

A. Burr

St. Simon's, August 31, 1804

I am now quite settled. My establishment consists of a housekeeper, cook, and chambermaid, seamstress, and two footmen. There
are, besides, two fishermen and four bargemen always at command.
The department of laundress is done abroad. The plantation affords
plenty of milk, cream, and butter; turkeys, fowls, kids, pigs, geese,
and mutton; fish, of course, in abundance. Of figs, peaches, and
mellons there are yet a few. Oranges and pomegranates just begin
to be eatable. The house affords Madeira wine, brandy, and porter.
Yesterday my neighbor, Mr. Couper, sent me an assortment of French
wines, consisting of Claret, Sauterne, and Champagne, all excellent;
and at least a twelve months' supply of orange shrub, which makes
a most delicious punch. Madame Couper added sweetmeats and
pickles. The plantations of Butler and Couper are divided by a small
creek, and the houses within one quarter of a mile of each other;
accessible, however, only by water. We have not a fly, moscheto, or
bug. I can sit a whole evening, with open windows and lighted candles,
without the least annoyance from insects; a circumstance which I have
never beheld in any other place. I have not even seen a cockroach.

At Mr. Couper's, besides his family, there are three young ladies,
visitors. One of them arrived about three months ago from France, to
join a brother who had been shipwrecked on this coast, liked the

country so much that he resolved to settle here, and sent for this sister and a younger brother. About the time of their arrival, the elder brother was accidently drowned; the younger went with views to make an establishment some miles inland, where he now lies dangerously ill. Both circumstances are concealed from the knowledge of Mademoiselle Nicholson. In any event, she will find refuge and protection in the benevolent house of Mr. Couper.

The cotton in this neighborhood, on the coast southward to the extremity of Florida, and northward as far as we have heard, has been totally destroyed. The crop of Mr. C. was supposed to be worth one hundred thousand dollars, and not an extravagant estimate, for he has eight hundred slaves. He will not get enough to pay half the expenses of the plantation. Yet he laughs about it with good humour and without affectation. Butler suffers about half this loss. Part of his force had been turned to rice. . . .

Now, verily, were it not for the intervention of one hundred miles of low, swampy pestiferous country, I would insist on your coming to see me. . . .

I still propose to visit Florida. To set off in three or four days, and to return hither about the 6th of September; beyond that I have at present no plan. It is my wish, God knows how ardently I wish, to return by land, and pass a week with you; but, being without horses, and there being no possibility of hiring or buying, the thing seems scarcely practicable. Two modes only offer themselves—either to embark in the kind of mail stage which goes from Darien through Savannah, Augusta, and Columbia, to Camden, or to take a water passage either to Charleston or Georgetown. Either of these being accomplished, new difficulties will occur in getting from Statesburg northward. I must be in New York the first week in November. Consult your husband, and write me of these matters. . . .

I erred a little in my history of the family of Mademoisele N. There are still two brothers here. One a man *d'une certaine age*. Though not wealthy, they are not destitute of property.

Mr. C. has just now gone with his boat for the dashers who live about thirty miles southwest on the main. He has requested me to escort Madame C. on Sunday to his plantation on the south end of this island, where we are to meet him and his party on Monday, and bring them home in our coach. Madame C. is still young, tall, comely, and well bred. . . . Will close this letter, for to-morrow it must go to the postoffice at Darien, which is only about twenty-two miles distant.

St. Simon's, September 3, 1804

You see me returned from Gaston's Bluff, now called *Hamilton's Bluff*, a London merchant, partner of Mr. Couper. We were four in the carriage; the three ladies and myself.

Mr. Morse informs you that this island is forty-five miles long, and that it lies north of the mouth [of the] Altamaha, commonly spelled Alatamaha. It is, in fact, twelve and a half miles in length, and lies southeast of that river. Its width is about two and a half miles. There are now residing on the island about twenty-five white families. Frederica, now known only by the name of *Old Town*, is on the west side of the island, and about midway between its northern and southern extremities. It was first settled by Governor Oglethorpe, and was, about fifty years ago, a very gay place, consisting of perhaps twenty-five or thirty houses. The walls of several of them still remain. Three or four families only now reside here. In the vicinity of the town several ruins were pointed out to me, as having been, formerly, county seats of the governor, and officers of the garrison, and gentlemen of the town. At present, nothing can be more gloomy than what was once called Frederica. The few families now remaining, or rather residing there, for they are all newcomers, have a sickly, melancholy appearance, well assorted with the ruins which surround them. The southern part of this island abounds with fetid swamps, which must render it very unhealthy. On the northern half I have seen no stagnant water.

Mr. Couper, with his escort of ladies, was to have met us this afternoon, but he has sent us word that he is taken ill on the way; that, owing to illness in the family of the ladies who were to have accompanied him, they have been obliged to renounce the visit. We therefore returned as we went. At Frederica and Gaston's Bluff we were convinced that insects can subsist on this island. Moschetoes, flies, and cockroaches abounded.

Thursday, September 6, 1804

Just returned from Darien. And what took you to Darien? To see the plantation of Mr. Butler on an island opposite that town, and to meet a day sooner the letters which I expected from you. In the last object I have been again disappointed, which I ascribe wholly to the irregularity of the mails. It is most mortifying and vexatious to be seven weeks without hearing of you or from you, and now a whole week must elapse before I can expect it.

You are probably ignorant that Darien is a settlement (called a

town) on the north bank of the Alatamaha, about eight miles from
its mouth. Major Butler's Island in this river is one mile below the
town. It must become a fine rice country, for the water is fresh four
miles below Major Butler's, and the tide rises from four to five feet,
and the flats or swamps are from five to seven miles in width for a
considerable distance up the river. The country, of course, presents no
scenes for a painter. I visited Little St. Simon's and several other
islands; frightened the crocodiles, shot some rice-birds, and caught
some trout. Honey of fine flavour is found in great abundance in the
woods about the mouth of the river, and, for aught I know, in every
part of the country. You perceive that I am constantly discovering
new luxuries for my table. Not having been able to kill a crocodile
(alligator), I have offered a reward for one, which I mean to eat,
dressed in soup, fricassees, and steaks. Oh! how you long to partake
of this repast.

Wednesday, September 12, 1804

On Friday last, hearing that Mr. Couper had returned and was
very seriously ill, I took a small canoe with two boys, and went to see
him. He lay in a high fever. When about to return in the evening, the
wind had risen so that, after an ineffectual attempt, I was obliged to
give it up, and remain at Mr. C's. In the morning the wind was still
higher. It continued to rise, and by noon blew a gale from the north,
which, together with the swelling of the water, became alarming.

From twelve to three, several of the out-houses had been destroyed;
most of the trees about the house were blown down. The house in
which we were shook and rocked so much that Mr. C. began to
express his apprehensions for our safety. Before three, part of the
piazza was carried away; two or three of the windows bursted in. The
house was inundated with water, and presently one of the chimneys
fell. Mr. C. then commanded a retreat to a storehouse about fifty
yards off, and we decamped, men, women, and children. You may
imagine, in this scene of confusion and dismay, a good many incidents
to amuse one if one had dared to be amused in a moment of much
anxiety. The house, however, did not blow down. The storm continued till four, and then very suddenly abated, and in ten minutes
it was almost calm. I seized the moment to return home. Before I had
got quite over, the gale rose from the southeast and threatened new
destruction. It lasted [a] great part of the night, but did not attain the

violence of that from the north; yet it contributed to raise still higher the water, which was the principal instrument of devastation.

The flood was about seven feet above the height of an ordinary high tide. This has been sufficient to inundate [a] great part of the coast; to destroy all the rice; to carry off most of the buildings which were on low lands, and to destroy the lives of many blacks. The roads are rendered impassable, and scarcely a boat has been preserved. Thus all intercourse is suspended. The mail-boat, which ought to have passed northward last Saturday, and by which it was intended to forward this letter, has not been heard of. This will go by a man who will attempt to get from Darien to Savannah on foot, being sent express by the manager of Major Butler; but how, or whether it will go from Savannah, is not imagined.

Major Butler has lost nineteen negroes (drowned), and I fear his whole crop of rice, being about two hundred and sixty acres. Mr. Brailsford, of Charleston, who cultivates in rice an island at the mouth of the Alatamaha, has lost, reports say, seventy-four blacks. The banks and the buildings on the low lands are greatly injured. We have heard nothing from the southward, nor farther than from Darien northward. I greatly fear that this hurricane, so it is here called, has extended to the Waccamaw.

*Winyaw Intelligencer* (Georgetown, South Carolina), April 24, 1819

## PRESIDENT MONROE VISITS SOUTH CAROLINA

*When President James Monroe made his Southern tour in the spring of 1819, he received an enthusiastic welcome. Not since George Washington's triumphant tour in 1790 had a President ventured so far from the seat of government.*

*President Monroe left Washington on March 30. In his official party were the Secretary of War, John C. Calhoun, and family, Monroe's private secretary, Samuel L. Gouverneur, and Major General Thomas Pinckney, who would be one of his hosts at his South Carolina plantation, El Dorado on the Santee.*

*His host at Prospect Hill, Benjamin Huger, served in the 6th, 7th, 8th and 14th Congresses, as a Representative from South Carolina. Robert Heriot, called the intendant, lived at Dirleton Plantation on*

the Peedee River in Georgetown County. A record dated January 1772
shows that the first Heriot owned 3,888 acres of land in Georgetown
County.

The President's tour, before he returned to Washington in August
included Norfolk, Georgetown, Charleston, Savannah, Augusta,
Athens, Tennessee via the Cherokee Nation, Louisville and Lexington.

Each of the twenty-two toasts proposed, and doubtless drunk, is
faithfully reported in the newspaper account.

GEORGETOWN, S. C.

The President of the United States, the Secretary of War, Lady
and family; Mr. Governeur, the President's Private Secretary; Lieut.
Monroe, Col. Condy, the Governor's aid (who had been sent to meet
the President at the boundary of South Carolina), accompanied by
a Committee of the citizens of All-Saints, reached Prospect Hill, the
residence of Benjamin Huger, esq., on Waccamaw on the morning of
Wednesday the 21st inst. Having been there received and entertained
with the attention and respect due to his high office and amiable
private character, and with the usual South Carolina hospitality, the
President and suite left Waccamaw about 11 o'clock on the following
day, Thursday, in Col. Alston's elegant New York barge, which was
rowed and steered by a competent number of respectable masters of
vessels (who had volunteered their service) and over which proudly
waved the star-spangled banner. As soon as the barge and boats accompanying it, made their appearance at the entrance of Sampit river, a
federal salute was fired from field pieces, manned by volunteer citizens.

The President landed at the market wharf where he was received
by the intendant, Robert Heriot, esq., the Town Council, the Committee appointed by the citizens, and a large concourse of the citizens of
the town and of the adjacent country. A procession was then formed,
and the whole proceeded on foot to the house prepared for the President and suite. On their arrival at which, an appropriate address was
delivered by Benjamin Huger, esq., Chairman of the Committee, and a
suitable answer returned by the President.

The President and suite afterwards partook of a dinner at which
the intendant presided and which was attended by a highly respectable
as well as a very large party of citizens.

After the cloth had been removed, the following toasts were drunk:

1. *The Federal Constitution*—The Americans' richest inheritance.

2. *The Union*—In it there is political health, strength and immortality.

3. *The National Legislature*—Like the Roman Senate, firm; like the Areopagus, incorruptible.

4. *The Congress of '76*—May their successors be always worthy of them.

5. *The Judiciary*—Independent, may they never forget the people made them so.

6. *The Army*—More daring than the Infant Hercules, they have bearded the Lion.

7. *The Militia*—The diamond tho' unpolished is not the less valuable.

8. *The Navy*—"Its march is on the mountain wave, its home upon the deep."

9. *The Victory at Trenton*, the first dawn of returning success to our revolutionary struggle—May we always cherish the memory of those who fought and bled in its achievement.

10. *The Memory of Washington*—His virtues like the Sun "effuse one dazzling undivided light."

11. *The Memory of Franklin*—The accomplished philosopher, statesman, and patriot.

12. *The Living Ex-Presidents*—Let the memory of the heart be always strong towards the retired patriots.

13. *Major Gen. Jackson*—A Son of South Carolina, and worthy of her.

14. *Our Naval Heroes*—Their fame like their cannon is re-echoed in both hemispheres.

15. *The Floridas*, our late brilliant acquisition—we welcome those who inhabit them as brethren of the great American family.

16. *The Heads of Departments*—"who from the diamond can single out each ray."

17. *The Patriots of the Revolution*—When Americans cease to cherish their memory, the republic will be no more.

18. *The freedom of election*—The best gift of the Revolution.

19. *The literary institutions of our country.*

20. *The genuine sons of Freedom, throughout the World*—may success attend their exertion.

21. *The Marquis de la Fayette*—an early and firm friend of our republic.

22. *The American Fair.*

In the afternoon, a brilliant and numerous company of ladies from town and country, assembled in an adjoining room, tastefully ornamented with roses and other flowers, to which the President retired from dinner and gratified the ladies with his presence. About 10 he withdrew, and the ladies highly pleased with their distinguished guest, closed the evening in dancing.

On yesterday, the President, Secretary of War, Intendant, &c. embarked in boats provided by the Committee, to view and examine Winyaw Bay, the entrance into our port, and the adjoining shores and waters, and returned to a late dinner. We understand our distinguished guest leaves Georgetown this morning and will be accompanied by the Committee as far as South-Santee, (which divides Georgetown and Charleston Districts). From thence the President proceeds to Eldorado, on a visit to Major General Thomas Pinckney, which will leave him time sufficient to reach Charleston on the morning of Monday. We are happy to add, that he appears in good health and spirits, and to be rather benefitted than otherwise by his journey. We sincerely wish him a continuation of the blessings in the long route he is about to take and a happy return to the seat of government and his family. . . .

Captain Basil Hall

### THESE HOSPITABLE PLANTERS

*In the course of his career in the Royal Navy, Captain Basil Hall of Edinburgh had become an alert, observant and articulate traveler.*

*During a fourteen months' sojourn in the United States, Captain Hall and his wife, accompanied by their little daughter Eliza and her governess, had visited most of the cities of the young country and had been received by many distinguished citizens.*

*In the early spring of 1828 the Halls arrived in Charleston. After a brief stay they set out for Savannah well supplied, in accordance with pleasant Southern custom, with letters of introduction to the planters whose homes lay along the Combahee River between Charleston and Savannah.*

*Stopping first at Mr. William Skirving's plantation, Oaklawn, near the town of Adams Run, Mrs. Hall was moved to remark that the house contained "everything that is luxurious. . . ."*

*Another gracious welcome awaited them at the Bluff, one of the seventeen plantations owned by Nathaniel Heyward, who was the son of Daniel Heyward and half brother of Thomas Heyward, one of the signers of the Declaration of Independence. He was married to Henrietta Manigault, and Charles, the eldest of their nine children, lived at near-by Rose Hill.*

*In 1817 when Carolina rice sold for seven cents per pound, Nathaniel Heyward made a profit of $120,000. At the time of his death in 1851, his estate amounted to $2,018,000. The value placed upon his 2,000 slaves was $1,000,000. In addition, he owned five thousand acres of rice lands. There were ninety-eight slaves living in the Bluff settlement, not including house servants.*

*At the home of William Heyward, a brother of Nathaniel, the Halls again enjoyed the exquisite hospitality characteristic of the region.*

We left Charleston on the 6th of March, 1828, in a clear frosty morning, and slept at Jacksonburg, a scattered little village, on the right or southern bank of the Edisto, a river of some magnitude, running with more velocity than any stream we had crossed since leaving the St. Lawrence. We passed over in a scow or flat-bottomed boat, common in that part of the country, which was drawn across by means of a stout hawser or rope stretched from side to side. . . .

Next day we proceeded to the plantation of one of our obliging Charleston friends, who, in the style of hospitality universal in the South, had begged us to make it a resting place. We had travelled 30 miles the first day, and went only 20 the next; for having freed ourselves from the despotism of stage coach drivers, we hired a carriage to go at our own pace. . . .

There was still a touch of hoar frost on the grass, as we drove from our night's quarters and entered the forest. The air was of that pleasant temperature which is not coldness, but not warmth, making shawls and great-coats agreeable, and the promise of a higher sun very welcome. Our road lay through pine barrens, interspersed at most places with underwood and creepers in endless entanglement—all in flower. We noticed in particular, white and yellow jessamine, honeysuckles of various colours, multitudes of full-blown white roses, laurels, myrtles, laurestinus, holly, and numerous other shrubs, the names of which were unknown to us. These were mixed with an occasional aloe, and here and there with a fan-shaped, dwarfish member of the palm tribe. Another very tropical-looking plant peeped out occasionally from the bushes; it is called on the spot, the bayonet palmetto, from each division of its broad leaf being in the form of that weapon.

Pines were not the only trees in this forest scene, for we came to many fine live oaks, scattered about the wood, not very unlike the oaks of England. . . .

It was a dead calm when we started, and a haziness which filled the air gave a softened effect to the distant objects seen through the openings, or glades, which we came to every now and then, where a portion of soil richer than the rest, or the course of a river, or both combined, had invited the settler to pause in his wanderings. At other times we could see but a little way, except directly before or behind us, where the road went off in a straight line towards its vanishing point, and made us feel as if we had been driving along a great tube, rather than a public highway. . . .

The ground was every where perfectly flat, and the trees rose from it in a direction so exactly perpendicular, and so entirely without lower branches, that an air of architectural symmetry was imparted to the forest, by no means unlike that of some gothic cathedrals.

At other spots further on, where the trees were less thickly clustered together, the scene was far more lively. The ground was there chequered, or rather streaked over, with such rays of the sun as could make their way through the roof of foliage, rendered still less pervious by a singular species of moss, suspended, not in graceful festoons, but in ugly bunches, or skeins, like so much hemp, from the branches of most of the trees. At times we met with it in such quantity, that it enveloped the branches and leaves completely, and hung down in long ringlets, of a mouse grey colour, quite over the trees, as if the forest had been covered with enormous spiders' webs. . . .

On this day, we saw the first specimens of rice cultivation. I recognized, at a glance, my old friends of the East, where the straight embankments, separating the half-drowned fields, cut across by narrow canals or trenches, give a very peculiar and formal character to this amphibious sort of agriculture. About noon the sun became so disagreeably hot, that on coming to an open and cleared part of the country, we looked out sharply for our friend's plantation. We had already made sufficient acquaintance with these hospitable planters to justify our hopes of finding very good things in their country seats. As yet, however, we had not visited any of them at home, so that we were quite in doubt what this house might prove, especially as the proprietor was absent, and our experience had not led us to think very highly of negro service, even when the master's eye was over it. The first glimpse of the mansion reassured us considerably, as we drove through a neat gate into a lawn, along a nicely gravelled approach, to the house, in front of which lay a small sheet of water, with an island in the middle of it, shaded by a willow tree.

The steps of the carriage were let down by the servants, who came out before the bell was rung. The head driver, Solomon by name, welcomed us to the country, placing himself, the house, and all which belonged to it, quite at our disposal. "Such," he said, "were the orders he had received from Charleston."

After we were settled, I dropped some hints about dinner. "O yes, master, surely. What hour master choose to take it? All the rooms ready for you—hope you stay long time, sir?"

At all events, we resolved to stay some hours, though previously we had been in doubt as to this point. On going up stairs, we found ourselves in the most comfortable suite of apartments we had seen in America; the floors nicely carpeted, the walls painted and papered, and the windows made to go up and down. From the drawing-room, we could walk into a verandah or piazza, from which, by a flight of steps, we found our way into a flower garden and shrubbery, rich with orange trees, laurels, myrtles, and weeping willows, and here and there a great spreading aloe. From the top of the bank, on which the house stood, we could see over a hedge into the rice fields which lay beyond, and stretched over the plain for several miles, their boundary line being the black edge of the untouched forest. One of the windows was well-nigh choked up with the leaves of an orange tree, on which, for the first time in our journey, we beheld this golden fruit growing in the centre of a clustre of blossoms. . . .

All these things, combined with Solomon's promise of showing us over the plantation, the alacrity of the servants, and the smug air of the whole establishment, decided us to make the most of a good thing, while it was within our reach. We therefore ordered the horses to be put up till next morning, and walked out with our new friend, to see the slave village of the plantation.

It appears that when the negroes go to the field in the morning, it is the custom to leave such children behind, as are too young to work. Accordingly, we found a sober old matron in charge of three dozen shining urchins, collected together in a house near the centre of the village. Over the fire hung a large pot of hominy, a preparation of Indian corn, making ready for the little folk's supper, and a very merry, happy-looking party they seemed. The parents, and such children as are old enough to be useful, go out to work at daybreak, taking their dinner with them to eat on the ground. They have another meal towards the close of the day after coming home. Generally, also, they manage to cook up a breakfast; but this must be provided by themselves, out of their own earnings, during those hours which it is the custom, in all plantations, to allow the negroes to work on their own account.

Generally speaking, the planters, who seem well aware of the advantage of not exacting too much service from their slaves, consider the intermission of one day, at the least, in the week, as a source rather of profit than of loss. A specific task for each slave is accordingly pointed out daily by the overseer; and as soon as this is completed in a proper manner, the labourer may go home to work at his own piece of ground, or tend his pigs and poultry, or play with his children,—in a word, to do as he pleases. The assigned task is sometimes got over by two o'clock in the day, though this is rare, as the work generally lasts till four or five o'clock. I often saw gangs of negroes at work till sunset.

We went into several of the cottages, which were uncommonly neat and comfortable, and might have shamed those of many countries I have seen. Each hut was divided into small rooms or compartments, fitted with regular bed places; besides which, they had all chimneys and doors, and some, though only a few of them, possessed the luxury of windows. I counted 28 huts, occupied by 140 souls, or about 5 in each. This number included 60 children.

On returning to dinner, we found every thing in perfect order. The goodness of the attendance in this house, together with the comfort, cleanliness, and cheerfulness of the whole establishment, satisfied me, that by a proper course of discipline, slaves may be made good servants—a fact of which, I confess, I had begun to question the possibility. . . .

After dinner we strolled over the plantation, under our friend Solomon's direction, and a most intelligent and agreeable guide he proved, —more so, indeed, than it had ever occurred to us any slave-driver could possibly be. The imagination pictures such a character flourishing his whip, and so far it is true, for this symbol of office is never laid down— but he made no use of it during our stay, and he appeared to be any thing but stern or tyrannical in his deportment, to the people under his orders. We found the principal body of the negroes making a dam to keep back the waters of an adjacent river, which had invaded some of the rice fields. The negroes were working in a long string, exactly like a row of ants, with baskets of earth on their heads, under the superintendence of two under drivers, likewise blacks. This labour appeared to be heavy, and as the day declined, some of the poor people, especially the women, looked tired enough.

This plantation, at the time of our visit, consisted of 270 acres of rice, 50 of cotton, 80 of Indian corn, and 12 of potatoes, besides some minor plots for vegetables; the whole being cultivated by eighty working hands. . . .

Next day, we left our hospitable friend's plantation, and proceeded to the southward. We had no difficulty in again finding shelter, for the considerate people of Charleston had supplied us amply with introductions, enjoining us, at the same time, to consider every house we came to, as open to receive us, if we had any wish to occupy it. An experienced traveller on this road, had given us a hint where we should be best entertained, and we accordingly drove up to a very promising establishment, which fully answered the description given of it. The master of the place was walking about the grounds, but the servants had orders, they said, to receive us, and begged us to walk in.

The day being hot and calm, all the doors and windows were thrown open, and we walked through the house to a pleasant garden, overhanging the Combahee River, flowing majestically past, in a direction from the sea. Our host, who soon joined us, explained that the current we saw, was caused by the flood tide, though the sea was distant full 30 miles. This ebb and flow of the rivers intersecting the level parts of South Carolina, is of the greatest consequence to the rice growers, as it enables them to irrigate their fields at the proper season, and in the proper quantity; an advantage which leads to the production of those magnificent crops, with which all the world is familiar.

During our stay at this extensive and skilfully managed plantation, we had an opportunity of being initiated into the mysteries of the cultivation of rice, the staple of Carolina. This grain is sown in rows, in the bottom of trenches made by slave labour entirely. These ridges lie about seventeen inches apart, from centre to centre. The rice is put in with the hand, generally by women, and is never scattered, but cast so as to fall in a line. This is done about the 17th of March. By means of flood-gates, the water is permitted to flow over the fields, and to remain on the ground five days, at the depth of several inches. The object of this drenching is to sprout the seeds, as it is technically called.

The water is next drawn off, and the ground allowed to dry, until the rice has risen to what is termed four leaves high, or between three and four inches. This requires about a month. The fields are again over-flowed, and they remain submerged for upwards of a fortnight, to destroy the grass and weeds. These processes bring matters to the 17th of May, after which the ground is allowed to remain dry till the 15th of July, during which interval it is repeatedly hoed, to remove such weeds as have not been effectually drowned, and also to loosen the soil. The water is then, for the last time, introduced, in order that the rice may be brought to maturity—and it actually ripens while standing in the water. The harvest commences about the end of August, and extends into October. It is all cut by the male slaves, who use a sickle, while the women make it up into bundles. As it seems that no ingenu-ity has yet been able to overcome the difficulty of thrashing the grains out by machinery, without breaking them, the whole of this part of the process is done with hand flails in a court-yard.

The cultivation of rice was described to me as by far the most unhealthy work in which the slaves were employed; and, in spite of every care, that they sank under it in great numbers. The causes of this dreadful mortality, are the constant moisture and heat of the atmosphere, together with the alternate floodings and dryings of the fields, on which the negroes are perpetually at work, often ankle deep in mud, with their bare heads exposed to the fierce rays of the sun. At such seasons every white man leaves the spot, as a matter of course, and proceeds inland to the high grounds; or, if he can afford it, he travels northward to the springs of Saratoga, or the Lakes of Canada.

Each plantation is furnished with a mill; and in most cases that fell in my way, the planters contrived to make this and every thing else, or very nearly every thing else which they require, on their own estates. All the blacksmiths' and carpenters' work, for example, was done by the slaves of each plantation. . . .

Our hospitable friend next showed us the slave village of his planta-tion, where every thing was neat and comfortable. In answer to our questions, he told us, that he interfered as little as possible with their domestic habits, except in matters of police. "We don't care what they do when their tasks are over—we lose sight of them till next day. Their morals and manners are in their own keeping. The men may have, for instance, as many wives as they please, so long as they do not quarrel about such matters."

I asked if they had any religion?

"I know little about that," he said; "there may perhaps be one or two Methodists in a hundred. Preachers are never prevented, by me at least, from coming amongst the negroes, upon a distinct and express stipulation, however, that they do not interfere with the duties of the slaves, towards their master."

"Can any of them read and write?"

"Certainly none," he answered; "that is entirely contrary to usage here, and contrary to law in some places. Such things would only make them discontented with their lot, and in fact would be quite repugnant to the whole system of slave discipline in this country."

Domestic slaves, he told me, were better fed and clothed, and generally better treated, than those employed out of doors; but, what was odd enough, he added, that every where the slaves preferred the field-work. . . .

The laws direct that the overseer of the plantation shall always be a white man. He is a very important personage, as may be supposed, since much of the success of an estate, as well as the happiness or misery of the negroes—which appears to be nearly the same thing—depend upon his character. The details of superintendence pass under his eye, and he has the power of directing punishments, which ought always to be inflicted in his presence on the spot, by the driver. . . .

It is the popular fashion in America, and I think elsewhere, to abuse these overseers as a class. But none of my enquiries led me to think so ill of them by any means as I had heard them reported. Their interest, as well as that of the planters, in the long run, is, unquestionably, to use the slaves well. An overseer who acquires a character for undue severity, is much scouted, and sooner or later discovers that his services are not valued or sought after, merely because he produces less effective work than a more judicious person would do. . . .

In these and other discussions we passed our time very agreeably on the banks of the Combahee; but our kind host, not content with entertaining us sumptuously while we remained with him, in the true spirit of that useful hospitality which prevails in those countries, took care, that after we left him we should be well lodged every where on the road. The inns, he said, were not good—besides which, his friends would never forgive him, if he allowed strangers to go away without introductions.

On the 9th of March we resumed our journey, passing on our way many pretty country seats belonging to the different planters between Charleston and Savannah. This district is fertilized by the waters of the numberless streams, great and small, which drain the rich State of South Carolina, of which the River Edisto, the Salt Ketcher, the Coosawhatchie, and the Pocotaligo, are the most remarkable.

We drove cheerfully along, not doubting that we should light on our feet somewhere, as it never once occurred to us that the gentleman at whose house we had been recommended to take up our night's quarters could possibly be absent. But, lo and behold! on driving into the grounds, we learnt that the master of the establishment was from home.

"My master is gone to town—some days ago, sir," was the answer of the head servant.

"That is very unfortunate; we had hoped to stop here to-night," I said with an air of disappointment.

The black groom of the chambers smiled most graciously at this imaginary difficulty of our starting, but made a private signal to the driver, who, from understanding the fashions of the country better than we did, had the trunks unstrapped before we could look round us. Our grinning friend, Dick, then marshalling the way, we found ourselves in two minutes delightfully settled, sole tenants of the plantation!

Next morning, on going away, I put a note for the owner of the house into the hands of the delighted Major-domo, to say how comfortably we had been lodged, how attentive all his people had been, and how well accustomed they seemed to the office of hospitality; for though we had taken them by surprise, we found every thing as completely provided for us as if a week's preparation had been made for our reception. . . .

I have no wish, God knows! to defend slavery in the abstract; neither do I say that it is the best state of things which might be supposed to exist in those countries; but I do think it is highly important that we should look this great and established evil fairly in the face, and consider its bearings with as little prejudice as possible. There is no other chance for its gradual improvements, I am well convinced, but this calm course, which has for its object the discovery of what is possible—not what is desirable.

One of the results which actual observation has left on my mind is, that there are few situations in life, where a man of sense and feeling can exert himself to better purpose, than in the management of slaves. So far, therefore, from thinking unkindly of slave-holders, an acquaintance with their proceedings has taught me to respect many of them in the highest degree; and nothing, during my recent journey, gave me more satisfaction than the conclusion to which I was gradually brought, that the planters of the Southern States of America, generally speaking, have a sincere desire to manage their estates with the least possible severity. . . .


John C. Calhoun

## AFFAIRS AT FORT HILL

*Fort Hill, near Pendleton, South Carolina, became the permanent home of John C. Calhoun during his first term as Vice-President in John Quincy Adams' administration.*

*The house—its name carried over from earlier days when the site had been fortified against Indian attack—white-columned and stately, was surrounded by more than eleven hundred acres of well-planted land. Boxwood lined the walks and in the near-by groves were a varnish tree, a gift of Stephen Decatur, a hemlock from Daniel Webster and an arborvitae from Henry Clay. In the handsome dining room, the principal setting of much of Fort Hill's hospitality, stood a long, shining mahogany table and sideboard, also a gift from Henry Clay.*

*Calhoun's political career kept him of necessity from Fort Hill for long periods, but nothing could displace his devoted concern for his plantation. He personally directed its affairs and his letters from the city are full of the true countryman's love of his land.*

*In the summer of 1831, the date of our first letter, the Calhoun family consisted of Mrs. Calhoun—Floride—and their children, Andrew, Anna Maria, Patrick, John Caldwell, Jr., Cornelia, James Edward and the two-months-old baby, William Lownes.*

*Anna Maria, Calhoun's eldest daughter, married Thomas C. Clemson, founder of Clemson College. In 1849 she was living in Belgium where her husband held a diplomatic post.*

*James Edward Calhoun was Mrs. Calhoun's brother. His home was Midway, near Abbeville.*

*There were some seventy or eighty slaves at Fort Hill. Calhoun, known as a kind and firm master, won a prize at the county fair in Pendleton for having the best slave quarters. They were built of stone.*

*Calhoun had another plantation at Bath.*

## TO JAMES EDWARD CALHOUN

Fort Hill 27th Aug$^t$ 1831

Dear James, The heavy rains and great rise in the water courses must of course make you solicitous to hear about your planting interest in this quarter. The river has been very full, all over the low grounds, and covering completely the crops, except on a few more elevated spots. It has subsided partially, but is not yet in the banks. The cotton I think is lost, and I fear the corn too. They are both covered over with mud, tho there is now falling a rain, which I hope may wash it off, and at least give a more cheerful appearance. I had 50 acres of cotton completely covered and all my corn, in the same condition, except about 3 acres. The cotton on the upland has suffered most from the wet. It has shed profusely. . . .

Aleck, our house servant, gave us the slip yesterday and is now in the woods. I expect he has made for my place, and may possibly take Midway on his course. I must ask of you the favour to keep a lookout for him, and to give Mr. Gibson my overseer immediate notice in order that he may be also on the lookout. I will thank you to inform him, if he should be taken, to have him severely whipped and sent back immediately. I give this trouble, which I am sure you will excuse, as I have a private opportunity of writing to you sooner than I could by mail to my plantation. He had offended your sister, and she threatened him, with a severe whipping. He ran away to avoid it; and has left us without a house servant, except females.

We are all well except your sister, who has not yet entirely recovered, but is much better. I will be glad to hear from you. Should you hear, I would be glad to learn, how I have fared on the River below, and whether Aleck has been seen or heard of.

## TO JAMES EDWARD CALHOUN

Fort Hill 10th Sept 1831

My Dear James, Your letter gave me the first information of the extent of my loss at Bath. That added to my loss here, which is literally everything, except about 50 acres of cotton, renders it a calamitous year to me. I will nothing like clear expenses. I am glad to hear, that your prospect is so much better. Your loss here is nothing like in proportion to mine, which is the heaviest on the river. The place is very low. It is a great objection. I send Lewis to bring up Harold and Aleck. The latter is at Abbeville. He was taken up on his way down. . . .

I wish you to get for me two bushels of corn from Mr. Halsey. It comes so early, that it may help me out next summer. Do not fail to obtain it early. . . .

Your sister and all the children desire their love to you.

### TO ANNA MARIA CALHOUN

Washington 3d April 1834

My dear Anna, . . . Your mother, as well as yourself, writes me, that she devotes much of her time to the yard and garden, which I am very glad to learn, as I have no doubt it will contribute much both to her health and enjoyment. I hope that you will participate with her in the exercise, and the enjoyment. You must select the vines and shrubs for your particular care. I have no doubt, that your mother's management will quite discredit mine. Whatever she undertakes she does well. I sincerely wish, I were at home, and participating with you all in your employment and amusement, instead of going through the drudgery and confinement which my duties compel me to do here. I have never been more anxious to return home and see you all. . . .

Your mother wrote me to send her some more garden seeds. In my answer, I said I would send them in a few days, but you must say to her, that when I came to examine her list, I find that the season is too late for them; and therefore I do not think it worth while to send them. I will bring such of them, as may be sowed in the fall. Say to her also, that I have written to Mr. Bonneau to send her the Water Melon seed, tho I think she will find a good supply of them among the old seed. I, at the same time, directed him to send up immediately a quarter Cask of best Madeira. . . . Write me often. . . .

### TO ANNA MARIA CALHOUN

Washington 14th May 1834

My dear Anna, Were it not for your letters, there are a thousand incidents that are daily occurring, where every incident, even the smallest, is interesting to me, of which I should remain ignorant. Your Mother and Brother write me on grave subjects of business, or what relates to the welfare of the family; but you fill up the interval with those little, but to me interesting details, which it is so agreeable to an absent father to know. Were it not for you, I would not have heard a word about the Humming birds, their familiarity, the vines, their blooms, the freshness of the spring, the green yard, the children's gardens, and finally Patrick's mechanical genius and his batteaux, every item of which excited agreeable associations, but accompanied with the painful recollection of my long absence, from those so dear to me. I hope the period is now near at hand, that will put a termination to my absence. The House of Representatives will probably pass a resolution, fixing the 16th of next month as the time of adjournment, and I trust, the Senate will concur in the time. If so, a month more, and my face will be turned homeward, to my great delight. We can for the present do little more, but to check the *progress* of usurpation, which I think has been pretty effectually done. . . .

TO MRS. T. G. CLEMSON

Fort Hill 10th April 1849

My Dear Daughter, I had a safe and pleasant journey home. The weather was pleasant and Spring was rapidly advancing. The Jessamine and Dogwood were in bloom, and the forest had just commenced clothing itself with green. The contrast was great between being pent up in a boarding house in Washington and breathing the pure fresh air of the country, made fragrant by the blossoms of Spring.

Patrick accompanied me to your Uncle James, where we met your Mother and Sister. They, with your Uncle, were well. I remained there four days, when we took our departure for Fort Hill, leaving Patrick with his Uncle. We found all well on our arrival, and the place in good order and business forward, considering that the measles had passed through the negro quarter during the winter, and that none, but a few had escaped, but with the loss of only one, an infant of a constitution too feeble to survive the attack. I shall finish planting cotton to day, and the whole of my crop this week. The small grain looks well, and the place bears the appearance of good order.

We have no local news, in which you would take interest.

John returned from Milledge Ville by the last Stage but one. He looks well and I think his health is much improved by the Water cure. . . .

TO MRS. T. G. CLEMSON

Fort Hill 15th June 1849

My Dear Daughter, I do hope by this time, you are all safe in London, after a pleasant voyage. I shall be on the lookout for a letter dated at London in about two weeks from now. . . .

We all felt, my dear daughter, as you described your feelings to be, at your departure. It is, indeed, distressing to be so far off and for so long a time from those so dear to us; but let us rather look forward to when we shall again meet, than indulge in unavailing sorrows. I trust two years at the utmost, will terminate your residence in Europe, and return you all safe again to our country. It is due to the children, that your stay should not be longer. Their habits and mode of thinking will, by that time, begin to be formed; and it is important, that they should be such, as to conform to the conditions of the country, which is to be their home. I often think of them, and how much delighted they would be, to be enjoying themselves in our green and shady yard. The season has been wet, and everything looks beautiful. Even the old field beyond the yard looks as green as a meadow. In the field beyond it, (Speeds field), now containing 125 acres, by the addition of clearing, has a fine crop of oats, just fully shot out, which completely covers the whole ground, presenting an unbroken mass of green in that direction. The big bottom on the other side is covered, with a superb crop of corn, the best at this season, I ever had on it, which covers the whole with a deep green. Back of it, lies Fort Hill, with its harvested wheat in shocks. The spring had been too cool and wet for cotton, but mine looks well, and, with my hill side drains and serpentine rows, really looks handsome. The place is, altogether, in fine order. I ride or walk, according to the weather twice a day, morning and evening, over it, for the double purpose of exercise and superintendence. I have no trouble, as Frederick has become a first rate overseer, and takes as much interest as I do in everything about the place. I would be delighted to have you and the children with me occasionally, in my walks. It would be wearisome to take them as often as I do.

My health and strength are as good, as I could expect at my time of life. . . .


Henry Barnard

## A NEW ENGLANDER IN SOUTH CAROLINA

*From Salisbury, North Carolina, where he visited Dr. Ashbel Smith, young Henry Barnard went on to South Carolina. In Charleston he dined with his classmate, Charles Legare Burden, who practiced law and later medicine, and in Beaufort, South Carolina. It was there he*

*heard much talk of a Southern Confederacy, and before returning to
his home he came to the conclusion that secession was inevitable.*

*Evident in these letters to his brother Chauncy and his sister Betty
are the personal qualities that later contributed so greatly to Barnard's
success as an educationist. Intelligence, warmth, friendliness and a
capacity for keen observation make them both entertaining and in-
formative.*

Beaufort, S. C. April 30th 1833

... I left Savannah yesterday morning for this place 80 miles distant,
where I expected to have seen Edmund Smith a classmate of mine—
but I was disappointed. He is now in Charleston. However I spent the
evening delightfully at his mother's and was served with the most delicious luxury I ever met with, and that was a dish holding 4 or 5 quarts
of large, ripe *strawberries,* a dish of sweet cream and a bowl of fine
white sugar. I never tasted anything so very fine. They have had strawberries for 3 weeks. . . . This is the first time in my life, that I have
tasted of strawberries and green peas in April.

Beaufort is a beautiful place—very quiet,—no commercial business
going on here—but planters whose estates lie among the islands—the
famous Sea Island cotton plantations—have their plantations here.
These plantations yield an enormous income. Several planters in this
district enjoy a fortune from 10—70000 a year, and yet they complain
of hard times. The district of Beaufort is probably the richest in the
U. States, excepting the great commercial cities. The climate in the
winter season is delightful, resembling that of the South of France.

I landed yesterday afternoon with a Mr. Eddings, a young wealthy
planter, but very dissipated. He was very anxious that I should go out
to his plantation, on an island 10 miles distant, and I partly agreed to.
But he got gloriously drunk before evening, and we parted in a very
cavalier like manner. Fortunately he was no Nullifier or he would
have blown my brains out without any ceremony.

The North is not disposed to give the Nullifiers of this State, sincerity in their threatenings to fight—for myself, judging from what I
have seen—and heard from Union men and all, I have no doubt of that
sincerity. They would have fought with the courage of desperation. It
was their intention if things actually came to war, to fight as long as
they could do in the open fields—then if they were obliged to give way,
to blow up their cities, and retire to their marshes and swamps and
carry on a "guerilla warfare." This would do in the winter, but in sum-

mer, a few nights would soon drive them from their lurking places or else sweep them into their graves.

The affair is not over yet however—that attachment to the Union which was once so universal, and so sacred, is gone, and I fear gone forever. It is the commonest thing in the world, to hear them speak of disunion—the certainty of its taking place in a few years. Unless a revolution in popular feeling takes place, I should not wonder if disunion does come, and in its train all the horrors of civil war and revolution.

I don't wonder that Jackson is so damnably unpopular here. The leading men of this State had the surest pledges that Jackson was with them in their views of the Constitution. Gov. [James] Hamilton has got a letter in his possession at this time, in which Jackson expresses his approbation of his views of State Rights etc. etc. They were all assured that the Executive was with them. Hence it is not to be wondered at that their hatred to the old truant is so deep and bitter. 3 months ago if Jackson had ventured into this state he would have been shot or stabbed in a short time. Their hatred of him amounts to madness—it is only surpassed by their hatred of the d—d Yankees.

I have had today a visit from Albert Smith, brother of Edmund, and a very hot headed Nullifier, he has gone over the whole matter with me. He too has got the notion that the North has a disposition to tamper with the slave question. He is a brother of Robert Barnwell Smith, who made such violent speeches in the convention against the Union. . . .

Charleston May 9th 1833

. . . There is a great deal of sensitiveness on the subject of slavery in this part of the country. It has been strengthened by the proposition in the British Parliament to Emancipate all the slaves in the British West Indies. The injudicious publications at the North, give some color to the charge, that we are disposed to interfere with the domestic relations of the South. I am convinced if that suspicion should become general there would be a unanimous rallying on the part of the South. A convention of the Slave holding States would be held, and the question of Union be agitated and decided positively.

It is the opinion of the many distinguished men here that S. Carolina has suffered more from the operation of Nullification, than she ever did or could from the Tariff. . . .

Charleston, May 11th, 1833

. . . I spend my time principally in visiting and calling on men whose

opinions may be valuable. I dined yesterday with my classmate Burden
—his father is a planter and lives in the healthy season on one of the
neighboring Islands. He had not yet moved his family to the city—of
course he keeps bachelor's Hall. But he served up a grand dinner to a
small party—first came a calves head stew as soup—then fish fried or
boiled—roast veal and ducks, with Irish and Sweet potatoes—boiled
rice (an article of which you can form no opinion from what we ordinarily meet with in the North) and fine bread—peas and beets—tur-
nips and salad. Then came the dessert—another fruit—fine large oranges—pineapple—plantain and bananas (tropical fruits which I have
never seen at the North but which resemble the richest pear in flavor)
—apples—raisins and almonds—prunes and ground nuts and to wash
down the whole of each the finest claret, sherry and madeira wine.

We adjourned a little after 7 after taking a good cup of coffee. . . .


Harriet Martineau

## COUNTRY LIFE IN THE SOUTH

*Harriet Martineau, English novelist, political economist and writer
for children, visited America in 1834. She was thirty-two years of age.
A woman of esteem in her own country, she failed to win the same
admiration in America. In a crusading spirit she attended and insisted
on speaking at Abolitionist meetings. She visited in New York, Massachusetts, Washington, D. C., Virginia, Georgia, Alabama and South
Carolina. She traveled down the Mississippi and had a look at Louisiana, Mississippi and Ohio.*

*The result of her visit was the publication of two censorious books:
Society in America (1837), and Retrospect of Western Travel (1838).*

There was no end to the kind cautions given me against travelling
through the Southern States; not only on account of my opinions on
slavery, but because of the badness of the roads and the poverty of the
wayside accommodations. . . . We had friends to visit at Charleston
and Columbia, South Carolina; Augusta, Georgia; Montgomery, Alabama; and Mobile. At Richmond we were cautioned about the journey
into South Carolina: at Charleston we met with dreadful reports of
travelling in Georgia: in Georgia people spoke of the horrors of Alabama, and so on: and, after all, nothing could well be easier than the

whole undertaking. I do not remember a single difficulty that occurred, all the way. . . .

Our stationary rural life in the South was various and pleasant enough: all shaded with the presence of slavery; but without any other drawback. There is something in the make-shift irregular mode of life which exisits where there are slaves that is amusing when the cause is forgotten.

The waking in the morning is accomplished by two or three black women staring at you from the bed-posts. Then it is five minutes' work to get them out of the room. Perhaps before you are half dressed, you are summoned to breakfast. You look at your watch, and listen whether it has stopped; for it seems not to be seven o'clock yet. You hasten, however, and find your hostess making the coffee. The young people drop in when the meal is half done, and then it is discovered that breakfast has been served an hour too early, because the clock has stopped, and the cook has ordered affairs according to her own conjectures. Every body laughs, and nothing ensues. After breakfast a farmer in homespun,—blue trousers and an orange-brown coat,—or all over grey,—comes to speak with your host. A drunken white has shot one of his negroes, and he fears no punishment can be obtained, because there were no witnesses of the deed but blacks. A consultation is held whether the affair shall go into court; and, before the farmer departs, he is offered cake and liqueur.

Your hostess, meantime, has given her orders, and is now engaged in a back room, or out in the piazza behind the house, cutting out clothes for her slaves;—very laborious work in warm weather. There may be a pretence of lessons among the young people; and something more than pretence, if they happen to have a tutor or governess: but the probability is that their occupations are as various as their tempers. Rosa cannot be found: she is lying on the bed in her own room, reading a novel: Clara is weeping for her canary, which has flown away while she was playing with it: Alfred is trying to ascertain how soon we may all go out to ride; and the little ones are lounging about the court, with their arms round the necks of blacks, of their own size. You sit down to the piano, or to read; and one slave or another enters every half hour to ask what is o'clock. Your hostess comes in, at length; and you sit down to work with her: she gratifies your curiosity about her "people;" telling you how soon they burn out their shoes at the toes, and wear out their winter woollens, and tear up their summer cottons; and how impossible it is to get black women to learn to cut out clothes without waste; and how she never inquires when and where the whipping is done, as it is the overseer's business, and not hers. She has not been seated many minutes when she is called away, and returns saying how babyish these people are, that they will not take medicine unless she gives it to them; and how careless of each other, so that she has been obliged to stand by and see Diana put clean linen upon her infant, and to compel Bet to get her sick husband some breakfast.

Morning visitors next arrive. It may be the clergyman, with some new book that you want to look at; and inquiries whether your host sees any prospect of getting the requisite number of professors for the new college; or whether the present head of the institution is to continue to fill all the chairs. It may be a lank judge from some raw district, with a quid in his cheek, a sword cane in his hand, and a legal doubt in his mind, which he wants your host to resolve. It may be a sensible woman, with courtesy in her countenance, and decision in her air, who is accustomed really to rule her household, and to make the most of such human material and such a human lot as are pressing around and upon her. If so, the conversation between her and your hostess becomes rapid and interesting,—full of tales of perplexity and trouble, of droll anecdotes, and serious and benevolent plans. Or it may be a lady of a different cast, who is delighted at the prospect of seeing you soon again. You look perplexed, and mention that you fear you shall be unable to return this way. O, but you will come and live here. You plead family, friends, and occupation in England,—to say nothing of England being your home. O, but you can bring your family and friends with you. You laughingly ask why. She draws up and replies, "for the honour and glory of living in a republic."

Meantime, Clara has dried her tears, for some one has recovered her canary, and the door of the cage is shut. The carriage and saddle-horses are scrambling on the gravel before the door, and the children run in to know if they may ride with you. Cake, fruit, and liqueurs, or perhaps tea, are brought in; and then the ladies depart. The clergyman thinks he will ride round with your party, hearing that you are going to inspect Mr. A.'s plantation. He warns you that it will not be "pleasant to see even the best plantations;" and your trembling heart fully agrees.

You admire the horsemanship of your host on his white horse, and the boys on their black ponies. The carriage goes at good speed, and yet the fast *pace* of the saddle-horses enables the party to keep together. While you are looking out upon a picturesque loghouse, peeping forth from a blossomy thicket, or admiring a splendid hedge of the

Cherokee rose, in straggling bloom, Rosa rouses herself from a reverie, and asks you to tell her all about Victoria.

"What shall I tell you?"

"What religion is she? A Unitarian, I suppose, like you."

Church of Englandism and dissent being explained, Rosa resumes, in a plaintive voice, "Is she betrothed yet?"

"Not that I know of."

"O, I hope she is! I wish I knew! When will she be queen? When she is eighteen, won't she?—O, I thought she was to be of age, and be made queen at eighteen. How long will she be a queen?"

"As long as she lives."

"As long as she lives! Why I thought——"

Rosa has no idea of rulers not being changed every four or eight years. Even her imagination is almost overpowered at the idea of being set above every body else for life.

The carriage stops, and you are invited to step out, and view the ravages of a tornado, a season or two ago; you see how clear a path it made for itself in the forest; and how it swept across the river, tearing down an answering gap through the tall cane-brake on the opposite bank. The prostrated trees lie sunk in swamp, half hidden by flowering reeds and bright mosses; while their stumps, twice as tall as yourself, are all cropped off, whatever may be their thickness, precisely at the same height; and so wrenched and twisted as to convince you that you never before conceived of the power of the winds. The boys show you a dry path down to the river side, that you may see the fish traps that are laid in the stream, and watch the couples of shad fishers— dark figures amidst the flashing waters,—who are pursuing their occupation in the glare of noon. The girls tell you how father remembers the time when there were bears in that cane-brake, and there was great trouble in getting them to come out of their thick covert to be killed. When father first came here, this side of the river was all cane-brake too. Is not a cane-brake very ugly?—It may not have any picturesque beauty; but your eye rests upon it with satisfaction, as a tropical feature in the scene.

You proceed, and point out with admiration a beautifully situated dwelling, which you declare takes your fancy more than any you have seen. The children are amused that you should suppose any one lives there, overshadowed with trees as it is, so that its inhabitants would be devoured by mosquitoes. Your hostess tells you that it is called Mr. B.'s Folly. He spent a good deal of money, and much taste upon it; but

it is uninhabitable from being rather too near the river. The fever
appeared so immediately and decisively that the family had to leave it
in three months; and there it stands, to be called B.'s Folly.

Your host paces up to the carriage window, to tell you that you are
now on A.'s plantation. You are overtaking a long train of negroes
going to their work from dinner. They look all over the colour of the
soil they are walking on: dusky in clothing, dusky in complexion. An
old man, blacker than the rest, is indicated to you as a native African;
and you point out a child so light as to make you doubt whether he be
a slave. A glance at the long heel settles the matter. You feel that it
would be a relief to be assured that this was a troop of monkeys
dressed up for sport, rather than that these dull, shuffling animals
should be human.

There is something inexpressibly disgusting in the sight of a slave
woman in the field. I do not share the horror of the Americans at the
idea of women being employed in out-door labour. It did not particularly gratify me to see the cows always milked by men (where there
were no slaves); and the hay and harvest fields would have looked
brighter in my eyes if women had been there to share the wholesome
and cheerful toil. But a negro woman behind the plough presents a
very different object from the English mother with her children in the
turnip field, or the Scotch lassie among the reapers. In her pre-emin-
ently ugly costume, the long, scanty, dirty woollen garment, with the
shabby large bonnet at the back of her head, the perspiration streaming down her dull face, the heavy tread of the splay foot, the slovenly
air with which she guides her plough,—a more hideous object cannot
well be conceived; unless it be the same woman at home, in the negro
quarter, as the cluster of slave dwellings is called.

You are now taken to the cotton-gin, the building to your left, where
you are shown how the cotton, as picked from the pods, is drawn between cylinders so as to leave the seeds behind; and how it is afterwards
packed, by hard pressure, into bales. The neighbouring creek is
dammed up to supply the water-wheel by which this gin is worked. You
afterwards see the cotton-seed laid in handfuls round the stalks of the
young springing corn, and used in the cotton field as manure.

Meantime, you attempt to talk with the slaves. You ask how old that
very aged man is, or that boy; they will give you no intelligible answer.
Slaves never know, or never will tell their ages; and this is the reason
why the census presents such extraordinary reports on this point; declaring a great number to be above a hundred years old. If they have

a kind master, they will boast to you of how much he gave for each of them, and what sums he has refused for them. If they have a hard master, they will tell you that they would have more to eat, and be less flogged, but that massa is busy, and has no time to come down, and see that they have enough to eat. Your hostess is well known on this plantation, and her kind face has been recognized from a distance; and already a negro woman has come to her with seven or eight eggs, for which she knows she shall receive a quarter dollar. You follow her to the negro quarter, where you see a tidy woman knitting, while the little children who are left in her charge are basking in the sun, or playing all kinds of antics in the road; little shining, plump, clear-eyed children, whose mirth makes you sad when you look round upon their parents, and see what these bright creatures are to come to. You enter one of the dwellings, where every thing seems to be of the same dusky hue: the crib against the wall, the walls themselves, and the floor, all look one yellow. More children are crouched round the wood fire, lying almost in the embers. You see a woman pressing up against the wall, like an idiot, with her shoulder turned towards you, and her apron held up to her face. You ask what is the matter with her, and are told that she is shy. You see a woman rolling herself about in a crib, with her head tied up. You ask if she is ill, and are told that she has not a good temper; that she struck at a girl she was jealous of with an axe; and the weapon being taken from her, she threw herself into the well, and was nearly drowned before she was taken out, with her head much hurt.

The overseer has, meantime, been telling your host about the fever having been more or less severe last season, and how well off he shall think himself if he has no more than so many days' illness this summer: how the vegetation has suffered from the late frosts, pointing out how many of the oranges have been cut off, but that the great magnolia in the centre of the court is safe. You are then invited to see the house, learning by the way the extent and value of the estate you are visiting, and of the "force" upon it. You admire the lofty, cool rooms, with their green blinds, and the width of the piazzas on both sides the house, built to compensate for the want of shade from trees, which cannot be allowed near the dwelling, for fear of mosquitoes. You visit the ice-house, and find it pretty full, the last winter having been a severe one. You learn that for three or four seasons after this ice-house was built, there was not a spike of ice in the State; and a cargo had to be imported from Massachusetts.

When you have walked in the field as long as the heat will allow, you step into the overseer's bare dwelling, within its bare enclosure, where fowls are strutting about, and refresh yourself with a small tumbler of milk,—a great luxury, which has been ordered for the party. The overseer's fishing tackle and rifle are on the wall: and there is a medicine chest, and a shelf of books. He is tall, sallow, and *nonchalant*, dropping nothing more about himself and his situation than that he does not know that he has had more than his share of sickness and trouble in his vocation, and so he is pretty well satisfied.

Your hostess reminds the party that they are going out to dinner, and that it is quite time to be returning to dress. So you go straight home by a shorter road, stopping no more, but looking out, now at a glorious trumpet honeysuckle dangling from a branch; now at a lofty, spreading green tree, red hot close to the ground, while a sheet of flame is spreading all about its roots, the flames looking orange and blue in the bright sunshine.

You are glad to find, on arriving at home, that you have half an hour to lie down before you dress, and are surprised, on rising, to feel how you are refreshed. You have not very far to go to dinner,—only to Mr. E.'s cottage on the Sand Hills. The E.'s have just come for the summer; the distant city being their winter residence. If you find the accommodations poor, you must excuse it, in consideration of their recent removal. The E.'s live in very good style in the city. The cottage is half way up a gentle ascent, with a deep, sandy road leading to the wooden steps of the front piazza, and pine forests in the rear. The entertainment to-day is not solely on your account: it is a parting dinner to young Mr. and Mrs. F., who are going to reside further west. They are leaving their parents and friends, and the family estate, and are to live in a loghouse till a proper dwelling can be built. Mrs. F. is rather low in spirits, but her mother means to send the old family nurse with her; so that she will have one comfort, at any rate, and will be able to trust her infant out of her sight now and then. As for Mrs. E., she informs you that she has come out to the cottage sooner than she usually does, as she is expecting her confinement. She has all her five children in her presence always; and as she cannot trust them for an hour with her "people," their noise and the heat would be intolerable in town; but here, where her room opens upon the piazza, she can have the children always in her sight or hearing, with less fatigue than in the city. You ask whether such a charge be not too much for her. Certainly; but there is no use in complaining, for it cannot be helped. She never had a nurse that was not more plague than use. It is not only that the servants tell the children improper things, and teach them falsehood, but it is impossible to get the little boys' faces washed without seeing it done; and the infant may, as likely as not, be dropped into the fire or out of the window. Ladies must make the best of their lot, for they cannot help themselves.

The dinner is plentiful, including, of course, turkey, ham, and sweet potatoes; excellent claret, and large blocks of ice-cream. A slave makes gentle war against the flies with an enormous bunch of peacock's feathers: and the agitation of the air is pleasant, while the ladies are engaged in eating, so that they cannot use their own fans, which are hung by loops on the backs of their chairs. The afternoon is spent in the piazza, where coffee is served. There the ladies sit, whisking their feather fans, jesting with the children, and talking over the last English poem or American novel; or complaining bitterly of the dreadful incendiary publications which Mr. E. heard from Mr. H., who heard it from Mr. M., that Judge R. had said that somebody had seen circulated among the negroes, by some vile agent of the horrid abolitionists of the North.

You go in to tea, and find the table strewed with prints, and the piano open; and Mrs. F. plays and sings. The gentlemen have done discussing the French war and the currency, and are praising the conduct of the Committee of Vigilance; frankly informing you, as a stranger, of the reasons of its formation, and the modes of its operation in deterring abolitionists from coming into the neighbourhood, in arresting them on any suspicion of tampering with the negroes, and in punishing them summarily, if any facts are established against them. While you are endeavouring to learn the nature of the crime and its evidence, you are summoned. There is going to be a storm, and your party must get home, if possible, before it comes on. In such a case, Mrs. E. will say nothing in opposition to your leaving her so early. She would not be the means of exposing you to the storm. You hasten away, and reach home during the first explosion of thunder.

You find there a bouquet, sent to you with Miss G.'s compliments; a splendid bunch of quince, yellow jessamine, arbor vitae, hyacinths, cherry, and other blossoms. It is not nearly bed-time yet; and you sit on the sofa, fanning yourself, with the table-lamp dimmed by the momentary glare of blue lightning. Your hostess learns from the servants that poor Miss Clara went to bed in great grief; the cat having killed her canary in the afternoon. It has been a sad day for poor Clara, from the adventures of her bird: but she is now fast asleep.

Your host amuses you with anecdotes of South country life. He asks you how you were struck with Mrs. L., whose call you returned yesterday. You reply that she seems a cheerful, hearty personage, who makes the best of a poor lot; and you relate how pleased you were at the frankness with which she owned, pointing to the stocking she was darning, that she knew little of books now-a-days, or of music, as she was making shirts and darning stockings for her sons, all the year round. You were sorry to see such evidences of poverty; chairs with broken backs, and a piano with three legs, and a cracked flute: but glad that Mrs. L. seemed able to look on the bright side of things. Your host throws himself back, and laughs for three minutes: and when he recovers, informs you that Mrs. L. is the wealthiest widow in the State. You protest that you looked upon her with respect as a meritorious widow, doing her best for a large family. Your host repeats that she is the richest widow in the State; and that she and all her family are odd about money. She has a sister in a neighbouring State, Mrs. M., who is even more bent upon economy. Last year Mrs. L. visited this sister, who lives in a country town. The sisters went out in Mrs. M.'s carriage, to make calls and do shopping. Mrs. L. observed that her sister's carriage was attended by a little mulatto girl, who let down the steps, and put them up, and mounted behind very dexterously. "The child is clever enough," said Mrs. L.: "but, sister, your carriage should have a proper footman. You should not be seen in town with a girl behind your carriage." Mrs. M. promised to consider the matter. The next day, a spruce mulatto lad was in waiting, of whom Mrs. L. fully approved. When she looked in his face, however, as he was letting down the steps at the entrance of a store, she was struck by his remarkable likeness to the girl of yesterday, and observed upon it. Mrs. M. laughed, and owned she had got a suit of boy's clothes made since yesterday, for the girl to wear during morning drives: and she thought this an excellent plan. Many such a story does your host amuse you with; observing that, though America has fewer humourists than England, they may be met with in abundance in rare settlements and retired districts, where they can indulge their fancies without much suffering from public opinion.

The storm abates. You are the oracle as to what o'clock it is; and, as you are confident that it is near eleven, the chamber lights are brought. You dismiss your dusky attendants, and throw yourself on your ample sofa for half an hour, to recall what you have seen and heard this day, and meditate on the scope and tendencies of Country Life in the Southern States.

G. W. Featherstonhaugh

## "I AM A SOUTH CAROLINIAN"

*G. W. Featherstonhaugh, the noted British geologist, made his first trip to the United States in 1806. He did not return until 1834 when he was accompanied by his wife and young son. While Mrs. Featherstonhaugh stayed with friends at the Sweet Springs of Virginia, Featherstonhaugh and his son embarked on a geological investigation that carried them south and west to the Mexican frontier.*

*The careful record that he kept of his tour was published upon his return to England. Of the book he said:*

*"The U. S. which lies to the south (southern slave-holding states) has received less attention from travellers than the north and west. It is to supply, to a certain extent, the want of information which exists respecting some portions of the southern states, that the author has drawn up the following pages."*

*Featherstonhaugh's friend, Dr. Thomas Cooper, became the second president of South Carolina State College in 1821.*

*The scientist's eye for detail together with Mr. Featherstonhaugh's genuine literary ability creates in the following selection a memorable impression of the spirit and character of South Carolina planters during the tumultuous 1830's.*

Almost the whole distance of eighty miles from Augusta to Columbia [South Carolina] is over a pine and sand country of the poorest character, the latter part of it being a dead flat. One mile from Columbia we crossed a long wooden bridge, thrown over the Congaree at the confluence of the Saluda and Broad Rivers, both of which have their sources in the mountains of North Carolina. Not far from the bridge this river falls over gneiss rocks penetrated by granitic veins, and a short railway is laid from the bridge up a gentle acclivity to the town, which contains about 4000 inhabitants. The streets, like those of the other towns, are broad, and planted with that gaudy tree, the Pride of China (Melia Azaderach). Having travelled several nights in that exposed and most comfortless and lumbrous contrivance, an American stage-coach, I determined to rest a day or two here and see a few acquaintances I had in the neighbourhood; so being fortunate enough to get a private room at the tavern, I proceeded to spruce myself up a little, a thing I had not done since I left New Orleans.

Columbia, the capital of South Carolina, is pleasantly situated, and in some of its airy streets there are genteel-looking houses, which at once indicate a respectable state of society. . . . Having walked through the streets to see what the town looked like, I rambled in the afternoon about two or three miles off to call upon Dr. [Thomas] Cooper, whom I had met before in New York. This gentleman, always conspicuous, had made himself particularly so of late, in the agitation of the *Nullification* question, which the Tariff law had given birth to, and which had so nearly brought the State of South Carolina into hostile collision with the power of the federal government under the administration of President Jackson. Although the excitement—which at one time threatened such fatal consequences—had been calmed by the judicious conduct of Mr. Clay and Mr. Calhoun in agreeing to the Compromise Act, yet the same question is of such vital consequence to South Carolina, and so important to the Northern manufacturers, that it is always liable to be agitated again. The leading planters of South Carolina are generally men who having inherited large estates with numerous slaves born upon them, and received liberal educations, consider themselves, not without some reason, *the gentlemen of America*; looking down upon the trading communities in the Northern States, where slavery does not exist, with that habitual sense of superiority which men born to command—and above all others slaveholders—always cherish when they are placed in competition with men engaged in mercantile pursuits, whom they consider to be by the nature of their avocations, incapable of rising to their level: to this feeling, the seeds of which are planted in infancy, is added a distrust sometimes amounting to hatred.

The planter, although his crops of cotton and rice often produce him an annual income far exceeding that of the cultivator of the North, and tempt him to live in a style corresponding to the rank he believes himself to hold in society, yet is frequently less independent than the opulent merchant or farmer he undervalues, his annual expenditures being large and certain, whilst his returns are somewhat precarious. He has perhaps to feed and clothe several hundred slaves, and it is not convenient for him to reduce his style of living; so that not unfrequently the merchant at the north, who is his agent, and to whom he consigns his productions for sale, sends him an account current, where, instead of small charges being deducted from large returns, he finds the advances made to him in money, the bills for feeding and clothing his slaves, his wines and luxuries, and other charges, swelled to an amount far exceeding the sum-total that his crops have sold for; perceiving himself therefore the debtor and quasi slave of the man he despises, his pride, his interest, and his passions, all combine to rouse his indignation: at such moments the agitated planter is easily led to follow in the wake of any politicians who flatter him with a prospect of redress.

When the politicians and manufacturers of the Northern States combined to enact the tariff act of 1828, "for the *protection* of home manufactures," alleging that the productions of the Southern States were admitted without competition into the ports of England, a general feeling of resistance arose in the State of South Carolina: the duties now to be levied upon those articles of British manufacture which the planter was compelled to purchase for the use of his slaves, must necessarily greatly augment his expenditures, and to this was added the apprehension of another evil of still greater magnitude, viz. that Great Britain might lay retaliatory duties upon his exports, and gradually look to other countries to be supplied with them. Politics and interests therefore combined in South Carolina to rouse the people into a resistance to that law, and the government of the State taking the lead, finished by declaring that when the United States government manifestly exceeded its powers—of which fact they held that the suffering State must be the best judge—every single State had a natural and constitutional right to "nullify its acts."

Armies now were raised, and everything was prepared for resistance, as much as if a foreign invader was about to enter their territory. Such was the indomitable spirit that appeared to prevail, and the determination not to permit the revenue laws of the United States to be executed in South Carolina, that if President Jackson, as it was believed he was disposed to do, had attempted to execute them by force, there is no doubt that a furious civil war would have raged in the State, of which the consequences—let the questionable result have been either one way or the other—must have been signally fatal; for no one can predict the ultimate consequences of giving military habits to a numerous slave population, which must upon so fatal a contingency have unavoidably taken place. Happily for the country, the wise compromise which took place, the effect of which was to provide for the gradual reduction of those oppressive tariff duties to an amount limited by the wants of the public revenue, and not by the demands for *protection*, averted this great danger. Mr. Clay, whom the protection-party claimed as their leader, and Mr. Calhoun, the avowed leader of the Nullifying party, patriotically concurred in making sacrifices in favour of peace, by carrying the measure called the Compromise Act through the national legislature.

No man had taken a more energetic and animated part in the dangerous agitation than the veteran Dr. Cooper, now approaching his eightieth year, and one of the most remarkable men that have emigrated from England—his native country—to the United States. Cooper was a philosophical élève of the famous Dr. Priestley, and finding that everything in England was too long or too short for him, he passed over to the "asylum of oppressed humanity," with the intention of making it his home for life. . . . On his arrival his talents procured him an official appointment of some distinction in Pennsylvania, but he soon contrived to be driven from it, and to be fined heavily into the bargain. At length he took refuge in South Carolina, was well received by the leading planters there, and placed in the honourable and lucrative situation of President of the College in the town of Columbia.

Here the Doctor might have flourshed in renown, and have pursued a career of usefulness, but the current was too gentle for him, and preferring troubled waters, he began to insinuate that it was unworthy of free men to be educated in religious prejudices, and ended by openly denouncing the Christian religion. . . . The Doctor having succeeded in driving away all those who were not disposed to imbibe his irreligious opinions, proceeded to practise the same tactics with those who would not agree with him in defying the government of the country, as established by law, in regard to Nullification; so that his students became at length very few in numbers, and not long before I reached Columbia, the friends of the college, to save it from total ruin, caused to Doctor to be removed from his situation. In doing this they acted with great delicacy and generosity, creating for him a sort of sinecure office, under which, unless he again oscillates out of his orbit, he may enjoy a very competent salary for the rest of his life.

I found Dr. Cooper in a pleasant little villa, which the ladies had furnished with a great many comforts. He received me very cordially, and although about eighty years old, began to talk with wonderful energy and vivacity upon a variety of subjects. . . .

At tea we were joined by some very well-bred neighbours, amongst whom were several ladies, to whom the Doctor, constantly paddling about amongst them, paid his lively compliments, and then returned to his chair to laugh and dispute about chemistry, geology, law, and, above all, religion and politics. . . .

The next morning I visited the college. On my return I learnt that some gentlemen, with whom I had been previously acquainted, had called upon me, and I willingly accepted an invitation to dine with one of them. Our party consisted of some gentlemen of the place, Dr. Cooper, and a few professors belonging to the college. Some of them were very intelligent men, and hearty in their manners. What particularly struck me at this dinner was the total want of caution and reserve in the ultra opinions they expressed about religion and politics; on these topics their conversation was not at all addressed to me, but seemed to be a resumption of the opinions they were accustomed to express whenever they met, and upon all occasions. A stranger dropped in amongst them from the clouds would hardly have supposed himself amongst Americans, the language they used and the opinions they expressed were so diametrically opposed to the self-laudatory strain they too generally indulge in when speaking of their country or themselves. It was quite new to me to hear men of the better class express themselves openly against a republican government, and to listen to discussions of great ability, the object of which was to show that there never can be a good government if it is not adminstered by gentlemen. Not having shared in the conversation, I ventured at one time to name Mr. Madison, at whose house I was in the habit of making autumnal visits, as a person that would have ranked as a gentleman in any country; but I was immediately stopped by a declaration that he was a false hypocritical dissembler, that he was one of the favourites of the Sovereign People, and one of the worst men the country had produced. . . . A short time after, something very extravagant having been said, I could not help asking, in a good-natured way, if they called themselves Americans yet; the gentleman who had interrupted me before, said, "If you ask *me* if I am an American, my answer is, No, sir, I am a South Carolinian."

G. W. Featherstonhaugh

## CALHOUN'S COUNTRY

*On a later trip, the purpose of which was to explore "those countries watered by the principal tributaries of the Mississippi River," Feather-*

*stonhaugh begged leave of John C. Calhoun, with whom he had been
long acquainted, to pay a visit to Fort Hill.*

*The superb description of the countryside and of the warm and easy
hospitality of Calhoun, "one of the most perfect gentlemen I ever
knew," are taken from A Canoe Voyage up the Minnay Sotor, published in England in 1847. Some of his spellings show a British gentleman's disregard of convention!*

*Featherstonhaugh went from Fort Hill to Portman Shoals, one of
the homes of his friend, Langdon Cheves. Cheves, a member of the
House of Representatives from 1810 to 1815 and its Speaker for the
last two years, declined appointment as Secretary of the Treasury in
Madison's cabinet to become president of the United States Bank. So
excellent was his management of the complex enterprise that he was
called its Hercules. In 1829 he returned to South Carolina, built a
house near Savannah called The Delta and devoted himself to rice
planting. Portman Shoals, the summer residence near Pendleton,
South Carolina, at which Featherstonhaugh was a guest, was one of six
houses built by Cheves. All of them were architecturally interesting
and this one was considered by some to be the most successful of all.*

*Cheves's wife was Mary Elizabeth Dulles. They were the parents of
sixteen children.*

August 18 [1837].—This was a beautiful morning. I was now on the
eastern slope of the chain that fronts the Atlantic, from whence the
country to the north-west is an elevated table land about sixty miles
broad, varied with ridges, valleys, hills and streams, and terminated by
the long line of the Oonáykay, or White Mountains. . . . At this charming rural situation a pretty little river, called the Keeowee, about one
hundred yards wide, runs near the village, and nothing can be more
tranquil than the place and its neighbourhood.

This loveliness of the mountain scenery in the Southern States is
almost unknown in other parts of the United States, except to those
gentlemen who occasionally retire to the mountains from the low
country on the coast, from the scorching effects of the sun. I have
travelled a great deal in the Northern States without having ever seen
so attractive a country. Indeed, in what country can more attractions
combine to gratify the traveller than where the last energies of an
aboriginal race, the most beautiful varieties of the mineral kingdom,
and the most obliging hospitalities instruct and gratify him whilst he
is wandering amongst the rarest and most beautiful of nature's scenes?

About 8 A.M. two servants arrived from Mr. C— [Calhoun] with a
riding-horse for myself, and a small vehicle with a mule to carry my
luggage. I now mounted and rode about fifteen miles through a pleasing country, entirely unsettled, all hill and dale, with occasional delightful pellucid streams. The road was literally strewed with semi-
transparent quartz and crystallized hornblende. The same sensitive
briar, the beautiful vicia, the passion flower, the convolvulus batata . . .
were growing here. Towards the close of the ride the country became
less hilly; and passing the house of Mr. John E. Calhoun, perched on
a hill, where I paid a visit last year, I at length reached Fort Hill, where
Mr. C— and his family received me in the most friendly manner. A
delightful room was assigned to me, and here I found myself in a
charming house, amidst all the refinement and comfort that are in-
separable from the conditions of well-bred and honourable persons.
After partaking of an excellent dinner we adjourned for the evening to
the portico, where with the aid of a guitar, accompanied by a pleasing
voice, and some capital curds and cream, we prolonged a most agreeable conversazione until a late hour. The air of this part of the country reminded me of that of Tuscany, in the Apennines, which is soft
and salubrious at every hour of the night.

August 19.—This was a beautiful Italian-like morning, and it tempted me to stroll out before breakfast. The woods about were strewed
with bunches of quartz crystals, and the most curious varieties of
crystallized hornblende. Our breakfast was admirable, excellent coffee
with delicious cream, and that capital, national dish of South Carolina, snow-white hominy brought hot to table like maccaroni, which
ought always to be eaten, with lumps of sweet fresh butter buried in it!
this is certainly one of the best things imaginable to begin the day liberally with. How exquisitely it is prepared at Mrs. C—'s! I passed the
rest of the morning writing letters, the sun being too intensely hot to
go out. At dinner we had Mr. Wayland, principal of the academy at
Pendleton, a town not far distant, a sensible odd-looking Englishman.
In the evening, Mr. C— and myself walked to Cold Spring, a quiet
rural residence on his estate, built for his mother, but inhabited at the
time by a German and his wife. . . . On our return to Fort Hill, the
family again assembled in the portico to pass a most agreeable evening.

August 20.—This was a beautiful, but most surprizingly hot morning. After breakfast, I went in the carriage with the ladies to the Epis-

copal Church at Pendleton, a neat temple prettily situated in a shady grove. The congregation was numerous, and principally composed of well-dressed and very genteel people. Eight or ten nice-looking carriages were drawn up, and the scene reminded me of an English country church in a good neighbourhood. The service was very appropriately performed, and I had the greatest satisfaction in assisting in it. . . . Here I had the good fortune to meet my old friend Mr. Ch— [Langdon Cheves], whom I had not seen since 1824, and promised to pay him a visit before I left the country. After a very pleasant dinner, Mr. C introduced me to a Colonel Warren, a veteran of the Revolution, with a wooden leg, who called to pay him a visit. The following anecdote was related to me of him: He left England when a youth to lend his aid to the colonists; and his aunt, a lady upon whom he depended, finding him obstinately bent upon taking up arms against his native country, said she hoped he would get a mark fixed upon him for his rebellious conduct. At the siege of Savannah his leg was shot off by a cannon-ball, upon which he had it put up in a box, and sent it to England with his duty to his aunt.

August 21.—After breakfast I made an arrangement with a Mr. Sloane [Sloan], a friend of Mr. C—'s, for an excursion to the mountains to embrace the Tolula Falls, the White Mountain, and thence proceed to the Cherokee country of Valley River. This tour would enable me to see the most interesting parts of the mountainous country; and I felt exceedingly obliged to Mr. C— for having procured me an agreeable companion, who was already acquainted with many parts of it. At dinner we had Colonel [Cotesworth] Pin[c]kney and the veteran Colonel Warren, with a great deal of interesting conversation. What an immense difference there is in the manners of the southern gentlemen, and most of those who are at the head of society in the middle and Northern States. Here the conversation was always liberal and instructive, and seldom suggested by selfish speculations of what they might gain by following particular lines of conduct. I observed a great solicitude here for the welfare of their slaves, especially on the part of the ladies, who give them a great deal of personal attendance when they are ill. The autumnal fevers are sometimes very malignant, and carry off slaves worth one thousand dollars each. This, of course, makes every one careful of their health; but, independent of that consideration, there was evidently a great deal of humanity and tenderness exercised to all who were born on the family plantation. Mr. C— cultivated both cotton and Indian corn, and was an excellent man of business. I learnt from those who knew him well, that he was a man of great punctuality in his dealings, and had never been known to run in debt, or enter into wild speculations. All looked up to him as the first man in South Carolina; and many who were embarrassed in their circumstances came to him for advice. Whilst he declined entering into pecuniary responsibilities for those who did not belong to his family, he always listened to their stories, gave them the most friendly advice, and frequently referred them to men of business, who could assist them if their affairs were retrievable. By persevering in this wise conduct, he was enabled to do good to all, and keep himself free from embarrassment. He himself had no embarrassments but those political struggles he was engaged in. Living, however, at so great a distance from the northern constituencies, it was impossible for them to be sufficiently acquainted with the sterling excellence of his character. If the purity of his private life could be as generally known in the State of New York as it is in South Carolina, no demagogues could prevent him from becoming universally popular.

August 22.—After breakfast I bade adieu to this amiable family, and mounting my horse, proceeded with Mr. Sloane to the head of twelve Mile Creek. . . .

September 9.—There being no stage-coach for some days, I determined to pay a visit to another distinguished South Carolinian, with whom I had been long acquainted, and rose early, and after breakfast again took leave, and Mr. C— being kind enough to lend me his carriage, I went in it to Mr. Ch—'s, whom I had met at church on the 20th of August. After driving eight miles through the woods I reached Mr. Ch—'s villa at Portman Shoal, where I was most kindly received by himself and his two charming daughters. The house of this distinguished gentleman was beautifully situated upon a knoll in the tranquil forest, with the Seneca River flowing in a graceful serpentine course from north to south. I had never seen a place with finer capabilities for improvement, and his house was one of the most curious and pleasing structures I had ever been in. The original intention of Mr. Ch— was merely to build a few log cabins, in two rows separated by an avenue perhaps twenty feet wide. But becoming attached to this quiet retreat, he put a general roof over them all, and added at the west end a hall or vestibule, with a parlour on the south side, and a good dining-room on the north, giving to the whole the form of a Latin cross.

The log cabins had now become spacious bed-rooms, 20 feet by 18, all of which opened into what was the former avenue, but was now become a very handsome hall, 80 feet long and 20 feet wide, through which the breezes circulated east and west from the portico. This hall was wainscoted, and the doors and ceiling were all of plain wood-work, the doors of the bed-rooms being capped with a plain gothic lanceolate ornament, so that the hall, when pacing it, resembled a cloister.

The effect of the whole was very pleasing, and nothing could be more commodious than this arrangement for a family that did not like the inconvenience of staircases. The apartments for servants, the coach-house, stables, and out-houses, were a little detached from the family mansion. At dinner we were joined by some gentlemen of the neighborhood. The day passed very pleasantly. Mr. Ch— was what I had always known him to be, full of information and pleasantry. Once occupying a large share of the public attention as a statesman and speaker of the House of Representatives, he now appeared disposed to retire altogether from the political world. At 10 P.M. I retired to one of the nice bed-rooms, where I found everything most conveniently and comfortably arranged.

September 10.—After breakfast I accompanied Mr. and Miss Ch— to the Episcopal Church at Pendleton, where, as upon a previous occasion, I saw a most respectful congregation, and again admired the well chosen and umbrageous situation of the church. In the afternoon we dined at Colonel H—'s [Pinckney Huger's], who had married the daughter of a gentleman whom I knew a great many years ago. I was very much struck with the beauty of Mrs. H—'s children. It is very clear that the real gentry of America are to be found amongst the land-holders. The dinner was a very handsome one, and the wines various and excellent. After passing a very pleasant evening, we returned home in the rain.

September 11.—A delightful morning, but a rather hot sun, which kept us in the house. We however got engaged in an agreeable conversation about the State of South Carolina in old times, when the whites were contending with the Indians, the Cherokee language, and the mineralogy of the country. Mr. Ch—'s daughters were superior women, eager for information and highly intellectual. In the

afternoon we drove six miles through the woods to Colonel Pin[c]k-
ney's to dinner. Here we met Colonel H—and other gentlemen, had a
most luxurious dinner, and the greatest profusion of fine French and
German wines. I was quite surprised at their excellence and variety, and
could not but express my astonishment to our host. He informed me
that every gentleman in the State lived in that manner, that the price
of his wines never gave him any concern, being only interested in the
quality; adding, that when his crops of rice and cotton were consigned
abroad, he always directed the amount of sales of ten barrels of rice, or
ten bales of cotton, or some other number, to be laid out in particular
wines *of the finest vintages*. These gentlemen have selected the most
lovely summer retreats for themselves, and contrive to enjoy life in a
very agreeable manner. You never hear the prices of things talked of at
their tables, or of money being held out as the great object of human
existence; they ridicule this in the northern commercial classes, but
enjoy what they have without talking about it, and surprise an Englishman with their knowledge of European politics and letters, and their
liberal and polite attentions to him. We returned from this agreeable
visit by moonlight.

September 12.—Notwithstanding a natural inclination to indulge
in such good quarters, I managed to rise early and take a walk before
breakfast. . . . The forest around was thickly growing up with underwood. In all the districts where I have been, which are now possessed
by the Indians, the woods are open, generally with a few trees sparsely
growing here and there, in consequence of the Indians firing the woods
annually in order to increase the herbage, and that they may better see
to pursue their game. But as soon as the Indians abandon a district,
and that destructive practice ceases, the underwood begins to grow up
again, as it is now doing here. After breakfast, I took leave of this kind
and pleasing family, and went in Mr. Ch—'s carriage to Pendleton. At
1 P.M. got into four-horse stage for Greenville. . . .

Frances Anne Kemble

## A GEORGIA PLANTATION

*Frances Anne Kemble, the celebrated English actress, came to
America with her father, Charles Kemble, in 1832. She and her father*

*toured up and down the country, from New York to New Orleans, for
two seasons. Fanny's success was immediate and sustained. Then, in
1834, she married Pierce Butler of Germantown, Pennsylvania, whose
grandfather, Major Pierce Butler, we have met in Georgia. Butler
had inherited plantations in Georgia, and in the winter of 1838 and
the following spring she visited for the first time her husband's southern estates. The Butlers were accompanied by their small children,
Sally, aged four, and Frances, seven months, and the children's nurse.
The family divided their time between Mr. Butler's rice and cotton
plantations at Butler Island near Darien, and Hampton Point on St.
Simon's Island.*

*Fanny had become close friends with the large and talented Sedg-
wick family of Stockton and Lenox, Massachusetts, and during her
residence in Georgia she wrote often and at length about her experiences and observations to Elizabeth Dwight Sedgwick of Stockton.*

*In 1845 Fanny returned to England with her two children and in
1848 Pierce Butler sued for divorce, charging desertion. Fanny had returned to America when the divorce was finally granted in 1849. Pierce
Butler died in 1867.*

*Fanny was urged to publish her letters when the War between the
States started and British support of the Confederacy seemed possible.
But by the time the book was finally published, in 1863, there was no
longer any question of British support of the South, and Fanny's book
exerted little influence so far as shaping public opinion was concerned.*

*After her divorce Fanny was faced with the necessity of earning a
living. She had never liked being an actress despite her great success.
She found an enthusiastic reception both in the United States and in
England for her new occupation, giving readings from Shakespeare.
After 1869 she gave up this work, dividing her time between her two
married daughters, the one the wife of a clergyman living in England,
and the other the wife of Owen J. Wister, Sr., of Germantown, Pennsylvania. Her grandson, Owen J. Wister, Jr., was the author of* Lady
Baltimore, The Virginian *and many other successful novels.*

*Fanny Kemble died in London, January 15, 1893.*

Darien, Georgia

Dear E.——

In taking my first walk on the island, I directed my steps toward the
rice mill, a large building on the banks of the river, within a few yards
of the house we occupy. . . . Now on this estate alone there are three

threshing mills—one worked by steam, one by the tide, and one by
horses; there are two private steam mills on plantations adjacent to
ours, and a public one at Savannah, where the planters who have none
on their own estates are in the habit of sending their rice to be
threshed at a certain percentage. . . .

[The rice mill] is worked by a steam-engine of thirty horse power,
and, besides threshing great part of our own rice, is kept constantly
employed by the neighboring planters, who send their grain to it in
preference to the more distant mill at Savannah, paying, of course, the
same percentage, which makes it a very profitable addition to the estate. Immediately opposite to this building is a small shed, which they
call the cook's shop, and where the daily allowance of rice and corn
grits of the people is boiled and distributed to them by an old woman,
whose special business this is. There are four settlements or villages
. . . on the island, consisting of from ten to twenty houses, and to each
settlement is annexed a cook's shop with capacious caldrons, and the
oldest wife of the settlement for officiating priestess.

Pursuing my walk along the river's bank, upon an artificial dike,
sufficiently high and broad to protect the fields from inundation by the
ordinary rising of the tide—for the whole island is below high-water
mark—I passed the blacksmith's and cooper's shops. At the first all
the common iron implements of husbandry or household use for the
estate are made, and at the latter all the rice barrels necessary for the
crop, besides tubs and buckets, large and small, for the use of the people, and cedar tubs, of noble dimensions and exceedingly neat workmanship, for our own household purposes. The fragrance of these
when they are first made, as well as their ample size, renders them
preferable as dressing-room furniture, in my opinion, to all the china
foot-tubs that ever came out of Staffordshire.

After this I got out of the vicinity of the settlement, and pursued
my way along a narrow dike—the river on the one hand, and, on the
other, a slimy, poisonous-looking swamp, all rattling with sedges of
enormous height, in which one might lose one's way as effectually as
in a forest of oaks. Beyond this, the low rice-fields, all clothed in their
rugged stubble, divided by dikes into monotonous squares, a species of
prospect by no means beautiful to the mere lover of the picturesque.
The only thing that I met with to attract my attention was a most
beautiful species of ivy, the leaf longer and more graceful than that of
the common English creeper, glittering with the highest varnish, delicately veined, and of a rich brown-green, growing in profuse garlands

from branch to branch of some stunted evergreen bushes which border the dike, and which the people call salt-water bush.

My walks are rather circumscribed, inasmuch as the dikes are the only promenades. On all sides of these lie either the marshy rice-fields, the brimming river, or the swampy patches of yet unreclaimed forest, where the huge cypress-trees and exquisite evergreen undergrowth spring up from a stagnant sweltering pool, that effectually forbids the foot of the explorer.

As I skirted one of these thickets to-day, I stood still to admire the beauty of the shrubbery. Every shade of green, every variety of form, every degree of varnish, and all in full leaf and beauty in the very depth of winter. The stunted dark-colored oak; the magnolia bay . . . which grows to a very great size; the wild myrtle, a beautiful and profuse shrub, rising to a height of six, eight, and ten feet, and branching on all sides in luxuriant tufted fullness; most beautiful of all, that pride of the South, the magnolia grandiflora, whose lustrous dark green perfect foliage would alone render it an object of admiration, without the queenly blossom whose color, size and perfume are unrivaled in the whole vegetable kingdom. . . .

The profusion of birds here is one thing that strikes me as curious, coming from the vicinity of Philadelphia, where even the robin redbreast, held sacred by the humanity of all other Christian people, is not safe from the *gunning* prowess of the unlicensed sportsmen of your free country. The negroes (of course) are not allowed the use of firearms, and their very simply constructed traps do not do much havoc among the feathered hordes that haunt the rice-fields. . . . Here our living consists very mainly of wild ducks, wild geese, wild turkeys, and venison. Now, perhaps, can one imagine the universal doom overtaking a creature with less misery than in the case of the bird who, in the very moment of his triumphant soaring, is brought dead to the ground. I should like to bargain for such a finis myself amazingly, I know, and have always thought that the death I should prefer would be to break my neck off the back of my horse at a full gallop on a fine day. . . .

Our servants—those who have been selected to wait upon us in the house—consist of a man, who is quite a tolerable cook; . . . a dairy-woman, who churns for us; a laundry-woman; her daughter, our house-maid, [named] Mary; and two young lads of from fifteen to twenty, who wait upon us in the capacity of footmen. . . .

. . . the slaves on this plantation are divided into field-hands and mechanics or artisans. The former, the great majority, are the more

stupid and brutish of the tribe; the others, who are regularly taught
their trades, are not only exceedingly expert at them, but exhibit a
greater general activity of intellect, which must necessarily result from
even a partial degree of cultivation. There are here a gang . . . of
coopers, of blacksmiths, of bricklayers, of carpenters, all well acquainted with their peculiar trades. The latter constructed the wash-
hand stands, clothes-presses, sofas, tables, etc., with which our house
is furnished, and they are very neat pieces of workmanship—neither
veneered or polished indeed, nor of very costly materials, but of the
white pine wood planed as smooth as marble—a species of furniture
not very luxurious perhaps, but all the better adapted therefore to the
house itself, which is certainly rather more devoid of the conveniences
and adornments of modern existence than anything I ever took up
my abode in before.

It consists of three small rooms, and three still smaller, which would
be more appropriately designated as closets, a wooden recess by way
of pantry, and a kitchen detached from the dwelling—a mere wooden
out-house, with no floor but the bare earth, and for furniture a congregation of filthy negroes, who lounge in and out of it like hungry
hounds at all hours of the day and night, picking up such scraps of
food as they can find about, which they discuss squatting down upon
their hams, in which interesting position and occupation I generally
find a number of them whenever I have sufficient hardihood to venture
within those precincts, the sight of which and its tenants is enough
to slacken the appetite of the hungriest hunter that ever lost all nice
regards in the mere animal desire for food.

Of our three apartments, one is sitting, eating, and *living* room, and
is sixteen feet by fifteen. The walls are plastered indeed, but neither
painted nor papered; it is divided from our bedroom (a similarly elegant and comfortable chamber) by a dingy wooden partition covered
all over with hooks, pegs, and nails, to which hats, caps, keys, etc., etc.,
are suspended in graceful irregularity. The doors open by wooden
latches, raised by means of small bits of pack-thread—I imagine, the
same primitive order of fastening celebrated in the touching chronicle
of Red Riding Hood; how they shut I will not attempt to describe, as
the shutting of a door is a process of extremely rare occurrence throughout the whole Southern country. The third room, a chamber with
sloping ceiling, immediately over our sitting-room and under the roof,
is appropriated to the nurse and my two babies.

Of the closets, one is Mr. ——, the overseer's, bedroom, the other his office or place of business; and the third, adjoining our bedroom, and opening immediately out of doors, is Mr. [Butler]'s dressing-room and cabinet d'affaires, where he gives audiences to the negroes, redresses grievances, distributes red woolen caps (a singular gratification to a slave), shaves himself, and performs the other offices of his toilet.

Such being our abode, I think you will allow there is little danger of my being dazzled by the luxurious splendors of a Southern slave residence. Our sole mode of summoning our attendants is by a pack-thread bell-rope suspended in the sitting room. From the bedrooms we have to raise the windows and our voices, and bring them by power of lungs, or help ourselves—which, I thank God, was never yet a hardship to me. . . .

I had a most ludicrous visit this morning from the midwife of the estate—rather an important personage both to master and slave, as to her unassisted skill and science the ushering of all the young negroes into their existence of bondage is intrusted. I heard a great deal of conversation in the dressing-room adjoining mine while performing my own toilet, and presently Mr. —— opened my room door, ushering in a dirty, fat, good-humored looking old negress, saying, "The midwife, Rose, wants to make your acquaintance." "Oh massa!" shrieked out the old creature, in a paroxysm of admiration, "where you get this lilly alabaster baby!" For a moment I looked round to see if she was speaking of my baby; but no, my dear, this superlative apostrophe was elicited by the fairness of *my skin*: so much for degrees of comparison. . . .

Soon after this visit, I was summoned into the wooden porch or piazza of the house, to see a poor woman who desired to speak to me. This was none other than the tall, emaciated-looking negress who, on the day of our arrival, had embraced me and my nurse with such irresistible zeal. She appeared very ill to-day, and presently unfolded to me a most distressing history of bodily afflictions. She was the mother of a very large family, and complained to me that, what with childbearing and hard field labor, her back was almost broken in two. With an almost savage vehemence of gesticulation, she suddenly tore up her scanty clothing, and exhibited a spectacle with which I was inconceivably shocked and sickened. . . . I promised to attend to her ailments and give her proper remedies. . . .

After the departure of this poor woman, I walked down the settlement toward the Infirmary or hospital, calling in at one or two of the houses along the row. These cabins consist of one room, about twelve

feet by fifteen, with a couple of closets smaller and closer than the
state-rooms of a ship, divided off from the main room and each other
by rough wooden partitions, in which the inhabitants sleep. They have
almost all of them a rude bedstead, with the gray moss of the forests
for mattress, and filthy, pestilential-looking blankets for covering.
Two families (sometimes eight and ten in number) reside in one of
these huts, which are mere wooden frames pinned, as it were, to the
earth by a brick chimney outside . . . A wide ditch runs immediately at
the back of these dwellings, which is filled and emptied daily by the
tide. Attached to each hovel is a small scrap of ground for a garden,
which, however, is for the most part untended and uncultivated. . . .
Firewood and shavings lay littered about the floors, while the half-
naked children were cowering round two or three smouldering cinders.
The moss with which the chinks and crannies of their ill-protecting
dwellings might have been stuffed was trailing in dirt and dust about
the ground, while the back door of the huts, opening upon a most
unsightly ditch, was left wide open for the fowls and ducks, which they
are allowed to raise, to travel in and out, increasing the filth of the cabin
by what they brought and left in every direction. In the midst of the
floor, or squatting round the cold hearth, would be four or five little
children from four to ten years old, the latter all with babies in their
arms, the care of the infants being taken from the mothers (who are
driven afield as soon as they recover from child labor), and devolved
upon these poor little nurses, as they are called, whose business it is
to watch the infant, and carry it to its mother whenever it may require
nourishment. . . .

The Infirmary is a large two-story building, terminating the broad
orange-planted space between the two rows of houses which form the
first settlement; it is built of whitewashed wood, and contains four
large-sized rooms. . . . But half the casements, of which there were six,
were glazed, and these were obscured with dirt, almost as much as the
other windowless ones were darkened by the dingy shutters, which the
shivering inmates had fastened to in order to protect themselves from
the cold. In the enormous chimney glimmered the powerless embers
of a few sticks of wood, round which, however, as many of the sick
women as could approach were cowering, some on wooden settles,
most of them on the ground, excluding those who were too ill to rise;
and these last poor wretches lay prostrate on the floor, without bed,
mattress, or pillow, buried in tattered and filthy blankets, which,
huddled round them as they lay strewed about, left hardly space to

move upon the floor. . . . I stood in the midst of them, perfectly unable to speak, the tears pouring from my eyes at this sad spectacle of their misery, myself and my emotion alike strange and incomprehensible to them. . . .

I left this refuge for Mr. ——'s sick dependents with my clothes covered with dust, and full of vermin, and with a heart heavy enough. . . . My morning's work had fatigued me not a little, and I was glad to return to the house, where I gave vent to my indignation and regret at the scene I had just witnessed to Mr. —— and his overseer, who, here, is a member of our family. The latter told me that the condition of the hospital had appeared to him, from his first entering upon his situation (only within the last year), to require a reform, and that he had proposed it to the former manager, Mr. K——, and Mr. ——'s brother, who is part proprietor of the estate, but, receiving no encouragement from them, had supposed that it was a matter of indifference to the owners, and had left it in the condition in which he had found it, in which condition it has been for the last nineteen years and upward. . . .

I am learning to row here, for circumscribed, as my walks necessarily are, impossible as it is to resort to my favorite exercise on horseback upon these narrow dikes, I must do something to prevent my blood from stagnating; and this broad brimming river, and the beautiful light canoes which lie moored at the steps, are very inviting persuaders to this species of exercise. . . .

In the evening Mr. ——, who had been over to Darien, mentioned that one of the storekeepers there had told him that, in the course of a few years, he had paid the negroes of this estate several thousand dollars for moss, which is a very profitable article of traffic with them: they collect it from the trees, dry and pick it, and then sell it to the people in Darien for mattresses, sofas, and all sorts of stuffing purposes. . . .

Monday, 20th

My Dearest E——,

. . . We have, as a sort of under nursemaid and assistant of my dear M——, whose white complexion . . . occasioned such indignation to my Southern fellow-travelers, and such extreme perplexity to the poor slaves on our arrival here, a much more orthodox servant for these parts, a young woman named Psyche, but commonly called Sack . . . she can not be much over twenty, has a very pretty figure, a graveful, gentle deportment, and a face which, but for its color (she is a dingy mulatto), would be pretty, and is extremely pleasing, from the perfect sweetness of its expression; she is always serious, not to say sad and silent, and has always an air of melancholy and timidity. . . .

I have never questioned Psyche as to her sadness . . . but, to my great astonishment, the other day M—— asked me if I knew to whom Psyche belonged, as the poor woman had inquired of her with much hesitation and anguish if she could tell her who owned her and her children. She has two nice little children under six years old, whom she keeps as clean and tidy, and who are sad and as silent as herself. My astonishment at this question was not small, and I forthwith sought out Psyche for an explanation. She was thrown into extreme perturbation at finding that her question had been referred to me, and it was some time before I could sufficiently reassure her to be able to comprehend, in the midst of her reiterated entreaties for pardon, and hopes that she had not offended me, that she did not know herself who owned her. She was, at one time, the property of Mr. K——, the former overseer . . . and who has just been paying Mr. —— a visit. He, like several of his predecessors in the management, has contrived to make a fortune upon it (though it yearly decreases in value to the owners . . .), and has purchased a plantation of his own in Alabama, I believe, or one of the Southwestern states. Whether she still belonged to Mr. K—— or not she did not know, and entreated me, if she did, to endeavor to persuade Mr. —— to buy her. Now you must know that this poor woman is the wife of one of Mr. B——'s slaves, a fine, intelligent, active, excellent young man. . . . I was so astonished at the (to me) extraordinary state of things revealed by poor Sack's petition, that I could only tell her that I had supposed all the negroes on the plantation were Mr. ——'s property, but that I would certainly inquire, and find out for her, if I could, to whom she belonged, and if I could, endeavor to get Mr. —— to purchase her, if she really was not his. . . .

I did not see Mr. —— until the evening; but, in the mean time, meeting Mr. O——, the overseer . . . I asked him about Psyche, and who was her proprietor, when, to my infinite surprise, he told me that *he* had bought her and her children from Mr. K——, who had offered them to him, saying that they would be rather troublesome to him than otherwise down where he was going; "and so," said Mr. O——, "as I had no objection to investing a little money that way, I bought them." With a heart much lightened, I flew to tell poor Psyche the news, so that, at any rate, she might be relieved from the dread of any immediate separation from her husband. You can imagine better than

I can tell you what her sensations were; but she still renewed her prayer that I would, if possible, induce Mr. —— to purchase her, and I promised to do so.

Early the next morning, while I was still dressing, I was suddenly startled by hearing voices in loud tones in Mr. ——'s dressing-room, which adjoins my bedroom, and the noise increasing until there was an absolute cry of despair uttered by some man I could restrain myself no longer, but opened the door of communication and saw Joe, the young man, poor Psyche's husband, raving almost in a state of frenzy, and in a voice broken with sobs and almost inarticulate with passion, reiterating his determination never to leave this plantation, never to go to Alabama, never to leave his old father and mother, his poor wife and children, and dashing his hat, which he was wringing like a cloth in his hands, upon the ground, he declared he would kill himself if he was compelled to follow Mr. K——.

I glanced from the poor wretch to Mr. ——, who was standing, leaning against a table with his arms folded, occasionally uttering a few words of counsel to his slave to be quiet and not fret, and not make a fuss about what there was no help for. I retreated immediately from the horrid scene, breathless with surprise and dismay, and stood for some time in my own room, with my heart and temples throbbing to such a degree that I could hardly support myself.

As soon as I recovered myself I again sought Mr. O——, and inquired of him if he knew the cause of poor Joe's distress. He then told me that Mr. ——, who is highly pleased with Mr. K——'s past administration of his property, wished, on his departure for his newly-acquired slave plantation, to give him some token of his satisfaction, and *had made him a present* of the man Joe, who had just received the intelligence that he was to go down to Alabama with his new owner the next day, leaving father, mother, wife, and children behind. You will not wonder that the man required a little judicious soothing under such circumstances, and you will also, I hope, admire the humanity of the sale of his wife and children by the owner who was going to take him to Alabama, because *they* would be encumbrances rather than otherwise down there. If Mr. K—— did not do this after he knew that the man was his, then Mr. —— gave him to be carried down to the South after his wife and children were sold to remain in Georgia. I do not know which was the real transaction, for I have not had the heart to ask; but you will easily imagine which of the two cases I prefer believing.

When I saw Mr. —— after this most wretched story became known to me in all its details, I appealed to him, for his own soul's sake, not to commit so great a cruelty. Poor Joe's agony while remonstrating with his master was hardly greater than mine while arguing with him upon this bitter piece of inhumanity—how I cried, and how I adjured, and how all my sense of justice, and of mercy, and of pity for the poor wretch, and of wretchedness at finding myself implicated in such a state of things, broke in torrents of words from my lips and tears from my eyes! It seemed to me that I was imploring Mr. —— to save himself more than to spare these wretches. He gave me no answer whatever, and I have since thought that the intemperate vehemence of my entreaties and expostulations perhaps deserved that he should leave me as he did without one single word of reply; and miserable enough I remained.

Toward evening, as I was sitting alone, my children having gone to bed, Mr. O—— came into the room. As he sat down looking over some accounts, I said to him, "Have you seen Joe this afternoon, Mr. O——?" (I give you our conversation as it took place).

"Yes, ma'am; he is a great deal happier than he was this morning."

"Why, how is that?" asked I, eagerly.

"Oh, he is not going to Alabama. Mr. K—— heard that he had kicked up a fuss about it, and said that if the fellow wasn't willing to go with him, he did not wish to be bothered with any niggers down there who were to be troublesome, so he might stay behind."

"And does Psyche know this?"

"Yes, ma'am, I suppose so."

I drew a long breath; and whereas my needle had stumbled through the stuff I was sewing for an hour before, as if my fingers could not guide it, the regularity and rapidity of its evolutions were now quite edifying. The man was for the present safe, and I remained silently pondering his deliverance and the whole proceeding, and the conduct of every one engaged in it, and, above all, Mr. ——'s share in the transaction, and I think, for the first time, almost a sense of horrible personal responsibility and implication took hold of my mind, and I felt the weight of an unimagined guilt upon my conscience; and yet, God knows, this feeling of self-condemnation is very gratuitous on my part, since when I married Mr. —— I knew nothing of these dreadful possessions of his, and even if I had I should have been puzzled to have formed any idea of the state of things in which I now find myself plunged, together with those whose well-doing is as vital to me almost as my own.

With these agreeable reflections I went to bed. Mr. —— said not a word to me upon the subject of these poor people all the next day . . . In the evening I was again with Mr. O—— alone in the strange, bare, wooden-walled sort of shanty which is our sitting-room, and revolving in my mind the means of rescuing Psyche from her miserable suspense . . . I suddenly accosted Mr. O——.

"Mr. O——, you will never sell Psyche and her children without first letting me know of your intention to do so, and giving me the option of buying them."

Mr. O—— is a remarkably deliberate man, and squints, so that, when he has taken a little time in directing his eyes to you, you are still unpleasantly unaware of any result in which you are concerned; he laid down a book he was reading, and directed his head and one of his eyes toward me and answered. "Dear me, ma'am, I am very sorry—I have sold them." My work fell down on the ground, and my mouth opened wide, and surprised; and he deliberately proceeded: "I didn't know, ma'am, you see, at all, that you entertained any idea of making an investment of that nature; for I'm sure, if I had, I would willingly have sold the woman to you; but I sold her and her children this morning to Mr. ——." . . .

I jumped up and left Mr. O—— still speaking, and ran to find Mr. ——, to thank him for what he had done. . . .

My letter has been interrupted, dear E——, by the breaking up of our residence on the rice plantation, and our arrival at St. Simon's, whence I now address you. We came down yesterday afternoon, and I was thankful enough of the fifteen miles' row to rest in, from the labor of leave-taking, with which the whole morning was taken up, and which, combined with packing and preparing all our own personalities and those of the children, was no sinecure. At every moment one or other of the poor people rushed in upon me to bid me good-by. Poor people! how little I have done, how little I can do for them. . . .

I have worked my fingers nearly off with making, for the last day or two, innumerable rolls of coarse little baby-clothes, layettes for the use of small new-born slaves. . . . We leave a good supply for the hospitals, and for the individual clients besides who have besieged me ever since my departure became imminent.

Our voyage from the rice to the cotton plantation was performed in the *Lily*, which looked like a soldier's baggage-wagon and an emigrant transport combined. Our crew consisted of eight men. Forward in the bow were miscellaneous live-stock, pots, pans, household furniture, kitchen utensils, and an indescribable variety of heterogeneous necessaries. Enthroned upon beds, bedding, tables, and other chattels, sat that poor pretty chattel Psyche, with her small chattel children. Midships sat the two tiny free women and myself, and in the stern Mr. ——— steering, And "all in the blue unclouded weather" we rowed down the huge stream, the men keeping time and tune to their oars with extemporaneous chants of adieu to the rice-island and its denizens. . . .

At the end of a fifteen miles' row we entered one among a perfect labyrinth of arms or branches, into which the broad river ravels like a fringe as it reaches the sea, a dismal navigation along a dismal tract, called "Five Pound," through a narrow cut or channel of water divided from the main stream. The conch was sounded, as at our arrival at the rice-island, and we made our descent on the famous long staple cotton island of St. Simon's, where we presently took up our abode in what had all the appearance of an old, half-decayed, rattling farm-house.

This morning . . . I peeped round its immediate neighborhood, and saw, to my inexpressible delight, within hail, some noble-looking evergreen oaks, and close to the house itself a tiny would-be garden, a plot of ground with one or two peach-trees in full blossom, tufts of silver narcissus and jonquils, a quantity of violets and an exquisite myrtle bush; wherefore I said my prayers with especial gratitude.

Dearest E.———, . . . The people . . . that I saw yesterday were remarkably clean and tidy . . . The whole day, till quite late in the afternoon, the house was surrounded by a crowd of our poor dependents, waiting to catch a glimpse of Mr. ———, myself, or the children; and until, from sheer weariness, I was obliged to shut the doors, an incessant stream poured in and out. . . .

In the afternoon I walked with ——— to see a new house in process of erection, which, when it is finished, is to be the overseer's abode and our residence during any future visits we may pay to the estate. I was horrified at the dismal site selected, and the hideous house erected on it. It is true that the central position is the principal consideration in the overseer's location; but both position and building seemed to me to witness to an inveterate love of ugliness, or at any rate, a deadness to every desire of beauty, nothing short of horrible; and, for my own part, I think it is intolerable to have to leave the point where the waters meet, and where a few fine picturesque old trees are scattered about, to come to this place even for the very short time I am ever likely to spend here.

In every direction our view, as we returned, was bounded by thickets of the most beautiful and various evergreen growth, which beckoned my inexperience most irresistibly. —— said, to my unutterable horror, that they were perfectly infested with rattlesnakes, and I must on no account go "beating about the bush" in these latitudes, as the game I should be likely to start would be any thing but agreeable to me. We saw quantities of wild plum trees all silvery with blossoms, and in lovely companionship and contrast with them a beautiful shrub covered with delicate pink bloom like a flowering peach-tree. . . .

After that life in the rice-swamps where the Altamaha kept looking over the dike at me all the time as I sat in the house writing or working, it is pleasant to be on *terra firma* again, and to know that the river is at the conventional, not to say natural, depth below its banks.

The two plantations are of diametrically opposite dispositions—that is all swamp, and this all sand; or, to speak more accurately, that is all swamp, and all of this that is not swamp is sand. . . .

Last Wednesday we drove to Hamilton, by far the finest estate on St. Simon's Island. The gentleman to whom it belongs lives, I believe, habitually in Paris; but Captain F—— resides on it, and, I suppose, is the real overseer of the plantation. . . . The negro huts on several of the plantations that we passed through were the most miserable human habitations I ever beheld. . . .

The planters' residences we passed were only three. It makes one ponder seriously when one thinks of the mere handful of white people on this island. In the midst of this large population of slaves, how absolutely helpless they would be if the blacks were to become restive! They could be destroyed to a man before human help could reach them from the main, or the tidings even of what was going on be carried across the surrounding waters. As we approached the southern end of the island we began to discover the line of the white sea-sands beyond the bushes and fields, and presently, above the sparkling, dazzling line of snowy white—for the sands were as white as our English chalk cliffs—stretched the deep blue sea-line of the great Atlantic Ocean.

Hamilton struck me very much—I mean the whole appearance of the place; the situation of the house, the noble water prospect it commanded, the magnificent old oaks near it, a luxuriant vine trellis, and a splendid hedge of yucca gloriosa, were all objects of great delight to me. . . .

At dinner we had some delicious green peas, so much in advance of you are we down here with the seasons. Don't you think one might accept the rattlesnakes, or perhaps indeed the slavery, for the sake of the green peas? 'Tis a world of compensations—a life of compromises, you know; and one should learn to set one thing against another if one means to thrive and fare well, i.e., eat green peas on the twenty-eighth of March.

After dinner I walked up and down before the house for a long while with Mrs. F——. She is a kind-hearted, intelligent woman; but, though she seemed to me to acquiesce, as a matter of inevitable necessity, in the social system in the midst of which she was born and lives, she did not appear to me, by several things she said, to be by any means in love with it. . . .

We drove home by moonlight; and as we came toward the woods in the middle of the island, the fireflies glittered out from the dusky thickets as if some magical golden veil was every now and then shaken out into the darkness. The air was enchantingly mild and soft, and the whole way through the silvery night delightful. . . .

Dearest E——, . . . I drove to pay a visit to old Mrs. A——, the lady proprietress whose estate immediately adjoins ours. On driving through my neighbor's grounds, I was disgusted more than I can express with the miserable negro huts of her people; they were not fit to shelter cattle—they were not fit to shelter any thing, they were literally in holes. To be sure, I will say, in excuse for their old mistress, her own habitation was but a few degrees less ruinous and disgusting. . . .

When I returned home I found that Mrs. F— had sent me some magnificent prawns. I think of having them served singly, and divided as one does a lobster—their size really suggests no less respect.

*Saturday, 31st.* I rode all through the burnt district and the bush to Mrs. W——'s field, in making my way out of which I was very nearly swamped, and, but for the valuable assistance of a certain sable Scipio who came up and extricated me, I might be floundering hopelessly there still. He got me out of my Slough of Despond, and put me in the way of a charming wood ride which runs between Mrs. W——'s and Colonel H——'s grounds. While going along this delightful boundary of these two neighboring estates, my mind not unnaturally dwelt upon the terms of deadly feud in whch the two families owning them are living with each other. A horrible quarrel has occurred quite lately upon the subject of the ownership of this very ground I was skirting, between Dr. H—— and young Mr. W——; they have challenged each other, and what I am going to tell you is a good sample of the sort of spirit which grows up among slave-holders. So read it, for it is curious to people who have not lived habitually among savages.

The terms of the challenge that has passed between them have appeared like a sort of advertisement in the local paper, and are to the effect that they are to fight at a certain distance with certain weapons—fire-arms, of course; that there is to be on the person of each a white paper, or mark, immediately over the region of the heart, as a point for direct aim; and whoever kills the other is to have the privilege of *cutting off his head, and sticking it up on a pole on the piece of land which was the origin of the debate.* . . .

*Sunday, 14th.* My dear E——, That horrid tragedy with which we have been threatened, and of which I was writing to you almost jestingly a few days ago, has been accomplished, and apparently without exciting any thing but the most passing and superficial sensation in this community. The duel between Dr. H—— and Mr. W—— did not take place, but an accidental encounter in the hotel at Brunswick did, and the former shot the latter dead on the spot. He has been brought home and buried here by the little church close to his mother's plantation; and the murderer, if he is even prosecuted, runs no risk of finding a jury in the whole length and breadth of Georgia who could convict him of any thing. It is horrible. . . .

I stopped before going into church to look at the new grave that has taken its place among the defaced stones, all overgrown with briers, that lie round it. Poor young W——! poor widowed mother, of whom he was the only son! What a savage horror! And no one seems to think any thing of it, more than a matter of course. My devotions were any thing but satisfactory or refreshing to me. My mind was dwelling incessantly upon the new grave under the great oaks outside, and the miserable mother in her home. The air of the church was perfectly thick with sand-flies; and the disgraceful carelessness of the congregation in responding and singing the hymns, and the entire neglect of the Prayer-book regulations for kneeling, disturbed and displeased me. . . . I thought we should surely have some reference to the event from the pulpit, some lesson of Christian command over furious passions. Nothing—nobody looked or spoke as if any thing unusual had occurred; and I left the church, rejoicing to think that I was going away from such a dreadful state of society. . . .

Dear E——, We shall leave this place next Thursday or Friday, and there will be an end to this record; meantime I am fulfilling all sorts of last duties, and especially those of taking leave of my neighbors, by whom the neglect of a farewell visit would be taken much amiss.

On Sunday I rode to a place called Frederica to call on a Mrs. A——, who came to see me some time ago. I rode straight through the island by the main road that leads to the little church.

How can I describe to you the exquisite spring beauty that is now adorning these woods, the variety of the fresh, new-born foliage, the fragrance of the sweet, wild perfumes that fill the air? Honeysuckles twine round every tree; the ground is covered with a low, white-blossomed shrub more fragrant than lilies of the valley. The accacuas are swinging their silver censers under the green roof of these wood temples; every stump is alike a classical altar to the sylvan gods, garlanded with flowers; every post, or stick, or slight stem, like a Bacchante's thyrsus, twined with wreaths of ivy and wild vine, waving in the tepid wind. Beautiful butterflies flicker like flying flowers among the bushes, and gorgeous birds, like winged jewels, dart from the boughs, and—and—a huge ground snake slid like a dark ribbon across the path while I was stopping to enjoy all this deliciousness, and so I became less enthusiastic, and cantered on past the little deserted church-yard, with the new-made grave beneath its grove of noble oaks, and a little farther on reached Mrs. A——'s cottage, half hidden in the midst of ruins and roses. . . .

I sat for a long time with Mrs. A——, and a friend of hers staying with her, a Mrs. A——, lately from Florida. The latter seemed to me a remarkable woman; her conversation was extremely interesting. She had been stopping at Brunswick, at the hotel where Dr. H—— murdered young W——, and said that the mingled ferocity and blackguardism of the men who frequented the house had induced her to cut short her stay there, and come on to her friend Mrs. A——'s. We spoke of that terible crime which had occurred only the day after she left Brunswick, and both ladies agreed that there was not the slightest chance of Dr. H——'s being punished in any way for the murder he had committed; that shooting down a man who had offended you was part of the morals and manners of the Southern gentry, and that the circumstance was one of quite too frequent occurrence to cause any sensation, even in the small community where it obliterated one of the principal members of the society. . . .

We had a long discussion on the subject of slavery, and they took, as usual, the old ground of justifying the system, *where* it was administered with kindness and indulgence. It is not surprising that women should regard the question from this point of view; they are very seldom *just*, and are generally treated with more indulgence than justice by men. They were very patient of my strong expressions of reprobation of the whole system, and Mrs. A——, bidding me good-by, said that, for aught she could tell, I might be right . . .

I rode home pondering on the strange fate that has brought me to this place so far from where I was born, this existence so different in all its elements from that of my early years and former associations. . . . On my return home I found a most enchanting bundle of flowers, sent to me by Mrs. G——; pomegranate blossoms, roses, honeysuckle, every thing that blooms two months later with us in Pennsylvania. . . .

Now, E——, I have often spoken with you and written to you of the disastrous effect of slavery upon the character of the white men implicated in it; many among themselves feel and acknowledge it to the fullest extent; but the devil must have his due, and men brought up in habits of peremptory command over their fellow-men, and under the constant apprehension of danger, and awful necessity of immediate readiness to meet it, acquire qualities precious to themselves and others in hours of supreme peril. . . . I know that the Southern men are apt to deny the fact that they do live under an habitual sense of danger; but a slave population, coerced into obedience, though unarmed and half fed, *is* a threatening source of constant insecurity, and every Southern *woman* to whom I have spoken on the subject has admitted to me that they live in terror of their slaves. . . .

Francis W. Pickens

## A PLANTER'S OBSERVATIONS

*Francis W. Pickens of Edgewood Plantation near Edgefield, South Carolina, was the son of Governor Andrew Pickens and the grandson of General Andrew Pickens. He owned several plantations and many hundreds of slaves.*

*Pickens served in the House of Representatives from 1834 to 1843.*

*Married in 1858 to Lucy Holcombe of Texas, he accepted, partly because the beautiful Lucy very much wanted him to, the post of Minister to Russia in that same year. Political unrest in South Carolina brought him home in 1860. He was governor of South Carolina from 1860 to 1862. A picture of Lucy Holcombe was engraved on Confederate currency and the Holcombe Legion of South Carolina was named in her honor.*

*Pickens' first wife, Margaret Eliza Simkins of Edgefield, died in 1842. His second was Marie Antoinette Dearing of Georgia. And Lucy was the third.*

*Pickens was thirty-six years old and a member of Congress when he wrote the following letters to his cousin, John C. Calhoun. Like Calhoun he was a Nullifier and a strong believer in States' Rights.*

*Colonel Patrick Noble, first cousin to Mrs. Calhoun, was governor of South Carolina from 1838 to 1840.*

*Captain J. Calhoun was John Ewing Calhoun, cousin and brother-in-law of John C. Calhoun.*

*Colonel Ward was Joshua John Ward of Brookgreen Plantation near Georgetown, South Carolina.*

*Franklin H. Elmore had served a term and a half in Congress before becoming president of the State Bank in 1839.*

*General James Hamilton went from South Carolina to Texas. He preceded Ashbel Smith as Texan envoy to London and Paris, but remained in Europe till September 1842.*

*"Cousin Floride" was Mrs. John C. Calhoun.*

### FRANCIS W. PICKENS TO JOHN C. CALHOUN

Edgewood [S.C.], 2d Oct. 1841

My Dear Sir:

I arrived home safely and found the most perfect health I ever knew at this season prevailing at all my places. I have not had a single case of fever at either plantation this year. I came by my river place and found that the most extraordinary freshet ever known had occurred on Thursday and Friday 16th. . . . I lost about 80 bags of cotton—the overseer thinks more but I do not. I had about 40 acres almost entirely lost, 60 more badly hurt, 100 slightly injured in the lower branches, and 100 not hurt at all. I have no doubt I would have made 10 bags to the hand or 3000 lbs. to the hand. I never saw such cotton in my life as what is left—much of it will produce 2000 lbs. per acre—no rot nor worm and matured to the top. As to my corn it was nothing as I have plenty of old corn to do the place another year, but still I have lost only about ⅓. The river was not very high 30 miles below me, at least not higher than it has often been. As to my home place, I have the worst cotton crop I ever saw on it. The overseer was drunk half the year, and neglected to work it until it was too late, and the late working only makes it grow without maturing. I shall not make ½ crop here unless the Fall is very late. My crop on Turkey Creek where I keep a negro overseer, is very fine. I think the cotton good for about 900 lbs. per acre, much better than common for that land. As to grain crop I allways make an abundance at any rate, and never sell anything of the kind, except wheat. . . .

I never knew as much land to be sold any Fall as at present, and also as many negroes. Several of our wealthiest citizens have died without wills lately. One of my neighbor's property is to be sold on one two and three years credit for division; 152 negroes and upwards of 7,000 acres of land. Artemus Watson is dead at the Ridge with a fine planta-tion and buildings and 100 negroes to be sold, and I hear about 500 negroes are soon to be sold from deaths in the same way not far off, from different estates. I understand the same is the case in Abbeville. Gov. Noble's land is to be sold—your Brother William's—Capt J. Calhoun's at the Hills—the finest uplands in the state almost—Capt. Elmore's etc. etc. What a settlement could be made of Elmore's and Capt. J. Calhoun's! . . .

Charleston [S.C.], 6 Feby. 1846

My Dear Sir

. . . I have been on a visit to Savannah and only returned a few days since. It is a beautiful and very hospitable city with great elegance and luxury. I visited the rice lands of that river and found them superior to anything I had conceived of. It is undoubtedly the most perfect system of agriculture in the world. The rice planters are realizing immense incomes. A friend of mine Col. Ward makes this year $360 clear to every hand that hoes. He gave $250 cash for rice lands adjoining him. His income this year is $96,000. And $300 to the hand is common. Rice lands, part of Genl. Hamilton's land, sold here a few weeks since at outcry for $130 per acre. Negroes average all round large gangs $425. The demand for the lower part of this state and Georgia is greater than in La. or Texas. I saw planters in Savannah from Early county who made this year 10 bags of cotton per hand. We have had a very cold

winter, so much so that the orange trees are injured very much. I learn
that it has been much colder in Edgefield. I suppose you see cotton has
gone down very low. I think the cause temporary, for the crop will not
exceed 2 millions of bags, I have just shipped 336 bags of mine to
Liverpool yesterday, to take the Spring market and to get the advantage
of the war fever, which I suppose will be fomented, to enable the Peel
ministry to sustain itself and call for supplies. . . .

As soon as my family are well (the infant being sick) I shall return
home. . . . I have 3 of my children here at school & have been devoting
myself to their improvement, as their prosperity is all I care for now.

Present me kindly to Cousin Floride.

Very truly<br>Fr. Pickens

Emily Wharton Sinkler

## "DEAREST PAPA"

*Eutaw Plantation in St. John's Parish, South Carolina, was built by
William Sinkler, whose forebears had been given a grant of 500 acres
in Craven County, South Carolina, by King George III in the year
1770. From his father, Captain James Sinkler, William had inherited
a great love of horses and horse racing and he built a race track where
his own racers were trained. Near by was the site where the Revolu-
tonary battle of Eutaw Springs was fought and where remnants of the
British fortifications could be seen.*

*To this plantation in 1842 came Emily Wharton of Philadelphia,
bride of William's son Charles. The following letters by the young
bride to her father, Thomas Wharton, relate her experiences in her
new home. The Christmas customs she found both delightful and
unique. The races and her husband's prize horse which ate the "most
dainty food" charmed the young Northerner. And her enjoyment of
the picturesque tilting tournament, a popular custom from Colonial
days, is recounted with delightful enthusiasm.*

*Charles and Emily Sinkler had two children, Elizabeth (Lizzie) and
Wharton. When she grew up Lizzie married Charles Coxe of Philadelphia.*

*It was a happy group at Eutaw. Emily refers affectionately to her
father-in-law as "the Beau-père," and she was evidently fond of*

*Charles's sister Anna and his brother William. Her own brother Henry
came down from Philadelphia for the tournament and the races.*

*Julius Porcher, of Walworth Plantation, who was so handsomely
costumed in full armor, rose to the rank of lieutenant colonel in the
Confederate Army. He was killed at Chickamauga and his body was
never recovered.*

*The unfortunate young knight, Rene Ravenel, was the son of the
noted botanist, Dr. Henry Ravenel.*

Eutaw, December 5th, 1842

Dear Papa,

I was very glad to receive your letter on Thursday. I had been on
the lookout for some time and at last at 6 o'clock in the eve I saw the
boy come galloping up the avenue with the bag on his arm. It was
brought to me and I was delighted to find one in your hand-writing
as I expected a treat. You ask how I pass my time. Breakfast is from
half-past eight to quarter of nine. I get up a little after seven. Mr.
Sinkler, five mornings out of seven, gets up at four or five and mounts
a horse and goes off to shoot English wild ducks or deer, or to fox
hunt. All the family assemble at breakfast at which there is a great
variety of hot cakes, waffles, biscuits. Soon after breakfast our little
carriage comes to the door and we're off to take a drive. The whole
equipage is quite *comme-il-faut*. The carriage is perfectly plain, just
holding two persons. The horses are very dark brown with plain black
harness. When we set out the dogs come running up so we have a
cortege of two grey-hounds and two terriers generally. We are always
preceded by the groom Samson on horseback to open gates. We are
home by twelve or one and then I read, sew etc. until dinner time.
Mr. Sinkler goes off with his brothers to hunt and shoot partridges
until dinner. They are always, as you see, on horseback. . . . We dine
between half-past three and four. . . .

The ice cream and jelly here are the best I ever tasted.

In the evening we have music, both piano and guitar. . . .

Love to all from your affectionate daughter,

EMILY

Eutaw, December 29th, 1842

My dear Papa,

. . . How much amused you would have been at everything here.
Early on Christmas morning before crack of day the negroes began

to arrive from the different plantations of Mr. Sinkler and I was soon
awakened by a loud knocking at my door and then "Merry Christmas
Mas' Charlie, may you live many, many year. Merry Christmas Miss
Emily, long life and *crosperity to you!*" They went to every door in the
house and made some such speech. One went to brother James and
said "Merry Christmas, Massa, may you live t'ousand year and have to
drive you hosses all de time." As soon as I came out of my room I
was surrounded by all the house servants eager to "catch" me, that is,
to say "Merry Christmas" first. Such laughing and screaming you never
heard. Before breakfast every one takes a glass of egg-nog and a slice
of cake. It is the universal custom and was not on this occasion
omitted by anyone. As Christmas was kept during four days egg-nog
was drunk regularly every morning. After breakfast a most amusing
thing took place. Every four or five minutes companies of women
arrived to give their presents and wish Merry Christmas. They bring
as presents each about half a dozen eggs and although they were all
intended for Missy (Sister Eliza) I insisted upon having half, always
to their great delight. I managed to collect about 100 eggs which of
course the next day I gave to Eliza for her domestic purposes. All of
the negroes had presents of new clothes made to them and it was a
perfect babel. Their Massa stood out on the piazza helping them and
of course a great deal of attention was paid to me as being "Mas'
Charlie new lady." Both he and I were very much congratulated all
Christmas morning. . . . Give my best love to Mama and tell her I
will write to her next mail day.

Goodbye, dear Papa,
Your affectionate daughter, EMILY

Charleston, October 7, 1844

Dearest Papa,

We got here safely on Friday the 4th and found everything waiting
for us and the city delightfully cool and *perfectly* healthy. There has
not been a single case of yellow fever or any other fever in Charleston
the whole summer. Last week there was not a single white death and
only two black. . . . I spent a short time in Columbia most delightfully
with Mrs. Manning. The people there are the most hospitable I ever
saw and I have made all sorts of promises for visits this winter. People
here think no more of asking me to spend the week with them than you
would in Philadelphia of inviting them for tea. I have promised to
spend the time of the session with Mrs. [Wade] Hampton. They are all

a very generous family and just when I was there gave 15 thousand dollars to build a new Episcopal Church in Columbia. . . .

Mrs. Middleton sent for me as soon as I got here and has been very kind in invitations. Mr. Sinkler is at the Navy Yard today so he cannot send you any message but he will write to you very soon. He is a great deal there and it is a very disagreeable place. He is the only officer there and the sailors are all negroes who are constantly in mutiny and he has the most unpleasant scenes—indeed I never feel perfectly easy. The Commodore is never there and there is but one white man beside himself at the Yard. . . . He hardly gets home before some one comes running for him to come back over there. . . .

Believe me ever your affectionate<br>E. S.

Eutaw, February 1843

My dear Papa:

. . . The races are just beginning in a country town about twenty miles from here and the gentlemen are full of it. The races begin tomorrow and last for three days. The Charleston races begin next week. They have sent five horses from the stables here but only one, however, belongs to Eutaw—the rest are sent here to be trained. Jeannette Berkeley is the name of our horse and she is going to run both here and in Charleston and they think she has a good chance. It is ridiculous the care they take of them. Each horse has two boys to take care of it and a groom to take care of all of them. The horses eat the most dainty food and have to be rubbed with whiskey and actually drink it too. Every day they take exercise they eat twenty eggs! One named Kate Converse used to belong to William Sinkler and he sold it to Mr. Sinkler for 3000 dollars after she had made 500 dollars in a race. . . .

April 25, 1851

. . . Wednesday was as bright and beautiful a day as could be desired and as cool as could be desired. Anna and I accompanied by Charles and the Beau-père, Lizzie, Wharton and Henry, repaired to the ground and took our places in the ladies stand. As we arrived early we got excellent places and had time to inspect the premises before the show began. There were about two hundred ladies present, some in carriages but mostly in the stand and from various parts of the country, from Columbia and Charleston. There were also strangers. The judges' stands were decorated with flags etc. and directly in front of the ladies stand was the ring suspended, it must be confessed, from something looking very much like a gallows. At last along the winding road the "Knights" were seen approaching at full speed, the trumpets sounding and as they drew near the band struck up Yankee Doodle—of all things for this anti-yankee state! At last they came before the stage, 30 in all, lances glittering and flags flying and after some maneuvering the steeds were drawn up, lances lowered and the ladies saluted. Mr. Mazyck Porcher was the King at Arms very handsomely dressed in Sir Walter Raleigh style. He directed the whole affair and deserves great credit. . . . He was attended by a Moor in full costume whose duty it was to pick up the ring when it fell which he did with great solemnity. He was a highly respected old negro belonging to Mr. Porcher and before going off one of the lades said to him, "Now if you do your part well you will be rewarded," upon which he answered "Thank you, ma'am, all I wish is to have my Moor's dress for my burial suit."

William Sinkler (Charles' brother) was herald; his dress was very handsome blue velvet trimmed with silver, hat plumes, gauntlets, etc. His horse was beautifully caparisoned. After the saluting was over, the tilting began. The object was to carry off the ring on the lance, a very difficult matter. Each knight came full speed, pointing his lance directly at the ring, many throwing it off on the ground and many failing entirely. At each attempt the trumpet would sound and the Herald and the Master of the Horse would announce the title of the knight. When each of the 27 had had a trial, they defiled past the place of starting. There were six trials and when it was all concluded, the Judges pronounced that the Knight of Carolina, a young man by the name of Morton Waring, had carried off the ring the greatest number of times and therefore was directed to choose a Queen which the poor youth did with great trepidation. He chose Miss Elizabeth Porcher. After this the Judges selected the Knight whose costume was the handsomest and he who had ridden most gracefully. Our friend Julius Porcher, "Knight of Walworth," was chosen for the former and Keating Palmer, "Knight of The Grove," for the latter. Julius Porcher's dress was a full suit of armor which was certainly appropriate and looked extremely well on horseback. He was very ceremonious in his conduct and when requested to select a maid-of-honor did so with much circumstance, pointing his lance and exclaiming in a voice "I'll select the fair Lady Inglesby."

Then came the ceremony of crowning. The victorious knight crowned the Queen with a wreath of white roses and she in return crowned him with a wreath of Laurel. The other two knights then, kneeling, received from the hands of their maids-of-honor the one a scarf for the best costume and the other a pair of spurs for the best riding. This over, the Herald (William) in the name of the King at Arms, the Master of the Horse and himself, invited the knights and the company to a collation to which of course all repaired. It was by this time three o'clock and the collation being very much like a supper at a ball, was very acceptable. In the evening there was a regular ball given by the knights to which Charles, Anna and I did not go. . . . The whole affair, to sum up, was very handsome and went off with but one interruption which nearly broke Lizzie's heart. A young man, Rene Ravenel, the Knight of Berkeley, rode a vicious horse much against his father's wish and on the first trial as he approached the Ring he lost all command of the animal and in a few moments was thrown. Fortunately, he was only marred, not hurt and in a few moments mounted another horse, came before the ladies stand accompanied by the Herald and the Master of the Horse and after lowering his lance said "The Knight of Berkeley comes before you without plume or spurs and craves the indulgence of the ladies for his disgrace."

He is quite a handsome young man and looked extremely pale and disconcerted. It was too much for poor Lizzie who burst into tears and thought of no one else all day. He went immediately to his father's carriage and Lizzie was somewhat relieved by the ladies sending him a bunch of flowers with a very complimentary message, requesting him to favor them with his company at the stand which he accordingly did and was quite as much a hero as the real victor—women, you know, having always a penchant for the knights in misfortune.

The rest of the riders acquitted themselves to admiration—in this part of the world they seem to be one with the horse and there were some splendid horses there. They were, of course, picked horses and I heard Mr. Brevort of N.Y. who was present saying that after seeing such splendid riding and horses, he could never mount a horse again. Our friend FitzSimons came very near getting the greatest number of rings. He was the Knight of Erin, dressed in green velvet with gold shamrocks on his hat, which was a French affair with plumes, and on his coat a scarf on which was embroidered the harp etc. of Ireland. There were many other handsome creatures, particularly Saladin, the Knight Templar, the Hungarian Knight and the Knight of Malta.

Now I am afraid I have tired you with this long account. I had no idea of going so much into detail when I began but my pen ran almost without my knowing it. . . .

Henry Benjamin Whipple

## A VISIT TO ST. MARYS

*Henry Benjamin Whipple was born in 1822 at Adams, New York. He was rector of Zion Church in Rome, New York, for seven years. In 1857 he served in the Free Church of the Holy Communion in Chicago and in 1859 he was made bishop of Minnesota. His work as a frontier missionary in behalf of the Indians brought him national recognition and ultimately secured official recognition of the terrible plight of the Indians, his "red children."*

*Before his death in 1901 he received many honors. Honorary degrees came to him from Durham, Oxford and Cambridge. He represented the Protestant Episcopal Church of America at the London celebration of the centenary of the formation of the Missionary Society where Queen Victoria herself paid tribute to his work.*

*But when he made the entries in his Southern Diaries these honors were far in a future rendered precarious by ill health. In November of 1843 the twenty-one-year-old Whipple arrived at St. Marys, Georgia, where he hoped to benefit from the mild southern climate. He was a guest of Mr. H. R. Sadler and was made welcome by many of Mr. Sadler's friends.*

*Among these friends was Brigadier General Duncan L. Clinch, to whom Whipple refers as "the hero of Withlacoochee." General Clinch fought in the War of 1812 and in Florida during the second Seminole War. He retired to his plantation near St. Marys in 1836. In 1844 and 1845 he represented the district in Congress.*

*Afterward Henry Whipple made a brief trip to Florida at the invitation of a Mr. Du Buske whom he had met in St. Marys.*

*Whipple's comments on Southern society as he found it are notable for their discrimination and solid good sense. The dangerous folly of rash and intemperate judgment on the part of Northerners and Southerners alike distressed him.*

*In later years he returned again and again to Florida, cherished for the warm friendships made during his youthful visit and for the genial climate.*

Nov. 25th [1843]. The people of the southern states are generally much more hospitable than northerners, and this difference must be attributed mainly to the fact that they are not such a money loving people. You do not see that low mean cupidity, that base selfishness so striking a characteristic of one portion of our restless Yankee brethren. But the energies of the south are crippled by the incubus of slavery. Indeed, as John Randolph says, were it not that their staples are not liable to competition with free labor, they could not sustain themselves, for if it did planters would be obliged to run away from their slaves if the slave did not run away from the master. I regret deeply that blind fanaticism should so warp the judgment of any portion of our citizens that they will detract and abuse men naturally so noble hearted as the intelligent and educated planters at the south. They feel the evils of slavery, but to free the slave would be ruin to the master and destruction to the slave. I am more & more convinced that most of the exaggerated stories of abolitionists exist only in imagination. And from personal observation I know that the efforts of abolitionists at the north have only served to injure the slave and to destroy that kind & fraternal feeling which should exist between the northern and southern states. The south are not blind to the evils of slavery, they can see its bad effects as well as the most sharp sighted abolitionists yet they cannot nor will they consent to have caustic remedies applied by unskillful hands which would only serve to increase rather than diminish the evil. No! if slavery ever is abolished it must be gradual and done at the desire of & in the manner which the slaveholder desires. The slaveholders are generally opposed to the internal slave trade, and the families of slaves are never separated unless owing to the embarrassed situation of the master.

This evening I took tea with Esq. H. R. Sadler and met there his accomplished daughter & Miss Clynch, Mr. Laud, Mr. Madison & Mr. & Mrs. Preston beside his wife and mother. The evening passed off pleasantly in agreeable conversation & in listening to sweet music discoursed to us by Miss S. Mr. Sadler is a thorough bred gentleman, simple & unostentatious in his habits & kind & manly in his intercourse with others. He pleases all by his frankness & his intelligence. Mr. S. gave me an insight into his management as a planter. He said it was true the government of the planter is despotic, as despotic as can be. The will of the master is law, yet this is not only necessary but kindness to the slave on account of his indolent degraded condition. Each family is allowed a piece of ground to cultivate for himself (he has 40 or

50 acres thus appropriated) and each slave has his task, which is generally finished from 12 to 2 o'clock. After that his time is his own to plant & sow for himself and his slaves have this year all of six hundred bushels of corn for sale the avails of which is entirely their own. They have the privilege of dancing, singing &c.&c. Mr. S. says it is greatly for the interest of the master to treat the slave kindly and although there are some cases of brutality at the south, yet we despise such men, said he, as much as do you. He invited me to visit him often.

Nov. 26, 1843. I accompanied Mr. Preston and several other gentlemen today on a sailing excursion down to Fernandina, a small settlement on the frontiers of Florida. We passed Cumberland Beach & I had pointed out to me the place where Babcock & Palosti fought, also on Amelia Island the spot where Floyd & Hopkins fought. This last was one of the bloodiest duels ever fought in this section of country. The arrangement was that each should be armed with a double barrelled gun loaded with buck shot, with a pair of pistols & a bowie knife. At the word they were to advance towards each other and fire at such time as they pleased. If the guns failed to kill they were to use the pistols & then finish with bowie knives & fight until one or the other was killed. They fought until both were very badly mutilated and then the seconds separated them. This Genl Floyd resides about 20 miles from here & has quite an armory. He appears to desire to keep about him the days of chivalry of old. The Floridians fight on Cumberland Island & the Georgians on Amelia Island. The one is in Georgia the other is in Florida only separated by a few miles & thus they are enabled to evade all law.

After we had rambled about a few hours we returned but as our wind had left us, two negroes, slaves of Mr. P. rowed us back and gave us a specimen of negro lyrics. All of these blacks sing and generally they choose a lively tune & invent words as they need them. . . .

They have a horrible dread of being sold into the southwestern states & many of their songs are about the horrors of those places. Their ear for music is good and they will sing in words which no one could twist into music by accenting some syllables very much & others little. . . . But altho' slavery may be less dreadful to the slave than many would fain make us believe, yet it is a curse to the whites. It prostrates the energy of the country & prevents the south from becoming that business country which it would have been had our fathers never imported slaves. And despite the assertions of others, I am fully con-

firmed in the belief that this is no place for the poor man. The tendency of the planting interest is to make the rich man richer & the poor
man poorer.

Nov. 28. Mr. Du Buske (a planter near Reids Bluff, Florida) invited
me to go over the river with him & spend the night and the next day
to accompany him to Nassau Court which was to be held on Thursday,
and as my friend Mr. Preston, a young lawyer of St. Marys, intended
to be there I concluded to go. Mr. Griswold, formerly of Utica, accompanied us. We left St. Marys about 3 o'clock P.M. and walked nearly a
half mile through bog & mire to a point on the river where he usually
left his boat and there shipped ourselves for a cruise to Florida. Our
boat was one of the cypress canoes so common here & for a long time
I rode under the delightful apprehension of upsetting & becoming
food either for sharks or alligators, a delectable choice truly. Mr. Du
Buske is a very agreeable man, somewhat witty & tells a story remarkably well. After a ride of three or four miles we landed and again took
to our trotters through open pine land & there a little hammock for a
mile & a half & came in sight of his plantation. He has about 30 negroes
& raises cotton. We found his house like most of southern plantation
houses in the woods, merely a good frame boarded up and floors laid
with lath partitions without plastering but his table amply repaid the
loss of a good northern house & I for one did it justice. We took a walk
through his plantation, visited his cotton house &c. &c. The cotton crop
when ready for picking is a beautiful sight. You can see the blossom,
the bud & the staple ready for picking. In a good season the plant will
not grow more than 3 or 2½ feet high altho' some of this was 7 feet
and upwards. The cotton is first picked from the boll in the field, then
sorted at the cotton house, then ginned and lastly packed for market.
The blossom is a beautiful yellow or straw resembling very much our
holly hocks at the north and has about as much fragrance. Mr. Du
Buske will have a poor crop, only about 100$^{lb}$ to the acre. It is a very
uncertain crop as almost every element seems combined to destroy
it and there is a small red insect which ruins a great deal every year. . . .

Nov. 30. We arose today very early to take a campaign to the Nassau
Court house about twelve miles through the woods. Mr. Du B & G's
took horses and in lieu of a horse I mounted a mule. Never did I laugh
so merrily in my life. . . . We returned home just at evening & spent
the evening very pleasantly in social chit chat. The day has been ex-

ceedingly hot & I do not think I ever suffered so much with the heat
in the world, altho my clothing was quite thin and there was a good
breeze. The last day of November & suffering with heat!

December 1. Today we returned to St. Marys and right glad was I
to get back, altho' such trips are very conducive to health. . . .

December 2nd 1843. I left St. Marys today in company with Mr.
Preston of this place for Jacksonville, Duval County, E. Florida. We
took the steamer Gaston and owing to the roughness of the sea we
suffered somewhat with that awfully disagreeable feeling, sea sickness.
I remained at Jacksonville four days and during that time saw quite
enough of the place. While here I visited the plantation of Mr. Sadler
and was much pleased with its order and general appearance. It is
beautifully situated on the river St. Johns about five miles from Jacksonville. He has quite a small village. Beside the plantation house &
the overseer's house there are about 30 negro houses and the cotton
houses &c. &c. His crop is mainly cotton. He puts up this year about
100,000 pounds of the best sea island cotton besides raising sugar cane,
corn & other grains. Mr. Sadler's management of his negroes is very
good. While I was there he broke his driver. He had been detected in
stealing peas and that only a week after 300 bushels had been distributed among the negroes. The fellow plead guilty & was flogged 75
lashes on the bare back and another appointed in his place. These
negroes have to be kept in rather strict, yet Mr. Sadler's negroes are
decidedly a happy set of negroes. . . .

December 6th 1843. St. Marys, Georgia. . . . The first frost of the
season appeared yesterday eve on the St. Johns and vicinity, but it was
so slight that it did not injure any plants. The weather is a little cooler,
but is still much like our warm fall weather. Everything has the appearance of summer and old dame nature clings to her gay robes of
green with a remarkable tenacity. I today met a very pleasant gentleman from Charleston, a very heavy dealer in cotton, and from him
learned something new of the cotton crop. He says that the prospects
for planters are poor. This must be the cry year after year under the
operation of slavery. For the sons of the planter are generally reared
in idleness & extravagance, so when he comes to act for himself he
rushes madly in debt and too often his ruin is effected. The legitimate
tendency of slavery is to make each generation more & more inefficient

and less & less moral. To say nothing of slavery as it regards the black population, it is ruinous to the whites. . . .

December 12, 1843. The more intimately I become acquainted with southern men and the peculiar institutions of the south the more do I notice their peculiarities. The southerner himself is different from the northerner in many striking particulars. He is more chivalrous, that is to say, he has more of that old English feeling common in the days of the feudal system & crusades. He is liberal in his feelings, high minded, a warm & generous friend but a malignant and bitter enemy. He forms his attachments easier and does not retain them as long as men of less ardent disposition. He is generous to a fault with his property, is fond of gaiety and pleasure & generally dislikes the routine of business. His habits are those of genteel idleness or of the man of leisure. Nothing is a too expensive gratification of appetitie or feeling, which his purse will permit him to buy. It is unfortunate that in a country where menial labour is performed entirely by slaves, that there industry is generally looked upon if not dishonorable, at least as of doubtful gentility. . . . The luxurious habits of southerners is ruinous in the extreme and it has resulted in the embarrassment and ruin of many planters. . . .

Dec. 16, 1843. At the invitation of Rev. Mr. Baird & Mr. Griswold I accompanied them today on a visit to the plantation of Col. Hallows, a half pay officer in the New Grenada service who served under Bolivar in the Columbian war. We found his place a beautiful one situated in a fine grove of large hickory trees & were cordially welcomed. Our ride lay through pine barrens & oak shrub for seven miles and the ride would have been excessively dull had it not been enlivened by humorous anecdotes by Mr. Baird. . . . Col. Hallows raises sugar cane & cotton in small quantities but his principal crop was arrow root this year. He puts up about 3000 lb for which he will receive about 30 cts. per lb. . . . I have never spent a pleasanter day away from home. Mrs. Hallows is a very pleasant and intelligent lady and a paragon of industry. We spent the morning very pleasantly in viewing his grounds & plantation and after dinner returned to St. Marys, all of us delighted with our visit. I saw roses blooming today in his garden & we had fine oranges for our dessert. . . .

Dec. 17 & 18. Extremely warm, thermometer stands at 75 in the shade. I saw a variety of roses and other flowers in full bloom today in the garden.

Dec. 25. Christmas day. At 12 o'clock we were all aroused from a sound sleep by the music of the negroes commencing the celebration of the Christmas holidays. A more motley group of dark skins I have never seen, all arrayed in their holiday dresses and full of joy and gladness at the return of their annual holidays. Their masters give them their time at this season of the year to celebrate the holidays and none can imagine the joy & enthusiasm with which a slave hails these seasons of festive enjoyment. As soon as we were up the servants were all waiting with laughing faces to wish us a Merry Christmas, expecting to receive a bit or so as a contribution. I was truly gratified at the joyous faces of the negroes who met me in the street and their cheerful "happy Christmas, massa" made me feel a part of their happiness in hailing the Christmas holidays. In company with Mr. Hill & Griswold I left St. Marys to visit the plantation of Genl Clinch, who resides about 27 miles from here upon the Satilla River. Our route lay through the pine barrens so common in the low country of Georgia. And we were astonished at the extreme sparseness of the population. We rode 23 miles only seeing 3 houses on our route and over as fine roads as I have ever seen. The road is dull and monotonous, as it is but one continual succession of pine trees thinly scattered over immense plains with no underbrush, and here and there we found small patches of swamp and hammock lands. We reached the residence of the Hero of Withlacoochee just before dinner and were cordially welcomed. After partaking of an excellent Christmas dinner and enjoying a quiet siesta of an hour or so we took a walk out over his plantation. Genl Clinch has one of the largest rice plantations in this section of country. He plants about 500 acres and has over one hundred field hands. The land is of the richest alluvial soil and owing to the deposits made upon it by the influx of the tide is inexhaustible. The land is surrounded by large embankments and laid out in squares of about 15 or 20 acres each, these intersected by ditches & embankments with flood gates to flow the land or to drain it so that one plot can be overflowed and another dry at the same time. The crop is planted in February and ripens about the last of August. After planting, the land is flowed until time for hoeing, then drained & hoed & then flowed again. The flowing of the land is beneficial in keeping down grass and weeds besides enriching the land. This land is worth from $100 to $200 per acre. It costs about 75 dollars to clear it and put into an excellent state of cultivation. After reaping it is threshed with a machine or flail, then winnowed and finally divested of the rough hull by means of mortars and pestles. Genl

Clinch raised this year about 25,000 bushels, which brings him about 60c per bushel. He raises about 70 bushels to the acre and its weight is about 46 lb to the bushel.

Genl Clinch is a good master and follows the task system. I found his daughters pleasant and agreeable as well as accomplished ladies. Here I found the negroes enjoying the holidays to the fill. Dancing was to be heard & seen from early dawn to 11 & 12 o'clock at night. The tamborine and fiddle were in constant use and the General's piazza in front of his house was used as the ball room. . . .

We spent the next day there and left after dinner & delighted with our visit. Long shall I remember the Christmas holidays in Georgia. The weather is quite warm, almost sultry. We reached Saint Marys about 10½ P. M fatigued with our long ride through the woods of Georgia.

Dec. 27. This is with the negroes the last day of the feast and with them the "great day." The negroes are out in great numbers arrayed in their best and their ebony faces shine with joy and happiness. Already have they paraded, with a corps of staff officers with red sashes, mock epaulettes & goose quill feathers, and a band of music composed of 3 fiddles, 1 tenor & 1 bass drum, 2 triangles & 2 tamborines and they are marching up & down the streets in great style. They are followed by others, some dancing, some walking & some hopping, others singing, all as lively as lively can be. . . . They levy contributions on all the whites they see & thus find themselves in pocket money. . . . It would make a northern abolitionist change his sentiments in reference to slavery could he see as I have seen the jollity & mirth of the black population during the Christmas holidays. Never have I seen any class of people who appeared to enjoy more than do these negroes. And during my visit to the plantation of Genl Clinch I was gratified by the kind feeling which seemed to exist between the master and his slave. On the breaking up of the dance each slave came in and bade his "massa good night" and all seemed to feel as if he were their dearest and best friend. There was none of that fear, that servile fear, that is the offspring of tyranny and cruelty. I know there are men who do not treat their slaves kindly, men whose slaves bear the looks of abject sorrow but these are the exceptions not the general rule.

Dec. 29. As we (Mr. Hill & myself) intend leaving St. Marys tomorrow I have spent this day in making farewell visits. I have formed some

very pleasant acquaintances here and some friends who will ever be
esteemed by me until life shall close. Among them are first Mr. Sadler
& family & Mr. J. Preston & family. Long shall I remember their kind
attentions and their hospitality. Mr. Sadler's family is such as you will
find few to equal it in the south. May they & all other friends & relatives altho obliged to be sundered in this world be united in a world
of eternal joy above. Farewell—to St. Marys and to its inhabitants. . . .

Sir Charles Lyell

## HOPETON PLANTATION AT DARIEN, GEORGIA

*To Sir Charles Lyell, the famous British naturalist and author of the
monumental* Principles of Geology, *travel was a highly pleasurable
necessity of life. He made two trips to the United States, one in 1841
and another in 1845. On both he spent some time in the Southern
states.*

*Sir Charles had exchanged letters with James Hamilton Couper, who
counted natural history among many interests, and during his second
trip he and his wife spent nine days visiting Hopeton, Couper's plantation near Darien, and his summer villa on St. Simon's Island.*

*After being graduated with honors from Yale in 1814, Couper had
devoted two years in Holland to studying the Dutch systems of water
control. When he assumed management of the 2,000-acre Hopeton
property, he set up a system of diking and drainage which became the
model for the rice growers. He had good results with cane also, and in
1829 Hopeton possessed the most complete and modern sugar mill in
the South, but by 1838 rice had almost entirely supplanted cane.
Among the many foreign plants with which Couper experimented successfully were olive trees and Bermuda grass.*

*His management of the large slave population at Hopeton excited
the praise and admiration of the numberless visitors who found the
plantation a revelation and an education.*

*Though he was himself opposed to Secession, when the war came
his five sons joined the Confederate forces. Hamilton, his eldest, and
John, a gifted artist, were both killed.*

*Under the pressures of war Hopeton rapidly declined and at its end
scarcely a trace of Couper's superb achievement remained. He died in
1866, broken in health and fortune, and lies buried at Fredrika on St.
Simon's.*

Dec. 31, 1845.—On the last day of the year we sailed in a steamer from Savannah to Darien, in Georgia, about 125 miles farther south, skirting a low coast, and having the Gulf-stream about sixty miles to the eastward of us. Our fellow-passengers consisted of planters, with several mercantile men from northern states. The latter usually maintained a prudent reserve on politics; yet one or two warm discussions arose, in which not only the chances of war with England and the policy of the party now in power, but the more exciting topic of slavery, and the doings at a recent anti-slavery meeting in Exeter Hall, London, were spoken of. . . . One of the most moderate of the planters, with whom I conversed apart, told me that the official avowal of the English government, that one of the reasons for acknowledging the independence of Texas was its tendency to promote the abolition of slavery, had done much to alienate the planters, and increase the anti-English feeling in the south. He also observed, that any thing like foreign dictation or intermeddling excited a spirit of resistance, and asked whether I thought the emancipation of the West Indian slaves would have been accelerated by meetings in the United States or Germany to promote that measure. . . .

Dec. 31.—At the end of a long day's sail, our steamer landed us safely at the village of Darien, on the sandy banks of the river Altamaha. The sky was clear, and the air mild, but refreshing, and we were told that we must walk to the inn, not far off. Five negroes were very officious in offering their services, and four of them at length adjusted all our packages on their backs. The other, having nothing else to do, assumed the command of the party. We passed under some of the noblest evergreen oaks I had yet seen, their large picturesque roots spreading on all sides, half out of the loose, sandy soil, and their boughs hung with unusually long weepers of Spanish moss. . . .

The next morning, while we were standing on the river's bank, we were joined by Mr. Hamilton Couper, with whom I had corresponded on geological matters, and whom I have already mentioned as the donor of a splendid collection of fossil remains to the museum at Washington, and, I may add, of other like treasures to that of Philadelphia. He came down the river to meet us in a long canoe, hollowed out of the trunk of a single cypress, and rowed by six negroes, who were singing loudly, and keeping time to the stroke of their oars. He brought us a packet of letters from England, which had been sent to his house;

and when we had glanced over their contents, we entered the boat and began to ascend the Altamaha.

The river was fringed on both sides with tall canes and with the cypress (*Cupressus disticha*), and many other trees, still leafless, which, being hung with gray moss, gave a somber tone to the scenery at this season, in spite of the green leaves of several species of laurel, myrtle, and magnolia. But wherever there was a break in the fringe of trees, which flourished luxuriantly in the swamps bordering the river, a forest of evergreen pines was seen in the back ground. For many a mile we saw no habitations, and the solitude was profound; but our black oarsmen made the woods echo to their song. One of them taking the lead, first improvised a verse, paying compliments to his master's family, and to a celebrated black beauty of the neighbourhood, who was compared to the "red bird." The other five then joined in chorus, always repeating the same words. Occasionally they struck up a hymn, taught them by the Methodists, in which the most sacred subjects were handled with strange familiarity.

Darien is on the left or northern bank of the Altamaha. About fifteen miles above it, on the opposite bank, we came to Hopeton, the residence of Mr. H. Couper, having first passed from the river into a canal, which traversed the low rice fields. Here we put up prodigious flights of the marsh blackbird, sometimes called the red-winged starling, because the male has some scarlet feathers in the upper part of his wing. When several thousands of them are in rapid motion at once, they darken the air like a cloud, and then, when the whole of them suddenly turn their wings edgeways, the cloud vanishes, to reappear as instantaneously the next moment. Mr. Couper encourages these birds, as they eat up all the loose grains of rice scattered over the field after the harvest has been gathered in. If these seeds were left, they spring up the year following, producing what is called volunteer rice, always of inferior quality to that which is regularly sown.

From the rice grounds we walked up a bank to a level table land, composed of sand, a few yards above the river, and covered with pines and a mixture of scrub oak. Here, in this genial climate, there are some wild flowers in bloom every day of the year. On this higher level, near the slope which faces the rice fields and the river, stands the house of Hopeton, where we spent our time very agreeably for a fortnight.

Much has been said of the hospitality of the southern planter, but they alone who have traveled in the southern states, can appreciate the perfect ease and politeness with which a stranger is made to feel himself at home. Horses, carriages, boats, servants, are all at his disposal.

Even his little comforts are thought of, and every thing is done as heartily and naturally as if no obligation were conferred. When northerners who are not very rich receive guests in the country, where domestic servants are few and expensive, they are often compelled, if they would insure the comfort of their visitors, to perform menial offices themselves. The sacrifices, therefore, made by the planter, are comparatively small, since he has a well-trained establishment of servants, and his habitual style of living is so free and liberal, that the expense of a few additional inmates in the family is scarcely felt. Still there is a warm and generous openness of character in the southerners, which mere wealth, and a retinue of servants cannot give; and they have often a dignity of manner, without stiffness, which is most agreeable.

The landed proprietors here visit each other in the style of English country gentlemen, sometimes dining out with their families and returning at night, or, if the distance be great, remaining to sleep and coming home the next morning. A considerable part of their food is derived from the produce of the land; but, as their houses are usually distant from large towns, they keep large stores of groceries and of clothing, as is the custom in country houses in some parts of Scotland.

Near the house of Hopeton there was a clearing in the forest, exhibiting a fine illustration of that natural rotation of crops, which excites, not without reason, the surprise of every one who sees it for the first time, and the true cause of which is still imperfectly understood. . . .

A few days after our arrival (January 4, 1846), Mr. Couper took us in a canoe down the river from Hopeton to one of the sea islands, called St. Simon's, fifteen miles distant, to visit his summer residence, and to give me an opportunity of exploring the geology of the coast and adjoining low country. We saw, on the banks of the river, the *Magnolia glauca*, attaining a height of thirty feet. . . .

On our way we landed on Butler's Island, where the banks of the river, as is usual in deltas, are higher than the ground immediately behind them. They are here adorned with orange trees, loaded with golden fruit, and very ornamental. We saw ricks of rice raised on props five feet high, to protect them from the sea, which, during hurricanes, has been known to rise five or six feet. The negro houses were neat, and whitewashed, all floored with wood, each with an apartment called the hall, two sleeping-rooms, and a loft for the children. . . .

When our canoe had proceeded into the brackish water, where the river banks consisted of marsh land covered with a tall reed-like grass, we came close up to an alligator, about nine feet long, basking in the sun. Had the day been warmer, he would have not allowed us to approach so near to him; for these reptiles are much shyer than formerly, since they have learned to dread the avenging rifle of the planter, whose stray hogs and sporting dogs they often devour. The oldest and largest individuals on the Altamaha have been killed, and they are now rarely twelve feet long, and never exceed sixteen and a half feet. . . .

We landed on the northeast end of St. Simon's Island, at Cannon's Point, where we were gratified by the sight of a curious monument of the Indians, the largest mound of shells left by the aborigines in any one of the sea islands. Here are no less than ten acres of ground elevated in some places ten feet, and on an average over the whole area, five feet above the general level, composed throughout that depth of myriads of cast-away oyster-shells, with some mussels, and here and there a modiolus and helix. . . .

We found Mr. Couper's villa, near the water's edge, shaded by a verandah and by a sage tree. There were also many lemon trees, somewhat injured by the late frost; but the olives, of which there is a fine grove here, are unharmed, and it is thought they may one day be cultivated with profit in the sea islands. We also admired five date palms, which bear fruit. They were brought from Bussora in Persia, and have not suffered by the cold. The oranges have been much hurt. Some of the trees planted by Oglethorpe's troops in 1742, after flourishing for ninety-three years, were cut off in February, 1835, and others, about a century and a half old, shared the same fate at St. Augustine in Florida. So long a period does it require to ascertain whether the climate of a new country is suitable to a particular species of plant.

The evergreen or live oaks are truly magnificent in this island; some of them, 73 feet in height, have been found to stretch with their boughs over an area 63 feet in diameter.

The island of St. Simon's is so low, that the lower part of it was under water in 1804 and 1824, when hurricanes set in with the wind from the northeast. Nearly the entire surface was submerged in 1756. In that year the sea rose, even as far north as Charleston, to the height of six feet above its ordinary level, and that city might have been destroyed, had the gale lasted in the same direction a few hours longer.

I went with Mr. Couper to Long Island, the outermost barrier of land between St. Simon's and the ocean, four miles long, and about half a mile wide, of recent formation, and consisting of parallel ranges of sand dunes, marking its growth by successive additions. . . .

Among the numerous sea birds, I particularly admired one called the sheer-water, with its shrill clear note, and most rapid flight.

On my return to Cannon's Point, I found, in the well-stored library of Mr. Couper, Audubon's Birds, Michaud's Forest Trees, and other costly works on natural history; also Catherwood's Antiquities of Central America, folio edition, in which the superior effect of the larger drawings of the monuments of Indian architecture struck me much, as compared to the reduced ones, given in Stephen's Central America, by the same artist, although these also are very descriptive.

During our excursion to the sea-beach, my wife had been visited by some ladies well acquainted with relations of her own, who formerly resided in this part of Georgia, and who, when they returned to England, had taken back with them an old negress. . . .

The sea islands produce the finest cotton, and we saw many women employed in separating the cotton from the seeds with their fingers, a neat and clean occupation.

We returned from St. Simon's to Hopeton, much pleased with our expedition. . . .

During a fortnight's stay at Hopeton, we had an opportunity of seeing how the planters live in the south, and the condition and prospects of the negroes on a well-managed estate. The relation of the slaves to their owners resembles nothing in the northern states. There is an hereditary regard and often attachment on both sides, more like that formerly existing between lords and their retainers in the old feudal times of Europe, than to any thing now to be found in America. The slaves identify themselves with the master, and their sense of their own importance rises with his success in life. But the responsibility of the owners is felt to be great, and to manage a plantation with profit is no easy task; so much judgment is required, and such a mixture of firmness, forbearance, and kindness.

The evils of the system of slavery are said to be exhibited in their worst light when new settlers come from the free states: northern men, who are full of activity, and who strive to make a rapid fortune, willing to risk their own lives in an unhealthy climate, and who can not make allowance for the repugnance to continuous labor of the negro race, or the diminished motive for exertion of the slave. To one who arrives in Georgia direct from Europe, with a vivid impression on his mind of the state of the peasantry there in many populous regions, their ignorance, intemperance, and improvidence, the difficulty of obtaining subsistence, and the small chance they have of bettering their lot, the condition of the black laborers on such a property as Hopeton, will afford but small ground for lamentation or despondency.

I had many opportunities while here of talking with the slaves alone,

or seeing them at work. I may be told that this was a favorable specimen of a well-managed estate; if so, I may at least affirm that mere
chance led me to pay this visit, that is to say, scientific objects wholly
unconnected with the "domestic institutions" of the south, or the character of the owner in relation to his slaves; and I may say the same in
regard to every other locality or proprietor visited by me in the course
of this tour. I can but relate what passed under my eyes, or what I
learnt from good authority, concealing nothing.

There are 500 negroes on the Hopeton estate, a great many of whom
are children, and some old and superannuated. The latter class, who
would be supported in a poor-house in England, enjoy here, to the end
of their days, the society of their neighbors and kinsfolk, and live at
large in separate houses assigned to them. The children have no regular work to do till they are ten or twelve years old. We see that some of
them, at this season, are set to pick up dead leaves from the paths,
others to attend the babies. When the mothers are at work, the young
children are looked after by an old negress called Mom Diana. The parents indulge their own fancies in naming their children, and display a
singular taste; for one is called January, another April, a third Monday,
and a fourth Hard Times. The fisherman on the estate rejoices in the
appellation of "Old Bacchus." Quash is the name of the favorite
preacher, and Bulally the African name of another negro.

The out-door laborers have separate houses provided for them; even
the domestic servants, except a few who are nurses to the white children, live apart from the great house—an arrangement not always convenient for the masters, as there is no one to answer a bell after a certain hour. But if we place ourselves in the condition of the majority of
the population, that of servants, we see at once how many advantages
we should enjoy over the white race in the same rank of life in England.
In the first place all can marry; and if a mistress should lay on any
young woman here the injunction so common in English newspaper
advertisements for a maid of all work, "no followers allowed," it would
be considered an extraordinary act of tyranny. The laborers begin work
at six o'clock in the morning, have an hour's rest at nine for breakfast,
and many have finished their assigned task by two o'clock, all of them
by three o'clock. In summer they divide their work differently, going
to bed in the middle of the day, then rising to finish their task, and
afterward spending a great part of the night in chatting, merry-making,
preaching, and psalm-singing. At Christmas they claim a week's holidays, when they hold a kind of Saturnalia, and the owners can get no
work done.

The winter, when the whites enjoy the best health, is the trying season for the negroes, who are rarely ill in the rice-grounds in summer, which are so fatal to the whites, that when the planters who have retreated to the sea-islands revisit their estates once a fortnight, they dare not sleep at home. Such is the indifference of the negroes to heat, that they are often found sleeping with their faces upward in a broiling sun, instead of lying under the shade of a tree hard by. We visited the hospital at Hopeton, which consists of three separate wards, all perfectly clean and well-ventilated. One is for men, another for women, and a third for lying-in women. The latter are always allowed a month's rest after their confinement, an advantage rarely enjoyed by hardworking English peasants. . . .

Jan. 9, 1846.—When I had finished my geological examination of the southern and maritime part of Georgia, near the mouth of the Altamaha river, I determined to return northward to Savannah. . . .

Having taken leave of our kind host, we waited some hours at Darien for a steamer, which was to touch there on its way from St. Augustine in Florida, and which conveyed us speedily to Savannah. . . .

Fredrika Bremer

## THREE PLANTATIONS

*Fredrika Bremer, a Swedish woman of letters, came to the United States in 1849 and remained for two years, traveling in some twenty-seven states. Her friend Andrew Jackson Downing of New York state, the first American landscape gardener, secured for her an invitation to the home of Mr. Poinsett of South Carolina.*

*Joel R. Poinsett was born in Charleston in 1779. He was the first accredited agent of a foreign government in Chile in 1810. In 1816 he was elected to the state legislature and in 1820 he succeeded Charles Pinckney in the Federal House of Representatives. In 1825 he was appointed first American Minister to Mexico. Memento of his somewhat turbulent Mexican experience was a lovely red flower that he brought back with him and which is named for him, the poinsettia.*

*In 1833 he married Mary Izard Pringle, widow of his neighbor, John Julius Pringle, and retired to his home, Casa Bianca, or the White House, near Georgetown. In 1837 President Van Buren appointed him Secretary of War, a post which he filled with signal success.*

In 1841 he again withdrew to his country home and though he continued to interest himself in the political fortunes of the nation he declined further active participation.

A little over a year after Miss Bremer's visit he died in Statesburg, Sumter County, South Carolina, and was buried in the cemetery of the Church of the Holy Cross.

From Casa Bianca Miss Bremer took ship for Florida. The steamer Magnolia on which she was traveling ran aground. After two futile days of waiting the passengers were transferred to another boat, leaving the Magnolia to await the next full moon and high tide to float off the sand bar.

From Ortega Plantation in Florida Miss Bremer went to St. Simon's Island where she was much impressed with that brilliant conversationalist, James Hamilton Couper.

During her travels Miss Bremer wrote often to her sister in Sweden. The letters describing her impressions of the United States were printed in her book, Homes of the New World, published in 1853.

Two days after Miss Bremer left Casa Bianca Joel Poinsett wrote to his friend, Mr. Gouverneur Kemble of Cold Spring, New York: "The peaceful banks of the Peedee have been enlivened for a fortnight past by the presence of the fair Swede Miss Bremer. I mean fair haired and fair skinned, for she is not at all pretty. . . . I do not know who her associates were in Boston and New York, but either her preconveived notions of this country and government were very erroneous or she has been misled by impracticable minds. . . . On the whole however we were much pleased with her visit and entertained with her talk. . . ." (From Signe Alice Rooth, Seeress of the North Land: Fredrika Bremer's American Journey, 1849-1851. Phil. American Swedish Historical Foundation, 1955, pp. 58-59.)

### SOUTH CAROLINA PLANTATION HOME OF JOEL POINSETT

Casa Bianca, April 16th 1850. I now write from a hermitage on the banks of the little River Pedee. It is a solitary, quiet abode; so solitary and quiet, that it almost astonishes me to find such an one in this lively, active part of the world, and among these company-loving people.

A fine old couple, Mr. Poinsett and his lady, who now remind me of Philemon and Baucis, live here quite alone, in the midst of negro slaves, rice plantations, and wild, sandy forest land. There is not a single white servant in the house. The overseer of the slaves, who always lives near the slave hamlet, is the only white person I have seen out of the house. Nevertheless, the old couple seem to me to live as safely as we do at our Aersta, and to be about as little careful of fastening the house-door at night. The house is an old one (N.B., for this young country), with antique furniture, and rooms testifying of good old-fashioned aristocratic taste and comfort.

Round the house is a park or garden, rich in the most beautiful trees, shrubs and plants of the country, planted by Mr. Poinsett himself, according to Mr. Downing's advice, and, as under the snow-covered roof at Concord, had I the pleasure of hearing the words, "Mr. Downing has done much for this country," so universal is the influence of Mr. Downing here in the improvement of taste, and the awakening a sense of the beautiful, as regards buildings, the cultivation of gardens, and the laying out of public grounds.

North America has also this peculiarity, that all kinds of trees and shrubs from other parts of the world may be removed here, become naturalized and flourish; in the grounds around *Casa Bianca* are a great number from foreign countries. Of all the trees here, I like best the native large live-oak, with its long, pendant growth of moss (two magnificent specimens of this tree stand opposite the house, on the banks of the Pedee, and form by their branches an immense portico, through which one sees the river and the landscape beyond), and the sober, lofty, dark-green magnolias. Outside my window, which is in the upper story, stands a *Cornus Floridae,* a tree whose crown now seems to be a mass of snow-white blossom, and early in the morning I hear and see the thrushes singing their rich morning song on its topmost branches; further off is the deliciously odoriferous *Olea fragrans* from Peru, and many beautiful rare trees and shrubs. Among these sing the thrushes and the mocking-birds, and swarms of blackbirds twitter and chatter, and build in the great live-oaks. Mrs. Poinsett will not allow them to be disturbed, and every morning after breakfast come little gray sparrows and the brilliant cardinal-birds (so called from the splendor of their plumage), quite familiarly, and pick up the rice-grains which she scatters for them in the piazza before the door.

On the quiet little River Pedee glides first one and then another canoe, paddled by negroes, and it is only by the steam-boats which now and then swing their tails of smoke over the River Waccamaw, beyond the Pedee and by sailing vessels which one sees on their way down to Cuba or China, that one observes that here also one lives in this trading and trafficking world.

Mr. Poinsett is a French *gentilhomme* in his whole exterior and demeanor (he is of a French family), and unites the refinement and natural courtesy of the Frenchman, with the truthful simplicity and straightforwardness which I so much like in the true American, the man of the New World. That fine figure is still slender and agile, although he suffers from asthma. He has seen much and been among much, and is an extremely agreeable person to converse with, in particular as relates to the internal political relationship of the United States, which he has assisted in forming, and the spirit and intention of which he thoroughly understands, while he has a warm compatriot heart. I have, in a couple of conversations with him in the evening after tea, learned more of these relationships, and those of the individual states to their common government, than I have learned from books, because I acquire this knowledge in a living manner from the sagacious old stateman; I can ask questions, make objections, and have them at once replied to.

He is the first man that I have met with in the South, with one exception, who speaks of slavery in a really candid and impartial spirit. He earnestly desires that his native land should free itself from this moral obliquity, and he has faith in its doing so; but he sees the whole thing at present involved in so many ways, and the difficulties attending any change so great, that he leaves the question to be solved by the future. He firmly believes in the onward progress of America, but he is far from satisfied with many things in the country, and especially in this very state. He is one of the New World's wise men, who more and more withdraw themselves from the world, looking calmly on from his hermitage, and apparently happy there with his excellent wife and his rural occupation.

In the morning, after I have eaten, with a good relish, my breakfast of rice, and egg, and cocoa, I help Mrs. Poinsett to feed the birds, and am delighted that the beautiful showy cardinal-birds will condescend to pick up my rice-grains. And then, if I rush out into the garden, ready to embrace the air, and the shrubs, and all nature, the good old lady laughs at me right heartily. Then out comes Mr. Poinsett, begs me to notice the beautiful *Lamarque* rose which Mr. Downing gave him, and which now is full of large clusters of yellowish-white flowers on the trellised walls of the house; and thence he takes me round the garden, and tells me the names of the plants which I do not know, and their peculiarities, for the old gentleman is a skillful botanist. He has also taken me round his rice-grounds, which are now being sown, after which they will lie under water. And it is this irrigation, and the exhalation therefrom, which makes the rice plantations so unwholesome for the white population during the hot season. Mr. Poinsett's plantations are not large, and seem not to have more than sixty negroes upon them. Several other plantations adjoin these, but neither are they large as it appeared, and my entertainers seemed not to be intimate with their proprietors.

I range about in the neighborhood, through the rice-fields and negro villages, which amuses me greatly. The slave villages consist of small, whitewashed wooden houses, for the most part built in two rows, forming a street, each house standing detached in its little yard or garden, and generally with two or three trees about it. The houses are neat and clean, and such a village, with its peach-trees in blossom, as they are just now, presents a pleasant appearance. The weather is heavenly; "true Carolina air," say the Carolina people, and it is delicious.

Yesterday—Sunday—there was, in the forenoon, divine service for the negroes in a wagon-shed, which had been emptied for that purpose. It was clean and airy, and the slaves assembled there, well dressed and well behaved. The sermon and the preacher (a white missionary) were unusually wooden. But I was astonished at the people's quick and glad reception of every single expression of beauty or of feeling. . . .

In the evening I wandered out to enjoy the beautiful evening and to look about me. I reached the slave village. The little white houses, overshadowed by the pink blossoming trees, with their little plot of garden-ground, looked charming; the little fat, black children leaped about, eating a large yellow root, the sweet potato, laughing if one only looked at them, and especially inclined to shake hands. But in the village itself every thing was very still and quiet. A few negro men and women were standing about, and they looked kind and well to do. I heard in one house a sound of prayer and zealous exhortation. . . .

I went on still further through wood and meadow, into the wild, silent country. When it began to grow dusk I turned back. I repassed the same slave village. Fires blazed in the little houses, but every thing was more silent and stiller than before. I saw a young negro with a good and handsome countenance, standing thoughtfully under a peach-tree, leaning against its bole. I accosted him, and asked him of one thing and another. Another slave came up, and then still another, and the conversation with them was as follows:

"At what time do you get up in the morning?"

"Before sunrise."

"When do you leave off in the evening?"

"When the sun sets—when it is dark."

"But when do you get time to look after your garden?"

"We must do that on Sunday or at night, for when we come home we are so tired that we could drop down."

"How do you get your dinners?"

"We have no dinner! It is all we can do if, while we are working, we can throw a bit of bread or some corn into us."

"But, my friend," said I, now a little mistrustful, "your appearance contradicts what you say; for you look in very good condition, and quite brisk."

"We endeavor to keep ourselves up as well as we can," replied the man by the tree; "what can we do unless we keep up a good heart? If we were to let it droop, we should die!"

The others responded to the song of lamentation.

I bade them good-night and went my way, suspecting that all was not true in the slaves' representation. But still, it *might* be true; it was true, if not here, yet in other places and under wicked masters; it might always be true in an institution which gives such irresponsible power at will; and all its actual and possible misery presented itself to me, and made me melancholy. The evening was so beautiful, the air so fragrant, the roses were all in bloom; nature semed to be arrayed as a bride; the heaven was bright; the new moon, with the old moon in her arms, was bright in the firmament, and the stars came out, clear and brilliant. The glory of the scene, and that poor, black, enslaved, degraded people—they did not at all agree! All my enjoyment was over.

I was glad, however, to have a man like Mr. Poinsett to talk with. And to him I confided, in the evening, my conversation and my thoughts. Mr. Poinsett maintains that the slaves have told me falsehoods. "One can never believe what they say," said he; adding, "that also is one of the evils of slavery. The people are made liars by it. Children learn from their parents to regard the white people with fear, and to deceive them. They are always suspicious, and endeavor by their complainings to get some advantage. But you may be sure that they have been imposing upon you. The slaves round here have a certain quantity of work set them for the day, and at this time of the year they have for the most part finished it by four or five o'clock in the afternoon. There is commonly kept on every plantation a male or female cook, who prepares the daily dinners at one o'clock. I have one for my people, and I have no doubt but that Mr. —— also has one for his people. It can not be otherwise. And I am certain that you would find it to be so if you would examine into the affair."

Mr. Poinsett does not deny but that abuse and maltreatment of slaves has often occurred and still occurs, but public opinion becomes more and more sternly opposed to it. Some years ago extreme cruelty was practiced against the slaves on a plantation in the neighborhood by an overseer, during the prolonged absence in England of the owner of the plantation. The planters in the neighborhood united, wrote to him, told him that they could not bear it, and requested that the overseer should be removed. And this was done. Mr. Poinsett considers that the system of slavery operates in many cases much more unfavorably on women than on men, and makes them not infrequently the hardest masters.

*18th.* I am just returned from a solitary ramble into the plantations, which had done me good, for it has shown me that the slaves under the peach-tree really did impose upon me. During my ramble I saw at one place in the rice-field a number of small copper vessels standing, each covered with a lid, from twenty-five to thirty in number, just as with us one sees the laborers' noggins and baskets standing together in the grass. I went up, lifted the lid of one, and saw that the vessel contained warm, steaming food, which smelled very good. Some of them were filled with brown beans, others with maize-pancakes. I now saw the slaves coming up from a distance, walking along the headland of the field. I waited till they came up, and then asked permission to taste their food, and I must confess that I have seldom tasted better or more savory viands. The brown beans were like our "princess beans," boiled soft with meat, and seasoned somewhat too highly for me. But it ate with a relish, and so did the maize-cakes and the other viands also. The people seated themselves upon the grass-sward and ate, some with spoons, others with splinters of wood, each one out of his own piggin, as these vessels are called, and which contained an abundant portion. They seemed contented, but were very silent. I told them that the poor working people in the country from which I came seldom had such good food as they had here. I was not come there to preach rebellion among the slaves, and the malady which I could not cure I would alleviate if it was in my power. Besides which, what I said was quite true.

On my homeward way I saw an old negro, very well dressed, who

was standing fishing in a little stream. He belonged to Mr. Poinsett,
but had been by him liberated from all kind of work in consequence
of his age. From this sensible old man I heard various things which
also pleased me. I saw in two other places likewise the people at their
meals, breakfast and dinner, and saw that here too the food was good
and abundant.

I passed by my negroes of the peach-tree yesterday afternoon, and
saw them coming home with a crowd of others at about six o'clock.
One of them sprang over a hedge when he saw me, and, grinning with
his white teeth, asked from me half a dollar.

*April 20th.* I have just had my second breakfast, at twelve o'clock, of
bananas. I am beginning to like this fruit. It is gentle and agreeable,
and has a wholesome effect, as well as the mild air here, that is to say,
when it is mild. But even here the climate is very changeable. Yesterday
the thermometer fell in one day twenty-four degrees, and it was so cold
that my fingers were stiff as icicles. Today, again, one is covered with
perspiration, even when one sits quietly in the shade. We have been
twice at great dinners with planters some miles from here, but I am
so annoyed by great dinners, and made so ill by the things I eat, that
I hope, with all my heart, not to go to any more. But my good hostess,
who has a youthful soul, in a heavy and somewhat lame body, heartily
enjoys being invited out.

*22d.* My life passes quietly, as quietly as the little river before my
window; but it is well for me. I have not passed a calmer time since I
have been in this country; for, with the exception of a few occasional
visits in the forenoon from neighbors, I live quite alone with my good,
old married pair. Every morning there is laid on the breakfast-table,
beside my plate, a bouquet of deliciously fragrant flowers, generally of
the Peruvian *Olea fragrans* (and any thing more delicious I do not
know), gathered by Mr. Poinsett. Every evening I sit with him and
Mrs. Poinsett alone, read and talk with him, or tell stories for the
good old lady, or give her riddles to guess, which very much amuses
her. She sits by the fire and takes a nap, or listens to what Mr. Poinsett
and I read by lamplight at the table. I wished to make him a little
acquainted with my friends the Transcendentalists and Idealists of
the North, and I have read to him portions of Emerson's Essays. But
they shoot over the head of the old statesman; he says it is all "un-
practical," and he often criticises it unjustly, and we quarrel. Then the

good old lady laughs by the fire, and nods to us, and is amazingly entertained. Mr. Poinsett is, nevertheless, struck with Emerson's brilliant aphorisms, and says he will buy his works. It is remarkable how very little, or not at all, the authors of the Northern States, even the best of them, are known in the South. They are afraid of admitting their liberal opinions into the Slave States.

Mr. Poinsett has traveled much, as well in Europe as in America. He seems weary of statesmanship and of the life of a statesman. Even Calhoun, the great and almost idolized statesman of Carolina, is not great in Mr. Poinsett's opinion, excepting in ambition. His whole life seems to have been a warfare in the service of ambition, and his death (for he is just dead, during the sitting of Congress at Washington) the result of this warfare in his breast, owing to the political feuds in which he perpetually lived.

It is very charming to see my two old friends together in everyday life. They are heartily attached to each other. One standing quarrel they have about a horrible old straw bonnet of Mrs. Poinsett's, which looks like an ancient up-turned boat, and which Mr. Poinsett can not bear the sight of, and which he threatens to make an end of, to burn, every time he sets eyes on it, but which she obstinately will keep, and which she defends with terror whenever he makes any hostile demonstration against it. But it is altogether a love-squabble, and as it has now lasted for ten years, I suppose it will last on to the days of their death. They have both of them a cough which they call "constitutional." I contemplate this good feeling between my old couple with delight, and see how true love can bloom in and beautify old age.

I spend the greater part of the forenoon in the garden, among the flowers, birds, and butterflies, all splendid and strangers to me, and which salute me here as anonymous beauty. During these hours spent amid this new and beautiful nature, thoughts visit me which give me great joy, and which in every way are a great comfort to me. I will explain: I have for some time felt as if I could scarcely bear to read, nor yet to write any thing which required the least exertion of mind, as it produces in me a degree of nervous suffering which is indescribable. I have, therefore, almost given up the hope of studying, and of making myself much acquainted with books during my residence in this country. This has been painful to me, and I have long striven against it, because study has always been my greatest pleasure, and now more than ever was it necessary for me to be able to devour books, so that I might be somewhat at home in the life and literature of this country.

Here, however, during these beautiful early mornings, in this beautiful, fragrant, silent world of trees and flowers, there has arisen within me a clearness, a certainty, something like the *inner light* of the Quakers, which tells me that it is best for me now to lay aside books, and altogether to yield myself up to live in that living life, to live free from care for the moment, and to take and accept that which the hour and the occasion present, without troubling myself with many plans or much thought. I must let things come to me as they may come, and determine for me as they will determine. A conviction has come to my mind that a higher guidance attends me, and that it will direct every thing for the best. . . .

And thus I go forth and converse with the flowers, and listen to the birds and to the whispering of the great live-oak. Oaks like these, with their long, depending trails of moss, must have inspired the oracle of Dodona.

The blackbirds, which build in them in great numbers, are about the size of our jackdaw, and have on each side their necks, below the head, a fine yellow ruff, like a half-round frill. The mocking-birds are gray, about as large as our Swedish nightingale, and their song is very intricate, and often really charming; but it wants the strong inspiration of the European nightingale and lark. It is as if the bird sang from memory; sang reminiscences, and imitated a number of sounds of other birds, and even animals. There are, however, in its song beautiful, peculiar tones, resembling those both of the thrush and the nightingale. People say that these birds dance minuets with each other. I, too, have seen them here figuring toward one another, tripping quite in a minuet fashion. I suppose this is their way of wooing. It is remarkable that people never succeed in rearing in cages the young of these birds which have been taken from the nest; they always die shortly after their captivity. It is asserted that the mothers come to them and give them poison. The full-grown birds in the country thrive very well and sing in cages.

I am sometimes interrupted in my forenoon musings by a merry negro girl, servant in the house, who says, "Missis has sent me to hunt you," and it is for me to come in to my luncheon. If I am writing, I remain in my own room, and then, generally at twelve o'clock, the good old lady herself comes up to me with bananas and a glass of milk. In the afternoon I generally go on some expedition of discovery. When I am returning home in the twilight, I often see my old folks coming to meet me, she walking with a crutch and supported by his arm.

*24th*. Last evening I had an old negro to row me in a little canoe down the Waccamaw River, spite of Mr. Poinsett's remonstrances, who fancied that no good would come of it. The moon rose and shone brightly on the river and its banks, over which hung various trees and plants in flower with which I was unacquainted. The negro, a kind old man, paddled the boat onward, and wherever I saw an enticing flower, thither we paddled and gathered it. Thus went we on for about two hours in that clear moonlight, and every thing was as solitary and silent on the river and on its banks as in a desert.

There had, however, been this day a great wedding on the banks of the Waccamaw, and all the neighbors had been invited; but either my host and hostess did not belong to their circle of acquaintance or the fame of my abolitionist views had prevented us being invited. Very good! for though I love to see brides and weddings, yet I love quietness now better than all.

My good host and hostess were glad to see me return from my river excursion, and Mr. Poinsett told me the names of the flowers which I gathered. One of these was the *Magnolia glauca*, a white flower something like our white water-lily; this grows on a smaller tree, with gray-green leaves. The celebrated, splendid flower of the South, the *Magnolia grandiflora*, does not blossom till the end of May.

I shall in a few days leave this place and return to Charleston. My kind entertainers wish me to remain yet longer, but I greatly desire to reach Savannah before the heat becomes too great, and I must therefore hasten. I have received much kindness here and much benefit from Mr. Poinsett's conversation. . . . It is time to be going. I now know how life looks in the plantations, know how the negro slaves live, and how rice and Indian corn are planted. . . .

### ORTEGA PLANTANTION

Ortega Plantation, Florida, May 23

Again on a bank, but not in a steam-boat (our poor little *Magnolia* is said to be lying there still, without any hope of getting off before the next full moon!), but on a maize plantation belonging to relatives of the MacI. family, where I am enjoying rest and refreshment with an amiable family, in a good and hospitable home.

The whole family has an expression of so much good-heartedness and gentleness, that one sees plain enough that the slaves can not suffer. But the drought is fearful; the maize plants on this plantation are withered in the sand, of which this plantation has more than its ordinary share; and the harvest of this year wears a mournful appearance. Even in this beautiful Florida, life is heavy and dry as regards the poor children of earth.

But when in the mornings early I wake and feel the balmy wind of Florida play through the white curtains round my bed, and hear the nightingale of America pouring forth, in its many tongues, its melodious inspirations in the trees before my window, then do I exalt the home of summer, and wonder not that Ferdinand de Soto and his young men were enchanted by it, and it seems to me almost unnatural that life here can be heavy or dark.

We remain here a couple of days in expectation of a good steamboat which will take us to Mr. C.'s plantation at Darien, whence we return to Savannah.

This plantation lies in a sandy tract, and the sand considerably encroaches upon the charms of nature and country life. There is here, however, a foot-path by the river which follows a wild and woody shore, than which nothing more picturesque can be conceived, in particular the masses of trees and wild boscage which rise like a lofty wall between the shore and the sloping cultivated land. Splendid magnolias, covered with white flowers, lift aloft among these their dark, shady crowns. The magnolia is the most magnificent tree of the Southern States. I wander here alone in the afternoons, wondering sometimes whether I shall hear, from the dense thickets, the warning signal of the rattlesnake—for this serpent gives warning before he makes an attack or approaches near. But, although rattlesnakes are numerous in Florida, I have not yet happened either to see or hear a living one. I however saw this afternoon one which the negroes had just killed on the plantation and brought to show the family. It might be about three yards long, and as thick as my arm. The head was much injured by the blows it had received, and the terrible poison-fangs were revealed. I have had the rattle, with its fourteen joints, given to me to take home with me to Sweden. A year ago a negro on the plantation was bitten on the leg by a rattlesnake; great endeavors were made to save the limb from amputation, but in vain; it was, in the end, obliged to be taken off, to put an end to the great and increasing suffering.

A pretty little village on the plantation is the home of the black nurse of the gentleman of the house, and there she rests from her labors, under circumstances which testify the tenderest care. She has her own neat little house, on a terrace by the river, and within it every convenience that an old person can desire; a comfortable rocking-chair is even among these, and children and children's children, whom she has faithfully nursed, visit her with love and presents. She has had many children of her own, but she acknowledged that the white children were dearest to her; and this affection of the black nurses, or foster-mothers, to the children of the whites is a well-known fact. Another fact also, which is often witnessed in the slave states, is the tender care which is bestowed upon these faithful black foster-mothers in their old age by the family.

### PLANTATION OF MR. J. C. ON ST. SIMON'S ISLAND

*St. Simon's Island, May 27th*

In front of my window runs, broad and clear, the western arm of the Altamaha River, and beside it sits the undersigned upon an island on the coast of Georgia, between the river and the Atlantic Ocean. I am now at the house of Mr. J. C., a planter, in the midst of gardens and olive-groves, where the family seeks for its summer pleasure and the salubrious air of the sea when fevers begin to ravage the large plantation at Darien, the principal residence of the family.

Mr. C. is one of the greatest planters in the south of the United States, and owns about two thousand negro slaves, whom he employs on his rice and cotton plantations. He had been mentioned to me as a reformer, who had introduced trial by jury among his slaves, with many other educational institutions, to prepare them for a future life of liberty. And this created in me a desire to become acquainted with him and his plantations. But I did not find him a reformer, merely a disciplinarian, with great practical tact, and also some benevolence in the treatment of the negroes. In other respects I found him to be a true representative of the gentlemen of the Southern States—a very polite man, possessing as much knowledge as an encyclopedia, and interesting to me in a high degree through the wealth and fascination of his conversation. He is distinguished for his knowledge of natural history; he has a beautiful collection of the natural productions of America, and the lecture which I heard him read this morning, in the midst of these, on the geology and the rock formation of America, has given me a clearer knowledge of the geological structure of this portion of the world than I ever possessed before.

Mr. C. has an unusual faculty for systematization, and for demonstrating the characteristic points of a subject. A conversation with him on any subject can not fail of being interesting, even if one differs from him in opinion.

But as Mr. C., on the question of slavery, unites with the good party in the South, who regard the colonization of Africa by the liberated negro slaves as the final result and object of the institution of slavery, it was any thing but difficult for me to converse with him on this subject, and that which naturally belongs to it. Neither could I do other than agree with him in the views he expressed regarding the peculiar faculties of the negro race and their future destiny, because they accorded with my own observations.

Mr. C. regards slavery in America as a school for the children of Africa, in which they may be educated for self-government on the soil of Africa. He was inclined to look at the institution of slavery as a benefit to them. And that it might be converted into a benefit is certain. But that it is the only means of imparting to Africa the blessings of Christianity and civilization may be safely denied. . . .

In urbanity and grace of conversation Mr. C. reminds me of Waldo Emerson; but, in a general way, the Southern gentleman has too small a development of the organ of ideality, even as in the gentleman of the North it is too large. Mr. C. corroborated the facility with which the negroes acquire a knowledge of handcraft trades, and their dexterity as artisans. They have in Georgia begun to employ them advantageously in manufactures. I now remember having visited, last year, a cotton factory near Augusta, in which colored work-people were employed. It was not a sight which caused me pleasure, because I could not believe that the blacks would voluntarily choose this occupation, with its noise, difficulty, and dusty, unwholesome atmosphere—they who had been accustomed to the labor of the open fields.

The home here is full of gay, youthful countenances, six boys and two girls, the youngest of which is the image and delight of her father; and Mrs. C. is a youthful, pretty, and happy mother of this handsome flock of children.

Not far from the house is a troop of little black children, seventy or eighty in number, whom I visited this evening, and who wanted mothers. A couple of witch-like negro women, with rods in their hands, governed the troop by fear and terror. I had been told that they also taught the children to pray. I gathered a little flock around me, and slowly repeated to them the Lord's Prayer, bidding them read the words after me. The children grinned, laughed, showed their white teeth, and evinced very plainly that none of them knew what that wonderful prayer meant, nor that they had a Father in heaven.

The children were well fed. They were kept here, separated from their parents, on account of fever raging on the plantations where they worked.

If I have not here the reformer whom I expected, I have heard of two such planters, the one in Florida, the other in Georgia, who have established schools for the children of their negro slaves, with the intention of preparing them for good and free human beings.

Why have I not before heard of these Christian labors? I would have made every possible effort to have witnessed them, to have seen with my own eyes. Such plantations in the slave states may be regarded as holy spots, to which pilgrimages would be made by those who seek for the soul's elevation, and for new power to hope and to believe. What, indeed, have I been so zealously seeking for, and inquiring after, in these Southern States, but for such places!

I parted from Mr. C. with sincere gratitude for his interesting society, and with a decided liking for one of the young sons of the plantation, whose broad forehead revealed a thoughtful, unprejudiced, and humorous turn of mind.

Almira Coffin

## "IF YOU DOUBT MY WORD COME AND SEE FOR YOURSELF"

*When Miss Almira Coffin of Buxton, Maine, went to visit the family of her cousin, Charles Royall Brewster, near Charleston, South Carolina, in the spring of 1851, she wrote a series of letters home to her friend Rebecca Martha Usher, Mrs. J. G. Osgood, that are as brisk and vigorous as an ocean breeze. Miss Coffin had a grand time and she did her best to share it.*

*Charles Royall Brewster had gone from Buxton to Charleston in 1831. He practiced law for a number of years with Chancellor Charles Faneuil Dunkin. He married Washington S. Prentiss, a sister-in-law of Chancellor Dunkin.*

*Miss Coffin stayed awhile at Midway, Chancellor Dunkin's home. A native of Massachusetts, Dunkin moved to South Carolina early in the nineteenth century and rose to be Chief Justice of the state. He was expecting the early arrival of his brother-in-law, Dr. Horatio Adams, of Waltham, Massachusetts, who was attending a medical convention in Charleston.*

At the Retreat on the Peedee River, Almira was a guest of the Chancellor's daughter Mary, Mrs. Cleland Kinloch Huger. There she met Mrs. Huger's father-in-law, Mr. Francis Kinloch Huger, son of Major Benjamin Huger, who had entertained Lafayette when he came to America in 1777. She was greatly impressed by the particularity with which Colonel Joshua John Ward, master of Brookgreen Plantation and the richest man on "the Neck," treated his slaves.

She rode over to Pawley's Island to see the youngest Dunkin daughter, Mrs. Charles Alston.

Georgetown County was a populous and productive rice-planting district. It was a region rich also in history. Here at the Oaks lived Theodosia Burr Alston, and from here she departed to sail on the Patriot from Georgetown to New York on December 30, 1812. Here in the Alston Cemetery is buried her husband, Governor Joseph Alston, and their little son, Aaron Burr Alston.

In Revolutionary days, Tarleton, and Francis Marion too, knew this region. George Washington was a visitor in 1791, and some years later, in 1819, President James Monroe was a guest at Prospect Hill Plantation.

### ALMIRA COFFIN TO MRS. J. G. OSGOOD

Charleston May 9th [10th] Saty Morng [1851]

My dear Mattie

. . . I have been a fortnight in the country since I recd your welcome letter, & a charming time I had too. I wished for you girls more than once, that you might see the beauties of a plantation with your eyes instead of through mine, for I can give you no idea of all.

We left here in a steamer at 9 o'clock A.M. & sailed in a northerly direction, near the coast, till we arrived at Winyaw Bay, which we entered, stopping awhile at Georgetown. After leaving our own harbor, there is not much of interest to be seen till we enter the bay, which is 20 miles long. While at G. we took a walk about the town which is quite pretty, much lumber business carried on & other trading, & is a little larger than Harrison, situated much like it, steam saw & other mills in abundance, saw many vessels from Maine & Mass. loading.

From there we went up the Waccamaw River 12 miles to Chancellor Dunkins place, a distance of 100 miles from here & arrived at 6 P.M. I enjoyed the sail up river highly & was continually asking questions.

The houses of the Planters are situated near the river on high land surrounded by huge live oaks, & some of them were very handsome. I was not prepared to see such large ones & was agreeably disappointed, but one cottage greeted my eye the whole distance. At the wharf I met the Chancellor & a bevy of ladies waiting to welcome me, they expected Dr. Adams & cousin, but I was alone & for want of somebody better were obliged to honour me! We walked from the wharf several hundred yards through a rice field, on a wide bank built up for the purpose of a path, then we came to the high land & entered through a big gate on either side of which was a tree called the "Pride of India" covered with purple flowers & a cherokee rose climbing to the top of one, & a multiflora the other, both having hundreds & perhaps thousands of roses on them. Wild orange hedges as high as my neck & some six feet broad we walked between to the house, which is a two story square one, white with green blinds, a Piazza on the north and south sides. The front rooms are used for parlor & drawingroom, & any other rooms, 11 in all, are fitted up for sleeping rooms because they need so many, with all the city company they entertain. There is a large circle in front of each piazza surrounded by hedges, filled with roses, flowering vines & evergreens, each can contain as many flowers as your whole flower garden, and all the trees in the yard are evergreen. Magnolia was in blossom when we left, the first flower of the kind I ever saw, live & water oaks, orange &c, which makes the place look nearly as inviting in winter as in summer.

The avenue for the carriages, leading to the main travelled road, is a quarter of a mile long, enclosed with a white fence & a *hundred oaks on each side* all planted several years since by Mrs. Dunkin's direction. When I tell you that the W River, nearly a mile broad, flowed along one side, & the large Rice fields covered with water, looking like immense ponds lying on the other, this avenue of oaks on a third & the corn fields & negro village on the fourth, you can imagine it presented a scene entirely new to me, but you cannot think how beautiful it was.

I forgot one other feature upon this landscape, which was a labyrinth of Hedges. You enter it, near the house, & the path will lead you about in a zigzag direction, in the center is a circle with a summer house covered with flowering vines &c, then you go on & on, round & round, first coming to a hedge of wild orange then again to Arbor-vitae, then to Casina, & between them are plots in a variety of shapes, filled with flowers. Some of the hedges are so high & broad that you can just peep over them & so thick that a chicken couldnt get through, &

trimmed beautifully, looking like one mass of deep green leaves, these looked best from the chamber window & gave one a better idea of a labyrinth to look down into it. It was the first one I had ever seen & many times a day, we girls would take a run through it. I not only became interested in the ornamental, but by a series of questions became as "Sam" would say, "well booked up," with regard to the useful.

Mr. D. has a large Rice pounding mill near the river which is moved by water power & is very curious, another one equally large for threshing rice & grinding corn & another smaller place where the grain is winnowed. Some planters have steam mills for these purposes, others have none, but send it here & have it hulled at an extensive set of steam mills & pay a certain amount of toll. Rice plantations are more valuable than cotton because it cannot be cultivated to any advantage except on tide rivers, as the fields have to be so often flowed & drained, which is done by means of having the banks of the river guarded by artificial levees & flood gates which can be opened or closed at will. These levees do not injure the beauty of the river as you might suppose at first, as they are covered with bushes & running vines, trees, &c. . . .

If you will look on the map you will see that the Waccamaw River is near the ocean, & the land between the two is called Waccamaw Neck & is from two to four miles wide only & is owned & cultivated by 18 or 20 planters up as far as 24 miles from the mouth. Each place has a name & many are very pretty. Mr. D.'s is "Midway" as it is about half way up, the next is "True Blue," one "Laurel Hill," "Strawberry Hill," "Fairway" &c &c, some have Indian names which I don't recollect. There are two churches on the Neck, one two miles above "Midway" & the other four below. Mr. [Alexander] Glennie, the Episcopal minister, officiates at both alternately on Sunday mornings; p.m.'s & evenings he preaches at the chapels on each plantation. These gentlemen furnish him a summer & winter house, give him nearly all the eatables he needs for his family and pay him 1200 dollars a year! One church is a plain wooden one, but the other is brick & rough cast with cement to imitate stone & is very handsome inside & out.

Mr. G. is a very interesting man, an Englishman, educated at Oxford, came over here for his health, finished studying his profession in Carolina & was settled at Waccamaw in '35, & they have paid his expenses to Europe twice since then! He fares better than our poor minister at Buxton! He has been with them so long & is such an amiable, kind man that the negroes love him very much & his example has as much influence over them as his preaching. We all went to the negro church one P.M. & I was very much pleased as well as amused. Those who live near enough attend the other churches, but when they are at any distance, Mr. G. goes to them. . . .

The Chancellor owns another plantation on the Pedee, called "Bienvenu" (the French for welcome) & on each place he has a hundred negroes, each family have a house of their own. Their tasks are only half day ones if they are ambitious, & then they can cultivate land for themselves, raise poultry, pigs & on some places cattle, catch fish, dig oysters or whatever they please. . . . Some of the gentlemen have more & some not so many. Col. Ward, the richest man on the Neck, owns 800, & he is the most particular man, everything is done by rule; he gives them half of every Saturday to scour & at night an inspector goes around & sees that every house & the wooden & tin ware is scoured & Sunday morning they are required to go to church with a clean suit, or if they are at home they must be dressed clean, as he makes ample provision. His receipts for rice last year were $90,000 & he calculated that it would take 30,000 to carry on the plantations. These gentlemen go to Europe frequently & travel north often which makes them very interesting & their style of living comes nearer to the English gentlemen than any other in this country I presume. They have so much wealth, their houses are furnished elegantly & the quantities of plate & cut glass is not small.

I passed a week at the "Retreat," a place on the Pedee River, with Mrs. Huger, a daughter of Mrs. Dunkin & had a nice time. We rode on horse back & in the carriage, walked &c. Mrs. H. is one of the most agreeable and fascinating women I ever knew & very intelligent. She tells a story admirably & kept us laughing all the time. She plays the piano better than any lady I ever heard. She is only 26 years old and has been married 9 years, has a first rate white woman for housekeeper who has the care of everything, & Mary has nothing to do but make herself agreeable. You girls, Ellen included, would enjoy a visit with her as much as with any other person whether north or south, I'll be bound to say, for your tastes are so much alike. Her husband is as interesting as she, tho quite different. If I ever see you, I will tell you many interesting things about them & his Father, who is an old gentleman, but one of the first men here. When a young man he was 18 months in solitary confinement at Olmutz for attempting to liberate Lafayette. This name is pronounced Ugee, as they are of French descent.

You are doubtless weary over this & I would advise you to lay this long story aside and rest upon it, but as I am not & time is precious I shall continue. I have so much to tell. . . .

The Pedee is a narrower river than the Waccamaw & not as beautiful but longer, for it takes another name in North Carolina. Steamboats go up 140 miles; creeks connect these rivers & we went over from one to the other in row boats, so level is the country through which they pass, it was 8 miles, not an hour row with the tide. The only unpleasant thing about living at one of these fine plantations is that they are obliged to leave them in May & not return till the first of Nov. on account of sickness, which they would be certain to have if they remained, called country fever. Some of them own houses here & come down to pass their summers, some on the Pedee go to a settlement, in a Pine land, called Plantersville, to be nearer their places & can visit them during the day. Others on the Waccamaw have houses on the islands, near the shore. I rode over to one (Pawley's Island) which is three miles long, with a fine beach on the ocean side, some 6 or 8 houses, plenty of trees &c, separated by a creek by the main land, which we forded. Mrs. Dunkin's youngest daughter (Mrs. Alston) is to pass this summer there & Mrs. Huger at Plantersville for the first time, before they have passed them in the city with their Mother, or else gone to Virginia Springs or Mass.

In purchasing a rice plantation they only count the rice land, the high land & buildings are thrown in! This high land is not valuable for tillage as it is too sandy; but by manureing the corn fields & gardens they manage to raise enough for their own consumption. The trees are pine, oak, sycamore, cypress &c, many pretty wild flowers & vines in them, but the ticks from the sheep are so troublesome that there is little pleasure gathering them, for if these ticks get on your skin they burrow under it & poison. I took several walks in the woods but saw none. . . . The washing & cooking kitchens were out of doors in another house nearby. The cows are the meanest looking animals you ever saw, no grass grows for them, & they are kept on rice straw & grain, and four of them are not as good as one of ours. The sheep are very decent, raised for the mutton & lamb entirely, of the wool they make mattresses, which are very nice. Hogs are small, but they only raise them for the hams & keep a hundred or more, it matters not. Mules are used entirely for work, but the carriage and saddle horses will compare favorably with any other place. Both Mrs. Huger & Alston had little ponies, which we used every day. . . .

I hear Ike is thinking of being married & is in pursuit of a house,

tell him if he can't find one to suit & don't wish to take rooms at the
"Astor House," he had better take his bride out here. He can take
charge of mills at Georgetown or on the Pedee River & coin money as
fast as he pleases. Several steam mills are in operation & carried on
usually by northern men, where they saw pine & oak lumber, make
staves for the rice tierces, shingles, & other things in the midst of a
splendid growth of pine & oak. One man has just left the Pedee for the
North who has made $100,000 in a very few years by lumbering. The
Southerners are trying very hard to get up manufactories of all kinds
to be prepared for *secession* but it takes northern men to set them
going. They have a shoe factory at Georgetown, but the leather, thread,
pegs, & lasts come from the North or Tennessee!! I laugh at them well
about these things, & how I find it out puzzles them. But I take some
unsuspecting one & ask if such is not the case & he innocently "owns
up." They can make more money here at Planting or by their professions & mercantile business than the Yankees but they don't take to
manufacturing. One reason is the nigs are too slow & stupid to be good
at trades or working by steam, they prefer the jog trot movement.
Some of them make very good painters, carpenters, blacksmiths, but
they need constant looking after as they lack judgment. . . .

But I must tell you no more lest you will think I have exaggerated
already, but if you doubt my word, come & see for yourself & then
you'll say with Katy Brown that the half has not been told. . . .


Ella Gertrude Clanton Thomas

FROM THE JOURNAL OF A YOUNG PLANTATION MISTRESS

*When Ella Gertrude Clanton became engaged to J. Jefferson
Thomas, he gave her "a most beautiful ring with nine large diamonds."
She proudly confided to her diary, "As I write I can see the light flash-
ing from it."*

*This journal she had started in 1847 before she went to college in
Macon, and she continued to make entries in it till 1889—the record
of an active life for more than forty years.*

*When the following extracts from it begin, Ella was twenty-one,
Jefferson twenty-four. They had a three-year-old son, named Turner for
her father.*

*Their home, some six miles from Augusta, Georgia, she had named*

*Belmont after Portia's seat in* The Merchant of Venice. *Three wide driveways led to the white-columned house; Negro quarters were to the left of it, barns to the right. Near by were the cotton plantations of the young couples' parents. Colonel Turner C. Clanton and his wife divided their time between their plantation and the town house in Augusta. At the Thomases' plantation, called Burke, Jefferson was almost constantly busy. Some of the slaves he and Ella had received as wedding presents were quartered at Belmont—Patsy, Isabella and Tamah, for example—and the others at Burke.*

*Ella mentions Thackeray at Charleston in 1856. He had been there before—in 1853—and on this second visit met again an old flame, Sally Baxter, who in the interval had married Frank Hampton, Wade Hampton's brother. He wrote friends in England: "Hampton is a fine young fellow—like an Englishman big broad honest handsome gentlemanlike quite unlike the N. York whippersnappers. His wife is very much improved by her marriage and our mutual flame extinguished most satisfactorily." (From* Letters and Private Papers of William Makepeace Thackeray, *edited by Gordon N. Ray, Harvard University Press.)*

*In less than six years after Ella wrote in her diary about her husband's happy attendance at the parade, he would be serving as lieutenant in General Joe Wheeler's cavalry. On Sherman's devastating approach in 1864 Jefferson burned five hundred bales of his carefully stored cotton rather than let them fall into Yankee hands.*

Belmont   *January the 18th 1856*

Again a long while since writing. But the pen with which I am writing is so good a one I'll probably while away some time in recording the events which have taken place.

"Little ills make up the sum of human life." And so it is, events which apparently in themselves are of little importance, go far towards increasing our pleasure or pain. This afternoon I have paid several calls. Mrs. Harris sent over today to know whether I would accompany her this afternoon to call on Mrs. Dr. Cox and Mrs. George Riggs. Although I had not been feeling well either yesterday or today I thought I would enjoy the ride and accompanied her. We called on Mrs. Allen, Mrs. Riggs and Mrs. Cox. The two first were from home. Mrs. Hull (Cornelia Allen) is living at her father's and her husband is planting at Martin's place. By the way speaking of Mrs. Hull reminds me of a repartee given by Mrs. N. of Charleston, which little Bob Allen told to

# A SELECTION OF
# PLANTATION HOUSES
# OF THE
# ANTE-BELLUM SOUTH

*Courtesy of the Carolina Art Association. Charleston, South Carolina*

DRAYTON HALL

the ancestral home of the Draytons of South Carolina was built in 1738 on the banks of the Ashley River.

THE ANCHORAGE

built before the Revolutionary War in Beaufort, South Carolina, by William Elliott, is now owned by Mrs. S. S. Stokes.

*Library of Congress Collection*

**HOUMAS HOUSE**

near Burnside, Louisiana, once belonged to the Wade Hampton
family of South Carolina. In 1857 it was sold to John Burnside.

THE SHADOWS
near New Iberia, Louisiana, was built by David Weeks in 1830.

MELROSE

DUNLEITH
near Natchez, Mississippi, was built in 1848. It was the home of the Carpenter family for five generations.

THE HERMITAGE
near Savannah, Georgia, was built by Henry McAlpin early in the 19th Century.

GAINSWOOD

in Marengo County, Alabama, was built for the Whitfield family in the middle of the 19th Century.

PINE HILL

*Courtesy of Susan W. and Alice B. Eppes of Tallahassee, Florida*

MONTICELLO
home of President Thomas Jefferson.

THE HERMITAGE

FORT HILL

at Clemson, South Carolina, was the home of John C. Calhoun. Its name derived from the site on which it was built having once been fortified against Indian attack.

FORT HILL, an interior

*Courtesy of Mrs. E. W. Cook of Clemson, South Carolina*

BELLAMY HOUSE
near Wilmington, North Carolina, was built in 1859 by the Bellamy
family.

me. When Thackeray was visiting Charleston where he was feted a good deal, he remarked in the presence of a crowd to Mrs. N. "I understand Mrs. N. you are a fast woman."

Every one present endeavored to suppress a smile while she with her usual vivacity instantly replied, "Ah, indeed! It appears we have both been under an erroneous impression. I have always understood that Mr. Thackeray was a gentleman."

This same lady, Mrs. Harris was telling me, is indeed a fast woman, her reputation being any thing but unblemished. When a girl, her father finding that she had an intrigue with some one interrogated her as to "who it was." Having long fancied Mr. N. and notwithstanding her fascination, never been able to entrap him into marriage, she assured her father in answer to his question that "it was Mr. N." Her father invited him to an oyster supper. A Catholic Priest was in attendance—and with the father and brother armed with sword and pistol standing on either side the marriage ceremony was performed. Of course no happiness could result from such a union and they are now separated. She is however a woman of decided talents being the author of [two books, one of] which I have read. . . . I was very much pleased with *Peg Woffington* and think the more I read of his works the more I would be pleased with Reade as an author.

Sunday Jan. the 6th was the last day I wrote in my Journal. The same day Dr. Means preached at Rosney Chapel. Mr. Thomas and I expected company home to dinner. It was so cold they did not come. He left for Burke the next morning. Mrs. Carmichael and Paul (her little son) came over soon after. While they were here Sis Anne and M. came. In the afternoon Brother J. came up. Both B. and W. have left for Davidson College in N. Carolina.

Friday I went in town. It commenced *snowing* just before I started but every thing was ready and I started. I had a warm brick in the carriage and plenty of Blankets, Shawls and &c. so I was not cold although it was coming faster and faster every minute.

*Friday morning Feb. the 8, 1856*

This is a dull, gloomy morning out. It has been raining; but the clouds are breaking away and I am in hopes it will soon be clear again. Here in my pleasant sitting room is quite a contrast to the gloom without. A cheerful fire is burning while the air of perfect comfort and cleanliness conveys a sensation of pleasure in looking around. Some one has said that "Cleanliness is next to Godliness." I am sure it must be nearly so. I am constituted with a keen sense of the elegant in life and unless every thing is in order I do not enjoy the occupation in which I am engaged. . . .

*Sunday night Feb. the 17th 1856*

Today has been an extremely windy, unpleasant day, yet notwithstanding I have accomplished more traveling than usual. Mrs. Carmichael sent us word that there was to be preaching at the Rosney Chapel this afternoon so we concluded to go. There has been so little preaching there I am perfectly willing to do all I can toward assisting in having regular services. During this last week Thackeray the author of "Vanity Fair," "The Newcomes," and "The Virginians" has delivered two lectures. I should have been delighted to have been in town to have heard them had I known of it previously. . . .

I scarcely remember how I spent that week. Friday night Mr. Thomas brought me home a present of a beautiful Gold Thimble, and bought himself a set of shirt buttons at the same time. The next day I was sewing and reading in the first volume of Prismes travels (while I am writing Buddy is engaged in a regular romp in his crib. He has said his prayers and been put to bed but he does not appear inclined for sleep). Sunday we went down to Mother's and heard old Mr. Gantt preach at the Chapel down there. Heard a very good plain sermon and saw a larger congregation out there than I expected. The next day Mr. Thomas, his father and brother Jeff left for Burke. The two former were to attend the sale of Mr. Anderson's estate and meet Pa down there the next day. Pa bought three negroes. Mr. Thomas bought an old woman by the name of Petunia, for whom he gave $100 dollars. *The first servant he has ever bought.* His father bought five negroes.

Monday I was sewing and mending a little. Tuesday afternoon Mother and I went down to see Mrs. Roth. Found her busy gardening. Place very much improved. She loaned me "Marmion" a novel said to be written by Sir Walter Scott and "Smike" and "The Child Wife" both taken from Dickens works and adapted for children. She also loaned me Miss Bremer's "Impressions of America."

Thursday morning we went up to see Mrs. Bess Harris. . . . We found Mr. Thomas at Mother's when we returned and in the afternoon we came home. They have a new teacher down there—Henry Lydenham—a pretty name and he appears to be a worthy young man. He is from England and is quite young. He has two volumes called "Chambers Information for the People." It appears to be a very valuable work

containing information upon almost any subject. Mother gave me a
good many seeds and I have planted a few Peas and a little Mustard,
Lettuce and Collards.

Mr. Thomas has been quite busy for a few days past setting out trees
and fruit trees. I have planted out two Magnolia trees which I am
in hopes will live. But we have had three of the worst possible days
upon the trees. So very windy.

Last night about half past two Mr. Thomas and I were aroused by
the wind howling around the house. We were speaking of the trees
blowing down upon the house when we were startled by a cry. Mr.
Thomas jumped up, ran out and heard John cry out "Fire!" Great
Heavens! What a sound in the night—in the country—and such a
night. The wind was sweeping in perfect gusts around and about everything. We at first thought the woods were on fire but speedily discovered that twas the kitchen. John waking discovered the house was on
fire. There was water in the Bucket which he threw upon the flame.
Mr. Thomas was crying for Water, Water, and then for An axe, An
Axe—I started Isabella with the Bucket—Patsy with the Bowl in which
was some water! *Fortunately, very* fortunately, the fire was soon arrested and with a heart filled with thankfulness I returned to bed. . . .

I expect to spend tomorrow in town and the next day we think of
leaving for Screven County to visit some of Mr. Thomas' relatives.

*Friday night February the 29th 1856*

The first opportunity for writing in a long while. My visit to Screven
and then having company absorbed my time. I enjoyed my visit very
much—leaving home Sunday February the 17th. We took dinner with
mother. We left there after dinner and went on down to the S. place
where we spent the night with Brother Joe. After tea I was looking over
"Georgia Scenes" by Dr. Longstreet—a more mirth provoking work I
have seldom seen. It has been some time since I have seen a copy. The
ringing of the large Bell for the negroes failed to arouse me, and when
at last I woke I found we were destined to have an unpleasant day. It
continued damp—occasionally raining through the course of the day.
We left soon after breakfast and rode thirty-two miles during the rain.
We passed Mill House, a place owned by Mr. Jones. The latter is living
there now. There is little or no arrangement in the disposition of the
buildings—all however giving evidence of wealth. Riding, my attention
was much interested in the peculiar growth of the Pines. Forests of
them with not a particle of undergrowth, thus presenting an expanse

of Pines as far as the eye could reach with a carpet of grass which now, yellow, in the Spring is a beautiful green. We got a little out of the way causing us to arrive later at Uncle John's. Mr. Thomas shot near twenty Birds and a Squirrel going down. Game appeared in great profusion and we also saw wild Turkeys. I was much pleased with Uncle John's family. He has married twice, sisters each time. We spent Wednesday and Thursday night with them.

Friday we went over to see Mrs. Williamson. They have the most beautiful Oaks I have ever seen. They are Evergreens and are extremely large having been planted near twenty years. Their house is very handsomely furnished, and the hand of taste is seen to preside over every thing from the arrangement of an elegant dinner to the displaying of a few violets in a vase. We went to ride Friday and Saturday afternoon. Passed the house of Dr. S. who committed suicide by shooting himself with a pistol; and the house of a woman who has visited Africa. Mr. Williamson is a very fine looking pleasant old gentleman. Mrs. W. and Georgia Bryan having promised to return with us, we remained till Monday.

Sunday we went to church—heard a very fine sermon and returned to dinner at Uncle John's. In the afternoon Georgia and Sallie Brewster came over. Sallie is a niece of Mr. Williamson who he is educating.

Monday morning we left Screven having spent quite a pleasant time. I brought up with me some Cape Jassamine, one Magnolia, and some Pear trees. We had a series of misfortunes coming up. Mr. Thomas' Buggy broke—so did our carriage. Mrs. W.'s horse refused to pull and George lost four Rings at once when we stopped for dinner and never found them. I gathered some pretty specimens of Rock there. Never have seen any like them. Arrived at Mother's Monday night and Mr. Thomas and I came on up home early Tuesday morning.

After coming home I was quite busy as I expected George and his Mother up the next day. I had the house thoroughly cleaned up and we fixed and hung shades in both rooms upstairs in our bed-room and a shade at the windows upstairs. Sent Daniel in town for a box of raisins, oranges and Cake. I had figs and almonds in the house. I had a Turkey and prepared as nice a dinner as I could. In the morning Mr. Thomas' mother and Brother Joe came and George and his mother. In the afternoon the two latter returned home the rest of us went to ride. We returned—hurried back only taking a cup of Coffee we left for Augusta to hear the Campbells.

*Tuesday March the 4th 1856*

We have just finished supper and Mr. Thomas has just returned from cutting up a Hog or attending to having it done. Turner has just caused this big blot upon the page. I have been feeling very unwell all day and having finished reading "Lily" by Mrs. King, I walked over to see Mrs. Harris this afternoon. Found her at home and although I was suffering from languor and headache, I spent quite a pleasant afternoon. She gave me "Our Cousin Veronica" to read and from the glance I have had of its contents I should judge it to be interesting. I have been reading a work called "The Match Girl" loaned me together with several others by Mrs. Gardner. She was kind enough to offer any others she had. . . . I have had little time for reading of late.

Thursday of last week we spent in Augusta with Ma. She had a very elegant dinner prepared for us. . . . In the afternoon we rode up to G.'s auctions rooms and saw some Pictures which were there to be sold on Friday. Then we came out home and Sis Anne came out in the Buggy with Mr. Thomas and spent the night with us. I had some very nice oysters for supper. In the morning Mr. Thomas carried Sis Anne to town. He attended the auction and bought four Pictures. One of "The Presentation of the Magna Charter"—one of the "Canterbury Pilgrims" making a pilgrimage to the tomb of Thomas a Becket, the other the opening of the "Sixth Seal" and the fourth "The Spanish Wife's Last Appeal."

Saturday it was raining all day and I spent the day sewing. . . .

*Monday night March the 10th 1856*

Tonight is Mr. Thomas' birthnight. He is twenty-five tonight. Since supper we have been holding an animated conversation with regard to Mr. and Mrs. Harris. I was arguing that had I a husband who gambled and drank to excess, that I should spend more and have my expenses more in proportion to his own. I was perhaps wrong yet it is *just* so. As it is I endeavor to economize in some degrees and assist Mr. Thomas in disengaging himself from his embarrassments. . . . I'll stop and kiss Mr. Thomas now. He is in bed having done one of the hardest days work he has done in a long while. He has moved the front yard fence out forty feet farther today. I think it quite an improvement. Today being Monday I did a great deal of work. Gave the Parlor and sitting room a thorough cleaning up. This afternoon planted some Peas.

All the servants were busy at the fence so I laid off the ground and planted them myself. Last Wednesday I spent at home sewing. Thursday Mr. Thomas left for Burke and I for Augusta.

*Sunday March 30th 1856*

Again a long interval—during which time Aunt Polly has come to Georgia on a visit bringing the little grandson. She is looking well indeed being over seventy years. Then I believe I have made no mention of Cousin B.'s visit. He came unexpectedly and remained near two weeks. He has improved very decidedly both in manner and personal appearance. Is wearing very black whiskers and mustache which is decidedly becoming to him. He was telling me some romantic love adventures which he has been engaged in. Among them an "affaire de coeur" with L. of Oak Barony who took first honors at Macon the year after I graduated. He was engaged to her and the engagement was broken off in consequence of her hearing that insanity was hereditary in his family. Of course there is no truth in such a supposition. He is now apparently much pleased with Miss Anne, a niece of Governor Gilmore. We have heard since Cousin B. left that Jimmie Clanton has been engaged in an unlucky affair in which he has shot and severely wounded a man.

In writing this month I appear to have been in a constant bustle of excitement. I have been a good deal in town. The merchants are beginning to receive their new goods. I have bought me a very pretty Blue silk and had it made by Cousin Mary C. Poor creature. She appears to have a hard time of it. She is nursing Jim C. and sewing for a means of subsistence. He has had rheumatism for a long while and for the last fifteen months has been constantly confined to his bed. I had rather I believe work for a sick husband than an idle trifling one like Mr. B. My dress makes up very prettily. Mrs. Galt has sold within the past week one hundred Bonnets. Sis Anne bought one, a straw from Mrs. M. at eight dollars, and one from Mrs. H. at fifteen dollars. She also bought from the latter a riding hat.

Mr. Thomas has joined a Cavalry company recently gotten up in Augusta. . . . On Sunday we were at St. Johns Church. In the afternoon of that Sabbath we went up to the Masonic Hall and heard a sermon from a German Lutheran. We had quite a small congregation. We then walked on down by the Market where a wandering missionary was preaching. He was attracting quite a crowd. We walked on down by the gardens and Aunty and I walked to the Graveyard, the first time I have been there since my little boy has been there. Somehow with a selfish feeling, I shrink from visiting a place so sacred. . . . But it is now late and we have been in town all day. . . .

*Wednesday April the 2, 1856*

I am writing at a usual time for the sun is setting and I will soon require the light of a candle. Aunt Polly and George have been with me for a few days past and today Sis Anne came out and spent the day. This afternoon Mr. Thomas and I intended going down to his Mother's but I was busy and had Edmund planting out a few things for me, so I was the cause of us not going. It was carelessness on my part, and I am sorry for it as Mr. Thomas appears quite annoyed at the postponement of his trip to Burke.

Mrs. Harris sent me over a book called "Caste" to read. I have merely looked at the Title. It is a work of Julien Cumming's.

My chicks are interesting me very much this Spring. I have two hens come off and have given to one of them twenty two chickens, and the other I will put up. In the morning I will take off another hen. Then I have nine others setting. . . . One day last week Mr. Thomas and I went up and spent the day with Mrs. Floyd Thomas on the Hill. She appears to be quite a fine lady. On Saturday when the Cavalry Company was out Mr. Thomas' horse kicked Mr. Cave and hurt him. Some fierce words passed between them but it was amicably settled after a while. We have been improving our place very much recently by extending the front paling forty feet farther in front and taking down the dividing fence between the house and kitchen. Then Mr. Thomas has run a fancy fence from the corner of the house.

*Friday night April the 4th 1856*

It is half after nine and my birth night. I had forgotten it entirely till I commenced to date a letter to M. I have written her two pages and am so tired I will postpone writing till in the morning. I have just received Mr. Thomas birth night kiss. He is in bed and Turner fast asleep in his Crib.

Written on my twenty-second birth night at my home in the Country.

*Sunday night April the 6th 1856*

I have just finished reading the last chapter of St. John. I commenced reading the New Testament the first day of this year. Last year I was reading the Bible and had nearly finished when I was confined

with my little boy. During the earlier period of my sickness I was not
permitted to read. I however finished it the last night of last year. I was
reading in bed while my babe lay *dying* in the arms of Mrs. Story. God
grant that its finishing chapter may never be made under similar circumstances. I believe I have never written of my illness at that time.
The week before I had been down to see Mother. Tuesday Mr. Thomas
was in town and returned to dinner. I had invited Ma, Aunty and Sis
Anne to drive with me the next day. I intended making considerable
preparation for approaching Christmas. That afternoon I rode over to
see Mrs. Harris. I knew Mrs. Harris was not at home and I also knew
I would soon be *compelled* to remain at home. She was not at home, so
we rode up as far as Mrs. Read's. Coming home I did not feel very well.
After getting out the Carriage and coming in the house I was in some
pain. It gradually increased till I became alarmed. Sent for Dr. E. and
also to town for Ma. Still I did not expect to be confined. Great was
the surprise when my Babe was born before the Doctor arrived. Such
a time I am in hopes I will never experience again. I had sent for Mrs.
Carmichael and she came over in a great hurry—but did not arrive till
after the birth of the babe. Mr. Thomas and Tamah were all that were
with me. Neither of them knew any thing. Mr. Thomas was dreadfully
frightened. I had a great deal of kindness shown me during my sickness.

But to return after so long a discussion, to the present time. My
twenty-second birthday passed without my giving one thought to the
fact. In the morning I was engaged sewing for some time. Then
mended a pair of Gloves for Mr. Thomas while he was busily engaged
in building a fence. I was out there with him. In the afternoon I took
Patsy and walked over to Mrs. Harris. Mr. Thomas was to send Daniel
for me. During the rest of the afternoon I was sewing and reading.
Yesterday morning Mr. Thomas and I went in town. Ma made me a
present of a beautiful blue silk scarf. In the afternoon we went up to
the Dancing School. Ma gave me some Bean seed. Pa gave Turner a
half dollar and Mr. Thomas and I a Beef which we will send for in the
morning. . . .

*Thursday April the 17th 1856*
Summer is coming at last. After our long dreary and cold winter how
delightful is Spring. We appear to appreciate it more since vegetation
has been so long budding out. Today has been rather a pleasant altho'
warm day. . . . Tuesday I was in town. Went up in the Buggy with Mr.
Thomas. I bought me a very pretty blue tissue silk. I have engaged

Miss W. to sew for me next week. The day I was in town Mr. and Mrs.
Carmichael called to see us, and left an invitation for us to spend the
next evening with them. Yesterday morning Mr. Thomas went in town
and I sent in for my blue silk dress. I spent quite a pleasant evening
and like these reunions of friends. I was fortunate enough to find a
Turkey nest with four eggs in it today. One of them is laying in the
Turkey House. I now have eighty-five little chickens.

*Sunday night, April the 27th 1856*
I have been quite busy sewing. Early Monday morning Daniel
brought Mrs. Calaway up with him to sew for me. On Wednesday I
was in town. Went in with Mr. Thomas. I bought me a white Bonnet.
I gave twelve dollars for it. Thursday Ma and Sis came by in the afternoon. Brought me some four o'clocks and dahlias to plant out. Yesterday Mr. Thomas' Mother and Father came by on their way to town. . . .

*Saturday night, May the 10th 1856*
Monday I sent over to Mrs. G.'s for the pattern of a dress and sent her
over one half of a bunch of asparagus and some other vegetables. The
same morning she sent me a waiter with a coconut pie, a saucer of
Pineapples, and a saucer of Strawberries. Wednesday Mr. Thomas left
for Burke and I for town. Found Ma quite alone—Aunty and Sis were
in the country, Aunt Polly in Columbia and Pa at the plantation. Mr.
Thomas came up on Sunday to attend the parade in the afternoon. . . .

*Monday night May the 12th 1856*
Today has been passed quietly but pleasantly. Mr. Thomas made
me two lattice pieces to train cypress vines upon. He also prepared a
place for a Honeysuckle to grow and shade the back Piazza. I did not
have time to finish an account of how last week was spent. I did not return home Monday as I expected to. Pa was going to Screven County
to visit Mobley Ponds, a plantation for sale there. He wished Mr.
Thomas to accompany him so not wishing to remain at home by myself I stayed in town. . . .

*Monday night May 26, 1856*
Today I have been quite busy in finishing cutting out the Pants for
the men at the plantation. I have sent them their shirts and the children their clothes. Mr. Thomas has a fine prospect for a crop this year
which I am heartily glad of for several reasons. One of them is that if
practicable I would like very much to travel somewhere. I am very well

prepared and then too I have no infant and I can not tell whether next summer I will be so free from care. . . .

Mr. Thomas went in town this morning and I expected Alethea R. out to spend several days with me but she was not well and did not come. So as Mr. Thomas is going to Burke I have concluded to go down with him to his Mother's and spend a day or two. I have not been there in some time. Saturday Sis Anne and Alethea came down and went over to the Rowell Place and returned back here to dinner. I had a Guinea for dinner and have taken quite a fancy to them. Intend raising a good many.

Yesterday (Sunday) went down to Sunday School carrying Turner with me and Isabella to take charge of him. Mrs. Carmichael and I were the only teachers there. She heard the girls and I the boys. I was quite interested in my class. We have decided to have Sunday School, hereafter at five oclock in the afternoon which I think will be better. On the 7th of this month I attended a celebration of the Methodist Sunday School over at S. Hill. It was to have been on Tuesday but it rained so was postponed till the next day. I enjoyed the day very well. I never saw a more bountiful dinner. The order of the day appeared to be to eat. Some of the little boys spoke—all spoke well too. I returned home the following Sunday. May the 11th I commenced a class in Sunday School. On Tuesday I went in town to the May Convention. The Friday previous I went over to see Mrs. Harris. Found her from home and then went over to see Mrs. Carmichael. Found Mrs. Gray and Mrs. Elliott there. I took tea with Mrs. C. The same evening Mrs. G. and Miss I. Harris come over to see me. I was from home and they then came over to Mrs. C.'s. She showed me how the water was conducted into the house. Every thing very nicely arranged.

*Sunday night June 1st 1856*

With a very decided disinclination to write I commence from a sense of duty for I have written so seldom of late that I feel as tho' I have almost lost an account of the past few weeks. Today we have spent at home till this afternoon we attended church at Rosney Chapel to hear Mr. C. preach. He gave us an excellent practical sermon. . . . I took Mrs. G. and Miss M. Harris home. Mr. Thomas went over in his Buggy. Upon my return home this afternoon I have had a Hen to come off with 14 chickens and I gave her two others which makes 16. I have a great many little chickens now. I expect 150. More than I have ever had before. I have ten little Turkeys. Have had

23 but have lost the rest. A little Dog (Mr. Thomas brought home a few days since) killed two of them. The convention week passed quite pleasantly. Tuesday May the 13th we went in town and in the afternoon Sis Anne, cousin Mary D. and Alice rode out in her open Carriage. Mine was there but as Pa had expressed a wish that we should go we went in hers. There were a great many strangers in town. It was extremely pleasant too. No dust as usually the case and it was quite cool. Wednesday Sis Anne and I were out visiting. The evening before we called to see Mrs. K. but she was from home. We only saw Mrs. Metcaff. She carried us down into the hot house and gardens. Wednesday we called to see Mrs. K. and Margaret S. who was with her. We then called on Ada H. I had not seen her since I graduated. Among other interesting items of news connected with College acquaintances she told me that Anna M. who married Mr. F. was living quite unhappily with her husband—had left him once and then returned to him and that recently her child had burned to death. Poor Anna I was much attracted to her when in College.

While we were there Mr. Thomas came up and was introduced to her and then accompanied us to the Planters Hotel to see Miss and Mrs. C. from Athens. They were out so we left our cards. Mr. Thomas left us and we then went around to Mrs. Martins to call. A visit to Mrs. M. completed the calls for the morning. Mr. Thomas wished to take Mr. K. to ride so sent John down for his Buggy. . . . It had a good deal the appearance of rain but we went on up to the Masonic Hall to the Fair given by the ladies of the Episcopal church. . . . Took a glass of Ice Cream with Henry G. . . . Saw Ada G. and told her Good Bye. It has been five years since I saw her last. I wonder how long it will be and *what changes* will take place before I see her again. . . . The next morning Thursday I left town. The next day, Friday May the 16th Mr. Thomas went in town to attend the Parade. They have elected him second Lieutenant and he appears quite enthusiastic. When he came back it was nearly eleven o'clock. . . .


An anonymous Englishman

### "THERE IS A PLEASANT LAND"

*"I will jot down a few random recollections of my travels to one or two nooks and corners a little out of the beaten track," wrote the anon-*

*ymous author of the following account to the readers of* Blackwood's
Magazine *in 1856 about his travels in the plantation country near
Georgetown, South Carolina, and the Acadian district of Louisiana.
He offers too a wryly humorous aside on the trials and terrors of Ameri-
can travel. He is an acute observer, but the length of his sentences must
break all records.*

There is a pleasant land, not far from the sea-shore of a celebrated
Southern State, watered by the Waccamaw, Great Peedee, and Winyah, noble rivers, whose names were new to me but upon whose waters
steamers actively ply, bearing to the ocean the rich produce of their
shores. A land it is of johnny-cakes and waffles, hoe-cakes and hominy,
very agreeable to look back upon. A belt of pine-barrens, fifty miles
broad, intervenes between it and the nearest railway—a most dreary
tract to traverse, along deep sandy roads, through an interminable
forest of pines, where the only variety is that some are notched for turpentine, and some are not. Turpentine oozes everywhere; even the
trees that are not gashed seem to be weeping tears of turpentine for
their unhappy comrades, whose gaping wounds are all mortal. A little
farther north this region sinks into the Peedee and Great Dismal
Swamps, . . . over which now the cars rattle with shrill whistle, and the
trestle on which they run, high above the tops of the highest trees,
trembles beneath them; and as you look out of the window there is
nothing between your eye and the morass but the pointed summits
of the waving pines.

It is at this point that the tourists of our own country listen intently
for the bay of blood-hounds and crane eagerly from the window, expecting to see some equivalent of Dred dashing madly through the
fen, and after him the field in full cry. Or if it be at night, they look
for "the fire of the midnight camp," and, failing to discover it, call
Mrs. Stowe an impostor, pull their nightcaps over their eyes, and dream
of anything but of getting out, as I did at two o'clock on a pitch-dark
morning, at a solitary log-hut, in the midst of that dreary region, where
the cars stopped for about five seconds.

In these swamps the above-named rivers rise, and after a winding
course approach the sea, and near it fertilize a vast extent of alluvial
country, where the rice-fields extend to the distant woods, and on the
river-banks neat comfortable mansions of opulent planters are situated,
with lawns reaching down to the water, surrounded by well-tended gardens, and sheltered by noble trees; while, a little way back, a street of

negro houses, like a country village, contains their living store of the
material wealth of the proprietors. Broad grinning visages greet you
merrily as you pass through it; and if the occasion of your arrival is
that also of the master, after his absence during the summer months,
great is the commotion which is created; all the field-hands come
trooping in to welcome him; the old and decrepit hobble out of their
cabins; and the juvenile portion of the population, under charge of
a stalwart matron, are drawn up, a somewhat mutinous-looking assem-
blage of curly heads; and a shaking of hands commences, beginning
with the master, and going through all his own family, and then on to
the guest, so that by the time the latter has grasped 3co hands, whose
owners are of both sexes, of every age, and are reeking at the moment
with the effects of every description of manual labour, he is abun-
dantly satisfied with the evidences of their good-will.

That this scene necessarily takes place every autumn is one of the
greatest drawbacks to the possession of property in this part of the
country. But so it is. Every spring the owners of all these plantations
are compelled by the unhealthiness of the climate during the summer
months, to vacate their homes, leaving their rice-fields to the care of a
sickly fever-eaten European overseer, to betake themselves to the gaie-
ties of the Virginia springs, or Newport, or, crossing the Atlantic, to
swell the crowd of Continental tourists, until the first frost proclaims
the setting-in of the cool weather, and the extinction of those noxious
influences which the malaria of the lowlands of South Carolina exercise upon all but the negro. But when that deadly season is over, families come flocking back, and open the doors of the hospitable houses
which have been closed for six months past, and the traveller who has
the good fortune to enter them may thank his lucky stars, and find that
his lines have fallen in pleasant places.

If life on a slave plantation is new to him, and he arrives with the
notion popular in England upon the subject, he will find the occupation interesting of becoming practically acquainted with the workings
of what Americans call "our peculiar institution." If his host be a good
master, he will have an opportunity of seeing it in operation under its
most favourable aspect; and whatever may have been his preconceived
notions upon the matter, he will find himself driven to the conclusion,
that however indefensible, in a moral point of view, he may be made
to conduce to a degree of happiness and contentment in the slave, as
much beyond ordinary experience of the peasantry of free countries, as
is that opposite extreme of misery and distress which the same system

is no less liable to involve. It is its peculiarity, that in its operations it
embraces the most widely different results.

It is seldom, however, that the traveller has an opporunity of witnessing for himself the more flagrant abuses of slavery; the probability
being that his friend is a gentleman and a humane master, or else he
would not have made his acquaintance, and become his guest. I have
often regretted that no tyrant, or even commonly cruel master, ever
asked me to stay with him; but it is not easy to be honored by an invitation from such a quarter, because, in all likelihood, such a man and
the friends whose guest you are, are not intimate, or, perhaps, even not
on speaking terms.

To stroll, then, through the negro houses, to visit one which is set
apart as an hospital, and others which contain curious fossil specimens
of negro humanity, whose working days have been past for thirty years,
and who have all that time been pensioned and cared for by their master and his wife, upon whose heads they have just strength and sense
enough left to mumble blessings as he enters; to listen to others, not yet
so far advanced in dotage, recall reminiscences of three or four generations back of the family to which they have belonged for nearly a century; to pass on to the other extreme, and inspect the nursery, where
the juvenile community are grinning and rioting and driving their
elderly guardian to despair; to extend our walk into rice-fields, and
watch all the papas and mammas of these little urchins at work, the
former taking it uncommonly easily, and the latter perpetually giggling
over jokes known to themselves, and very ready to shake hands upon all
occasions, and afterwards to titter and blush unseen;—to go through
an experience of this sort on divers plantations, will, to say the least of
it, conduce to a certain modification of the idea which possesses most
of my countrymen, that misery is the rule, and happiness the exception,
with the negro in the Southern States of America. . . .

If we push our aquatic expedition farther than usual, we reach at
length the little port of Georgetown, to which the tradition alone remains of its former importance, when the first colonists from England
made it their seat of government. Now, it lives upon the necessities of
the neighbouring planters, and is a dull unhealthy place, containing
about two thousand inhabitants. It is, however, conveniently situated
on the Winyah for the export of the productions of the surrounding
country, about eighteen miles from the sea. Steamers ply to Charleston, which they reach in ten or twelve hours. But it is not necessary
to pass through Georgetown to reach the sea; there is a short cut from

most of the plantations through a belt of pine forest to the shore, which differ materially from what is called the beach, inasmuch as the latter consists of a bank of sand separated from the pine-fringed shore by a narrow lagoon, which must be crossed in order to reach the summer-houses of the planters, who find that this strip of water importantly affects the salubrity of the climate, and whose wooden erections are consequently placed on the sand, with the sea-spray almost beating into the front windows, and the waters of the lagoon washing their back-stairs—the whole arrangement presenting a very desert-island aspect indeed; and at this season, except for curiosity, there is no object in visiting it.

A more profitable way of spending the declining hours of the day is to explore the neighborhood, driving or riding among the surrounding plantations, or to navigate, under pleasant guidance, the numerous channels which connect the large streams, and which afford a convenient mode of intercommunication; or, for the sake of variety, to sit with a gun upon the ridge of a rice-field; and as dense flocks of wild-ducks, of numerous varieties, come winding past in long single-file, or, closing their ranks, settle in dense single-file, with noisy quack and flutter, all round you, to provide for the larder until it becomes so dark that, though you can hear them paddling and scuffling about in a most tantalizing proximity, you are compelled to relinquish your occupation with regret.

Meantime we grieve to say that we must allow no attractions of this or any other sort to induce us to prolong our stay; the time has come when we must steel our breasts against all hospitable entreaties, and once more prepare ourselves to undergo afresh the usual experience of American travel—to pass some nights to come in the state-rooms of river steamboats, and on the uncomfortable seats of crowded cars; to eat a series of dinners at gaunt hotels, at the risk of dying of indigestion; to swallow incredible quantities of boiling-hot oyster-soup at miserable stations; to be jostled in omnibuses, through large towns, from one terminus to another, and then to find that the connection has been broken, and that we are condemned to pass the six small hours of the cold morning on a platform, waiting to start; to imbibe innumerable drinks, at divers bars, of infinite variety of composition, with a miscellaneous succession of travelling companions whom we are continually fraternizing and parting with, as we each follow our respective routes; to run off the rails at one place; to be nearly burnt in a steamer loaded with cotton in another; to become reconciled at last

to all our miseries, and quite sorry that the journey is over, because we
have performed the last half of it with some really charming family,
and have laughed in company at what we groaned at alone.

All these are, I say, incidents of American travel, more or less of
which all who venture upon that species of excitement may be prepared to expect.

Charles Mackay

## GENERAL JAMES GADSDEN'S RICE PLANTATION

*Charles Mackay, former editor of the* Illustrated London News, *left
London in October of 1857 for a tour of the United States and Canada.
The fulfillment of this "long cherished desire" resulted in a book called*
Life and Liberty in America.

*In his preface Mackay said: "It is not to be expected that in a resi-
dence of less than a twelve-month in America the author can have
acquired a thorough acquaintance with the institutions of the country. He has contented himself with describing 'Life' as he saw it, and
'Liberty' as he studied it. . . . He has returned from America with a
greater respect for the people than when he first set foot upon the
soil. . . . Progress crawls in Europe, but gallops in America."*

*Mackay concluded his account with this observation: "Between
Massachusetts and South Carolina, between Vermont and Arkansas,
between Connecticut and Alabama, there exists almost as great a difference in everything, except language and the style of dress and architecture, as there does between Scotland and Portugal, England and Na-
ples, Wales and the Ionian Islands. . . ."*

*Charles Mackay reached South Carolina in the spring of 1858 and
accepted an invitation to visit General James Gadsden's rice plantation at Pimlico, some twenty-seven miles from Charleston. Born in
Charleston, May 15, 1788, the grandson of Christopher Gadsden of
Revolutionary War fame, General Gadsden, Minister to Mexico during Pierce's administration, retired to his plantation in 1856. His death,
on December 26, 1858, followed shortly after that of his wife, Susanna
Gibbes Hort.*

*Among the distinguished Tattnalls of Bonaventure was Josiah, who,
though opposed to Secession, resigned his commission in the United
States Navy to become senior flag officer, and later, commander of*

*naval defenses in Virginia waters, in the Confederate Navy. His flag-*
*ship was the ironclad* Merrimac, *renamed the* Virginia.

I had received many invitations while in the South to visit plantations of cotton, sugar, and rice, that I might see the slaves in their
homes, and watch them at their labors in the field or the swamp, and
judge for myself whether they were well or ill treated, and whether
their owners were men of the patriarchal type, like Abraham of old,
or of the type of Blunderbore in the child's story—ogres of cruelty and
oppression. I was unable to accept any of these invitations until my arrival in Charleston, when I gladly availed myself of the opportunity
afforded me by the courteous hospitality of General Gadsden to visit
his rice plantation at Pimlico. The general is known both to Europe
and America as the negotiator of the famous Gadsden Treaty with
Mexico, by means of which a portion of the large province of Sonora
was annexed to the already overgrown dominion of Brother Jonathan
[i.e., "Uncle Sam"]. His estate at Pimlico is situated about twenty-
seven miles from Charleston. The general owns on this property between two and three hundred slaves, but only resides upon it for a
small portion of the year, having possessions in Florida and other
parts of the Union, and being compelled, like all other men of European blood, to avoid, in the warm weather, the marshy regions favorable to rice cultivation.

From Charleston the railway for twenty miles runs as straight as an
arrow's flight through a forest of primeval pine. These melancholy
trees form the most conspicuous feature of the landscape in the two
Carolinas and in Georgia. Often for whole days, and for hundreds of
miles, the traveler sees no other vegetation but this rank, monotonous
forest growth. Here and there a clearing, here and there a swamp, here
and there a village, dignified with the title of a town or of a city, and
one unvarying level of rich but uncultivated land—such is the general characteristic of the "sunny South" as the traveler leaves the seaboard and penetrates inward to the great valley of the Mississippi.

In less than an hour and a half our train stopped at a station at which
there was neither clerk, nor check-taker, nor porter, nor official of any
kind. Having descended, luggage in hand, we saw our train dart away
into the long-receding vista of the forest, and awaited in solitude the
vehicle which had been ordered from Pimlico to convey us to the plantation. We being before, or the negro-driver after the appointed time,

we had to remain about a quarter of an hour at the station, and amuse ourselves as best we might. Though the station itself was deserted, a small log hut and inclosure almost immediately opposite swarmed with life. A whole troop of ragged children, with fair hair and blue eyes, played about the clearing; a donkey browsed upon the scanty undergrowth; cocks crowed upon the fence; hens cackled in the yard; and lean pigs prowled about in every direction, seeking what they might devour. The loneliness of the place, with the deep, thick pine woods all around it, and the shiny lines of rail stretching as far as the vision could penetrate in one unbroken parallel into the wilderness, suggested the inquiry as to who and what were the inhabitants of the log hut.

"The pest of the neighborhood," was the reply. "Here lives a German and his family, who keep a store for the accommodation of the negroes."

"And how a pest?"

"The negroes require no accommodation. They are supplied by their owners with every thing necessary for their health and comfort; but they resort to places like this with property which they steal from their masters, and which the men exchange, at most nefarious profit to the Jew receiver, for whisky and tobacco, and which the females barter for ribbons and tawdry finery. Wherever there is a large plantation, these German traders—if it be not a desecration of the name of trade to apply it to their business—squat in the neighborhood, build up a wooden shanty, and open a store. If a saddle, a coat, or a watch be lost, the planter may be tolerably certain that it has been bartered by his negroes at some such place as this for whisky or tobacco. The business is so profitable that, although the delinquent may be sometimes detected and imprisoned, he soon contrives to make money enough to remove with his ill-gotten gains to the Far West, where his antecedents are unknown and never inquired after."

A drive of five miles through the forest, in the course of which we had to cross a swamp two feet deep with water, brought us to Pimlico and its mansion, pleasantly embowered among trees of greater beauty and variety than we had passed on our way. Among them, the live or evergreen oak, the cypress, the cedar, and the magnolia, were the most conspicuous. The mansion, like most of the houses in the South, where trees are abundant and stone is scarce, was built of wood, and gave but little exterior promise of the comfort and elegance to be found within. Here we fared sumptuously, having our choice of drinks, from

London porter and Allsop's India ale, to Hock and Claret, and Catawba and Isabella, of Longworth's choicest growth. The food was of every variety, including fish with names unknown in Europe, but of most excellent quality, and game in an abundance with which Europe can scarcely claim equality. The greatest novelty was the small turtle called the "cooter," similar to, but smaller than the "terrapin," so well known and esteemed in Baltimore, Philadelphia, and Washington. The "cooter" is, it appears, a perquisite of the slaves. They will not themselves eat it, looking upon its flesh with loathing and aversion, but in their leisure moments they seek it in the water-courses and trenches, or at the borders of the streams, and sell it to their masters. Among other privileges which they are allowed may be here mentioned that of keeping poultry on their own account, the profits of which enable them to buy tobacco for themselves and finery for their wives.

In the morning we sallied over the plantation, under the guidance of the general, and saw the whole art and mystery of rice cultivation. At high water, the river, which gives the estate its value, is five feet above the level of the rice-ground, so that by means of sluices it is easy to flood the plantation, or any part of it, and just as easy to let off the water as soon as the growing crop has received a sufficient steeping. The rice is submitted to three several floodings before it is fit to be harvested. The first, in the early spring, is called "the sprout flow;" the second, or intermediate, when the green stalks have acquired a certain strength and height, is called "the long flow;" and the last, "the harvest flow."

Between each "flow," the slaves, male and female, are employed in gangs, under the superintendence of the overseer, in hoeing among the roots. In this occupation we found about a hundred and fifty of them in different parts of the estate. They were coarsely but comfortably clad, and wore that cheerful good-humored expression of countenance which seems to be the equivalent and the compensation granted by paternal Providence for their loss of freedom. Measured by mere physical enjoyment, and absence of care or thought of the morrow, the slave is, doubtless, as a general rule, far happier than his master. His wants are few, he is easily satisfied, and his toil is not excessive.

Rambling along the raised dikes and sluices, the strangers of the party were surprised to see the immense flocks of birds which suddenly rose from the ground or from the low bushes that fringed the stream, and which sometimes settled upon a tree in countless thousands till the branches seemed to bend beneath their weight. They were declared to be blackbirds; but a boy of about twelve years of age, the adopted son of the general, who had been out all the morning with his gun making havoc among them, having brought one for our inspection, it was found to be very different from the blackbird of Europe. It wanted the golden bill and the glowing plumage, and had, instead of them, a white bill and a breast speckled like that of the English thrush.

It was too early in the season for the alligators to make their appearance; but they swarm in the river in the months of June and July, and commit sad depredation, not only among the fish, but among the ducks and geese, or wild-fowl that frequent the stream. Alligators are said to be quite equal to the Chinese in their partiality for dogs and cats when they can get hold of them; but cats are proverbial for their dislike of water, and dogs are too knowing to treat themselves to the luxury of a bath in any stream where the alligator is found, so that the poor alligator seldom enjoys the dainty that he most loves. But the bark of a dog excites him as much as the sight of a live turtle does a London alderman; and you have but to bring a dog to the brink of a river and make him bark, when the alligators, unless they suspect mischief, will pop their long noses out of the water, and yearn for the delicacy which hard Fate has denied them.

From the rice-grounds our party proceeded to the negro village where the slaves resided. Most of the occupiers were at work in the fields; but we entered some of the tenements, and found nothing to object to on the score of comfort. To each hut was attached a plot of ground for a garden; but none of the gardens were cultivated, or gave the slightest promise of a flower. In one there was a luxuriant peach-tree in full bloom—a perfect blaze of crimson beauty—but, as a general rule, the negro has either no love of gardens, or no time to attend to their cultivation. From all I could gather here and elsewhere, and as the result of my own observation, the former and not the latter reason explains the neglect of this beautiful and innocent means of enjoyment which both climate and circumstances place within the reach of the black population.

In the village there were a hospital, an infirmary for the sick, a chapel, where twice every Sunday Divine service was performed by a missionary, allowed to have access to the slaves upon condition of not preaching freedom to them, and a nursery, where the young children, from the earliest age upward to fourteen, were taken care of during the absence of their parents in the fields. The elder boys and girls were made useful in nursing the infants; and the whole swarm, to the number of nearly seventy, were drawn up by the side of the road, and favored us with several specimens of their vocal powers. The general declared them to be "hominy-eaters" and not workers; and they certainly looked as if hominy agreed with them, for a plumper and more joyous set of children it would have been difficult to assemble together in any country under the sun. Their songs were somewhat more hearty than musical. The entertainment was concluded by the Methodist hymn, "And that will be joyful, joyful," which the vociferous singers contrived unconsciously to turn into a comic song.

We were next introduced to "Uncle Tom"—such was the name by which he had been known long before the publication of Mrs. Stowe's novel—a venerable negro who had been fifty years upon the plantation. His exact age was not known, but he was a strong hearty man when brought from the coast of Africa in the year 1808. "Tom" had been sold by some petty African king or chief at the small price of an ounce of tobacco, and had been brought over with upward of two hundred similar unfortunates by an American slaver. He was still hale and vigorous, and had within a few years married a young wife belonging to a neighboring planter. He was told by the general that I had come to take him back to Africa; an announcement which seemed to startle and distress him, for he suddenly fell on his knees before me, clasped his hands, and implored me in very imperfect English to let him stay where he was. Every one that he had known in Africa must have long since died; the ways of his own country would be strange to him, and perhaps his own countrymen would put him to death, or sell him again into slavery to some new master.

He was much relieved to find that my intentions were neither so large nor so benevolent, though malevolent would perhaps be a better word to express the idea which impressed itself upon his mind in reference to my object in visiting him. The old man was presented with a cigar by one of our party, and with a glass of whisky by the general's orders, and he courteously drank the health of every one present, both collectively and individually. Drinking to a lady, he expressed the gallant wish that she might grow more beautiful as she grew older; and to the donor of the cigar, he uttered his hope that at the last day "Gor Almighty might hide him in someplace where the devil not know where to find him."

On this plantation I have no doubt, from what I saw, that the slaves are kindly treated, and that the patriarchal relation in all its best aspects exists between the master and his poor dependents. But I do not wish to depict this one as a sample of all, but confine myself to a simple narrative of what I saw. . . .

### FROM CHARLESTON TO SAVANNAH

From Charleston to Savannah by sea is a distance of one hundred miles. Taking my passage in the tidy little boat, the *St. Mary's*, bound for the St. John's River in Florida, and touching at Savannah, I found myself in comfortable quarters. The crew consisted entirely of negro slaves; the only white men on board, the passengers excepted, being the captain and the clerk. There are two routes to Savannah by sea— one the outer, and one the inner—and the *St. Mary's* being more of a river than a sea boat, only ventures on the outer passage when the weather is calm. Such being the case on this particular day, we made a short and pleasant passage, leaving the harbor of Charleston at nine in the morning, and arriving at Savannah before seven in the evening.

It was not until we arrived at the mouth of the Savannah River, and began to steam up for eighteen miles to the city, that the scenery offered any attractions. On each side was a low, flat, fertile country, with reeds twenty feet high—the summer haunts of the alligator— growing upon the bank, and the land studded with palmetto trees, rice plantations, and negro villages. As the night darkened the blaze of a burning forest lit up the whole of the landward horizon, and gave lurid evidence that man was at work, and displacing the wilderness to make room for rice and cotton. The flocks of wild-fowl upon the Savannah positively darkened the air, and, when the birds descended to feed or rest, it seemed as if black clouds, moved by their own voli- tion, had taken refuge among the reeds and canes. . . .

But of all the scenery in and about Savannah, the Cemetery of Bonaventure is the most remarkable. There is nothing like it in Amer- ica, or perhaps in the world. Its melancholy loveliness, once seen, can never be forgotten. Dull indeed must be the imagination, and cold the fancy of any one who could wander through its weird and fairy avenues without being deeply impressed with its solemnity and appropriateness for the last resting-place of the dead. One melancholy enthusiast, a clergyman, weary of his life, disgusted with the world, with a brain weakened by long brooding over a disappointed affection, happened in an evil moment to stray into this place. He had often meditated suicide, and the insane desire took possession of his mind with more than its usual intensity as he lingered in this solemn and haunted spot. For days and nights he wandered about it and through it, and at last determined in his melancholy frenzy that to die for the satisfaction of

being buried in that place would be the supremest happiness the world
could offer. He wrote his last sad wishes upon a piece of paper, left it
upon a tomb, and leaped into the Savannah River. His body was discovered some days afterwards; but—alas for the vanity of human
wishes!—his dying request was not complied with, and it was decided
by the authorities that he should be buried in the city of Savannah.
So he died as he lived—in vain.

And why is the Cemetery of Bonaventura so eminently beautiful?
Let me try to describe it. The place was formerly the country seat
of an early settler named Tattnall, one of the founders of the colony
of Georgia. This gentleman, though he came to a forest land where
trees were considered a nuisance, admired the park-like beauty around
the great country mansions of the nobility and gentry in his native
England, and, while every one else in the colony was cutting down
trees, made himself busy in planting them. Having built himself a
house on the estate of Bonaventura, he planted an avenue or carriage-
drive leading up to its porch, and the tree he chose for the purpose
was the evergreen oak, next to the cypress and the magnolia the noblest
tree in the Southern States of America. In due time, long after the
good man's death, the trees attained a commanding height, and from
their boughs hung the long, feathery festoons of the tillandsia, or
Spanish moss, that lends such melancholy beauty to all the Southern
landscape.

In the shadow of the wild wood around this place the Tattnalls are
buried; but the mansion-house, which was of wood—as nearly all the
rural dwellings are in Georgia and the Carolinas—having taken fire one
Christmas evening, when a large party were assembled, and being
utterly destroyed, with the sole exception of the chimneys and a little
brick-work, the then owner took a dislike to the place, and never rebuilt
the dwelling. The estate was ultimately sold, and now belongs to Mr.
Wiltberger, the proprietor of the Pulaski House at Savannah, who,
finding the tombstones of the Tattnalls and others in the ground, had
a portion set aside for the purposes of a public cemetery. Never was a
place more beautifully adapted by nature for such an object. The
mournful avenue of live oak, and the equally mournful glades that
pierce on every side into the profuse and tangled wilderness, are all
hung with the funeral drapery of the tillandsia.

To those who have never seen this peculiar vegetation it may be
difficult to convey an adequate idea of its sadness and loveliness. It
looks as if the very trees, instinct with life, had veiled themselves like

mourners at a grave, or as if the fogs and vapors from the marshes had been solidified by some stroke of electricity, and hung from the trees in palpable wreaths, swinging and swaying to every motion of the winds. Many of them are so long as to trail upon the ground from a height of twenty or thirty feet, and many of the same length, drooping from the topmost branches of oak and cypress, dangle in mid air. What adds to the awe inspired by the remarkable beauty of this parasitic plant is the alleged fact that wherever it flourishes the yellow fever is from time to time a visitant. . . .

As I had determined to return to Charleston by sea, I gladly awaited at Savannah the return of the *St. Mary's* from Florida. It was not until thirty hours after her appointed time that the little steamer, with her white captain and her black crew, reappeared in the river. She had met with strong head winds at sea, and, the bad weather still continuing, the captain determined to try the inner instead of the outer passage. This arrangement was in every way to my taste, as it would afford me the opportunity of sailing through the countless and picturesque mazes of the Sea Islands. These islands extend from Charleston downward to Savannah, and as far south as the great peninsula of Florida, and are famous for the production of the fine staple so well known and esteemed in all the cotton markets of the world—from New Orleans, Mobile, and Charleston, to Liverpool, Manchester, and Glasgow—as the "Sea Island cotton." In the summer this region is not habitable by the whites, but in the early spring there is neither fog nor fever, and the climate is delicious. Though the storm raged in the outer sea, the weather was calm, sunny, and beautiful as the *St. Mary's* threaded her way for a hundred and fifty miles through the narrow channels amid these low and fertile islands, some as large as the Isle of Wight or the Isle of Man, others as small as the islets of Venice.

At times the water-way was like that of a noble river, broad as the Mississippi, but without its currents, and at others not wider than the Regent's Canal, or the New River at Islington. So narrow was it at times that we could have jumped ashore from either side of the deck. The tall rushes and reeds grew up to the height of the deck; and had it been midsummer, we might have disturbed many an alligator as we wound our way, north and south, east and west, far into the bowels of the land, and then out again toward the sea, in this intricate navigation.

From the deck we could look over a large expanse of country, studded with cotton-fields, with the white mansions of the planters, with negro villages, and with here and there a stretch of pasture land in which cattle were feeding. Amid the swamp the palmetto, sometimes singly, sometimes in clusters, raised its graceful branches, while on the higher grounds, and sometimes on the bank of the channel, were clumps of pines and evergreen oaks, all hung with the graceful but melancholy drapery of the tillandsia. At one turn we came suddenly upon a negro village, and several little "darkies," from the ages of three to ten, some entirely and others partially naked, who were upon a dungheap, set up a shout of delight on our arrival, which speedily brought forth the elders of the place, as well as the dogs, to take a look at us; the adults grinning and showing their white teeth, the dogs and the children vying with each other who should make the most noise in our honor. Many of the planters' houses which we passed were large and commodious, and surrounded by groves of oak, cedar, and magnolia, giving the place the leafy attractions of an English midsummer all through the winter.

There is throughout all this country a very considerable population engaged in the cultivation of the Sea Island cotton, and the villages as well as country mansions were numerous as we passed. Here, for four or five months in the year, the planter lives like a patriarch of the olden time, or like a petty despotic monarch, surrounded by his obedient subjects, with a white "oikonomos," or overseer, for his prime minister, who, on his part, is condemned to endure the climate the whole year, that the slaves may be kept in order, while the master himself hurries away with his family to the far North—to New York or to Newport, and very often to London and Paris—to spend the abundant revenues of his cotton crop. We passed one considerable town or city—that of Beaufort, the capital of the Sea Islands, and pleasantly as well as imposingly situated—and then, steaming through the broad channel of the Whapoo, reached Charleston after a long but by no means disagreeable passage of forty-eight hours.

Irving E. Lowery

## A MEMOIR OF SLAVERY

*The Reverend Irving E. Lowery was born in Sumter, South Carolina, in 1850. Both his parents were slaves but later his father purchased his freedom. In his childhood Irving Lowery belonged to John Frierson, a planter of Sumter County. He served as "waiting-boy" to his master. As such he lived in the plantation house, attended family prayers, drove the family carriage and was given a pony named Charlie to ride when he went for the mail and to take care of other errands.*

*After the war he attended Baker's Institute in Charleston, a school organized by the Methodist Episcopal Church to train young men for the ministry. He later attended Claflin University in South Carolina and Wesleyan Academy in Wilbraham, Massachusetts.*

But how shall I begin to describe this wonderful old plantation? As I write the scene comes fresh before my vision. I imagine I can see the old farm house, where the white folks lived, nestled in the midst of a clump of stately old water oaks. There was a front and back piazza and there was a brick chimney at each end. It was a one-story building, with an ell running back, in which was located the dining room. About thirty feet east of the building was the kitchen, and about the same distance in the rear of the dining room stood the smoke-house and the store-room. That smoke-house was never without meat and lard, and that store-room contained barrels of flour, barrels of sugar, barrels of molasses and sacks of coffee from one year to another. And the corn, oh, there was no end to that. There were several barns, some big and some little, but when the corn was gathered and the "corn-shucking" was over and the crop was housed, the barns were full to overflowing. There was very little cotton raised on that plantation. Four or five bales were considered a good crop. But the corn, peas, potatoes, hogs, cattle, sheep and goats, there was no end to these. It was a rare thing to buy anything to eat on that plantation save sugar and coffee. Shoes were bought, but the clothing for the white folks and the slaves were made at home. It was the good old "homespun." On rainy days, when it was too wet to do outdoor work, the men and boys got out corn, as they said in plantation language, for the mill, while the women and girls carded and spun cotton and wool. A task of so many hanks of yarn was given them for a day's work, which was a reasonable task, and when it was finished they carded and spun for themselves. They more or less completed their tasks before night, and by working after night they were enabled to do almost as much for themselves as they did for the white folks during the day. The weaving was almost invariably done by the young white ladies, or by some one of the servant girls who was taught especially to do it. Thus everybody on the place was kept well clothed, both the white folks and the slaves. . . .

On the east side of the white folks' house was the orchard. It occu-

pied a space of about five or six acres and contained a large number of
fruit trees of every description. On the west side was a large vegetable
garden, which contained, in addition to the supply of vegetables for the
table, several varieties of grapes. And the slaves got their portion of all
these delicious fruits.

At some distance in the rear of the white folks' house stood the barns
and other outhouses, and a little to the east of these was the large
horse and cow lot and the stables. In front was a beautiful avenue
skirted on each side with lovely oaks of different varieties. And, strange
to say, about three hundred yards in front of the white folks' house,
and to the east of this beautiful avenue, was located the "negro quarters." On most plantations the "negro quarters" was located in the
rear, or at least some distance from the white folks' house. But not so
in this case, for these were located in front, but a little distance from
the house and from the avenue. But there is another thing that goes to
show that the owners and managers of this plantation were people of
education, culture and refinement, and that was even the fields were
given names. At some distance eastward from the "big house" was a
large field called "Sykes field." In the midst of this field stood a large
and beautiful walnut tree. It was customary to plant wheat, oats or rye
in this field, and when the crop was harvested, which usually took place
in June, the field was then made a pasture. Every field of the plantation
had a good fence around it, and after the crops were taken off the
horses, cattle and sheep were turned in. It was a charming sight to see
these creatures during the early morning grazing in different parts of
the "Sykes field," and when the sun waxed hot they would gather together and lie down under this tree and rest. Still east of the "Sykes
field," and across the swamp, were two large fields called the upper and
lower "Forks." North of these was another called the "Island field."
Then there were the "New Ground field," the "Gin House field," the
"Middle field," the "Graveyard field" and the "West field." It was necessary that these fields should all have names so that it could be ascer-
tained where the hands were working, or where the horses or cows were
being pastured.

There were six horses and two mules on the place, and they, too,
had names. There was "Old Reuben," "Old Gray," "Old Lep," "Fan-
nie," "John" and "Charlie." John and Charlie were young horses
raised on the place. The mules were "Jack" and "Ginnie."

It will be noticed that the word "old" precedes the names of these
horses. This does not signify that they were naturally old, but it was

simply a designation given to them by the slaves, and the white folks accepted it and so styled the horses also. The slaves were adept at giving nicknames to animals, to each other and even to the white folks. But the white folks seldom caught on to the nicknames given to them.

To the north was Mr. Isaac Keels and his father, Mr. Billie Keels; east was Mr. Alex Lemons; south was Mr. Chris Player, and west was Mr. Fullwood and Mr. Jack Player. These were all slaveholders, but none of them were cruel to their slaves. They knew their slaves were valuable property, and, therefore, took care of them. Mr. Fullwood died, leaving a widow and a number of small children, and the estate could not be settled up until the youngest child became of age. This made it necessary to put the plantation in the hands of an overseer, and that overseer was Mr. Rance Player, a brother of Mr. Chris Player and Jack Player. He was pretty strict in his discipline, but not cruel. Such things as bloodhounds and nigger traders were scarce in that community. It was a rare thing for slaves to be bought and sold in that neighborhood. . . .

The owner of this farm was a remarkable character. His name was Mr. John Frierson. His age I do not know.

He was a Christian. I am told that he was educated for the Christian ministry in early life, but he never entered that holy calling. It was said that he was the best educated man in all that region of country. . . .

Mr. Frierson was married three times. By his first wife there was born but one child—a boy—whom he named Mack; by his second wife there were born five children: Mary Ann, Isabella, Rush, Adolphus and Janie. By his last wife there was no issue. . . .

Mr. Rush grew up to a beautiful young manhood . . . he was among the first to enter the Confederate army. His leaving the old plantation to go to the front was a sad occasion. Well do I remember the morning. The handsome young soldier in a beautiful new uniform of gray with shining buttons bade the family and servants good-bye, never to return. In less than two years he fell on one of the battlefields of Virginia. When the news of his death reached the old plantation there was mourning and weeping among the white folks and the slaves. His body was never brought home, but was buried in that far-off land along with his comrades in battle. . . .

Mr. Frierson invariably observed family worship twice a day—morning and evening. The Scriptures were read in course at each service. Singing was usually omitted except on special occasions, when perhaps there was a minister present, one who could sing. But he was never in such a hurry that he did not have time for family devotions.

It mattered not in what season of the year and how busy they might be in the farm, his prayers he would say

Mr. Frierson always looked carefully after the morals of his slaves. He did everything he could to teach them to be truthful, to be honest, and to be morally upright. He had it understood on his plantation that there should be no little bastard slaves there. When the boys and girls reached a marriageable age he advised them to marry, but marry some one on the plantation, and he would see to it that they should not be separated. But if they married some one from the adjoining plantations, they might be separated eventually by the "nigger traders," as they were called. But Mr. Frierson was never known to separate a man and his wife by sale or by trading. Nor was he ever known to separate mother and child.

There were some free colored people in the neighborhood. Some of these were free-born, but others bought their freedom. But all of them, according to the then existing laws, had to have some white man to be their guardian. And Mr. Frierson was chosen by some of these free colored people as their guardian. He was a kind-hearted man and never failed to respond to the call of distress. . . .

He was greatly beloved by all his neighbors. His children, his slaves and all his white associates loved and admired him. . . .

The number that constituted the body of slaves on this plantation was not very large, but they were a fine-looking set of human beings. They were warmly clad, well fed and humanely treated. . . . When the Emancipation Proclamation was issued by Mr. Lincoln, there were perhaps forty or fifty slaves on this plantation.

But one of the most important characters among them all was Granny, the cook. She was slightly lame in one leg. When she was a little girl she and other children were playing in a bed of deep sand. She ran and jumped into the sand, and as her feet sunk into it she suddenly turned around and this twisted her leg at the knee. The injury at first did not seem to be serious and no doctor was called, but her leg grew crooked and she became lame for life. Because of this lameness she was favored to the extent that she was not made a field hand, but was kept about the house and taught to cook. And right well did she learn her trade; for she became one of the most expert cooks in all that region of country. All they had to do was to give Granny the materials and tell her what to do with them, and it was done. She always carefully followed the instructions given by Mrs. Frierson or Miss Mary Ann, and all was right. . . .

Granny could not be excelled in making and baking bread. Her biscuits, her light bread and her johnnie cakes were "just out of sight." If you have never inhaled the odor nor tasted a johnnie cake I am sure I shall have some difficulty in making you understand what it is.

It was not baked in an oven nor in a stove, but before the fire. A board was made out of oak, hickory or ash wood. It was about six inches wide and twelve inches long, and highly polished. The ingredients of the johnnie cake were: corn meal and sweet potatoes for flour, butter for lard and pure sweet milk for water. I think eggs were also used and some other seasoning which I cannot recall. These things were carefully mixed in and then the dough was spread out over the johnnie cake board and placed on the hearth before an oak fire. The board was slightly tilted so as to throw the cake squarely before the fire. It would soon "brown," as they said, and when Granny pronounced it done, the very sight, to say nothing of the odor, would make anybody's mouth water. . . .

But Granny was great along other lines and for other things than that of cooking. When Mr. Frierson lost his first wife she left a little motherless baby behind. It was a little boy, and his name was Mack. But Granny came to the child's rescue and acted a mother's part. She raised him. She prepared his food and fed him. She bathed him, dressed him, took him on her lap, tied his shoes, combed his hair and taught him his prayers. He slept in Granny's own bed with his lily white arms around her black neck. Little Mack loved Granny and Granny loved little Mack. And when he became a man he always entertained a high regard for her, and loved her to the end.

Granny, though she was black, considered herself the mistress on that plantation. When Granny gave orders those orders had to be obeyed. White and colored respected and obeyed her. . . .

In some way or other the slaves very often connected sickness and death with voodooism or conjuration. This belief and practice of voodooism and conjuration originated in Africa, and was brought over to America when the native African was brought here and made a slave. The idea is deeply rooted in the negro thought and life. . . .

There was a girl on the Frierson plantation by the name of Mary. She was a black girl of medium size, but rather good looking. She was quite a favorite among the young men of the place and neighborhood. Several, so to speak, were cutting after her. Mary was the daughter of Aunt Peggie and Uncle Sam. But it came to pass that she took sick, and, after a lingering illness of possibly four or six months' duration, she died, leaving behind her a little infant. During the entire period of her sickness it was whispered around on the plantation, also on the adjoining plantations, that Mary had been conjured. Of course, this meant that she had been poisoned. There was a woman who lived on a plantation not far away, whose name was Epsey. This woman was said to have been Mary's rival in a love scrape, and, therefore, was accused of being the one who administered the dose. Some conjurer of the neighborhood prepared the dose for her, so it was said. This thing— Mary's sickness and death, and the talk of her being conjured—stirred the negroes on all the plantations for miles around.

But the white folks took no stock in all these rumors and gossip. They knew that Mary was sick, therefore they sent for Dr. Adolphus Higgins Frierson. He was a brother of the proprietor of the old plantation, and was a graduate of a medical college in Philadelphia, Pa. He was a learned man and a very competent physician. He was the family physician for the white folks, and also attended the slaves.

Dr. Frierson treated Mary, but the slaves did not think that he understood the case. Therefore they employed a voodoo doctor. This voodoo doctor said he understood the case perfectly well. He said Mary had been "hurt" or "conjured," and that he alone could cure her. So he treated her secretly at the same time that Dr. Frierson was treating her. But it came to pass that Mary died and her funeral was the largest ever held in all that region of the country.

Death always made a very profound impression upon the slaves. They could not understand it. Their dead was invariably buried at night or on the Sabbath, at which time the slaves from the adjoining plantations attended in large numbers. Mary's funeral took place at night.

The coffin, a rough home-made affair, was placed upon a cart, which was drawn by old Gray, and the multitude formed in a line in the rear, marching two deep. The procession was something like a quarter of a mile long. Perhaps every fifteenth person down the line carried an uplifted torch. As the procession moved slowly toward "the lonesome graveyard" down by the side of the swamp, they sung the well-known hymn of Dr. Isaac Watts:

> "When I can read my title clear
> To mansions in the skies,
> I bid farewell to every fear
> And wipe my weeping eyes."

Mary's baby was taken to the graveyard by its grandmother, and before the corpse was deposited in the earth, the baby was passed from one person to another across the coffin. The slaves believed that if this was not done it would be impossible to raise the infant. The mother's spirit would come back for her baby and take it to herself. . . .

After this performance the corpse was lowered into the grave and covered, each person throwing a handful of dirt into the grave as a last and farewell act of kindness to the dead, and while this was being done the leader announced that other hymn of Dr. Watts:

> "Hark! from the tombs a doleful sound
> My ears, attend the cry;
> Ye living men, come view the ground
> Where you must shortly lie."

A prayer was offered, the doxology sung and the benediction was pronounced. This concluded the services at the grave. . . .

I. Jenkins Mikell

## POINT SAINT PIERRE ON EDISTO ISLAND

*Edisto Island, twelve miles long and five miles wide, was settled largely by Scots and Irish who came to Carolina at the end of the seventeenth century and early in the eighteenth. They raised both rice and indigo, but the fact that the land was ill adapted to rice and a sharp decline in the market for indigo forced them to experiment with the cotton plant. The first crop, planted in 1796, was immediately successful.*

*"The inhabitants of Edisto may be justly represented as an industrious description of planters," said David Ramsey in his* History of South Carolina from Its First Settlement in 1670, to the Year 1808.

*The Mikell family has been identified with Edisto since before 1686. Isaac Jenkins Mikell was born there in 1808. After being graduated from Princeton he returned to become one of the leading cotton planters of the South. He was married four times and was the father of sixteen children. The Mikell plantation home was called Point Saint Pierre or Peter's Point.*

*The sea islands were ordered abandoned when war came between the States and the young members of the Mikell family moved to Aiken. Three sons entered the Confederate service. Townsend Mikell, betrayed by an island Negro, was captured in 1863 and imprisoned at Hilton Head. After the war the family returned to Edisto to find their house and plantation in the hands of former slaves.*

*I. Jenkins Mikell, who tells the following story, was born on Edisto in 1851. He was graduated from the University of Georgia in 1871 and later became a civil engineer and the author of a number of books and articles.*

My life, as a young boy, was—like Gaul, of Caesar's time—divided into three parts. One-third I spent in Charleston, one-third on the plantation, while the other third did not matter. The lives of my young negro playmates and guardians were closely interwoven with mine. . . . As in the higher planes of life, we had our affinities. Andrew became mine. He was the younger son of the stroke oar of the old "Nullifier." James and Primus were set apart to "mind" me (watch over me). Primus was my own, individual slave. They were older than I, and their sole duty was to be responsible for my welfare. . . .

Many a hunt we had together, as boy and man, master and slave. . . . Our talk was on a problem that was ever a serious one to the slaveholder of the South, and equally so to the slave himself—the "run away." The romance of it appealed to me. The tragedy of it to him and his race. The impression left on my child mind, as the summing up of these talks was to the effect that, in the first instance, in nearly every case, it was to escape the moral degradation which he (the slave) and his family had been forced to suffer. The cause of his absenting himself from his work by running away, could not be attributed directly to the "Master." Punishment of a legitimate kind was looked for and not resented. Nor was the trouble, to any extent, from the white "overseer"—the assistant to the owner. No! It was from their own color, from one among themselves, the hated "driver," who gave the blasting degradation which they could not escape in any other way. Even then, they could not escape the memory of it, except by leaving the place and scene of their humiliation.

These "drivers" were selected from among them, in most cases, for the moral effect—well, hardly that; say, "masterful" effect of a splendid physique, an indication of power. Their power was supposed to be limited and negligible, when, in fact, it was absolute and intolerable. He was seldom reported for abuse of that power. It was useless. His authority had to be maintained. Favoritism goverened his discipline; and to dispute his fancied rights or deny his wishes meant continued persecution in intangible ways that made complaints futile. In a word, he was the serpent in the domestic Eden of many a young family. One had to submit and appear not to see, kill the offender, or run away from the scene of one's disgrace. The latter was generally the alternative accepted. . . .

I see before me that grand old colonial house, with its twelve great rooms, with white and colored marble for its inside adornment; the spiral "flying stair;" its brown stone front steps; its double piazzas; its groves of oranges, its figs, its pomegranates, its jujubes; with its extensive grounds of ornamental shrubs and imported cedars, trimmed into fantastic shapes, done by a master hand—all enclosed with moss-covered live oaks, on a point where two rivers meet on their journey to the sea three miles away, with not a tree to obstruct the view. I must not forget the artificial fish pond, made not for beauty alone, but as a reservoir for our winter supply of fish, which occupied the time of a slave for the whole summer to keep it stocked for winter use. Oh, that pond! It was the joy of my young life! It was no play pond. It combined beauty and utility in a marked degree. It was no holiday work to build it. It required means, time, patience and unlimited command of labor. It would require a bullet fired from a high powered pistol to carry across its length. It was a parallelogram having one of its long sides bricked up, on the shore side, and a grove of immense live oaks overshadowing it. The other three sides were dykes reclaiming it from the river, planted with salt-water cedars for beautifying the walks and to protect it from erosion. The pond was of sufficient depth to maintain its briny inhabitants at all stages of the tide, and the water was renewed twice daily by the rise and fall of the tides of the ocean, three miles away. There were several Venetian bridges thrown across it and small islands covered with fancy shrubbery scattered at intervals over its area, each island about the size of a medium dwelling-room, on which diminutive Chinese "tea gardens" were built, reached only by a little skiff. There was built out from the outer side of the pond, into and over the river, a small house, on palmetto logs, connected with the shore by a bridge, from the piazzas of which one might fish in the river with hand line or pole. And in the floor was a trap door, through which, in case of rain, one might catch sheepshead in satisfying quantities. . . .

The pond was kept stocked by the entire efforts of one man during the summer. The dreamlike beauty of it passes description. In the moonlight of a late Spring evening, one might wander on its banks under the evergreen live oaks and hear our Southern mocking bird singing its song of Spring. .... One might hear the splash of the channel bass and see its phosphorescent pathway as it darted at its prey beneath the surface of the lake. One might hear the "boom"! "boom" of the drum-fish, as it signals to its mate; the sharp, angry "snap" of the trout, as it takes its prey, a shrimp, in its mouth, the clear, silvery leap and splash of the mullet, as it rises from the water in sheer ecstasy of living, and, if very still, one might get a swift glimpse of an otter as it steals along the bank in his nocturnal depredations on the finny tribe within. In the bright moonlight, one might see rise, almost directly beneath, a little black spot on the water not there a moment before. A sound, and it would vanish. It was the head of a "diamond-backed terrapin."

The two greatest enemies of the pond, measuring extremes in size, were the alligator and the little "fiddler" crab, the first, destroying numbers of fish; the latter, constantly at work, burrowing into the banks, and permitting the water of the river to seep through, thus weakening the structure of the dam.

This was our home, "Point Saint Pierre," anglicized into "Peter's Point." We do not claim any tradition in the family that it was so named because St. Peter once landed there. Its name simply came down to us. We do claim, however, that Lafayette re-embarked on his steamer from here in his Southern itinerary, 1825-6.

Can you wonder at my heart-ache as a boy, my homesickness when I had to leave it? Or the alacrity with which invitations were accepted to spend Christmas on this favored spot? Young men and maidens with their dogs and guns and saddle horses are starting for their morning's sport. Young matrons are cooing over their first-born and making them fashion plates in friendly rivalry. Our young Cuban guest, a young man attending Mr. Carroll's school in Charleston, to whom we were asked to give a taste of country life in the United States, was looking wistfully across the waters that separated him from his sugar plantation on the island south of us. I hear the mistress in her soft silken attire giving directions to old Jerry as to the number to be seated at the six o'clock Christmas dinner. And not the least, the master of it all, happy in the happiness of all around him. The day has passed in enjoyment unbroken by any untoward incident. The hallowed hour of meeting around the family altar just before retiring has arrived. We are all on our knees, following the master in his fervent prayer. Suddenly there is a howl! The voice of our Cuban guest rings out: "*Madre de Dios!* A rat has run up my trouser leg!" With a hop, skip and a jump, up the stairs he goes—three steps at a time, hollering as fast as he can utter the words: *"Madre de Dios!* I am bit! Help!" When the excitement died down—and the laughter—we see before us the innocent cause of it all—the cat! It had brought in a live rat, which, escaping, sought the Cuban gentleman's trouser leg as a refuge.

Christmas week all work was suspended. Master and slave alike rested from all labor. Among the planters, it constituted a social clearing-house, in which all obligations of a festive kind for the past year were liquidated. And one had to keep busy to get around. The annual "oyster roast" of the Honorable John Townsend to his family connections at his baronial home "Bleak Hall" was at hand. It was called "oyster roast" for want of a more comprehensive name. The "roast" was no more than the salad course, so to speak, in the entertainment. . . .

Some two weeks before Christmas, to forestall any other engagement or invitation, our grand old man, citizen, statesman and writer, quietly remarked to father at church one Sabbath: "We hope to see you and yours at Bleak Hall on the 27th to join us in our Christmas festivities—an oyster roast." Nothing more. All knew what this meant. No one ever declined an invitation there. . . .

On the day before the 27th, all arrangements possible to be made before "the" day were made. It was to be a full day's work for the host. Rustic tables and seats for twenty-five or more were put in place. Cords of oak, hickory and cedar—for the aroma—ten feet long, were brought in and placed ready for the torch. The roads and bridges on the long causeway leading to Botany Bay were smoothed off and put in order for the carriages of the guests. This "Botany Bay" was an adjunct to the plantation, an island of live oaks, palmettoes and cedar—a tropical jungle, impenetrable twenty yards from the beach, five miles long and one half wide, inhabited only by half-wild and lawless cattle (hence the name "Botany Bay"), wild hogs and marsh tackeys. Deer abounded in a wild state and the beach was unsurpassed on the Atlantic coast. The "white foot" oysters were obtained a few yards from the "Camp" and left in the salt water until the last minute so as to preserve their peculiar flavor and tang of the sea, for which they are noted. They were named after the tribe of "White-foot" Indians, a subdivision of the Edistoes, who claimed and maintained their dominion over the territory on many a hard fought battleground among themselves. . . .

The morning of the 27th broke bright and temperate. By sunrise, wagons were moving, containing everything pertaining to an elaborate feast, from the humble oven to drinking water (not, however, used to any great extent), from the ancestral silver and table napery to the aristocratic champagne glass, accompanied by a host of household and kitchen servants. With soldier-like exactness and punctuality the arrangements were carried out. At noon, the fire for the roast was started. At one o'clock when the guests arrived, the oysters were poured on the live coals by barrelfuls, and were soon ready. The oyster course had begun.

As the guests seated themselves, at each place was an individual plate mat of coarse linen to hold the wooden platters of oysters, an oyster cloth on the left, an oyster knife, with protective guards, on the right. A tumbler for each was not left off. First came the butler, with a silver pitcher of steaming hot punch, filling the glasses; hot, old-time-knock-down-drag-out whiskey punch . . . made of lemons, hot water, sugar and double-proof, imported Irish peat whisky. . . . The lighter wines were in reserve for the main course—the dinner proper. . . . The host arose and inclined his grand old classic head. Then lifting his glass he simply said: "To our kinsfolk, our guests—welcome!" Immediately a dozen little picanninnies rushed from the fire with platters filled with hot, sputtering oysters and placed one before each person, and for a time nothing was heard save the knife struggling with an obdurate oyster. The trimmings to this course were also in evidence. Not too much—they were purposely limited, dinner was only one hour off. . . .

Recess, and a stroll or ride along the beach was now in order for an hour, to revive and bring to life the drooping appetite and to allow for the great transformation scene, the change from a bare table to one elaborately clothed. No sooner had the guests retired to the beach than a rapidly driven wagon came up with the dinner from the home kitchen, packed in extemporized "fireless cookers," so that it lost none of its heat, none of its savor. Lucullus "had nothing on it" in the way of a feast. True, we did not have nightingale's tongues, but we had, to offset these, diamond-backed terrapin, which was much more sensible. And we had what I know he did not have—palmetto cabbage. Every "cabbage"—or heart, more correctly—used, means the death of the palmetto tree. It has the combined taste of cauliflower, burr artichoke and asparagus, with a most fascinating predominant taste of its own. Lucullus doubtless had an orchestra. Ours was the sighing of the wind through the moss-bearded oaks; the ceaseless chatter of the palmetto fronds, the soft booming of the surf one hundred yards away, interspersed with the frequent high staccato pop of a champagne cork. The hour had passed all too rapidly, when the vibrant sound of a hunter's horn called the guests to dinner. To some it had not been a satisfactory hour. Perhaps the "old, old question" had been asked and not answered. To others the hour had not been long enough, for appetite had not returned in its pristine vigor. But the summons came and was obeyed.

At three o'clock in the  afternoon we took our seats, at five o'clock we were still sitting—some unable to rise. But all things have an end. The sun had set. The horses in the carriages were pawing and restless to get away. Goodbyes were said and homeward we moved. Late that night, when most of the guests were slumbering, the rumble of wagons might still be heard. The "clearing up" was still going on. . . .

A unique feature of life among us was that we had no poverty. Our slaves, if from no other policy than a business proposition, were well cared for. All enjoyed an abundance of means, even amounting to riches. All were on a social equality, which made a close scrutiny of one's visiting list quite unnecessary. Most had a craving for a higher education and a pride in its possession which Princeton, Harvard or Yale alone could satisfy.

Our system of agriculture—our only business—was rather feudal in character, in some of the diversified forms of that system, and resembled the system of the old English landholder of an earlier age. The utter indifference to all business, outside of the plantation, was characteristic and seemed to be a matter of pride with some. To be obliged to attend to business implied restricted means. . . . The Factor was the factotum of our business life, our commission merchant, our banker, our book keeper, our advisor, our collector and disburser, who honored our checks and paid our bills. Many of the planters did not really always know what money they possessed. One year's accounts would overlap another's and sometimes years would pass before the accounts were balanced and settlement made. The planter did not worry, so long as he could draw what money he called for. . . .

The Island planter's occupation was both remunerative and of the lightest kind, and mostly carried on by proxy. His education was not surpassed by that of any other people of the State. It may well be asked, what was the raison d'être of his life; what was his goal, motive, object, ambition? This question he seldom asked himself. Time passed with the indisposition to extra activity characteristic of the somnolence of a semi-tropical climate. He followed the line of least resistance, and enjoyed life after his own idea. If forced to be specific, would assert that politics and the Church stood out most prominently and more

generally occupied his attention than other things. It was either one
or the other—sometimes both at one time—that was the storm center.
We had no party division. We were all of the same Southern politics.
But domestic politics, local politics, state politics, were all worked
overtime and fully occupied our time and temper. . . .

We might split on local politics, but when the honor and pride of
the community was involved we were all there.

> "We vex our own with word and tone,
> But love our own the best."

# PART III

## *Cotton!*

### TENNESSEE—ALABAMA—MISSISSIPPI—
### LOUISIANA—TEXAS—ARKANSAS

"Cotton: a king: omnipotent and omnipresent: a destiny of which
. . . the plow and the axe had been merely the tools; not plow and axe
which had effaced the wilderness, but Cotton: petty globules of motion
weightless and myriad even in the hand of a child . . . not the rifle nor
the plow which drove at last the bear and deer and panther into the
last jungle fastness of the river bottoms, but Cotton; not the soaring
cupola of the courthouse drawing people into the country, but the same
white tide sweeping them in: that tender skim covering the winter's
brown earth, burgeoning through spring and summer into September's
white surf crashing against the flanks of gin and warehouse and ringing
like bells on the marble counters of the banks. . . ."

WILLIAM FAULKNER, *Requiem for a Nun*

John Anthony Quitman

## THE PLANTERS ARE THE PROMINENT FEATURE

*Born in Rhinebeck, New York, in 1798, the son of a Lutheran pastor and educator, John Anthony Quitman was graduated from the Hart-wick Academy at Otsego where he acted also as tutor. Having decided against the ministry as a profession, Quitman went to Delaware, Ohio, to begin his study of law. He became a member of the bar there in 1821, but he had long felt drawn to the South.*

*When he settled in Natchez, Mississippi, in 1822 he found warm welcome on all sides. Taken into the law offices of William B. Griffith, he soon was admitted to practice in his adopted state. In 1824 he married Eliza Turner, daughter of Judge Edward Turner of Woodlands Plantation, and became the owner of Monmouth Plantation where he lived for the rest of his life. With his brother Albert, he bought also a sugar plantation in Louisiana.*

*Quitman was a member of the Mississippi House of Representatives in 1826-1827. He was chancellor from 1828 till he resigned in 1835 to become a member of the state Senate. During the Mexican War he was commissioned brigadier general of volunteers and served at first under General Zachary Taylor. His command was the first to enter the defeated city of Monterey, of which General Scott appointed him governor. In 1850 Quitman began his term of office as governor of Mississippi. From 1855 till his death at Monmouth in 1858 he served in the national House of Representatives.*

*Why young John Quitman became a Southerner is seen through his enthusiastic letters to his father, his brother and Colonel Platt Brush.*

*It was at the home of the widow of General F. L. Claiborne that Quitman took refuge when yellow fever ravaged Natchez. Mrs. Claiborne was a close friend of Mrs. Griffith, wife of the lawyer who welcomed Quitman to his office when he came to Natchez.*

JOHN A. QUITMAN TO HIS FATHER, THE REVEREND DR.
FREDERICK H. QUITMAN

Natchez, Jan. 16th, 1822

I write, dear father, because I know your solicitude for me. . . . I had at first much anxiety as to how I could live here for the first few months, and until some business offered. My funds were very low, living high, and I could not bear the notion of running into debt. A few days after my arrival, however, conceive my joy when Mr. Griffith proposed to me to assist him in his office for a year, and, in the mean time, he would guarantee my support, hinting, likewise, that he would put other business in my hands to bring me some income. I am now, much to my satisfaction, located in his fine, large office, with an extensive library, and can reap the same instruction from his large practice as though it were my own. In short, my situation is as advantageous as you could wish. . . . No part of the United States holds out better prospects for a young lawyer. . . .

In the city proper, and the surrounding country, there is genteel and well-regulated society. The religious classes are chiefly Presbyterians and Methodists—a few Episcopalians and Catholics. The planters are the prominent feature. They ride fine horses, are followed by well-dressed and very aristocratic servants, but affect great simplicity of costume themselves—straw hats and no neck-cloths in summer, and in winter coarse shoes and blanket overcoats. They live profusely; drink costly Port, Madeira, and sherry, after the English fashion, and are exceedingly hospitable. Cotton-planting is the most lucrative business that can be followed. Some of the planters net $50,000 from a single crop.

I spent New Year's Day at "The Forest," the residence of the late Sir William Dunbar, now owned by his son, Dr. Dunbar. The mansion, the stately oaks, the extensive park, and the vast, undulating sweep of cultivated fields, are really magnificent. On the table we had green peas, lettuce, radishes, artichokes, new potatoes, and spinach, grown in the open air, and roses, jessamines, jonquils, and pinks in profusion. What a delightful climate! The peach and plum are in full bloom, and the birds sing merrily in the honeysuckles around my bedchamber.

Natchez is a bustling place. The streets are lined with carriages, drays, and wagons. The rush to the river is incessant. Every hour we hear the roar of cannon, announcing the arrival and departure of steamers. Hundreds of arks, or flat-boats, loaded with the produce of the Western States, even from the interior of Pennsylvania, here line the landing for half a mile, often lying five tier deep!

On the 8th I was examined before the Supreme Court, and am now a licensed attorney and counselor in the State of Mississippi. . . .

## TO HIS FATHER

Natchez, August 12, 1822

. . . Intermittent and bilious fevers are common now. I have not
taken a dose of medicine; my health is perfect. If necessary, I can retreat to the country. I have made friends, and have several invitations.
Dr. Dunbar, Mrs. Gen. [F. L.] Claiborne, and Judge [Edward] Turner, have all invited me to their delightful homes, more as an inmate
of their families than as a guest. Cordial hospitality is one of the characteristics of the Southern people. Their very servants catch the feeling
of their owners, and anticipate one's wants. Your coffee in the morning before sunrise; little stews and sudorifics at night, and warm foot-
baths, if you have a cold; bouquets of fresh flowers and mint-juleps
sent to your apartment; a horse and saddle at your disposal; every thing
free and easy, and cheerful and cordial. It is really fascinating, and I
seem to be leading a charmed life compared with my pilgrimage
elsewhere. . . .

## TO COLONEL PLATT BRUSH

Soldier's Retreat, near Natchez, August 23d, 1823

Since my last letter, my dear Col. Brush, I have been a refugee from
Natchez where the yellow fever is raging. Our bar is quartered at various country-seats—not boarding; a Mississippi planter would be in-
sulted by such a proposal; but we are enjoying the hospitalities that
are offered to us on all sides. The awful pestilence in the city brings
out, in strong relief, the peculiar virtues of this people. The mansions
of the planters are thrown open to all comers and goers free of charge.
Whole families have free quarters during the epidemic, and country
wagons are sent daily to the verge of the smitten city with fowls, vegetables, etc., for gratuitous distribution to the poor.

I am now writing from one of those old mansions, and I can give
you no better notion of life at the South than by describing the routine
of a day. The owner is the widow of a Virginia gentleman of distinction, a brave officer, who died in the public service during the last war
with Great Britain. She herself is a native of this vicinity, of English
parents settled here in Spanish times. She is an intimate friend of my
first friend, Mrs. Griffith, and I have been in the habit of visiting her

house ever since I came South. The whole aim of this excellent lady seems to be to make others happy. I do not believe she ever thinks of herself. She is growing old, but her parlor is constantly thronged with the young and gay, attracted by her cheerful and never-failing kindness. There are two large families from the city staying here, and every day some ten or a dozen transient guests. Mint-juleps in the morning are sent to our rooms, and then follows a delightful breakfast in the open veranda. We hunt, ride, fish, pay morning visits, play chess, read or lounge until dinner, which is served at two P.M. in great variety, and most delicately cooked in what is here called the Creole style—very rich, and many made or mixed dishes. In two hours afterward every body—white and black—has disappeared. The whole household is asleep—the *siesta* of the Italians. The ladies retire to their apartments, and the gentlemen on sofas, settees, benches, hammocks, and often, gipsy fashion, on the grass under the spreading oaks. Here, too, in fine weather, the tea-table is always set before sunset, and then, until bed-time, we stroll, sing, play whist, or croquet. It is an indolent, yet charming life, and one quits thinking and takes to dreaming.

This excellent lady is not rich, merely independent; but by thrifty housewifery, and a good dairy and garden, she contrives to dispense the most liberal hospitality. Her slaves appear to be, in a manner, free, yet are obedient and polite, and the farm is well worked. With all her gayety of disposition and fondness for the young, she is truly pious, and in her own apartment every night she has family prayer with her slaves, one or more of them being often called on to sing and pray. When a minister visits the house, which happens very frequently, prayers night and morning are always said, and on these occasions the whole household and the guests assemble in the parlor; chairs are provided for the servants. They are married by a clergyman of their own color, and a sumptuous supper is always prepared. On public holidays they have dinners equal to an Ohio barbecue, and Christmas, for a week or ten days, is a protracted festival for the blacks. They are a happy, careless, unreflecting, good-natured race, who, left to themselves, would degenerate into drones or brutes, but, subjected to wholesome restraint and stimulus, become the best and most contented of laborers. They are strongly attached to "old massa" and "old missus," but their devotion to "young massa" and "young missus" amounts to enthusiasm. . . . In short, these "niggers," as you call them, are the happiest people I have ever seen, and some of them, in form, features, and movement, are real sultanas. So far from being fed on "salted cotton-seed," as we

used to believe in Ohio, they are oily, sleek, bountifully fed, well
clothed, well taken care of, and one hears them at all times whistling
and singing cheerily at their work. . . . Compared with the ague-smitten
and suffering settlers that you and I have seen in Ohio, or the sickly
and starved operators we read of in factories and in mines, these
Southern slaves are indeed to be envied. They are treated with great
humanity and kindness. I have only heard of one or two exceptions.
And the only drawback to their happiness is that their owners, sometimes from extravagance or other bad management, die insolvent, and
then they must be sold to the highest bidder, must leave the old homestead and the old family, and pass into the hands of strangers. I have
witnessed one of these scenes, and but one, though they occur often,
and I never saw such profound grief as the poor creatures manifested.
I am opposed, as you know, to all relief laws, but, I confess, I never
hear of the sale of old family servants without wishing that there was
some provision by which some of them, at least, might be retained as
inalienable. It is a grave question for those interested in slavery to determine whether some protection of this nature is not a necessary
adjunct of slavery itself. . . .

### TO HIS BROTHER

Greenfields, near Natchez, October 1st, 1823

I have been for a week or more at this charming abode, where Mr.
Griffith and his family are likewise guests. We shall not return to town
until December. Whole families there have been exterminated. I
have lost several warm friends. Country air seems to be the antidote for
this dreadful scourge. Outside the city—even a hundred yards beyond
the corporation—it is as healthy as any part of the world. Sick persons,
brought from the city, are received into crowded households, and
nursed without fear of contagion, and I have heard of no instance of
the fever being thus contracted.

Four weeks ago I left this county to ride the circuit of the first judi-
cial district, about 150 miles. I returned three days since, and now
enjoy, I assure you, the repose of country life. Hunting and angling
constitute our amusements. The neighborhood is wealthy and populous. We meet in the morning, hunt or fish until dinner-time, and
then turn in to the house of the nearest planter, and never fail to get a
good dinner, with the choicest wines. The planters here are famous
for their claret and Madeira. Many fine packs of hounds are kept, and
they are always at our service.

Henry A. Wise

## HONEYMOON AT THE HERMITAGE

*When Henry A. Wise of Virginia married Anna Eliza Jennings of*
*Nashville he was twenty-two years old. His father was Major John*
*Wise who served in the Virginia House of Delegates from 1791 to*
*1802. Henry was a graduate of Washington College in Pennsylvania,*
*and had studied law under Judge Henry St. George Tucker in Win-*
*chester, Virginia. In less than five months after Henry and Anna Eliza*
*had spent their honeymoon at the Hermitage, their host, Andrew Jack-*
*son, would be inaugurated President of the United States, and their*
*hostess, Rachel Donelson Jackson, would be at rest in her garden grave.*

*After practicing law in Nashville for two years, Mr. Wise returned*
*to his plantation in Accomac County, Virginia. He served in Congress*
*from 1833 to 1844; as minister to Brazil in 1844; as governor of Vir-*
*ginia from 1856 to 1860; and as a major general in the Confederate*
*Army.*

*Three years after the death of his first wife in 1837 he married Sarah*
*Sergeant of Philadelphia. John S. Wise, whom we have already met,*
*was his son by this second marriage. Sarah died in 1852. The governor's*
*third wife was Mary Elizabeth Lyons of Richmond.*

*A full account of Major "Black Horse Harry" Lee, whose portrait is*
*painted in such lively colors by Mr. Wise, may be found in the first*
*volume of R. E. Lee: A Biography, by Dr. Douglas Southall Freeman.*
*While Lee resided at the Hermitage he arranged General Jackson's*
*military papers. For this service and for several polemics he wrote on*
*behalf of "Old Hickory," Jackson, when he became President, ap-*
*pointed him United States consul to Morocco. But he had barely*
*reached his post before an unsavory love affair became a public scan-*
*dal. He resigned and went into self-imposed exile in Paris. Because of*
*unpleasant references to his father, "Light Horse Harry," in Ran-*
*dolph's edition of Jefferson's correspondence, "Black Horse Harry"*
*wrote in exile a terrific indictment of Jefferson in 1832. He died in 1837.*

In the month of August, 1828, with a law license in hand, we left
our native Eastern Shore of Virginia for Baltimore, on our way to
Nashville to be married and settled for life. . . .

In a month or more we were at Nashville, and married the daughter of the Reverend Dr. O. Jennings, the Presbyterian pastor of Andrew Jackson, who honored him with tender reverence and respect. The general tendered his daughter the hospitalities of the Hermitage, and ordered our attendance there, the day after the wedding, to make his house the home of our honey-moon. The marriage was on the 8th of October, and our whole wedding-party was punctually at the Hermitage on the day appointed. We desired to study General Jackson in his slipshod ways at home.

The weather had been wet, and the roads were exceedingly bad in that soil of unbroken limestone. The bridesmaids and groomsmen were on horseback, and the bride and groom rode in a gig which had been driven all the way from Baltimore, in a travel full of incidents, but without a serious accident. Escape from all disasters in a travel of eight hundred and fifty miles had made us too confident for a drive of only twelve miles, the distance to the Hermitage from Nashville. On the way we noticed a narrow defile of rock and mud-holes on one side, and stumps on the Murfreesborough road on the other side of the track, which required a nice eye, good light, a steady rein, and a strong horse, quick to obey every touch of the rein.

We arrived at the Hermitage to dinner, and were shown to a bridal chamber magnificently furnished with articles which were the rich and costly presents of the city of New Orleans to its noble defender.

Had we not seen General Jackson before, we would have taken him for a visitor, not the host of the mansion. He greeted us cordially, and bade us feel at home, but gave us distinctly to understand that he took no trouble to look after any but his lady guests; as for the gentlemen, there were the parlor, the dining-room, the library, the sideboard and its refreshments; there were the servants, and, if anything was wanting, all that was necessary was to ring. He was as good as his word. He did not sit at the head of his table, but mingled with his guests, and always preferred a seat between two ladies, obviously seeking a chair between different ones at various times.

He was very easy and graceful in his attentions; free, and often playful, but always dignified and earnest, in his conversation. He was quick to perceive every point of word or manner, was gracious in approval, but did not hesitate to dissent with courtesy when he differed. He obviously had a hidden vein of humor, loved aphorism, and could politely convey a sense of smart travesty. If put upon his mettle, he was very positive, but gravely respectful. He conversed freely, and seemed to be absorbed in attention to what the ladies were saying; but if a word of note was uttered at any distance from him audibly, he caught it by a quick and pertinent comment, without losing or leaving the subject about which he was talking to another person—such was his ease of sociability, without levity or lightness of activity, and without being oracular or heavy in his remarks. He had great power of attention and concentration, without being prying, curt, or brusque. Strong good sense and warm kindness of manner put every word of his pleasantly and pointedly in its right place. He conversed wonderfully well, but at times pronounced incorrectly and misused words; and it was remarkable, too, that when he did so it was with emphasis on the error of speech, and he would give it a marked prominence in diction.

The Hermitage house was a solid, plain, substantial, commodious country mansion, built of brick, and two stories high. The front was south. You entered through a porch, a spacious hall, in which the stairs ascended, airy and well lighted. It contained four rooms on the lower floor, each entering the passage and each on either side opening into the one adjoining. The northwest room was the dining-room, the southeast and southwest rooms were sitting-rooms, and the northeast room had a door entering into the garden. The house was full of guests. There were visitors from all parts of the United States, numbering from twenty to fifty a day, constantly coming and going, all made welcome, and all well attended to.

The cost of the coming Presidency was even then very great and burdensome; but the general showed no signs of impatience, and was alive and active in his attention to all comers and goers. He affected no style, and put on no airs of greatness, but was plainly and simply, though impulsively, polite to all. Besides his own family he had his wife's relatives, Mr. Stokely and Andrew J. Donelson, around him every day, and his adopted son, Andrew Jackson, relieved him of all the minuter attentions to guests.

Henry Lee, of Virginia, was, we may say, resident for the time with him, as he was engaged in writing for his election some of the finest campaign papers ever penned in this country.

He was not handsome as his half-brother, General Robert E. Lee, but rather ugly in face,—a mouth without a line of the bow of Diana about it, and nose not clean and classic, but rather meaty and, if we may make a word, "bloody-beety;" but he was one of the most attractive men in conversation we ever listened to. He, Harry Lee, who was so severe upon Mr. Jefferson and his writings because of his "Arcana" about his father, Light-Horse Harry Lee of the Revolution, was then, in fact, the entertaining host of the Hermitage, and attracted the crowd of visitors around his glowing words of commentary on the election.

The first or second evening of our stay, Mr. Lee had drawn around him his usual crowd of listeners; but we were the more special guests of Mrs. Jackson. She was a descendant of Colonel Stokely, of our native county, Accomack, Virginia, and we had often seen his old mansion, an old Hanoverian hip-roofed house, standing on the seaside, not far above Metompkin; and she had often heard her mother talk of old Assawaman Church, not very far above Colonel Stokely's house. Thus she was not only a good Presbyterian, whose pastor's daughter was the bride, and she a Presbyterian too, but the groom was from the county of her ancestors, in Virginia, and could tell her something about traditions she had heard of the family from which she sprung. With pious devotion to her mother's family, she desired to have a talk with us particularly, and formed a cosy group of quiet chat in the northeast corner room leading to the garden. The room had a north window, diagonal from the door leading to the garden. At this door her group was formed, fronting, in a semicircle, this north window of the room, the garden door on our right. . . . Mrs. Jackson was for an hour or two questioning us about her people and their place in Accomack. . . .

After several days of delightful delay, we moved to leave the Hermitage, but day after day were detained by the entreaty of General Jackson and his lady. At last we were resolved positively to start; still, we were not allowed to leave until after dinner, and the hour for dining was as late as 4 P.M. We apprehended anxiously the danger of the defile of stumps and mud-holes on the Murfreesborough road, on the way back to Nashville. The road was not paved, and it would certainly be dark when we arrived at the point of danger. We urged this necessity for early departure but in vain. After dinner the general insisted it was too late, but ordered the horses, and whilst awaiting their being brought to the door, he took his pipe, sat on the sill of the front door, and with a group in the porch around him, consisting of several of the family and guests, repeatedly warned us that it would be dark before we could travel half the way, that the road was unsafe, and that we would certainly meet with disaster. This led to tales by one and another of the group of "hairbreadth 'scapes." In every instance narrated of disaster we noticed that he pointedly and oracularly said, "Ah! young man, you did not trust in Providence." This was repeatedly said, adding, "Never encounter danger if you can avoid it: if inevitable, meet it more than half-way; but whether to avoid or encounter it, trust altogether in Providence." We were struck by his repeated remarks of this sort. . . .

The gig came to the door. He rose to wait on the bride; and in handing her up the step, he said to her, "I have tried my best to protect you, madam, but your chosen one seems too self-reliant to heed your safety or my admonitions; I fear he don't trust in Providence, and will meet with disaster on the way. I shall be anxious until I meet you at church, safe in Nashville, Sabbath next. Trust in Providence, and you will not be hurt; and you have a goodly escort to help you in time of need. May Providence protect you!—it seems your husband thinks he can protect himself."

We drove off, and hurried on faster than the saddle-horses traveled, in order to reach the "stumps and holes" before dark; but darkness overtook us; and, on approaching the place, the road was scrutinized; we drove slowly and steadily, but vision was perfectly deceived. The wagon-wheels, daubed with the mortar of stiff clay, had to pass so close to an inclined stump that the dripping mud had fallen on the stump and colored it precisely like the bed of the road and the offal on the stump on the opposite side of the road looked black, and was taken for the stump itself; and this led the left wheel directly up and over it, overturning the gig to the right in the mortar of clay in the road.

The horse was a generous lion of draught, and, though spirited, perfectly broken. The right shaft was broken, and the fragments pricked his right hind leg and made him restive; but we remained perfectly still, steadily grasping the reins until the bride could creep out into the road, and then, gradually relaxing the rein, we too crawled into the mud. The breeching and traces were immediately undone and slipped out, and we found a dry spot of leaves on the roadside to stand on. So far was the bride from being put out or frightened, that she joined in the proposition to tie the horse in the woods and hide ourselves behind a large tree until the cavalcade escort should come up.

In a short time they arrived at the spot, and, finding the gig upset and broken in the road, and no sign of the horse, or harness, or ourselves, they set up a wail of agony most distressing. We could conceal ourselves no longer, but ran out and relieved the party. Fortunately a four-horse wagon soon drove up, and the driver having an axe and other tools with which to cut a pole and straps to lash on the broken shaft, it was repaired, and we reached Nashville safe, but very muddy, in the wedding fine clothes.

The next Sabbath General Jackson and his lady came into Mr. John
C. McLemore's, and, calling at the house of Dr. Jennings, at once inquired for our safety; when told of our "escape" from hurt, again he
repeated, "Ah, young man, you did not trust in Providence! You would
not be advised to avoid danger when you could. But for your trusting
wife, it would have been worse for both."

We then began to perceive what he meant by trusting in Providence. It was no inactive belief, no blind faith; but it was to do what
was prudent, careful, and obviously most safe, and leave the "whole
care" of the result to God.

## Dick Hardaway Eggleston

### FROM A COTTON PLANTER'S JOURNAL

*Dick Eggleston was a cotton planter who lived at Learmont Plan-
tation near Woodville, Mississippi, with his wife, Elizabeth Gildart
Eggleston, and their children, James, Margery, Lucy and Mahala.
During the year 1830 he kept a diary from which the following entries
have been taken.*

*Both he and his wife Betsy had many relatives and friends in the
neighborhood and their activities play an important part in the diary.
Betsy's mother, Sophia Gildart, lived at near-by Ashley Plantation.*

*However, all social activities are mere background for the all-im-
portant business of the plantation—the planting, picking, ginning and,
finally, the sale of the cotton. Dick Eggleston must have been pleased
with his 1830 crop. Certainly Nature was in his favor, for he frequently
notes, "The weather is very fine indeed for picking cotton."*

Learmont Plantation
Friday January 1st 1830

My negroes clearing new-ground, sawing, splitting up rails; spinning
&c. Mr. Caleb Hall & Richard C. Archer here. The weather is pretty
good. I was over at Timothy Chambers & dined with Judge Randolph.

Saturday January 2nd

My negroes employed very much as on yesterday. Mr. Elam of Ches-
terfield County, Virginia, old Mrs. Sally Randolph & her two grand-

daughters, Julia & Cornelia Randolph, Judge Peter Randolph, Mr. Phineas Gardiner & Mr. John W. Gildart dine with us.

### Sunday 3rd of January

We went to Woodville today, and heard a sermon in the Episcopal Church from Mr. Richmond, originally of the City of New York, but latterly of Pittsburg. We then dined at John W. Gildart's Esqr. & home in the evening.

### Monday 4th January

Miss Mary Brown came over here today from home, the weather is very fine though cool. My negroes are mauling of rails, hauling them, & making up the cane in the field, gleaning of cotton picking, sawing for garden rails, spinning &c. &c. A Pedler was here at dinner, also Richard C. Archer and Mr. Samuel Wilder. We expended with the pedler, or rather I bought of him in the amount of $18.50. . . .

### Tuesday January 5th

My negroes getting of rails, mauling rails, hauling rails to make up the lane by the gin-house—sawing for the garden—picking a little gleaning of cotton &c. Betsy, Miss Mary Brown & myself went to Woodville. R$^t$ Rev$^d$ Bishop Brownell of Connecticut preached.

### Wednesday 6th of January

[Bishop Brownell] also ordained to Priesthood Mr. Porter—consecrated the Episcopal Church, & administered the confirmation in *Christening to such as desired it.* Miss Mary Brown is here; also Richard C. Archer. My negroes at work pretty much as on yesterday.

### Thursday 7th of January

Ploughing. On yesterday I dined at Mr. Moses Liddell's, having gone to Woodville and expended with Dunn for two ploughs $10, & for sundries with Col. Oswald $2.25. Mrs. Sophia Gildart came here on yesterday & returned home this evening. We dined at G.W.G. on Tuesday.

### Friday 8th January

James Brown came here to dinner—also Miss Mary Sims, & Caroline Hamilton. Miss Mary Brown is here. We went up to the Ball at Woodville at Buckner's & Canfield's Tavern—rain last night—$4 Cash for the Ball.

Saturday 9th

We returned here in the night, last night from Woodville. Judge Prosser & his son Hylton called here yesterday. James Brown, Miss Mary Brown, Misses Mary Sims & Caroline Hamilton still here. Some rain today & quite cool.

Sunday 10th

Mr. Brown & his sister Mary went home, so did Misses Hamilton & Sims, Richard C. Archer is still here. Betsy & myself remained all day at home. Rain today.

Monday 11th

On Thursday last I started two ploughs to break up the ground I had in corn last year; my negroes clearing land, sawing, about the garden, spinning—ploughing &c. . . . In the afternoon I rode down to Judge Randolph's & then home. The weather is very cool. Richard C. Archer got here in the evening.

Tuesday 12th of January

I went to Woodville today & dined with Dr. Read. . . . Very fine weather. My negroes sawing, cutting down cornstalks, ploughing, ginning the last of my cotton, clearing land &c.

Wednesday 13th

My negroes are employed pretty much as on yesterday. A little rain today, the weather continues cool. John Irdell went down on yesterday, with our carriage to Jackson, La. with Mrs. Abram Scott, & some young Ladies to school.

Thursday 14th

We had rain today, though not enough to stop me from running one plough. *Saw* on yesterday & today ginning. . . .

Friday 15th

. . . Betsy & myself went to Ashly to dinner. I called at Gov<sup>r</sup> [George] Poindexter's. Tolerably good weather. No one is here.

Saturday 16th

I went to see Mr. Caleb Hall last evening, but came back to Ashly. For Flour $5, Irish potatoes $2, from Bayou Sarah by Mr. Deloach.

I gave Mahala 12 cts. & Betsy $1.50. It rained very hard; we returned
home from Ashly in the evening.

### Sunday 17th

Poor Betsy has suffered very much for the last three or four days with
a violent pain in her jaw & head. Judge Randolph & Fielding Davis
was here in the morning, Mrs. Randolph & Misses Julia & Cornelia
called in the evening.

### Monday 18th

Jesse is ploughing; about garden pails—clearing new ground, beating
down cotton stalks; I send 14 Bales of cotton to Bayou Sarah by Daniel Tom. . . . I was down at Judge Randolph's to supper & then home
in the evening. . . .

### Tuesday 19th of January

I went to Woodville & paid in Bank $200 for H. N. Gildart's Estate—
also paid Chisholm & Vase $26.75, for grog 18¾ cts. Hylton Prosser
(the Young Judge) called here. Cool & fine weather. Mr. Seagers came
home with me from Woodville. My negroes employed as on yesterday.
Sam carried down 5 bales of cotton. . . .

### Wednesday 20th

Before daybreak Mr. Seagers & myself set off, I for Bayou Sarah &
thence to New Orleans in the Steam Boat *Columbia*. . . . I got to Bayou
Sarah by 9 o'clock A.M. but the *Columbia* did not leave there until
dark; some rain in the afternoon. My negroes working at home.

### Thursday 21st

We arrived in New Orleans about 9 o'clock P.M. Judge Randolph,
Judge Magee, Thos. Smith Sen$^{tr}$, Walter Stewart, & Woodard of this
County went down in the *Columbia* with me. Pretty fair & cool
weather. Col. Frances of Powhatan County, Va. got on board the Boat
at Donaldssonville, La.

### Friday 22nd

I was very busy in New Orleans, paid Ogilvie & Co. $139 for groceries
of last year, T. W. Oakley & Co. $30.50 & for dry goods Rogers Slocumb
& Co. $4.12½ for hardware in 1829. Paid Bonner & Baker $41.50 for
clothes, $6 for a coat, $5.50 for a bonnet, & $9 for a cloak for Betsy.
L. C. Archer here.

Saturday 23rd
I staid last night with my friend Wm. R. Falconer of New Orleans. I
was at the play last night of *Virginia*   $2 for myself & Falconer. I ex-
pended in cash at Bayou Sarah & New Orleans in all $370.75; I paid Mr.
Mumford the clerk of the Steam Boat *Columbia* $31.63. Very good
weather.

Sunday 24th
I spent the night with Mr. Lemuet Pitcher, very fine weather though
cool. My accts on credit were with T. W. Oakley & Co. $109.72, with
James Ogilvie & Co. $72.74, with Wm. R. Falconer $33.25, with
Palmer Smith $17.50.

Monday 25th
The Steam Boat *Columbia* set off from New Orleans at 10 o'clock A.M.
on yesterday. The weather was cool & dry. We got to Bayou Sarah at
9 o'clock P.M. Hugh Connell & Judge Randolph with myself took an
oyster supper with Michael Woods. My last Bales of cotton—14 in
number—were carried down today. . . .

Learmont 1830 Tuesday January 26th
Hugh Connell & myself left Bayou Sarah about 11 o'clock A.M. having
breakfasted on board the Steam Boat *Columbia*. I got home about
sunset & found Mrs. Amy Randolph & Mrs. Sophia Gildart with my
wife,—all are well. My negroes about the Garden Pails—clearing up
the land—ploughing in last year's corn ground, though for cotton this
year.

Wednesday 27th
I went over to Captain Adam Hope's & bought two mules for $75 each,
making $150. Captain Hope & Wesley Chambers came home with me
to dine on oysters, we found here Mr. Cato C. West & wife, Mrs. Wes-
ley Chambers, also Mrs. Amy Randolph & Mrs. Sophia Gildart. Quite
cool—negroes working as on yesterday.

Thursday 28th
I was breaking up my orchard on yesterday to sow oats in it. Mrs.
Gildart & Mrs. Randolph went to Ashley, so did my wife. I dined at
Judge Randolph's & in the evening called at Gov. Poindexter's and
then to Ashly myself.

Friday 29th

I was at Mrs. Gildart's; then at Francis Gildart's, & dined at Judge
Prosser's. Betsy went through Woodville, dined with John Gildart's
wife & then home—she spent in Woodville $2.12½. Miss Mary Brown
went with Betsy to Ashly & returned with her; also Mrs. M. F. Gildart
& child. . . .

Saturday 30th

Today we went up to Gov. Poindexter's & returned here to dinner.
My negroes working as usual. Mr. Reuben P. Cattlete dined here, so
did Mrs. Susan Gildart, & Mrs. Brown & his sister.

Sunday 31st

Last evening Mr. Seagars came here & Richard C. Archer, Mr. Caleb
Hall, Mr. Seagars, Richard Archer, Mrs. Mary F. Gildart & child, Mrs.
Susan Gildart & Isaac, Miss H. Baillie dined here. Delightful weather.
For oats $3.

Learmont Plantation
Friday July 16th 1830

R. S. Gildart, Thos. Baillie and George Poindexter dined here. After
supper my wife & self accompanied Mr. G. L. Poindexter & Miss Henrietta Baillie to Woodville & they were married by Mr. Daniel Bass,
Justice of the Peace; & came back here. . . . Pulling fodder &c. No rain.

Saturday July 17th

A little shower of rain here, & a good deal of wind, my fine peach tree
in the garden was broken down. My negroes are pulling down fodder. . . .

Sunday 18th

No rain. We all went to Woodville to preaching & dined with Mr. J.
W. Gildart. We returned home in the evening. Mrs. G. L. Poindexter
& himself are here.

Monday 19th

No rain here yet of any consequence. My negroes are pulling fodder.
Mrs. Henrietta Poindexter & George L. Poindexter are here. . . .

Wednesday 21st

My negroes were mostly engaged today in making preparation for my intended frolic on tomorrow, such as making an arbour &c. Mrs. Eliz. Randolph, & Miss Julia here, so are Mrs. Susan Gildart, & Mrs. J. W. Gildart, Miss Mary Brown, Poindexter & his wife.

Thursday 22nd

My wife & self gave a dinner today with a party in the evening to the late married couple or rather more expressly to Henrietta, she having lived with us. We had about one hundred persons here. Some rain this evening about 4 o'clock.

Learmont Plantation
Wednesday Sept. 1st 1830

My negroes picked 2354 lbs cotton East of the House & in the cornfield. My wife is very sick. Old Mrs. Gildart dined here; so did Barr Hall, Judge Prosser, Fielding & Mrs. Elizabeth Randolph called twice; Mr. H. M. Orr, Mrs. Liddell; Mrs. Poindexter also called. Mr. Fleshman took supper here; so did Dr. Read & he spent the night. The weather is warm.

Thursday September 2nd

My hands only picked 1500 lbs seed cotton 1006 West of the House & 494 lbs East of House. We had a prodigiously hard rain with much wind & some hail. Mrs. Prosser got here to supper. Mrs. Eliz. Randolph & Miss Lucinda took tea here. Mr. & Mrs. Poindexter are here.

Friday September 3rd

Being a rainy & bad day I was at Mr. Collier's. My negroes did not pick cotton but worked in the young pease, in late Oat-patch & gathered corn 3 loads in all. My wife is still very sick. Dr. Read came here last night & staid till tomorrow morning. Mrs. Poindexter is here. James is sick.

Saturday September 4th

My negroes picked only 762 lbs of seed cotton, West of the House. Mrs. Mary & Mrs. Sophia Gildart came here on yesterday. Robt. Gildart was here on yesterday. Margery got sick today. James continues sick. My wife is ill.

Sunday September 5th

Mrs. Mary Gildart & her child left us today. Mrs. Sophia & Mrs. Susan Gildart with her husband dined here, as also Mrs. G. L. Poindexter & her husband.

Monday 6th

My negroes picked 1235 lbs of cotton West of the House. Mr. Ben Collier was here, I gave him $1 for Beef in Donegal. Mrs. Sophia Gildart & Mrs. Prosser left here. Dr. Read dined here. Mrs. Randolph, Miss Julia & Mrs. Charlotte Chambers supped here. Mrs. C. E. West & Mrs. W. Haile called & Mr. & Mrs. Poindexter are here.

Tuesday 7th

My negroes picked 1430 lbs of seed cotton West of the House. My wife & self rode out this morning, she is still very unwell. James and Margery are still sick. . . .

Wednesday 8th

My negroes picked 1575 lbs of seed cotton West of the House. . . . Took tea at Gov<sup>r</sup> Poindexter's. Mrs. Read dined here. Mrs. Randolph & Miss Julia were here in the evening. Mr. G. L. Poindexter returned & his wife is here. Mr. Richmond took supper here. Very good weather, though it rained today.

Thursday 9th

My negroes picked 1325 lbs seed cotton West of the House. . . . No rain today. My wife is still very unwell. James & Margery are yet sick.

Friday 10th

My hands picked 1945 lbs. of cotton today; viz. 1735 East & 210 West of the House. Mrs. Henrietta Poindexter & her husband left here to go to live in Woodville. . . . Betsy breakfasted in Woodville & then went to her Mother's. Very pretty weather indeed. . . .

Saturday 11th

My negroes picked 1495 lbs. East, & 175 West of the House, in all 1670 lbs. seed cotton. . . . Very pleasant weather. James & Margery are still sick.

Sunday 12th

. . . Betsy & the children returned home. Margery & James are still sick. . . .

Monday 13th

My negroes picked 2085 lbs. of seed cotton East of the House. . . .
Betsy & myself with the children rode over to Judge Randolph's and
took tea there before we returned home. The weather is very fine &
clear.

Tuesday 14th

My negroes picked 1725 lbs. of seed cotton East of the House. Sam,
Watt, & Willis are at the Gin; old Herod & Lucinda are at the cotton
scaffolds. . . . The weather is good. James & Margery still sick.

Wednesday 15th

My negroes picked 1595 lbs. of Cotton East of the House, mostly in
the new ground. . . . My whole white family including myself are
unwell. Dry, pleasant, weather.

Thurs. September 16th

My negroes picked 1840 lbs. of cotton East of the House, stay in South
new ground till dinner time, & in the afternoon, in North new ground.
John Hampden Randolph was here in the morning, & in the evening
Mrs. Frances Poindexter called. Betsy went with her to Judge Randolph's. They returned here to supper. James is yet sick. The weather
is good.

Friday 17th

My negroes picked in North new ground 1220 lbs. & in the cotton in
corn Field 845 lbs. in all 2065 lbs. East of the House, today. Betsy
rode up to Woodville to buy Mahala a Doll   cost $0.75, snuff 6¼ cts.
for having a tooth drawn. I rode up to Gov^r Poindexter's & then we
went to Judge Randolph's where we took supper. Fine weather for
picking cotton.

Sat. 18th

My negroes picked 1890 lbs of seed cotton East of the House, or rather
in Corn Field Ground. . . . Betsy went to Sligo to see Captain Sims,
the children went with her—Lucy is a little sick today, so are James &
Margery. Very cool, windy & dry weather. . . .

Sunday 19th

Messrs. Ben Ferguson, Thos Pearce, Joseph Wright, Adam Hope &
Pleasant Robertson breakfasted here, the same dined here with the

addition of Messrs. Caleb Hall, R. S. Gildart, and Walthall Burton.
. . . On the evening Betsy & myself rode up to Gov$^r$ Poindexter's. Very
cold last night & cool, pleasant & dry today. . . .

Monday 20th

My negroes picked 1875 lbs West of the House, & 325 lbs East of
the House, cornfield ground in all 2190 lbs of seed cotton. I was at
Moses Liddell's Esqr. in the morning. . . . home to weigh cotton. Jesse
is sick. James, Margery, & Lucy were unwell. The weather is cool;
though pleasant.

Tuesday 21st

My negroes picked 2415 lbs of seed cotton West of the House. . . .
I ginned some cotton myself today. . . . The weather is very fine indeed
for picking cotton; some distant thunder.

Wednesday 22nd

My negroes picked 2615 lbs. of cotton West of the House. . . . The
weather is very fine & pleasant for picking cotton a little thunder in
the evening—must have rained below here.

Thursday 23rd

My negroes picked again today West of the House 2615 lbs. of seed
cotton. Betsy & the children dined at Judge Prosser's went through
Woodville, where she expended $5. I dined at Prosser's, in the evening,
we all went to Ashly. The weather is very good & fine.

Friday 24th

My negroes picked 2545 lbs. of cotton East of the House. Having
dined with my family at Ashly in the afternoon . . . rode over to see
Mr. Caleb Hall. I returned home so did my family, & I found here
my friend William R. Falconer of New Orleans.

Saturday 25th

My negroes picked 2350 lbs. West & 65 lbs. East of the House in all
2415 lbs. of seed cotton. Mr. William Falconer & myself spent the day
here, in the evening Mr. Francie Dabney & Mrs. Poindexter came
down & took supper here. There are some little appearances of rain.

Sunday, September 26th
Betsy & the children rode up to Woodville & returned here to dinner. In the evening, Mr. Falconer & myself (Mahala also with us) rode up to see Mr. Dabney, & home here to supper. . . .

Mon. 27th
My negroes picked 2265 lbs of seed cotton East of the House. . . . Betsy & the children dined at Gov^r Poindexter's & in the evening to Woodville, spent there $6, & then they came home. Good weather.

Tuesday 28th
My negroes only picked 1270 lbs. of seed cotton East of the House. . . . I went on to Woodville, Mr. Falconer got here in the evening, as well as myself, but we came near losing our lives by his horse running away with his barouche. . . .

Wed. 29th
My negroes are gathering of corn & peas in the piece South of the Gin house & Potato Patch & Pea Patch. . . . General Joor dined here.

Thurs. 30th
My negroes are working as on yesterday. My Gin has been running ever since Tuesday. Mr. Moses Liddell, & Genl. Joor called here, we rode to see Genl. Joor's new fashion gin invented by Mr. Phineas Gardiner, having a double set of cylinder's for the saws, one above & the other beneath, we returned here to dinner, Mr. Francis Dabney dined with us. Very dry, & dusty.

G. W. Featherstonhaugh

## "COTTON NOW BECOMES THE STAPLE OF THE COUNTRY"

*Continuing his geological tour of the Southern states in 1834, G. W. Featherstonhaugh found the comparison of Tennessee as it had been in 1806 with what he found in 1834 quite astounding. A howling wilderness then was now transformed into a land of rich plantations, one of the most celebrated being President Andrew Jackson's Hermitage, near the handsome capital city of Nashville.*

*The scientist noted with approval that Tennessee had employed a
state geologist. His salary was five hundred dollars a year.*

*When Featherstonhaugh reached Texas, at that time still a part of
Mexico, he found violent political sentiment, reminiscent of the feeling he had encountered in South Carolina. The American colonists
were in revolt against the dictatorship of Santa Anna and were soon to
make their bloody and victorious stand against Mexico.*

On the 19th of September 1834, at the dawn of day, we resumed
our places in the stage-coach for Nashville. . . . The openness of the
woods gives a park-like appearance to the country, and enables you to
see through the forest for a great distance, which is very pleasing. The
white men, however, having now driven the ancient race out of their
country, the underwood is beginning to spring up quite thick, as the
old settlers say, in comparison to its ancient state. The soil was always
prone to produce a lofty wild grass; and as this prevented the Indians
from seeing and pursuing their game, they were in the habit of annually setting fire to it, and this kept the underwood down.

During the morning we crossed Caneyfork, a fine branch of Cumberland River. . . . Our road was now up and down steep limestone
slopes to a place called Liberty, where, as well as we could judge from
the exterior, there was a decent tavern; and as we had ridden thirty-
three miles without breaking our fast, we told the people we hoped to
get a good breakfast. . . .

At night we arrived at Lebanon, a place which is tolerably well laid
out, and contains some good buildings. . . .

By daylight on the 20th we were again in the stage-coach, proceeding
through a country of flat limestone covered with a deposit of fine
soil. Cotton now becomes the staple of the country. We stopped at a
poor tavern and got a wretched breakfast, a not uncommon occurrence
in these districts. Travellers always fare much better in farming than
in cotton-planting countries, where butter, milk, eggs, flour, &c. receive
very little attention from the small settlers.

We now drove on to the Hermitage, the plantation of General
Jackson, the President. I had seen at a tavern in Virginia a box directed
to him, and learnt accidentally that it had been waiting there several
weeks, the contractor of the stage having refused to forward it because
the carriage was not paid, and because he was opposed to the General
in politics. I therefore took it under my care, and mentioning the circumstances to him when I met him at Campbell's station, the old

gentleman told me that the box contained his favorite saddle, and that he had been inconvenienced for the want of it during the short holiday he had been indulging in from the seat of government.

The mansion-house at the Hermitage—where I stopped to deliver this box—is built of brick, and is tolerably large; everything was neat and clean around it, the fences were well kept up, and it looked like the substantial residence of an opulent planter. The estate is said to be a very fine one, to consist of from seven to eight hundred acres of cleared land, two hundred acres of which are in cotton at this time, and to extend to the Cumberland river. The quantity of cotton which the land yields in this part of Tennessee is small compared with the great productiveness of the rich bottom lands in the 33rd and 32nd degrees of latitude farther south, where the plant comes much nearer to perfection.

A plain farmer of the neighbourhood who got into the stage with us, not far from the Hermitage, to go to Nashville, and who had lived near General Jackson betwixt twenty and thirty years, gave us a very interesting account of this distinguished man; which, making allowances for the partiality of a neighbour who shared his political opinions, I have no doubt is founded in truth. He said the General was an industrious, managing man, always up to all his undertakings, and most punctual in the performance of his business engagements: that his private conduct was remarkable for uniformly inclining to justice, generosity, and humanity: that he was an excellent master to his slaves, and never permitted his overseers to ill-treat them. As to his house, he said it was constantly full of people, being in fact open to everybody; those whom he had never heard of before being asked to dine when they called, and those they had room for being always furnished with beds. For these reasons, he said, everybody respected him, and most people loved him.

As to his public conduct, he observed that he was rather an uncompromising man, and liked to have his own way, but that his own way was always a very good one, and a very sensible one, if he was left to himself. He was a man of strong passions, and had once been very much addicted to cock-fighting, horse-racing, and "considerable cursing and swearing," but that he had "quit all these," and was in earnest about doing good to the country. And he added, that if the General was not always right, it was to be laid to the score of some of his political friends, who imposed upon him for their own private ends, a thing not very difficult to do, because when he thought a man his friend he was

too apt to go to great lengths with him. These remarks, which fell from
our fellow-traveller in a quiet sensible manner, are so much in accordance with what I have observed and seen of one of the most remarkable
men the United States have yet produced. . . .

About 1 o'clock P.M. we fell in with an excellent macadamised road,
leading to Shelbyville, and soon after came in sight of Nashville, the
centre of civilization of the western country. Its appearance was pre-
possessing. We soon reached the public square, and alighted at a good-
looking inn, called the City Hotel, where at last we found some comforts, after getting over 900 miles in one way or another since the 1st
of August.

In the afternoon, after reading the numerous letters I found waiting
for me at the post-office, and taking a hasty look at the town, I walked
out to a villa in the neighbourhood where my friend Monsieur Pageot,
of the French legation, was passing some of the summer months with
his lady, who is a native of the State of Tennessee. We were delighted
to meet in this distant part of the world, and I remained chatting with
them until sunset. On reaching my quarters I began the serious work
of answering my letters. . . .

No traveller who comes into the country as I have done, can feel
anything but respect for what he sees around him in this place. When
I first visited North America, in 1806, the word Tennessee was mentioned as a kind of Ultima Thule. Now it is a Sovereign State, with a
population of upwards of 700,000 inhabitants, has given a President to
the United States, and has established a geological chair in the wilderness. The first log-hut ever erected in Nashville was in 1780; now there
is a handsome town, good substantial brick houses, with public edifices that would embellish any city in America, and certainly, as far as
architecture is concerned, one of the most chaste Episcopal churches
in the United States. . . . It adds greatly too to the interest of the place,
that a few of the hardy individuals who, with their rifles on their
shoulders, penetrated here, and became the first settlers, still live to see
the extraordinary changes which have taken place.

In one of my geological walks I called at the residence of one of
these venerable men, a Mr. Ridley, who possesses a plantation about
four miles from Nashville. Going along the road, a group of wooden
buildings of a rude and comparatively antique structure could not but
attract my attention, especially one of them which stood alone, and
different from all the others. On entering a room of the dwelling-house
I found a tall strapping young negro wench reeling cotton, with a

machine that made such a detestable creaking, that I could scarce hear my own voice when I asked her if there was a spring of water near. As soon as she pointed it out, my son took a gourd shell, kept for the purpose, and went for water: in the mean time I passed into the court-yard, where I found an elderly woman, rather masculine in her manner, very stout in her person, and strong in her movements. Upon my asking her if she was the mistress of the house, she very civilly replied that she was not, "but that her mammy was," who was coming. I now perceived a much older woman, extremely emaciated and sallow, but erect in her person, and very lively in her manner of speaking, coming from a log-hut which served as a kitchen. This aged person having obligingly asked me if I would go into the house and take a chair, I went towards it, and near the door found an aged man with a hoary head, eyes that would scarcely bear the light, and every mark of extreme old age about him. He shook hands kindly with me, and asked me various questions, who I was, where I came from, where I was going to, and was particularly anxious to know how old I was, seeing that my hair was grey. I spent the morning with this patriarchal family, and ingra-tiated myself so much with them, that they imparted their history to me.

The old man, Daniel Ridley, was ninety-five years old, or would be so the 1st of January, 1835, being born on the first day of the year 1740, in the reign of George II. The emaciated woman was his second wife; she was eighty years old, and during the fifty-four years they had been man and wife, she had borne him eight children. Miss Betsy, the stout woman—for so she was called by the slaves—was a daughter by his first marriage, and was now sixty-two years old: she had been mar-ried twice, and already had great grandchildren. The patriarch him-self, of course, had great great grandchildren, one of whom, a de-scendant of his oldest son, now in his seventy-second year, was to be married next year, so he may yet live to bless his fifth generation. He told me he had a short time ago been counting his descendants, but after getting as far as three hundred, he found it very troublesome, and had given it up. These had sprung from sixteen children, the produce of both his marriages. . . .

Old Mr. Ridley informed me that he was a native of Williamsburg, in Virginia, that he emigrated from thence on marrying his second wife in 1780, and established himself on the north fork of the Holston, where they lived betwixt ten and eleven years, continually engaged in troublesome contests with the Indians; but this he did not mind, he was naturally industrious, and having eight children by his first wife, to whom he was married before he was twenty, it was necessary for him to work hard. He had also been a soldier in General Braddock's army, and was thoroughly inured to fatigue and danger. Hearing of a settlement that was making on the Cumberland River, he joined a large party, who, having built boats, came down the Holston, the Tennessee, and the Cumberland rivers, about eight hundred miles, to Nashville, where they landed in 1790.

The families composing this expedition proceeding to settle themselves, he selected the site he now lived on for his plantation. His first care was to clear an acre of ground for his fort, and construct a strong stockade around it, with a gate, as the Choctaw, Chickasaw, and Cherokee Indians were fiercely contending against this intrusion into their hunting-grounds. Within the stockade he built a double log-house, consisting, in accordance with the general custom, of two rooms, with a spacious passage between them, putting the whole under one roof. One of the rooms served the family to sleep in, the other for a kitchen, and the passage was a convenient place to eat and sit in. A few yards from this he erected a well-constructed block-house, for the family to fly to if the stockade was forced. This block-house yet stands on the N.E. corner of the fort, and was the building which we had observed was so different from the others. On the S.E. corner of the fort he placed another block-house, and on the S.W. corner another. On the N.W. corner he had not built one, because it was protected by the others. Within the area were a few other buildings for the convenience of their horses and cattle.

This was the general plan adopted by the whites for the protection of their families against the Indians. . . .

Mr. Ridley never was attacked in his fort; but a neighbouring one, on the plantation of his son-in-law, Mr. Buchanan, became the scene of an affair still talked of by many of the inhabitants of Nashville with great interest, and of which I had the details from the Ridley family. Mr. Buchanan resided about two miles from the Ridleys: they had moved into Tennessee together, had settled near each other, and Mr. Buchanan's son had married Mr. Ridley's daughter, Sally, a woman of very large dimensions, weighing 260 lbs. She had a courageous spirit corresponding to her size, and having been trained from her early youth amidst dangers, had always—as her father informed me—been remarkable for her personal resolution, and her patient endurance of hardships. The fort of old Mr. Buchanan had once been surprised by the Cherokees and Choctaws, when the Indians, rushing into the room where the old pair had taken refuge, butchered the old man in the presence of his wife, who, kneeling with her back to the wall, and imploring their mercy, had the muzzles of their guns pushed close to her face to frighten her. She was, however, spared.

"I once asked her," said old Mrs. Ridley to me, "how she felt when she saw her old man she had lived with so long tomahawked in that way; but she gave me no answer, and putting her hands before her face cried so, I thought she would have broken her heart."

In 1792, when the attack upon the fort which is going to be narrated took place, Mr. Ridley's son-in-law, Buchanan, had possession of it.

The Indians had been gathering for some time, and the white settlers had been informed through their spies that it was their intention first to attack and subdue Buchanan's fort, then Ridley's, and afterwards another on the Cumberland. Four hundred settlers had assembled, and had waited from day to day at Buchanan's, but it being rumoured that the Indians had given up their intentions, almost the whole of them returned to their own homes, the insecurity of their families keeping them in continued anxiety, so that only nineteen of the whole muster remained, all of whom belonged to the immediate vicinity. One Saturday evening, a Frenchman, and a half-blooded Indian, arrived in great haste at the fort, to say that the Indians were on their way, and would soon be there. They were not believed, even when the half-blood told them they might cut his head off if the savages did not reach the place in a few hours. Two men, however, were dispatched to reconnoitre, and proceeding heedlessly, they fell into an ambush, and were both of them killed and scalped. These messengers not returning, it was concluded that they had extended their reconnaissance, and that therefore the Indians could not be near: the consequence was that the Frenchman and the half-blood, who had professed to have come amongst them to take white wives, were now looked upon with great suspicion.

In this state of things all the men of the fort retired to rest, leaving Sally Buchanan to sit up in the kitchen. Whilst she was listening in the dead of the night to a noise at a distance, which she at first supposed indicated the approach of the messengers, suddenly she heard the horses and cows struggling and running about in the enclosure in great agitation—for, as Mrs. Ridley said, "Cows is mortal feared, as well as horses, of them parfict devils the Indians;"—and understanding the signs, she immediately roused the men with the cry of "Indians, boys! Indians!" Instantly arming themselves, the men flew to the gate, which 900 warriors of the Cherokees, Choctaws, and Chickasaws were attempting to force. The gate was thoroughly well secured, or it must have given way to their efforts; but the Indians fortunately making no diversion at any other point, the brave men inside had but this to direct their attention to; and animated by a noble determination to defend the place to the last extremity, they made an active and vigorous defence, answering to the deafening yells of the savages by a shot at them whenever a chance occurred of its taking effect.

In the mean time, it being discovered that the absentees had taken almost all the bullets with them, the heroic Sally Buchanan, thinking the men would be more effectually employed at the stockade, undertook the task of supplying them, and at the kitchen-fire actually cast almost all the bullets that were fired, whilst a female relative who was staying with her clipped the necks off. As fast as they were ready, Sally would run out with them, and cry aloud, "Here, boys, here's bullets for you; but mind you don't sarve 'em out till you're sure of knocking some of them screaming devils over."

This incident is equal to any thing we read of in history; and so much were the men encouraged by the indomitable spirit of Sally, that the Indians, after a fruitless attempt to force their way in, which lasted several hours, becoming apprehensive that the report of the rifles and the uproar—which Mrs. Ridley heard very distinctly two miles off— would bring succours to the garrison, drew off before daylight, after losing several of their number. And thus the garrison, by its prompt and gallant resistance, not only saved itself, but all the other forts which the Indians had laid their account in capturing.

At this period the most unquenchable hatred existed betwixt the Indians and the white settlers, the first struggling for their hunting grounds, the last for their lives. The Indians never spared the male whites when they could destroy them, and very seldom the females. As they were not always in sufficient force to attack the settlements openly, they prowled about in small parties, and placed themselves in ambush where the whites were accustomed to pass. Mr. Buchanan had a grist-mill near his fort, to which the neighbours used to resort to have their flour made. Upon an occasion, when Indians were not supposed to be near, one of their female acquaintances who lived in the vicinity sent her four young boys to the mill for grist for the family, thinking they would not only be able to assist each other, but would be a mutual protection. These little fellows were unsuspectingly surprised by some savages not far from the house, and the wretched mother had the unspeakable misery of seeing them all dragged into the woods to be scalped. Two of these boys survived and got renewed scalps, but they were always bald.

Upon another occasion, a young girl was going on horseback to a friend's not more than two miles distant, and persuaded another young female, her friend, to get up behind and accompany her. Before they had got halfway, however, the girl who rode behind was shot down by some Indians, and the other escaped by the fleetness of her horse, which she urged with desperation, and with which she took such a desperate leap as to be the wonder of the generation she belonged to.

Still influenced by a feeling of unmitigable and unsatiated revenge against the Indians for practising such inhuman warfare, it is not surprising that when General Jackson went against the Creeks in 1813, the enthusiasm of the Tennesseans to serve under the bravest and most warm-hearted of their citizens should have been general. Four of old Mr. Ridley's sons accompanied him.

"The boys would go," said the old man to me: "I couldn't have stopped them if I had wished; but I did not wish to do it."

"Ay," added his old wife, "I told my boys they were as welcome to go with Jackson as they were to sit down to dinner."

"Yes," said Miss Betsy, the sister of the Amazonian Sally, and the great-grandmother of several children, "I'd fight for Jackson myself, any day."

And when I took leave of this fine honest family, the old man grasped my hand in his, and said, "When you get to Washington, tell Jackson I was sorry he did not call on me; it is the first time he went away without calling; but I know he couldn't come; he sent me word he couldn't. Tell him," said he, and the old man, to the great admiration of my son and myself, absolutely sobbed, whilst his aged eyes were suffused with tears, "tell him I love him—I love him better than I love any body; he has always been kind to me; there was always a good understanding betwixt us." As I was going out at the door, he added, "Tell Jackson to send me a pair of specs: if I could only see to read the Testament, it would not be so hard to live; but I can scarce see at all."

I am rather afraid this was a piece of stinginess in the old patriarch, who could have found plenty of spectacles in Nashville. But he is a great economist; for a carpenter, who was doing a job to his house, having got it done a couple of hours before night, the old man, seeing a plank or two to spare, obliged him to stay the two hours out and make up the planks into a coffin for himself, which he actually keeps under his bed; and there being still some stuff to spare, he told the carpenter it was a great pity there was not enough to make another for Mrs. Ridley. . . .

### A COTTON PLANTATION IN TEXAS

I pursued my way to Red River, following the southern slope of the pine hills, which show a great many beds of ferruginous sandstone. At the foot of these hills the rich and broad bottom land of Red River commences, which is considered to be of the very first class of cotton lands in this part of North America. A portion of it had just been sold at the public land-sale at Washington, and some of the sections had brought as high a price as ten, and even thirteen dollars an acre. The bottom is about a mile in width on the north side of the river, and is densely covered with lowland timber, such as cotton wood (*Populus monilifera*), the huge branches of which are as white as snow, other trees of the sycamore kind, deciduous cypress, and immense canes 20 to 30 feet high. . . .

On reaching the banks of Red River, although I was very much delighted at having successfully penetrated to this extreme frontier of the broad territory of the United States, yet I could not but perceive that nothing could be less beautiful or picturesque than the river and its shores. The stream was here about 200 yards wide, sluggish, muddy, and chocolate coloured; deriving its colour from the deep red earth it has in ancient times deposited, and through which it now flows; and exhibiting on its banks an impenetrable wilderness of briars, plants of various kinds, and lofty canes of from 20 to 30 feet high.

The next thing was to cross the river at what is called Dooley's Ferry, to the Texas side, where, on account of the present low stage of the water, there was an extensive beach of 200 yards or more. As soon as the ferryboat touched the Mexican shore, I hastened to lead my horse over the beach as rapidly as I could, for the ferryman told me that it was very dangerous, would scarcely bear the weight of a horse, and might *suck* him in, if I loitered. I soon saw this was good advice, for the bog shook in a treacherous manner, and Missouri, who did not appear to like this unusual surface, aiding with great agility, we soon reached the hard land, and found ourselves in what the ferryman called "Spain."

We now were upon an exceedingly fertile bottom between three and four miles wide, densely full of plants and trees, amongst which I recognized for the first time the Palmetto, with its graceful fanlike shape. Having got through it, we came upon drier and blacker land, and then to a locality called *Lost Prairie*, which is a tract of about 2000 acres of incredible beauty and fertility, bearing extraordinary crops of cotton, and gracefully surrounded by picturesque woods. I had never seen the cotton plant growing in perfection before, for in the cotton districts I had already passed through, the plant was a low dwarfed bush not exceeding two feet high; but here the whole country was filled with stately and umbrageous bushes five feet high, covered with innumerable pods resembling large white roses. Having found out where the plantation of a Dr. Jones was, to whom I had a letter of introduction, I rode there, and learned that he was from home, but his family offering to receive me, I determined to remain at their house for the night, that I might have an opportunity of looking at the immediate neighbourhood. It was a charming sunny day, the thermometer (Dec. 11) stood at 74° out of doors, and not a cloud in the sky.

It had occurred to me, before I crossed Red River, that it would be prudent not to prolong my stay in Texas at this time. All the persons whom I had had any intercourse with, appeared to be of one opinion as to the expediency and propriety of occupying and detaching this province from the Mexican Government, and it was easy to see that they thought the moment for action was drawing nigh. Upon several occasions, when this important subject was earnestly discussed in my presence, I had remained silent; and as this was unusual in a quarter where all men had some plan or other to offer to accelerate their design, I was by many regarded as a spy upon them. If I had waited here until my son joined me, and then advanced farther into the country, some outbreak might take place, and we might become involved in its consequences, or have found it difficult to return. I determined, therefore, as the most prudent course, to defer my examination of the interior of the province until I could do it with the permission of the Mexican authorities, or until the country had become quiet enough to admit of my moving about without observation. In the mean time there was something to see here, and I set about making the best use I could of the time I intended to stay.

It is impossible to exaggerate the extraordinary fertility of the soil of Lost Prairie. I had an opportunity of examining the nature of the deposit in a well just dug to the depth of thirty feet from the surface; the first three feet went through a rich black vegetable mould, and the remaining twenty-seven through a reddish-coloured argillacco-calcareous earth, so that it would seem impossible to exhaust a soil of this kind. In favourable seasons they gather from 1500 to 2500 lbs. of cotton in the seed to the acre, which, when the seed is taken out by the cotton gin, leaves from twenty-five to thirty per cent, in weight of marketable raw cotton. It is considered a fair crop if it produces one bale of 450 lbs. of such cotton to the acre, and where for every working negro on the plantation six or eight bales can be turned out.

I observed that it was not the same species of plant I had seen growing in Tennessee, and was told it was the Mexican white-seeded cotton, which was preferred in this part of the country, because it yields more to the acre and is much easier gathered. Some of the plants were near six feet high, and sent forth branches in great profusion, covered with large white bolls resembling the Guelder Rose when in full perfection. I counted 300 bolls on one stem, but Dr. Jones's overseer told me that he had counted as many as 360 on one stem this season. The field these plants were in contained 300 acres, and it was so dazzling white to look upon as to create rather a painful sensation to the eyes. . . .

Notwithstanding it was so late in the year, only one half of this field was gathered, and the proprietor was now on a journey to purchase an additional gang of slaves, intending to plant 400 acres the next season.

However lightly these people may hold the Mexicans, whose superiors they undoubtedly are in industry and enterprise, yet the Mexicans stand at a proud moral distance from them in regard to slavery, which is abolished in their republic. . . . The poor slaves I saw here did not appear to me to stand any higher in the scale of animal existence than the horse: the horse does his daily task, eats his changeless provender, and at night is driven to his stable to be shut in, until he is again drawn forth at the earliest dawn to go through the same unpitied routine until he dies. This is the history of the slave in Texas, differing in nothing from that of the horse, except that instead of maize and straw he is supplied with a little salt pork to his maize, day after day, without any change, until death relieves him from his wearisome existence. The occupation of Texas by the Americans, where there are so many millions of acres of the most fertile cotton lands, will convert the old slave-holding part of the United States into a disgusting nursery for young slaves, because the *black crop* will produce more money to the proprietors than any other crop they can cultivate. . . .

Seating myself upon my faithful Missouri, I turned my back upon the fair and sunny fields of Texas, now doomed to the curse of slave-labour, and on as serene, beautiful, and soft a December morning as ever was graced by a cloudless sky in Italy, I once more reached the banks of Red River.

Victoria V. Clayton

## "HERE WE LIVED IN THIS QUIET COUNTRY HOME"

*V. V. gives us a discerning, faithful picture of farm life for white and black in Barbour County, southeastern Alabama, in the middle of the nineteenth century—a system of life inherited and accepted.*

*The young man "recently graduated with the highest honors from a college in Virginia," who had the good sense to seek her prompt acquaintance and win her hand, was Henry D. Clayton. In 1857 he was elected to the state legislature where he served until the war began. Then he organized the First and the Thirty-ninth Alabama regiments. He took part in the Pensacola, Kentucky, Tennessee and Georgia campaigns and rose to the rank of major general. After the war he served for fourteen years as judge of the Circuit Court of Alabama. In 1888 he became president of the University of Alabama. He died in Tuscaloosa in 1892.*

My father, John Linguard Hunter, was of English and Scottish descent, his ancestors belonging to the Gentry. He was a planter by profession, owning at one time two large plantations in the State of South Carolina.

In 1835, hearing many marvelous stories of the great productiveness of the land in the State of Alabama, he was induced to sell his plantations in his old native State and move to Alabama. Here he found everything in a crude, unsettled condition. I was only two years old, and consequently know nothing of the country at that time except from hearing the older members of the family tell about it.

The little town selected for our home was merely an Indian village then. Many tribes of these natives roved over the country. Oftentimes they were very troublesome, and finally became so hostile to the white settlers that they were obliged, in self-defense, to resort to some means of driving them out. This meant war, which began in February, 1836. My father and oldest brother joined the army formed for the purpose of making the red man take up his march towards the setting sun. My mother and her children were sent up into middle Georgia to remain while these hostilities, called the Indian War, lasted.

When peace was restored and it was safe for us to return, we came back to our home in Irwinton, now Eufaula. A house for our occupation had been almost finished in the village before our flight, and my mother found on our return that the soldiers had used it as a barracks, and in consequence it was injured to some extent. She cared not, though, for this; she was so thankful to be free from savage faces peeping and prying around the premises. She had been very much afraid of these savages, and when the squaws visited her she used to give them anything they asked for; and in this way we were often deprived of a favorite dress or of other things which we prized greatly. Being fond of gay colors, they were always sure to want the red dresses, and, to our discomfort, carried them off.

Upon his return to Irwinton, my father began to put his house in order, arranging for the white family in the village, and for the most part of the colored familes on the plantation. The plantation lay on the banks of the Chattahoochie River, about two miles from the village. Here the greater number of his slaves lived. My father was a slave-holder by inheritance, never having known anything else. "Our thoughts, our morals, our most fixed beliefs, are consequences of our place of birth."

When fond memory carries me back to my childhood's happy days, these colored friends on the old plantation occupy a very important place. I recall the commodious carriage, the bay horses, and old Uncle Abram seated on the driver's seat to take us, the children, through the beautiful woods, to make a visit to the old "maumers" down on the plantation. Our mother taught us to respect age in whatever position we found it, and we always called the older women "maumers" as marks of respect due their years.

Every slave family possessed a garden, truck patch, chicken house and a lot of hens, and, from these sources, always had something nice to present to us, their young "misses." We cherished these humble presents, peanuts, fresh eggs, and the like, as though they were of intrinsic value. Their little cottages were arranged so as to form streets. After making the round of visits, not slighting any, but going in to see every one at home, sitting and chatting with all, we usually finished our calls at Uncle Sam's house. He was the foreman on the plantation, and had a more pretentious home. His wife, maum Flora, would entertain us most royally with bread and milk under the grand old oaks that sheltered the space around the door. The old man was a Methodist preacher, and close by his house stood a neat little building, in which he gathered all the children on Sunday morning to teach them their duty to God and man. Later in the day the adults assembled for worship. Frequently a visiting preacher would assist Uncle Sam in ministering to these people on a Sunday. The old man could read the Bible, but his education did not extend much beyond that and weighing the cotton as it was gathered from the fields, and putting down the weights for my father's inspection. Uncle Sam was, I believe, a good Christian man, and these people looked up to him with almost reverence.

My father was a kind, indulgent master, and I think I have never in the world met with happier people than were these simple uneducated blacks. . . .

An old aunt of my mother had come to make her home with us. She was a peculiar woman and a devotedly zealous Methodist. She built the first Methodist church in Barbour County. Many a day have I spent, when about eight years old, going round calling with Aunt Polly, as everybody called her. She was a Mrs. Barefield, but few knew her except as Aunt Polly. She never left home without her sack, which she wore suspended from her waist, containing a bottle of cologne, one of paregoric, one of liquid assafoetida, and a silver teaspoon. All these were fitted in their respective places, and this strange contrivance was concealed by her over-dress. She also carried an umbrella and fan. Thus she was always ready for heat, cold or sunshine, sickness or health.

In the spring of 1843 this aunt was taken to Paradise. Very soon after, our darling mother followed, and our happy home was broken up. The older children had married and gone, but there were four of us left. My father sent the two older girls to a boarding school, so my youngest sister and I were left with father in our sad old home. The servants were as good to us as they could be, but Father's business necessitated his absence a considerable portion of the time; consequently he determined it best for us to go and live with our married sisters. I spent several years very happily in my sister Violetta's family.

Our once rustic little village had by this time grown to be quite a town, and supported good schools. My brother, with whom I was now staying, had a friend living some miles in the country, who had a daughter he wished to send in town to attend school. She came to stay with us, and shared my room. After her sojourn with us for several months, her father came to take her home for a few days, and invited me to accompany her to their country home, some fifteen miles distant. When we reached Abbie's home, the news of a marriage near by greeted us, and the next day we attended this real country wedding. The following day I was still more excited by the novelty of events. The entire neighborhood was invited to what they called an "infair" at my friend's house. Early in the morning the crowd began to gather from the surrounding country for many miles and no sooner had they assembled than dancing began; the Cotillion and Virginia Reel.

I remained in my sister's family until my fifteenth year, when my father, who was an Episcopalian, took me to the school of Bishop Stephen Elliott. The Bishop at that time had the supervision of Christ College, a female institute belonging to the Diocese of Georgia, situated at Montpelier, about fourteen miles from Macon. There I remained two years. The school generally numbered about one hundred girls. Many of our teachers were from the North, and were very intellectual and highly cultivated ladies, and I was much attached to several of them.

After two years' stay at boarding school, I returned to the old homestead and found my father all alone except the faithful family slaves. In those days, with the better class of citizens, such servants were numerous, and each had his special charge. In our household there were Middleton, who waited on my father and kept the dining room in order; the cook, maum Louisa; the washwoman, maum Kate; and Uncle Abram, the man-servant who cared for the horses. There were all these servants with so little to occupy them; yet they were cared for as members of the family, fed and clothed, and attended by the family doctor when sick. They were not taken on social equality with their owners, any more than the servants at the North would be. My father's slaves all looked up to him with loving respect. On my return home, a girl of twelve summers was brought in from the plantation for my special service.

On the death of my mother, her estate, which consisted of slaves, was divided among the children. In the number that came to my inheritance was a bright, intelligent boy. He acted as errand boy about the premises and was very useful. One day he asked permission to go with another boy of nearly the same age to gather blackberries. After some importunity on his part I consented to let him go. The two boys ran off in glee, promising to be good boys. It was the last time that Daniel was ever seen. His comrade returned to say that Daniel was drowned in the river. We had a search made and the shore watched, but never could find his body. This incident was a great sorrow to my young heart, for I had become much attached to him.

In our dear old home I found the management of domestic duties in the hands of the negroes. I at once proceeded to take the supervision of the household into my own hands, not only the little every-day matters about the house, but also the weighing-out and providing supplies to be sent down to the plantation. All these things had been entrusted to the negroes by my father.

I staid closely at home attending to these duties. I did not know that any one in town was taking note of my conduct. A young man recently graduated with the highest honors from a college in Virginia, came to Eufaula for the purpose of studying law, and hearing of me, he remarked, "Must seek her acquaintance; she will make a good wife." This young man studied law, was admitted to the bar, and soon procured the position of assistant in the Circuit Clerk's office at Clayton, the county seat. He bought a home there and finally asked me to share it with him.

On the ninth day of January, in the year of 1850, we were married at my father's house in Eufaula. I was in my eighteenth year and Mr. Clayton in his twenty-second, a youthful couple, happy and joyous, full of hope for the long future that lay before us.

He took me to a dear little home in Clayton where we began housekeeping, with three servants; my cook, Harriet, inherited from my mother's estate; a boy, Ned, given my husband by his father; and little Annie, Harriet's daughter.

We lived in this house two years, when my husband having saved up enough money, purchased a farm near by, and we came into the inheritance of more slaves. We sold our dear little first home and moved to the farm. We gathered together our slaves and began a new life. Rules were made and everything was organized with reference to the comfort of all and profit to ourselves.

We had only eight grown negroes. One woman did the cooking for the whole household and the washing for the white family. I, with the help of my little girl, Annie, discharged the other duties of the house. The negroes were all called up early in the morning and went to the field before breakfast. The breakfast was prepared and sent to them. Their breakfast generally consisted of meat, ordinarily bacon, sometimes beef, hot coffee, and bread. At twelve o'clock they all returned to the house to feed the mules, eat their midday meal, and rest. The dinner consisted of meat, vegetables of different kinds, and bread, often fruit pies, especially in the summer season, and old fashioned pot pies cooked in a big oven. Apples baked with honey was a great dish for all at our house. After two hours' rest, the slaves returned to the field and remained until the setting sun warned them of the near approach of night. The evening meal was generally lighter than the others, milk taking the place of meat. Many of our farmers weighed out the rations weekly to their hands, letting them prepare their own meals; but my husband adopted his father's way of doing; having their meals cooked for them, so that the time allotted for rest could be spent literally at rest.

By and by the family became large, both through natural increase of the negroes, and because my husband, at the close of each year, having saved up money enough to invest in something to increase our income, was naturally disposed to invest in slaves as being then the most available and profitable property in our section of the country.

We never raised the question for one moment as to whether slavery was right. We had inherited the institution from devout Christian parents. Slaves were held by pious relatives and friends and clergymen to whom we were accustomed to look up. The system of slave-holding was incorporated into our laws, and was regulated and protected by them. We read our Bible and accepted its teachings as the true guide in faith and morals. We understood literally our Lord's instructions to His chosen people, and applied them to our circumstances and surroundings.

Both thy bond-men, and thy bond-maids, which thou shalt have, shall be of the heathen that are round about you; of them shall ye buy bond-men and bond-maids. Moreover, of the children of the strangers that sojourn among you, of them shall ye buy and of their families that are with you, which they begot in your land; and they shall be your possession. And ye shall take them as an inheritance for your children after you, to inherit them for a possession; they shall be your bond-men forever; but over your brethren the children of Israel, ye shall not rule over another with rigour. (Levit. XXV, 44-46). . . .

We simply and naturally understood that our slaves must be treated kindly and cared for spiritually, and so they were. We felt that we were responsible to God for our entire household.

I found it necessary to keep two cooks now instead of one, as heretofore. Every morning I would take my key basket on my arm and make the rounds, giving out to each cook the various articles of food to be cooked for both white and colored families for the ensuing day. I gave the preparation of the food my careful attention. And their clothes were comfortable, each garment cut out with my own hands.

In these days of plenty there was a meat house filled with good home-cured meat, a cellar filled with sugar, syrup, wine, vinegar, and soap, a potato house filled with sweet potatoes, and also a store room containing the breadstuffs, and so forth.

Every Sunday morning the mothers brought their little ones up to see me. Then I could satisfy myself as to the care they gave them, whether they had received a bath and suitable clothing for the holy day. Later the larger children presented themselves to be taught the Catechism. I used the little *Calvary Catechism*, prepared by Mrs. D. C. Weston. The adults were permitted to attend the different churches in town as they pleased, but when the sun hid himself behind the western hills, all were compelled to return home to feed and care for the horses, cows, etc. When the evening meal was over my dining room was in readiness for the reception of all the grown members of the family. They gathered there and took their respective seats. They were taught the Creed of the Holy Apostolic Church, the Lord's Prayer, and the Ten Commandments; that is, all who could be taught, for some of them never could learn to repeat them, but understood the meaning sufficiently to lead a right life. Sometimes I would read a short sermon to them. They sang hymns, and we closed with prayer to our Heavenly Father.

Here we lived in this quiet country home. . . .

Susan Dabney Smedes

## BURLEIGH PLANTATION

*When Thomas Dabney and his family arrived in Hinds County, Mississippi, in 1835 the conditions they found were primitive by any standards and in comparison with what they had left behind in Virginia stark indeed. But all the slaves had chosen to come to the new country rather than be left behind in Virginia. The following account from Susan Dabney's biography of her father tells about the making of a plantation under his superb, considerate management.*

*The baby who had to be shielded from rain pouring through the*

*leaky roof that first year in Mississippi was Virginius Dabney. He served*
*throughout the war in the Confederate forces. In peacetime he became*
*director of the New York Latin School and wrote a whimsical satire,*
The Story of Don Miff.

In selecting his plantation, Thomas showed his usual sound judgment in practical matters. It comprised four thousand acres in a com-
pact body, not all bought at one time, but as he saw opportunity to secure the property of small farmers whose land adjoined his. In this way
he shaped his place to suit himself; and it was characteristic of his exact
methods that after making his final purchase the section lines fell so as
to form an almost exact square, with Tallahala Creek crossing it diag-
onally from northeast to southwest. The lowland bordering the creek,
called "The Bottom," was inexhaustibly fertile, and ensured heavy
crops in the dryest season. From the creek-bottom the land gradually
rises and runs back in a series of hills and plateaus. Those not already
cleared for cultivation were covered with a magnificent growth of timber,—oaks of many species, yellow pine, hickory, elm, sweet and black-
gum, besides countless other trees and shrubs of less value. Walnut-
trees of magnificent size, magnolia, beech, and laurel grew on the
banks of the creek.

Crops raised on the hills flourished best in wet weather; so with
the admirable diversity of soil on the plantation there was never a
failure of a whole crop in the most unfavorable season.

The land was well watered throughout by Tallahala Creek, with its
tributary branches, Indian Jumper and Snake Creek, and a number
of smaller bayous. In the hills springs bubbled out, giving rise to spring
"branches," which did not go dry in the most prolonged drought.
There was always pasturage for cattle along these water-courses, and
in the bitterest cold of winter they found abundant green food in the
canebrakes of the creek. Many wild flowers adorn the fields and woods
till late in the fall. Tiny blue innocents dot the grass as early as January. Later come wild violets, roses, the wild lily, rhododendron, cle-
matis, woodbine, snap-dragon, and a host of flowering trees, shrubs,
and vines. Among these we find the red-bud, maple, dogwood, crab-
apple, hawthorn, and wild peach; but supreme in beauty and in fragrance we have the yellow jasmine. It is the crown and glory of Southern woods, throwing its drapery of golden bells over trees and shrubs
for whole acres.

It was Thomas's plan in the management of this large estate to bring under cultivation a certain portion of new land every year. His rule was to clear one hundred acres each season. The cotton-plant delights in a virgin soil, and he counted on making a bale and a half of cotton to the acre on all new ground. This was, of course, above the average. In the hill country a planter thinks himself rewarded for his labor by an average yield of half a bale to the acre. Thomas one year made six hundred bales on six hundred acres, but that was an exceptional season. . . .

In entering on this pioneer life many difficulties had to be met that were a new experience to people coming from lower Virginia. One of the first was the unavoidable delay in getting supplies of meat for the servants. For two weeks after their arrival they had none.

The roof of the house in which Thomas had to put his wife and children was so leaky, that he had sometimes at night when it rained to sit up in bed and hold an umbrella over her and the baby.

There were no railroads, and the cotton crop had to be hauled in wagons forty miles, to Grand Gulf. The roads were so bad that to trust the teams to negro-drivers alone was not to be thought of, and the master went with every wagon. . . .

There was no doctor nearer than Raymond, which was ten miles from Burleigh. The country people around the plantation, seeing that Thomas knew how to take care of his servants, began to send for him when they were sick. . . .

His plantation was considered a model one, and was visited by planters anxious to learn his methods. He was asked how he made his negroes do good work. His answer was that a laboring man could do more work and better work in five and a half days than in six. He used to give the half of Saturdays to his negroes, unless there was a great press of work; but a system of rewards was more efficacious than any other method. He distributed prizes of money among his cotton-pickers every week during the season, which lasted four or five months. One dollar was the first prize, a Mexican coin valued at eighty-seven and a half cents the second, seventy-five cents the third, and so on, down to the smallest prize, a small Mexican coin called picayune, which was valued at six and a quarter cents. The decimal nomenclature was not in use there. The coins were spoken of as "bits." Eighty-seven and a half cents were seven bits, fifty cents four bits, twenty-five cents two bits. The master gave money to all who worked well for the prizes, whether they won them or not. When one person picked six hundred pounds in a day, a five-dollar goldpiece was the reward.

On most other plantations four hundred pounds or three hundred and fifty or three hundred was considered a good day's work, but on the Burleigh place many picked five hundred pounds. All had to be picked free of trash. No one could do this who had not been trained in childhood. To get five hundred pounds a picker had to use both hands at once. Those who went into the cotton-fields after they were grown only knew how to pull out cotton by holding on to the stalk with one hand and picking it out with the other. Two hundred pounds a day would be a liberal estimate of what the most industrious could do in this manner. A very tall and lithe young woman, one of mammy's "brer Billy's" children, was the best cotton-picker at Burleigh. She picked two rows at a time, going down the middle with both arms extended and grasping the cotton-bolls with each hand. At Christmas Nelly's share of the prize-money was something over seventeen dollars. Her pride in going up to the master's desk to receive it, in the presence of the assembled negroes, as the acknowledged leader of the cotton-pickers, was a matter of as great interest to the white family as to her own race. . . .

For some years the master accompanied every wagon loaded with cotton that went to market from his plantation. He slept on these journeys under the wagons, and sometimes on awakening in the morning he found that his great-coat, in which he was wrapped, was frozen hard to the ground. His negro drivers were more heavily clad than himself, each one being provided with a thick woolen great-coat that reached to his heels, home-knit woolen socks and gloves, and an enormous comforter for the neck. No illness resulted from the exposure. In the morning a hot meal, cooked by one of the negroes—and all the race are admirable cooks—was shared by the master and his men. . . .

Thomas owned more negroes than could work with advantage on one place. He was advised to put a part on a second plantation, but he refused to let a consideration of profit induce him to place his servants where he could not personally attend to their welfare. All the negroes were encouraged to come freely to the house to see the master and mistress, and they were very fond of making visits there, even when there was nothing more important to say than to ask after the young masters off at college, and to send their how-d'ye to them. They had their favorites among the growing-up sons and daughters, and chose their future owners, and spoke of themselves as belonging to the ones selected.

The master and mistress taught the negroes truthfulness and honesty, as they taught their own children, by not tempting them, and by trusting them. It was a maxim with the master that it made a child honest and truthful to believe its word. He was by nature so unsuspicious that it required no effort to carry this out in his daily life. . . .

Thomas had the control of about five hundred negroes. About two hundred were his own, and on the Burleigh plantation. The others belonged to his wards, and were nearly all family negroes, closely related to his, and living on neighboring plantations. He had the management of four estates belonging to minors. It was a saying in the family that the estates of his wards were better managed than his own, and their property increased faster than his. "Of course, I put the best overseers on their plantations," he said. "You see, I am here to look after my own." The negroes of these came to him as to their master, and he treated them as his own. . . .

The children delighted in teaching the house-servants. One night the whole family were formally invited, the master, mistress, governess, and guests, by a twelve-year-old school-mistress to hear her pupils recite poetry. She had about a dozen of the maids, old and young. One of the guests was quite astonished to see his own servant, whom he had with him spending several months at Burleigh, get up and recite a piece of poetry that had been learned with pains for this occasion.

The cook at Burleigh had always a scullion or two to help her, besides a man to cut her wood and put it on the huge andirons. The scullions brought the water and prepared the vegetables, and made themselves generally useful. The vegetables were gathered and brought from the garden by the gardener, or by one of the half-dozen women whom he frequently had to help him. A second cook made the deserts, sweetmeats, etc. As children, we thought that the main business of the head cook was to scold the scullion and ourselves, and to pin a dish-rag to us if we ventured into her kitchen. Four women and a boy were in charge of the dairy. The boy brought the cows up, sometimes with one of the women to help him. Two of the women milked; the third held the semi-sinecure office, taking charge of the milk; and the fourth churned.

During the spring and summer lambs were butchered twice a week, or oftener if required. The hides from the beeves almost supplied the plantation with shoes. Two of the negro men were tanners and shoemakers. A Southern plantation, well managed, had nearly everything necessary to life done within its bounds. At Burleigh there were two carpenters in the carpenter-shop, two blacksmiths in the blacksmith-shop, two millers in the mill, and usually five seamstresses in the house. In the laundry there were two of the strongest and most capable women on the plantation. Boys were kept about, ready to ride for the mail or to take notes around the neighborhood. There were twenty-seven servants in the service of the house.

The land in cultivation looked like a lady's garden, scarcely a blade of grass to be seen in hundreds of acres. The rows and hills and furrows were laid off so carefully as to be a pleasure to the eye. The fences and bridges, gates and roads, were in good order. His wagons never broke down. All these details may seem quite out of place and superfluous. But they show the character of the man in a country where many such things were neglected for the one important consideration—the cotton crop.

Managing a plantation was something like managing a kingdom. The ruler had need of a great store, not only of wisdom, but of tact and patience as well.

When there was trouble in the house the real kindness and sympathy of the servants came out. They seemed to anticipate every wish. In a thousand touching little ways they showed their desire to give all the comfort and help that lay in their power. They seemed to claim a right to share in the sorrow that was their master's, and to make it their own. It was small wonder that the master and mistress were forbearing and patient when the same servants who sorrowed with them in their affliction should, at times, be perverse in their days of prosperity. Many persons said that the Burleigh servants were treated with over-indulgence. It is true that at times some of them acted like spoiled children, seeming not to know what they would have. Nothing went quite to their taste at these times. The white family would say among themselves, "What is the matter now? Why these martyr-like looks?" Mammy Maria usually threw light on these occasions. She was disgusted with her race for posing as martyrs when there was no grievance.

Thomas was never an early riser. He maintained that it did not so much matter when a man got up as what he did after he was up. He woke up in the morning as gay as a boy, and when Sophia, fully dressed, informed him that it was time to get up, received the announcement with one of his liveliest tunes.

He did not go in to breakfast till he had danced the Fisher's Hornpipe for the baby, singing along with the steps. All the nursery flocked about him at the signal, one or two of the little tots joining in the capering. Then he walked with his quick, half-military step, the laugh still on his face, into the dining-room, where breakfast was already in progress. It was not a ceremonious meal he maintained. Dinner was. . . . Everyone was expected to be ready, and sitting with the family in the hall or drawing-room or dining-room not less than five minutes before the last bell rang.

Tutors were employed to teach in the family until the boys were old enough to be sent off to college. In order to make the boys study with more interest, the children of the neighbors were received into the school. When the three sons were sent off to college, a governess was employed to teach the daughters. The teachers at Burleigh were treated like guests and friends. Thomas said that he did not wish any but ladies to have the charge of his daughters, and they should be treated as ladies. . . .

Letters to James Knox Polk

## AFFAIRS AT YALOBUSHA

*In 1837 when James Knox Polk was serving in the House of Representatives he purchased, in partnership with his younger brother William and his brother-in-law, Dr. Silas M. Caldwell, a plantation in Yalobusha County, Mississippi. The original purchase included a thousand acres and some thirty-six slaves. Both William and Dr. Caldwell sold their shares in the plantation to Polk.*

*The following letters from William Polk, who helped manage the plantation until George A. Bratton was hired as overseer; from Bratton; from Polk's agents, Albert F. McNeil and the M. D. Cooper Company in New Orleans; and from James Cowan and J. T. Leigh, whose plantations were near his—all give glimpses of the hard work and the small detail that had to be constantly attended to if a plantation were to prosper. It must be assumed that Overseer Bratton received occasional help in the writing of his letters.*

*The distinguished Tennessean never lived on his Mississippi plantation. Mr. Leigh's letter was a gesture of neighborly courtesy since the two men obviously had never met.*

*James Walker was another of Polk's brothers-in-law.*

Columbia [Tenn.] December 2, 1837

Dear Brother:

I reached home a day or two ago. I would have written to you from
the plantation had I not thought it best to defer it until my arrival
at home as I would be more properly able to give you a detailed account
of the situation of the plantation. The crop was fairly represented to
us, as the best in the neighborhood, it has proved itself so. We, is
true, had a better stand of cotton, being less injured by the late frost
in the spring. We will make from seventy five to eighty Bales, aver-
aging in weight about 450 lbs., with 100 Bls [barrels] of corn to sell, over
and above what will support the *farm*, and raise our Pork next year.
We have about fifty shoats half grown, with an equal number propor-
tioned in size down to suckling pigs, all of which will answer for Pork
*next year*.

The negroes are all well with the exception of Dicy who is very
weakly, unable to do anything, and Phil who still attends to his business but has to be favoured on account of a weakness in the *Breast*.
Barbary had a spell of fever in the summer, from which she has not
entirely recovered. Her mother (Lucy) says from her complaints of
her breast, she fears she is going in the manner in which Alston, Hamp
and Charity did, though it may be only the fears of a mother occasioned by solicitude for her welfare.

I have employed Mr. Bratton for the next year at $500. There was
no Pork in market when I left Coffeeville. I left money, $500.00, with
Albert McNeal to purchase it for us, the probability is that it will sell
for more, as I met a great quantity making for that market. I apprised
A. McNeal, from Bolivar by letter, of the number I had met so as to put
him on his guard against purchasing too soon. From the quantity I
met on the road making for that place, the market must be surfeited,
and of consequence sell low. When I left the plantation they had made
42 Bales of Cotton, a part of which I had sent to the River and left
word for them to haul it, as fast as it was bailed. . . .

February 5, 1838

Dear Brother:

In your Letter, which I this evening received, you desire me to give
you a statement of the expences of the plantation for the past year. It

is not in my power to do so entirely, as the store accounts which are inconsiderate [*sic*] were not presented to me when down, and if they had been, I had no means to pay them, having to incur when down other expenses sufficient to consume all the means I possessed. The Doct. Bill was not presented, of which I am unable to tell the amount. Exclusive of these and a ballance due Bratton 250$, my expences, money laid out for our joint interest amts to $1385.07½ including the purchase of three mules, at $100.00 each, and another mule bought by George Moore last summer and sent to the plantation, at $125.00, and the Horse purchased by Bratton, at $72.00, and the $150.00 paid to Bratton in part for his services. Also $500.00 deposited with Albert McNeal to buy our pork, and other little expences not necessary to mention, which will make out the amount stated above. I have all the articles set down in my book. Albert McNeal has purchased our Pork at *seven cents.* . . . The money for the rents had not been paid in, and McNeal could not pay me any. I told him when it was collected to pay himself out of it, for the negro clothing which you purchased of him and sent to the plantation last fall. . . .

I have purchased since you left Alfred Nicholson's place, near town. I gave him $8000, payable in one, two and three years. There is in the tract 275 acres, 180 of which is woodland, which woodland is worth the money and more. I am at this time living on it, farming on a small scale. I had but one negro to hire. Doct. Dickinson furnished me with hands to work it, and a good cook. You I know will disapprove of it, and I have no excuse to offer except that I *wanted a home.* . . .

Please write to me, your opinion about selling our plantation. I may be after this year constrained to do it, though it depends greatly upon circumstances. It may be our interest to sell, if landed property and Negroes should rise to their former fictitious value. You will ascribe my desire to sell, to my embarrassed situation, occasioned by the purchase of this place, on which I now live, but it is not the case. I can pay for it by selling my district land. You as I said above will disapprove of the purchase, and you are the only one to whom I acknowledge the right of disapproving. . . .

**FROM ALBERT F. MCNEAL**

Coffeeville, Mississippi, June 15, 1838

Cousin James:

Your favour of the 21st ult. reached me a few days since. I visited the plantation the day after it was received and rode over the farm. In consequence of an unusually cold spring, it is generally thought the cotton crop in Mississippi will not be so good as it was last year, but it is difficult at present to say how that will be, much depending upon the fall season. The corn crop however will be better. Bratton has in cultivation one hundred and sixty or sixty five acres in cotton and one hundred acres in corn. He will evidently make a better crop of corn than he did last year, and I think the prospect fair for a good crop of cotton. The stand is equally as good as it was last year, but the cotton not so large and flourishing as it was this time last June. Bratton says he will make Eighty five or Ninety Bales of cotton. He is somewhat in the grass, but promises with fair weather, which we now have, to be out in two weeks. He seems to have the negroes completely under his control *now* and I was glad to hear him praising them for their good conduct. They were no doubt spoiled by the inefficient and trifling overseer who preceded him. There has been some sickness among them this spring (principally a kind of dysentery) and consequent loss of time. The girls Nancy and Elizabeth have not yet sufficiently recovered to be able to work. Bratton says he has a hundred barrels of corn that he can spare for sale, that the hogs on the plantation will furnish from three to four thousand weight of pork next fall. This, I think, better than buying. It would certainly be well for William to visit Yala Busha at least twice a year, say in the spring and fall. Any advice or aid in my power will be most freely given to the overseer. . . .

### FROM GEORGE A. BRATTON

[September 7, 1838]

Dear Fren:

after my best respects to yo I now will let yo now that wear all well at this time   your crop is indiferent   i shall not mak a crop of cotton bu aplenty of corn   i hav not had any rane since the 20 of May until the 19 of Augus and i hav not had any since with boles a fauling of faster than tha cum on   the cotton crops in this naberhood are now dead   i am now picken out coton barbry piks out one hundred and seventy five   the resn i did not wright Mcneal said that he wood wright evry 20 days   I have the rise of one hundred head of hogs and will be able to kill three thousand and one hundred pounds of pork   i ad no more at present.

## FROM GEORGE A. BRATTON

[September 13, 1838]

Sir:

i take the presant time to rite a few lines after my respects to you i will inform you that myself and family is well   the negros is all well i understand from a letter to McNeil that you would be down the first of October   i wish you to not fail to come   on last munday Gilbert left home and we believe is aiming to git to Dr Caldwell   i think you had best come by thir for I have serct the neighberhood and Cannot hear of him   i do not no what took him of unles it was becaus he had ben stealing   i have not struck him one lick in a year nor yet thretend him   i would advis you to not sell him for if you do Henry Carter will be sirten to foller   i rite no more.

## FROM GEORGE A. BRATTON

November 24, 1838

Dear Sir:

we are all well at present   I shall soon be done gathering of my crop of cotten   I think that I shall make about seventy bales of cotten   I have made the arrange with James Minter and Chisholm agreeable to your request about your cotten.   There has not no cotten gone of yet the rive has not rise yet   I think I shall have my cotten all ready for shipping by the first rise.

You rote me that you wanted a good crop made   if I can have seasones I shall make you as good a crop as you want if health will permit and strength   If I can keep before I can do putty well   I think I have keep before this year.

I will make the exchange of negroes at the time appointed.  Losa died the sixteenth of this month. I had good attention paid to her   I call in another phisian to Loosa   she died with the brest complaint.

As it respect your cotten that was sunk on the river last winter Minter sas he took the insurance polacy out leagally and mailed it at Vixburge to Harris and Careathers Co   Minter told me that they got out three or four bales of the cotten and was sold for the benefit of insurence company not for yours at all an yur merchants are a swindled you.

## FROM GEORGE A. BRATTON

December 24, 1838

Dear Sir:

After my best respects to you I have the pleasure to say to you that I and family are all well and also all the negroes belonging to the plantation. I am almost most through with the cotton. I have delivered 50 some odd bales at Troy. I think I will get through in a week. I expect to be able to ship Seventy some odd.

As to the cotton that was lost by the sinking of the boat Gladiator last fall was a year ago, I saw Minter a few days since   he requested me to say to you that a protest was drawn up by A. C. Blaine Esqr and and made oath that your cotton was not damaged. the protest was served on the managers of the boat and qualified before Esqr Boon then returned by Minter to the Insurance Company and its service by them acknowledged. the cotton then was reshipped on the Gladiator belonging to the insurance company. after getting up some of the cotton it was then sold for the benefit of the Insurance Company. Esqr Minter says that at any time that he is called on he will render any assistance necessary.

I now have further to say to you that I do earnestly and wishfully look for one or two negro men as my force is too weak for the place at best  as one of the women will be of little or no service in April and May   if you can in any way send your waiting boy here I have no doubt but he will make a good hand. If you cant get him here try and swap him with Wm for the one he took away. T. R. Reed has never wrote to me respecting the bill you sent him. I have made a punctual contract about the Insurance of the present crop   please write immediately.

## FROM GEORGE A. BRATTON

January 25, 1839

Dear Sir:

i now inform you that wee are all well   the negroes is all well   i have finished the Cotton crop and has delivered it all at the river   i made seventy four bailes   i have killed thirty eight hundred pounds of pork i am better than half done making the Cross fence   i have got my cotton land the half of it cleaned up and is running four plows   i have marked you 38 bailes and the bail numbered 38 is your tole cotton   i send you your bill of laden   the mule that julis rode to hardaman i instructed Alfred McNeil to sell it for one hundred dollars  i have not saw McNeil since he returned but when I see him I will rite to you whare he left it   thaire is five of your bailes that has not left Troy yet.

### FROM M. D. COOPER AND COMPANY

New Orleans February 12, 1839

... We received 34 Bales of your cotton last week. Since its arrival the weather has been very unfavorable to outdoor business. A day or two before its arrival there had been very heavy transactions in the Cotton Market at prices in favour of the holders from ½ to ¾ cent, since which time the Market has been rather calmer. Upon Sampling your Cotton we find the Staple and Colour good, but it is rather trashy. We ask 14 cents for it, having great confidence in the firmness of present prices, and anticipating favourable accounts from Liverpool which we are daily expecting of a late date, we will not take less, although it is a fraction above the present market. The Yazoo and Yallobusha Rivers are now navigable, and we will look for the balance of your Cotton shortly. if we make a sale, in time for a letter to reach Washington by 1st March, we will forward you acct. sales there, if not to Columbia. Your Bill of Groceries shall receive due attention. ...

### FROM GEORGE A. BRATTON

March 13, 1839

Dear Sir:

we are all well at present and at work as hard as we can drive   I have commenced planting of corn on monday morning and I think that I shall get nearly done planting of corn this week if the weather holds good I can plant all of my crop in good time   I am planting a good deal more land this year than I did last year with the calculation of them hands you promised to send me when you come home and you must not fail to bring them   if you do I cannot tend my crop. the mule that Julius rode to Tennessee is at James Walkers plantation the produce that he sent on all come safe but one plow mule.

I want you to buy me a negro woman young and likely and be sertin that she is sound on the best terms you can bring her down with you and I will work her on the plantation this year.

### FROM GEORGE A. BRATTON

May 31, 1839

Sir:

i will inform you that we are all well at this time   the negros is all well only Maria   she has bin in bad health since the first of March and is likely not to be able to do any sirvice   i have the promisingist Crop that I have had since i have been in the miss   i will finish in a few ours going over the cotton the first time   the mule that you sent me i can sell it for what you give for it an i will keep it untill you come   my negros and mules is all fat and you think go a hed and i say go a hed and a good Crop is the object.

Thir is a lot of negros to be sold in Coffiville the first of August and for cash and i expect will be barganes to be bought and wish your assistance

### FROM GEORGE A. BRATTON

June 4, 1839

Dear Sir:

Myself and family is only but tolarable well   we have ben sick a grate deal all this year   the negroes is complaining a good many of them   Maria is down and is like to be   Elizabeth has done nothing since Crismas   i do not think that they are dangerous   i have a first rate cotton Crop and the Corn is good but it is sufering seriously for rain   rite to me when you will be down in this country.

### FROM JAMES COWAN

July 2, 1839

Dear Sir:

I have been here for some two months on my farm, and my place is entirely healthy, and the neighbourhood generally except the Bowel complaint, which has been very prevalent, and fatal in many instances. The Crops of Cotton are generally fine, the corn has suffered much for rain, but if we are blessed with it in a few days, it will be a fair crop. The object of this short epistle, is to inform you that your manager, Mr. Geo. Bratton, died this morning with the Bowel Complaint, and perhaps the fever in addition. I learn that his wife is not expected to live. I also learn that your agent, Mr. McNeil, is absent on a visit to Tennessee. Under all these circumstances, I regret, that I do not know how I could serve you agreeable to your wishes. Managers are scarce, and good ones not to be had, and bad ones worse than none. Upon the whole I would advise you to send some one from home, on receipt of this, for if you do not, whoever takes your farm, *now*, will want your crop for pay. I expect to leave for Mount Holyoke, Hy. County, Tenn., in a few days, say two, after a long absence. If I was not so situated, I do believe I would see and do what I thot right for your Int. and that of Blk family and take the Responsibility. Please be assured of my good wishes for your prosperity, here as well as elsewhere, and be assured that nothing would afford me more pleasure than to serve you or anyone else under similar circumstances. . . .

I merely write you this hasty sketch as the stage will pass in a few minutes. In the meantime I'll send my overseer over this evng, to see how matters are, and may inform you by next mail, which will reach you 4 days later than this. McNeil being absent, I thot it a duty due you or any one else to give you the earliest information.

### FROM J. T. LEIGH

August 13, 1839

Dear Sir:

Mrs. Bratton (widow of your late Overseer George Bratton) requests me to write you to inform you of her present situation. She has had to leave your place to make room for the overseer who succeeded her husband. She has removed some 8 or 10 miles off in the neighborhood of Coffeeville, is poor and in want of money to procure necessaries to live on, is anxious to know whether you will come down to your plantation this fall and at what time. She wishes to see you for the purpose of settling her husbands accounts and to obtain money to live on. She left me a book containing some accounts, and some of her husbands papers (I reside adjoining your plantation). If you will inform me at what time you will be down I will send for her to my house, where I will be glad to see you.

Your crop is very fine. Direct to Oakachickama P. Office.

Bennet H. Barrow

## "NEVER HAVE SEEN AS MEAN A SPRING"

*Bennet H. Barrow of Highland Plantation in West Feliciana Parish, Louisiana, kept a diary from 1836 to 1846. His entries for 1840 are a* *typical planter's journal. Though spring had been a trying time, on May 25 the cotton bloomed and on September 3 the first bales were shipped to New Orleans. Barrow's crop amounted to 508 bales, for which he received $17,565.16.*

*Bennet Barrow began his planting career when he was twenty years old. He was twenty-nine when he kept this journal. From his father, William Barrow II, who had migrated from North Carolina to Louisiana in 1795, Bennet inherited three large tracts of land. Later he acquired the Clark and Gibson properties. Barrow owned some two hundred slaves. In addition to cotton he planted two hundred acres of corn. He experimented with sugar cane, grew his own tobacco and raised garden truck and vegetables. He also maintained a large stable of race horses.*

*Finley and Company of New Orleans were his cotton factors.*

*At the age of nineteen Bennet married Emily Joor, on December 16, 1830. Of their eight children, six lived to maturity. Emily died on August 22, 1845. A year later he married her widowed sister, Mrs. Nancy Haile. Barrow died on May 29, 1854.*

[May] 25  Cloudy  cool . . . verry pleasant evening, fine rain, yet it barely moistened the ground. Cotten Bluming, several blumes this evening

26  Clear   cool morning, went Driving with A.G.B.  J. Joor. 4 Deer ran to them   none Killed   I snaped at one 15 feet—never before

27  Clear, night quit cool—hoeing Cotten third time  scraping through it on acct. of the cut worms  in fine order, B.S.Joor came down this morning, James & John found a run-aways cloths in the pasture

28  Clear morning  cool. . . . Took short Drive . . . swamp still rising—Fish moving up the swamp. . . .

30  Clear, nights cool for some time past, run one furrow with plough & the harrows in the middles yesterday—stoped the harrows to day. Went to Town

31  Clear  warm—Want rain. . . . Taking the Cencus of the United States—the products, cotten   corn   horses   mules   cattle   Hogs sheep  Potatoes  Poultry, quantity cloth made, Fodder  hay

*June* 1 Clear verry warm . . . never had as fine cotten 1st of June, as on hills at Gns crop generally the same as last year this time, from 10 inches to over knee high, blumes much Early than I ever knew them, bugs Eating cotten in *spots*. . . .

5 Clear verry warm, Want rain verry much, several sick, one with inflamation of the Palate, two with verry sore Eyes, verry much pleased with my Crop, in fine order. The Distemper has made its appearance among my Hounds.

6 Rain at 6 A.M. barely laid the dust, appearance of verry hard rain above, negros holliday, nearly over crop 3d time with hoes, never had a finer look Potatoe Patch, fine rain at 9 ok cleared of since, nothing can be more beautifull than the Cotten & corn since the rain, *Laid the dust well*

7 Few clouds & morning pleasant, gave the negros permission to go over to Robt. H. Barrows to preaching. . . . being near & leaving home but seldom, granted them permission

8 Clear pleasant morning, working piece of corn, thining it & replanting Peas. . . .

10 Cloudy verry warm—little negro "Marcus" taken last night 12 or 1 O. very ill senseless—continued spasms can't wake him—number of sick ones, asked Dr. Hail to see Marcus and a more undecisive man I never saw. made great many attempts to bleed him, but failed & large veins at that. Died at 11 ok Walker came but could do no good. Fine rain at the House, barely laid the dust in the field, corn wants a good rain. . . .

11 Few clouds pleasant morning, Hoe hands waiting for work for 6 days past, worked piece of new ground cotten fourth time "scraped" —Finished ploughing all first planting by 10 O. 3d time, 160 Acres to plough, Cotten from half leg to hip high, first rate. Except Where the bugs have Eaten it, ground Works beautifull. . . .

12 Clear warm went Driving Killed two Deer. the standers missed 3. Working young cotten above, thick with vines bug Eaten verry much

13  Clear  verry warm . . . hands holliday since dinner. . . .

15  Clear verry warm—several came to go a Driving & verry much against my wish—went & Killed two Deer, very poor. Several children sick, son Bat & all my children with verry bad colds, influenza through the country

16  Few clouds, warm. Finished ploughing & working cotten 3d time this morning  could have finished some days since, new land cotten not good  verry much eaten by Grass hoppers, verry little work for hoe hands, started 12 scrapers this morning, ground very loose.

17  Cloudy, warm nights for week past. Cotten improving. . . . hoeing corn & replanting Peas in the cool part of the day, ploughing Where the Harrows ran & corn  new ground cotten the 4th time  I have the worst stand of Cotten I've seen. . . .

18  Raining since yesterday dusk, first rainey night I ever noticed in June, slow steady rain, several negro children sick  worms. . . . June Peaches ripe  great many of them, women spinning. men shelling corn, and putting up chimneys, ground barely moistened, lost two thirds of the day from appearance of the morning, had the Horses turned out &c. one Large Crib full of corn

19  Appearance of a bad day  raining. Some Wild hogs have in-jured my corn very much, more little children sick than I ever knew at one time, bad colds and worms. Cotten looks fine this morning Excepting upper new land "young cotten." . . .

20  Cloudy damp morning  several showers at the House  now in the field. appearance of a hard rain above & below me, negros holliday from 10 O.

21  Damp. Foggy morning  verry warm. . . . First water Mellon to day, verry sweet, fine large seed. Fine shower on part of the planta-tion, do not like my crop "generally," some verry good  say half  the other bad stand  irregular and too green. . . .

23  Cloudy  verry warm morning, scraping Cotten, corn improving verry much. Cotten improving in some places others growing too fast.

plenty of large Boles. . . . Women spinning  men daubing chimneys &
hoeing piece of new ground corn. Patience told me a lie this morning,
to my surprise Margaret told one with her. &c. Patience is decidedly as
mean as she can be.

24  Cloudy  warm  all hands hoeing—went Driving, caught a
wild cat, rained at noon. . . .

26  Clear  verry warm, Cotten improving verry fast. Some as fine
as can be. corn remarkably fine, some parts of the plantation the rain
fell verry heavy & some wind. . . .

27  Clear  morning pleasant. hoeing  L Gate cut & P bottom
some Kind of insect or Louse is doing great damages to my crop in
spots about  Cotten nearly destroyed. . . .

28  Few clouds  warm in the sun, but pleasant breeze for three
days past, lost a little negro yesterday, neglect of the Mother "Maria"
in telling me of its situation the day before never spoke after I saw it,
inflamation &c. . . .

30  Clear verry warm, started 10 scrapers this morning running
two furrows in a row to make the hoeing lighter for hoes, old Land
cotten below best I ever saw on it, Excepting Where the bugs or Lice
have et. Several Sick. Appearance of rain in the East  thundering
verry warm

*July* 1  Clear  verry warm  Fine rain at dinner & hard rain at Gns
worked the Lane

2  Few clouds, damp—hoeing above  too wet at Gns, Corn crops
uncommonly Good, Cotten improving. . . . 300 acres good cotten  300
inferior,  never felt A more pleasant day, ground in beautiful order
to work. . . . Learned that Woodward was shot  Lives near Woodville
a meaner man never Lived  choked his wife nearly to Death, and made
an attack on the carriage of her son, Ladies in it. had the carriage
stoped by two negros, accompanied by his two brothers  fired three
times in the carriage, Frazier and his brother succeeded in killing him,
one of the Fraziers lost his arm, &c.

3  Clear   cold   wind from the North . . . George Frazier died on Tuesday from the wound, shot by Arad Woodward, there never was a more cowardly circumstance, W. Woodward had made all the property over to his wife, his reason for doing it, was he ran off with a Loose woman—afterwards returned, Mrs. Woodward recd him, feeling some gratitude for the moment did it, has treated her cruelly ever since and, attempting to force a release from her

4  Clear Beautifull day, Wish the prospects of every one were as bright, as this *memorable* day, preparations for great doings at Douces to day   Barn dance &c.   will not go   having been started by a few Loco Focos Who have the impudence to call themselves democrats, such men as the Howells figure Largely, Political Excitement is such that the greater the sycophant the more notice does he get. old Capt Howells breed are a head of any thing in these diggins, Killed more negros by their cruelty, & find them dead in the stocks, and yet A. G. Howell calls himself a big man. . . .

5  Few clouds, warm   negroes appeared quit Lively last night. . . .

6  Clear   warm, Hoeing at the Gb place, part verry grassy "fine" Cotten looks as well there as usual, to day is Election day through out Louisiana. . . .

7  Sprinkle of rain this morning & warm—verry heavy rain this afternoon, Hardest rain that has fallen this season, went to Town Voted for Ruggin & Ratliff for Legislators & Dawson for Congress— regret voting for Dawson. . . .

9  Cloudy   verry warm, my right fore finger has a rising on it and never any thing to trouble me more.

10  some clouds, verry warm   Finished hoeing 5th time   crop in fine order & looks well, from ½ thigh to over head high

11  Few clouds, verry warm—hard shower at dinner time, Gave the negros a dinner

12  Clear morning, verry warm   my hand is improving, Ruffin & Ratliff elected to the Legislature, & Dawson to Congress by 13 votes

majority "only" the District has allways given Dawson a Large majority. glad to see the people getting right 'again' men change principalls never do

13 Verry warm, Went to Town Executed a Mortgage to Louisiana Bank.

14 Cloudy verry warm, My Finger well, 5 hands sick shower rain on part of the Plantation Pulling Fodder

15 Few clouds, Cotten improved verry much, never had better prospects for a Large crop—from waist to over head high, well branched & bolled. . . . Coming home last evening saw a bundle of Fodder stoped my horse & attempted to pick it up on him, as I reached down and got hold of it my horse Wheeled round several times & down I came, no support but left hand in the main

16 Clear verry warm, Felt no bad effects from my Fall, light rain at dinner, all hands taking up Fodder this evening. . . .

18 Some clouds verry warm Went to assist Courtney in looking for some of his runaway negros. . . .

21 Cloudy verry warm, hands worked worse yesterday than they have this year, several sick, never saw ground look worse than P.R. bottom. owing to heavy rain on Sunday. Cotten small, best crop at Gns I ever had at this time of the year, hard rain at dinner, & rainey evening. My son Bat. is decidedly the finest looking child I ever saw, the most beautiful head of hair, Eyes as black as can be. Cotten opening in every part of the field. Emily unwell. There appears to be no doubt but that Daniel Woodward murdered Genl. Joor from the confessions of his negro Who was with him, the same negro was with him When he attacked Frazier & family. . . . He died too Easy a Death

22 Cloudy bad looking day, all hands hoeing at Gns never saw a place washed as the two last rains have washed my plantation, P.R. bottom covered with water yesterday & Sunday, several sick, Women spinning. . . .

25 Clear pleasant Morning Went to Town, 15 ploughs running

26 Clear  verry warm, threatening rain since dinner—gave the negros Mucheto Bars

27 Clear  very warm—never have been so out done with sickness before in my life, common practice dont cure them as it use to, violent pains in the back  red Tongue, 10 sick  Cotten opening very fast, can plough in places "only," verry heavy rain this evening  stormy appearance. . . . my best young dog was killed by son John running his horse over him. . . .

30 Clear  verry pleasant morning, to day appears more like settled weather than for two weeks past. . . . never saw a better Crop, good Fall & no storm will make 10 Bales to the hand, 9 sick "convalescent." My cook ran away day before yesterday, in riding round the field this morning found her, Lavenia thought she had been whipped unjustly owing to Jane (the Cook), let Lavenia give her a good drubing &c. Two thirds of my crop verry superior. . . .

*August* 3  Morning warm  Few clouds  There is a great deal of talk through the Country about abolition &c. Yet the people submit to Amalgamation in its worse Form in this Parish, Josias Grey takes his mulatto children with him and to public places &c. and receives similar company from New Orleans, fine carriage & Horses, What is every bodys buisness is no bodys buisness, I made it my buisness yesterday Greys son with two of his visitors from the City had the impudence to pass here & through my Quarter, on a visit to see Purnells family. I ordered the negros if they returned this way to stop them, I rode in the field and When I returned found them stoped by all my negros (Who seemed to enter into it with prospects of fun) dressed as fine as could be, never were creatures worse scared. Alfred suffered them to Enter one Gate then shut both  And had them completely Enclosed, they asked him What he meant by it. nothing says Alfred but you have to stay here 'till Master comes. As I rode up to them with a stick in my hand, and asked how dare they to pass here & through my Quarter, I never [saw] any thing humble as quick as they did, forget all their *high breeding* and self greatness, and as Levi said he wondered if they could have seen *Miss Purnell* if she had of passed at the time, after appearing as though I intended Whipping them all. (their guide, an old negro of Greys Who had passed here frequently they said he took them through the Quarter & he acknowledged it) I told them to take the road as fast as they could and never to pass this way again, 'twas amusing to see which should not be behind in getting out of the gate (Levi says they all went out abreast) not more than 4 feet wide, the old negro was in the crowd one of them hit his horse saying stay behind John & take your Whipping, the rest leaving saying with hats off thank you sir repeatedly, I asked the negro if he was not a preacher after hitting him with my stick, he said no sir but I am *Fidler*, told him he could go, thus Ended the chapter &c. this will cause some chat in the country & may have a good effect, all it wants is a start &c. . . . Ten Ploughs running now. . . .

6 Clear verry warm. . . . Cotten *opening* verry fast. Picking cotten since dinner. . . .

7 Clear verry warm—several sick, picked over 180 weight Cotten to day. . . . Mrs. Hall & family here this morning & Finly of N.O.

10 Clear cool morning. . . . all hands Picking Cotten Since dinner 9 sick, Sun verry Hot. . . .

18 Clear warm morning all hands picking since yesterday, 10 sick Verry warm. raised Press this morning. Cotten opening verry fast. Av[erag]ed yesterday 153¾—49 Picking. . . .

22 Clear verry Hot—never had a better crop taking it generally, bolled to the top & large. . . .

25 Clear warm. great deal of Thundering last night, in the North. two negroes verry sick yesterday high Fever & violent pain in the head. . . . Picking Cotten at Gns never had as good a crop such a season from this as last would make 10 Bales or more to every thing that works in the field. ground that never produced cotton more than waist & shoulder high now 7 feet & well Bolled. . . .

*Sept.* 3 . . . Shiped 36 Bales yesterday. . . .

Varina Howell Davis

## MISSISSIPPI WEDDING

*Mr. Joseph Emory Davis, cotton planter of Warren County, Mississippi, welcomed among his guests at Christmas 1843 seventeen-year-old Varina Howell who came from her home near Natchez. Davis' plantation, The Hurricane, was located on the river some twenty miles below Vicksburg.*

*Near by was Brierfield, home of his younger brother, Jefferson, who had been living in "great seclusion" since the death of his young wife (Zachary Taylor's daughter, Sarah) some years before. Jefferson Davis also was a cotton planter, but recently he had been taking an active interest in state politics.*

My father, W. B. Howell, lived in a large old-fashioned house called "The Briers," on a bluff near Natchez, Mississippi. The ground sloped on each side, on the west to a "dry bayou" about one hundred feet or more deep, the sides of which were covered with pines, oaks, and magnolia trees. On the west there were deep caving bayous, washed in the yellow clay by the drainage to the river bank, about one-eighth of a mile from us.

Mr. Joseph E. Davis came to see the family when I was sixteen, and urged my mother to let me go to him for a visit. After much insistence the request was accorded; but as I was reading hard then to finish my course of English and Latin classics, it was not until the next year that the visit was made.

The only mode of communication was by boat, or by going to Vicksburg and driving thirty-six miles back down stream. Therefore, under the care of our lifelong and intimate friend, Judge George Winchester, of Salem, Mass., a jurist of renown in Mississippi, we took the old Magnolia steamboat, the week before Christmas, 1843, and went up to the Diamond Place, the home of Mrs. David McCaleb, the eldest daughter of Mr. Joseph E. Davis, whose plantation is thirteen miles north of "The Hurricane."

The steam-boats were literally floating palaces of ease and luxury. I have never seen any hotel where the food was so exquisitely prepared or the provision of dainties so great. Fresh fruits and the most beautiful flowers were sent to the captain at almost every stopping-place by the planters and their families, to whom "the boat" meant ice, new books, and every other luxury New Orleans could furnish or their purses command. A journey on one of these packets was an ideal mode of travel.

I hope I may be excused for paying here a passing tribute to Judge Winchester, a saintly man, to whom I owe the little learning I have acquired. He was an eminent lawyer, an incorruptible jurist, a strong thinker, and a devoted, self-sacrificing, faithful friend. He taught me for twelve years gratuitously, and in the hard methods that a learned man is apt to adopt who has no experience in the art of pedagogics. During that period the most valuable lessons I learned were not from the Latin or English classics—in the former of which he was a proficient scholar, and remembered them well because he loved them— but from the pure, high standard of right of which his course was the exemplar.

His politics, like my father's, were what was then called Whig, as, indeed, were those of most of the gentlefolk of Natchez. Everybody took the *National Intelligencer*, then edited by Messrs. Gales & Seaton, who were men of sterling honesty, with strong Federal views. They held Mr. Van Buren's name and fame as anathema. They believed all they published, and, as a consequence, the Whigs believed them. In every argument the statements of the *National Intelligencer* were of frequent reference, and as to facts, accepted by both sides. These papers gave, in stately periods, the six weeks' old news from the "under world," and, as they were English, London was often the theme. We knew then more about Lord Brougham than about the Czar of Russia, more of the Duke of Wellington than of Bonaparte. General Jackson had removed the Treasury deposits from the national banks, thereby ruining half the people of the South; and this added to the detestation felt by "the best people" for the Democratic principles and theories. Texas was not yet admitted into the Union, and the poor fellows who were ruined by their speculating proclivities had gone there by the thousand to wipe off the long score against them and begin anew.

The Whig ladies, many of them, had what were called "sub-Treasury brooches"—small shell cameo-pins on which was carved a strong box with immense locks, and a little blood-hound chained to the lock and lying on watch. The Whig children were told, "Martin Van Buren wants to set these dogs on your family."

Mr. Davis, on his way to a preliminary caucus at Vicksburg, his first essay in political life, came by the Diamond Place on horseback, *en route*. He brought a message from his brother that he would expect me at once. The next day Miss Mary Bradford, Mr. Davis's niece, came up on horseback, accompanied by a servant-man leading a horse with a lady's side-saddle. The high swung carriage and pair came also to bring my *impedimenta*, and "all in the blue unclouded weather" we rode over the rustling leaves through the thick trees to "The Hurricane."

Mr. Davis was then thirty-six years old, and looked about thirty; erect, well-proportioned, and active as a boy. He rode with more grace than any man I have ever seen, and gave one the impression of being incapable either of being unseated or fatigued. From an old letter to my mother I quote my first impressions of him:

> Today Uncle Joe sent, by his younger brother, an urgent invitation to me to go at once to "The Hurricane." I do not know whether this Mr. Jefferson Davis is young or old. He looks both at times; but I believe he is old, for from what I hear he is only two years younger than you are. He impresses me as a remarkable kind of man, but of uncertain temper, and has a way of taking for granted that everybody agrees with him when he expresses an opinion, which offends me; yet he is most agreeable and has a peculiarly sweet voice and a winning manner of asserting himself. The fact is, he is the kind of person I should expect to rescue one from a mad dog at any risk, but to insist upon a stoical indifference to the fright afterward. I do not think I shall ever like him as I do his brother Joe. Would you believe it, he is refined and cultivated, and yet he is a Democrat!

"The Hurricane" house stood in many acres of splendid oaks, and the main part of the building had low ceilings; a wide hall with four rooms on the lower floor, as many on the second story, and the same number in the attic. The windows were small, the walls were thick, and the doors were panelled below, and had six small panes of glass above. On the right-hand side of the hall were the drawing-room and the "tea-room," where the ladies sat; on the other, was a bedchamber and the "office." There the brothers sat when they were not riding over their plantations, and talked of books, of elementary law, of agricultural experiments, commented upon the day's doings, and made and perfected theories about everything in heaven and on earth.

Mr. Jefferson Davis read aloud to his brother the Congressional debates, and often when his eyes were tired one of the ladies was summoned to finish the speech under consideration. While I was there I often took my turn, and greatly enjoyed their comments.

The house was surrounded by wide galleries that ran nearly all around it, upstairs and down. Below, the floor was paved with bricks, which were reddened industriously. To the west was a large annex of two rooms forty-three feet long and twenty-five wide. The lower one was a dining-room, paved also and cemented. The upper one was arched and called the "music-room," where the young people sang and played, acted charades, gave mock concerts, and improvised games, while the family portraits looked stolidly down upon our antics.

There was a little store-room adjoining Mr. Davis's bedroom below stairs, out of which came, in the most astonishing and unexpected variety, candy, negro shoes, field implements, new saddles and bridles, fancy plaid linsey or calico dresses for the negro women who needed consolation for a death in their families; guns and ammunition for hunting, pocket-knives, nails and screws. This little closet was an ark, of which Mr. J. E. Davis kept the key, and made provision for the accidental needs of "each one after his kind." At the back of the house was an immense garden of rare roses and shrubs, flanked by eight acres of peaches, figs, and apples.

On the east side of the house was a very large barn and stable, in which thirty stalls contained horses—a part for the use of the family and the guests, and the rest for the brood horses owned by the brothers. The riding-horses were fast rackers, broken with care and ridden enough by stablemen and the innumerable guests to make them gentle. Here was Highland Henry, a large red bay, that glowed golden in the sun; his lean head and popped eyes, as he craned his neck over the fence, always commanded the admiration of the lovers of horses and elicited a cake from the ladies of the house. He was both fast and strong, but, his eyes having failed, his former owners had withdrawn him from the turf, after he had won several races, and sold him. Black Oliver, a Canadian horse that had also won several races, went like the wind, and he stretched out so in running that he came alarmingly near the ground; he was the sire of the then-renowned Davis pacing stock. There was the gray Medley, an iron-gray horse, coarser than the other two, strong-limbed and of wonderful muscle, but of most vicious temper; and a wild horse from the plains west of the Rocky Mountains, dun-colored, with black legs, mane, and tail. He had a certain rolling of the eyes, and a free, airy motion of the head and neck that gave a suggestion of a deer. All his colts had the same carriage, united to a wonderful amount of endurance.

Both the brothers were good and fearless horsemen, and they were pitiful to their beasts, and talked of them in the most affectionate tones; they often gave them to friends, but never sold one. It was the gray Medley which gave rise to my husband's constant expression about tergiversating politicians. The gray Medley's groom was a dwarfish, odd, little negro called Randall. He had been very often warned about the temper of the horse, but grew careless, approached too close to him, and at last was mortally injured. Mr. J. E. Davis was leaning over the poor fellow, much distressed, when Randall sighed out, "It is in the breed of them gray Medleys, you never kin trust 'em," and died. From that time, when Mr. Davis distrusted a man he said, "He is a gray Medley, and it's in the breed of them."

While engaged in these quiet and varied pursuits Mr. Davis was called to run in the autumn of 1843-44, as a forlorn hope for the legislature from Warren County, knowing that the county was Whig by a large majority, and that he could not be elected. He was defeated, of course, but decreased the Whig vote considerably. Next year, 1844, he was nominated elector for Polk and Dallas, and went out on an active campaign.

Before Mr. Davis's departure, in January, we became engaged, and early in February I returned home. He followed within a week, and after a short visit addressed himself to the work he had undertaken. Riding in the sun, and late in the dew, in midsummer, always gave him malarial fever. So these journeys were generally succeeded by long attacks of illness, and the fever affected his eyes greatly; finally, they brought on an attack of amaurosis, and impaired the sight of one.

After the canvass for Mr. Polk had closed with his election, in the spring of 1845, Mr. Davis came down to Natchez for his wedding. I had been quite ill, and could not then undertake the ceremony; but some three weeks afterwards he came on a short visit, and we concluded to marry then.

On February 26, 1845, at "The Briers," in the presence of my family and some of his, we were married. After a breakfast to our friends, we left on a tour of visits to his family at Bayou Sara and Woodville, and from thence to New Orleans.

On our visit to Woodville I was introduced to Mr. Davis's mother, who, though she could not leave her chair, and had attained her eighty-fifth year, was still fair to look upon. Her eyes were bright, her hair was a soft brown, and her complexion clear and white as a child's. His dutiful attentions to her, and the tender love he evinced for his sisters and family, impressed me greatly.

After our visit was finished we went to the St. Charles, then the first hotel in New Orleans. A great many fashionable people were there, but one of those I remember most clearly now was Mr. Wilde the poet, whose sonnet, "My Life is like a Summer Rose," had made quite a local success. He was the uncle, I think, of the poet Oscar Wilde.

A soiree was given the evening we reached the hotel. . . .

In about six weeks we returned to Brierfield, our home, and took up our abode in a "cat and clayed" house, situated in the centre of, and behind, a magnificent grove of oaks, and flanked by thrifty fig-trees; the Quarter houses being to the right and left of us. The building was one of my husband's experiments as an architect, and he and his friend and servant, James Pemberton, built it with the help of the negroes on the plantation. The rooms were of fair size, and opened on a paved brick gallery, surrounded by lattice-work; but some miscalculation about the windows had placed the sills almost breast high. The outer doors were six feet wide, but on these he especially dwelt as most desirable for admitting plenty of cool air; however, when they were opened, the side of the house seemed to be taken down. The fireplaces were very deep, and looked as though they had been built in Queen Elizabeth's time, to roast a sheep whole. It was a cool house, comfortably furnished, and we passed many happy days there, enlivened by daily rides, in which we indulged in many races when the road was smooth. The game was more abundant then than the chickens are now. Wild-geese, in great flocks, made fat by the waste corn in the fields; wild-ducks by the thousand, and white and blue cranes adorned almost every slough, standing on one leg among the immense lily-pads that yet cover the low places with lemon-colored flowers as large as coffee-cups.

In these scenes and occupations we passed many happy days, looking after the sick negroes, reading and writing, and visiting our neighbors and the Hurricane every day. We always expected to build another house, but it was not finished for five years after our marriage, and, though it was much more pretentious—indeed for that day a fine house—the other always seemed "home" to me.

Mahala Eggleston Roach

## "THIS HAS BEEN A BUSY, BUT VERY HAPPY DAY"

*We met Mahala Eggleston at Learmont Plantation. She was five years old when her father, Dick Eggleston, noted in his diary: "Betsy rode to Woodville to buy Mahala a Doll." Her father died in 1837. At nineteen she married James Roach and became mistress of her own home near Vicksburg. In that first December she began a Christmas diary. In it she would not only recount the excitements of the holiday celebration—Mahala seems to have introduced the German Christmas tree into Mississippi—but often go on to mention important family events of the year past: the births, the deaths, the sicknesses, the notable visits paid and received—all in all a unique record of a contented woman. She made her last entry in 1866.*

*Many relatives and friends flit over these Christmas pages. Uncle Jeff and Varina Davis at Brierfield are often mentioned, and the Hurricane, home of Joseph Davis. On June 6, 1846, Colonel Jefferson Davis left to serve with distinction in the war with Mexico. If Varina was grieved that Christmas because she had no children, she would be solaced: she became the mother of six. Mahala's brother Dick, for whom the house on Farmer Street in Vicksburg was being readied by his mother, was killed at the battle of Buena Vista. His mother lived on to work untiringly for the Confederate cause.*

Wednesday, December 25th, 1844
Clear and mild. When I burned my diaries last month, I never meant to resume them again, but I cannot so easily break off the habit of four years. Now I will only keep a record of noted days, anniversaries, etc. This is my first Christmas as a married woman, and housekeeper; for one month I have been married, and am very happy; rather lonely today, for no one is here but my good husband and myself; my country home is very quiet; and usually I like it, but today I want to be at home with my dear Mother, my little Brothers, my sweet little Sister, fond Aunts and devoted Uncles—how they all pet and love me! Last night I received many beautiful presents, by the cars; books from Mr. Peck (our groomsman), Mr. Woodman, and Mrs. Robins, and some little things from home. Had a good dinner, then Mr. Roach and I took a

long walk on the railroad. I am homesick tonight. Christmas day does not seem like it use to when I was a child. It is so dull now.

Christmas, 1845

Cold and snowy. Have spent a sweet, quiet home day, no time for sadness, or homesick repinings now; my little cottage is the happiest spot on earth to me, it holds my whole heart, my beloved husband and my little three-months old boy, my little Tom Robins. He is a delicate looking, pretty babe, and all the world to me. My good husband gave me a pretty carriage and a pair of ponies for my Christmas present. We have both been well all this year; everything has prospered with us, and I am perfectly happy. Mother, brothers, sisters (in New Orleans and in Vicksburg) are well; and more pretty presents have been given me than I can count. God has showered his blessings on me too.

Christmas, 1846

Mild and damp. Returned last night from a three weeks visit to my friends on the river, and in Vicksburg; went first to *Hurricane* and *Brierfield*, where I spent ten days most delightfully; a large party of young folks were there, and several engaged couples among them. Our good Mr. Davis pets the baby, Uncle Jeff is fond of him; Varina has no children, which is a source of grief to her tho' Uncle Jeff bears it, as he does everything else, stoically. Mrs. Robins came down to meet me, and we went "home" together. My baby walked across the room, for the first time, while we were at *Hurricane;* he is so sweet, and good. Mr. Patterson baptized him last Thursday while we were in town. Mrs. Robins urged me to spend Christmas with her at the *Castle;* Mother and Aunt wanted me to stay with them, but my dear husband preferred coming to our home; and I was glad to come with him, he is so good and kind to me. This has been a happy year to us, though a troubled one politically. The Mexican War is still going on, and my dear Brother Dick, tho' so young, is in the army; he is now near Monte Rey, and we hear good accounts of him from Dr. Halsey, and from Col. Davis from whom letters came while I was at *Brierfield.* Varina is very anxious about him. Mother has bought a comfortable house on Farmer Street (through my dear husband's kindness), and has gone to housekeeping anticipating Dick's return.

Christmas, 1847

Cold and rainy. Christmas seems more as it use to in old times, now that I have two little "angels" in my home, my darling Tom, and my

six-months old Nora, the sweetest, best little thing that ever was. Tom
can appreciate Christmas, and had a quantity of pretty toys sent him
from our New York relations and my own family; mine are the only
grandchildren in the family. Nora came to console us for the loss of my
gallant brother who fell at Buena Vista. This sorrow has saddened my
life. . . . My husband is, if possible, more devoted than ever, and I am
the happiest wife and mother in this world.

                                                                Christmas, 1851
Thursday, warm and cloudy. Rain after dinner. The cares of a family
were too much for even my fondness for writing, so I have not written
for several years (four) until now. My husband urges me so strongly to
resume my former habit, and has bought me such a pretty book that
I will yield to his persuasions and again "keep a journal." My treasures have increased since I last wrote, for beside Tom and Nora, are
beautiful little Sophy, and tiny little Mahala Eggleston "the image of
her mother," as every one says; she was born on the sixth of this month.
I am not very strong, but am well enough to be up, and have company.
Our dear Bishop Greene came up from Natchez last evening, stayed
with us until after dinner today; he is such a good man and true friend.
The children had such a number of gifts that I made a Christmas tree
for them; Mother, Aunt and Liz came down to see it; all said it was
something new to them. I never saw one but learned [of it] from some
of the German stories I had been reading. All the servants from Mother's came down, and our servants had a regular dinner party. Dear husband gave me a beautiful book; Aunt, a pair of sleeves; Mother a pair
of preserve dishes; etc. etc. I gave all the servants some present, and did
not scold a single time. Husband says, "I am good and pretty, today."
Well, I am old enough to be "good." I am twenty-seven. No, only
twenty-six last September. The children are perfectly happy tonight, so
is their Mother, Thank God!

                                                                Christmas, 1852
Saturday; warm and rainy, no fire. Truly we "live our youth over again
in our children." Christmas which was for some five or six years, rather
a gloomy time, contrasted with the Merry Christmas of my youth, is
now almost as much a season of joy and merriment, as when I was a
believer in "Santa Claus," except that I am now at the head of a little
family of "believers" and have to provide for their amusement, instead of being amused myself; but after all, the truest pleasure lies in

caring for the enjoyment and pleasure of others; so that I have spent a "Merry Christmas" and one of deep, true happiness, and gratitude to God for His goodness. All are well here and at Mother's, but dear Aunt Sophy is in great trouble; dear kind Uncle died in September, and we all mourned for him. . . . I improved on my Christmas tree and had a nice one today. All the family came to see it, and add their presents. Mr. Jim Gray came with Sister Lizzie; I believe he is in love with the little woman. Had six gentlemen friends of dear husband's to dinner today. . . . Little Hala can walk very well, and is very good. Nora is ugly, but good and quiet, while Sophia is a beauty, and good too. Tom is a little fellow. I am content.

Christmas, 1853

Sunday, cold, icy, everything frozen up. Weak, sick and nervous all day. Spent the greater part of it in bed, my only enjoyment was in seeing our dear little children happy. . . . The yellow fever left both husband and me very weak, and we have had chills ever since. . . . The yellow fever scourged us terribly this fall; our good minister, Mr. Patterson, was taken from us, and many dear friends. I roused myself before dinner and got along nicely. Had Messrs. Cunningham, Tharp, Howe, and Daniels to dine with us, and then the servants had a "dining." Mother, Liz and Fanny Fox are to dine with me tomorrow Children well, husband better.

Christmas, 1854

Monday, warm and rainy; cleared off at night. One sweet name which shown on my pages last year, cannot be there now . . . our sweet, precious Lizzie, my only sister, Mother's beautiful idol, died last August. . . . My dear brother was married a few days ago, to a dear, good girl, Mary Read, so poor Mother is alone. She will not come to live with us, though our home is large enough. This has been a "Merry Christmas" indeed to my dear little children. . . . The yellow fever has visited our little town again this Summer. I had two young men here, friends of Mr. Roach, and we nursed them through the fever. Mr. Parker and Mr. Askew; both dined with us today; also Mr. Barber (Mr. Roach's confidential clerk), and Mr. Barney. Mr. Beaumont came to tea, and all spent the evening. Mr. Parker sent me an exquisite desk filled with everything needful. I am ashamed to receive such a magnificent present. He says "he owes his life to me." Cakes, oranges, oysters, preserves, etc., etc., have poured in on us today and I am tired of laughing, talking and playing with my sweet little children. Hala is my "baby" still, and four better children never lived (we think).

Christmas, 1855

Tuesday; bitter cold; ground covered with snow. Real old fashioned Christmas weather, the ground covered with snow, which fell yesterday and last night. Day before yesterday it was quite warm, and there has been no weather sufficiently cold to injure the flowers. So soon as I felt the weather changing, husband and I gathered all the flowers, so as to keep them for the Presbyterian Ladies who had a supper last night. . . . We had a magnificent dinner, and husband declared my pudding was perfect. I am perfectly happy. This is the twelfth Christmas since we were married, and I believe each has been happier then the last. This has been a busy, but very happy day. Thank God.

Christmas, 1856

Thursday, clear and warm; one of the mildest and most delightful Christmas days I have ever known, and everyone about me has seemed to enjoy themselves. We had only Mr. Barbour and Mr. Adams to dinner; had a nice dinner, and sent some both cooked and un-cooked to our neighbors. The children were up before light to see the contents of their stockings, which were well and tastefully filled. . . . The sweet peace, deep happiness, and perfect content are Heaven's own gifts, for which I pray to be made sufficiently grateful. I have never known a happier time, and should add our baby boy to the rest of my Christmas gifts, for he has been given since last Christmas and is truly a blessed gift. . . . All the dear ones, my Tom, Nora, Sophy and Hala are good, and like their mother, say they have spent a "Happy Christmas." My life is so full and perfect, that my heart is overflowing with love and thanks to the Giver of my blessings. My beloved hus-band, five sweet children, loving Mother, many dear friends, health, wealth and this sweet home, what more can a human wish? Nothing.

Sir Charles Lyell

## WOODLANDS IN ALABAMA

*From the Georgia sea islands where he had been a guest of James Hamilton Couper, Sir Charles Lyell continued his geological tour*

*through the Southern states. In Alabama he was received at several*
*plantations and found the planters interested in his work and eager to*
*be of help.*

*It was Dr. William Carpenter of New Orleans who introduced Sir*
*Charles to Mr. Faulkner at Fontania. Dr. Carpenter had recently ac-*
*companied Sir Charles on one of his scientific excursions. Sir Charles*
*said of him: "His knowledge of botany and geology, as well as his amia-*
*ble manners, made him a most useful and agreeable companion."*

Wednesday, Jan. 28, 1846.—The steamer Amaranth was lying at the
bluff at Montgomery on the Alabama River, and was advertised to sail
for Mobile, a navigation of more than 300 miles, at ten o'clock in the
morning. From information obtained here, I had determined to follow
up my geological inquiries by going next to Tuscaloosa, on the Black
Warrior River, about 100 miles distant by land, in a northwesterly direction. Every one agreed, however, that it was better for me to go 800
miles by water, instead of taking the direct road; so I determined to go
first to Mobile, due south, and then up the Tombeckbee to the capital
of Alabama, being assured that I should gain, both in time and money,
by this great detour. . . .

It was the first of these magnificent southern river boats we had
seen, fitted up for the two-fold purpose of carrying as many bales of
cotton as can be heaped upon them without their sinking, and taking
in as many passengers as can enjoy the luxuries which southern manners and a hot climate require, especially spacious cabins, abundance
of fresh air, and protection from the heat of the sun.

The pilot put into my hands a list of the landings on the Alabama
River from Wetumpka to Mobile, no less than 200 of them in a distance of 434 miles. A small part only of these consisted of bluffs, or
those points where the high land comes up to the river's edge—in other
words, where there is no alluvial plain between the great stream and the
higher country. These spots, being the only ones not liable to inundation, and which can therefore serve as inland ports when the river is
full, or when the largest boat can sail up and down, are of great importance in the inland navigation of the country. A proprietor whose
farm is thus advantageously situated, usually builds a warehouse, not
only for storing up for embarkation the produce of his own land, but
large enough to take in the cotton of his neighbor. A long and steeply-
inclined plane is cut in the high bank, down which one heavy bale after
another is made to slide. Had I not been engaged in geological in-

quiries, I should probably have had my patience severely tried by such repeated stoppings at every river cliff; but it so happened that the captain always wanted to tarry at the precise points where alone any sections of the cretaceous and tertiary strata were visible, and was often obliged to wait long enough to enable me to make a tolerably extensive collection of the most characteristic fossils. . . .

In a southern steamer abundant opportunities are afforded of witnessing the inconveniences arising out of the singular relation subsisting between the negroes, whether free or slave, and the white race. The succession of breakfasts, dinners, and suppers entailed by it appears endless. First, the cabin passengers dine; then come the white nurses, children, and officers of the ship; thirdly, the deck passengers, being white, answering to our steerage; fourthly, the white waiters, waited upon by colored men; fifthly, colored passengers, free or slave, and colored waiters. To a European this exclusiveness seems the more unnatural and offensive in the southern states, because they make louder professions even than the northerners of democratic principles and love of equality. I must do them the justice, however, to admit, that they are willing to carry out their principles to great lengths when the white race alone is concerned. I heard of a newly-arrived Irish ditcher at Chehaw, who was astonished when invited to sit down at table with his employer, a proprietor in the neighborhood, who thought it necessary to recognize him as an equal. On one occasion when I visited a lawyer at his country-house in Alabama—one accustomed to the best society of a large city, and the ladies of whose family were refined and cultivated—he felt it incumbent on him, to my great discomfiture, to invite the driver of my gig, a half-caste Indian, who traveled without any change of clothes, to sit down with us at table. He was of a dark shade, but the blood was Indian not African, and he was therefore one of the southern aristocracy. The man was modest and unobtrusive, and scarcely spoke; but it need scarcely be said, that his presence checked the freedom of conversation, and I was glad when his duties in the stable called him away.

In the course of the night we were informed that the Amaranth had reached Claiborne. . . .

From Claiborne we crossed the Alabama River, and were hospitably received by Mr. Blount, to whom I had a letter of introduction from Mr. Hamilton Couper. While my wife staid with Mrs. Blount at Woodlands, he took me in his carriage through the forest, to the country town of Macon, where he had business as a magistrate. The district we passed through was situated in the fork of the Alabama and

Tombeckbee rivers, where the aboriginal forest was only broken here and there by a few clearings. To travel with an accomplished and agreeable resident proprietor, who could entirely sympathize with my feelings and opinions, in a district so recently deserted by the Indians, was no small advantage. . . .

The uncertainty of the cotton crops, and the sudden fluctuations in the value of cotton from year to year, have been the ruin of many, and have turned almost every landowner into a merchant and speculator. The maize, or Indian corn, appears to be almost as precarious a crop, for this year it has entirely failed in many places, owing to the intense summer heat. I passed some mills in which the grain, cob, and husk were all ground up together for the cattle and hogs, and they are said to thrive more on this mixture than on the grain alone. . . .

I passed my time agreeably and profitably in Alabama, for every one, as I have usually found in newly peopled districts, was hospitable and obliging to a stranger. Instead of the ignorant wonder, very commonly expressed in out-of-the-way districts of England, France, or Italy, at travelers who devote money and time to a search for fossil bones and shells, each planter seemed to vie with another in his anxiety to give me information in regard to the precise spots where organic remains had been discovered. Many were curious to learn my opinion as to the kind of animal to which the huge vertebrae, against which their plows sometimes strike, may have belonged. Dr. Buckley informed me that on the estate of Judge Creagh, which I visited, he had assisted in digging out one skeleton, where the vertebral column, almost unbroken, extended to the length of seventy feet. On the same plantation, part of another backbone, fifty feet long, was dug up, and a third was met with at no great distance. . . .

Feb. 5.—On my return from this excursion, I rejoined my wife at Mr. Blount's, and we then went back to the inn at Claiborne to wait for a steamer bound for Mobile. The first large vessel which touched for a moment at the landing, came up the river from that city, and stopped to know if there were any passengers. The answer was, "No, what news?" To which they replied, "Cotton up one eighth—no war."

### FONTANIA NEAR PORT HUDSON, LOUISIANA

After I had examined the bluff below Port Hudson, I went down the river in my boat to Fontania, a few miles to the south, to pay a visit to Mr. Faulkner, a proprietor to whom Dr. Carpenter had given me a letter of introduction. He received me with great politeness, and, at my request, accompanied me at once to see a crescent-shaped sheet of water on his estate, called Lake Solitude, evidently an ancient bed of the Mississippi, now deserted. It is one of the few examples of old channels which occur to the east of the great river, the general tendency of which is always to move from west to east. . . . One of my fellow passengers in the Rainbow had urged me to visit Lake Solitude, "because," said he, "there is a floating island in it, well wooded, on which a friend of mine once landed from a canoe, when, to his surprise, it began to sink with his weight. In great alarm he climbed a cypress tree, which also began immediately to go down with him as fast as he ascended. He mounted higher and higher into its boughs, until at length it ceased to subside, and, looking round, he saw in every direction, for a distance of fifty yards, the whole wood in motion." I wished much to know what foundation there could be for so marvelous a tale. . . .

Lake Solitude, situated in lat. 31° N. is two miles and a half in circuit, and is most appropriately named, being a retired sheet of water, its borders overhung by the swamp willow, now just coming into leaf, and skirted by the tall cypress, from which long streamers of Spanish moss are hanging. On the east it is bounded by high ground, a prolongation of the bluff at Port Hudson, on which the hickory, the oak, and many splendid magnolias, with the beech, walnut, tulip tree, and holly, and a variety of beautiful shrubs are seen. The surface of the lake (except near the shore, where it is covered with the water lily) faithfully reflects the trees and sky, presenting, in this respect, a marked contrast to the yellow waters of the Mississippi. It is inhabited by hundreds of alligators and countless fish, and so many birds were swimming on it, or flying over it, that it seemed as if all the wild creatures which the steamers had scared away from the main river had taken refuge here. Several alligators were lying motionless, with their noses just above the surface of the water, resembling black logs. . . .

On the boughs of the willows were perched several white cranes, white herons, cormorants, and water-rails were swimming on the lake, their various notes adding to the wildness of the scene. Shriller than all, as the evening came on, we heard the voice of the large bull-frog.

As we went back to the house, over the high ground, we saw three kinds of squirrels and many birds. So skillful was my companion with his rifle, that he brought down every bird which came within shot— owls, rice-birds, woodpeckers, and jays—that I might examine their plumage. I admired a beautiful cluster of the flowers and fruit of the red maple, about twenty feet above our heads. He offered to pick them for me, and, without delay, took aim, so dexterously, as to sever the stem from the bough just below the blossom, without seeming to have injured the flower by a single shot. . . .

From these heights south of Port Hudson, we had a grand view of the great plain of the Mississippi, far to the south and west, an endless labyrinth of uninhabited swamps, covered with a variety of timber, and threaded with bayous, one resembling another so exactly, that many a stranger, who has entered them in a canoe, has wandered for days without being able to extricate himself from their woody mazes. Among these morasses, one called the Devil's Swamp was in sight, and I found a curious account of the origin of its name in a MS. dated 1776, of Caleb Carpenter, a relation of my New Orleans friend.

A German emigrant having settled near the bank of the Mississippi, in 1776, felled, with great labor, some lofty cypresses; but, happening one day to make a false turn in his canoe, entered, by mistake, a neighboring bayou. Every feature was so exactly like the scene where he had been toiling for weeks, that he could not question the identity of the spot. He saw all the same bends, both in the larger and smaller channels. He made out distinctly the same trees, among others the very individual cypresses which he had cut down. There they stood, erect and entire, without retaining one mark of his ax. He concluded that some evil spirit had, in a single night, undone all the labors of many weeks; and, seized with superstitious terror, he fled from the enchanted wood, never to return.

In order that I might not spend an indefinite time on the Mississippi, I determined to be prepared for a start in the first chance steamer which might be bound for Natchez, 140 miles distant, whenever an opportunity should offer, whether by day or night. I was told by my host that a trusty black servant had been already appointed to look out for a steamer, which was to convey some farm produce to a proprietor far off on the Red River. He proposed, therefore, to give orders to this negro to wake me if any boat bound for Natchez should appear in sight before morning. Accordingly, about an hour after midnight, I was roused from my slumbers, and went down over a sloping lawn to the steam-boat landing on the river's bank. The sky was clear, and it was bright moonlight, and the distant cries of the owls, and other night birds around Lake Solitude, were distinctly heard, mingled with the chirping of myriads of frogs. On the low bank my watchman had

lighted a signal fire, and I heard the puffing of a steamer in the distance ascending the stream. She soon neared us, and, on being hailed,
answered, "La Belle Creole, bound for Bayou Sara." This port was far
short of my destination, and when we shouted "Natchez," the captain
first asked if we had any wood to sell, and on learning there was none,
sailed away.

I returned to the house, and took another nap of several hours, when
I received a second summons from my faithful sentinel. The scene
was entirely changed; it was nearly day-break, and the fogs rising from
the marshes had begun to cover the river. I was in despair, fearing that
our signal fire would not be discerned through the mist. Soon, however, we heard the loud gasping of the two steam-pipes sounding
nearer and nearer, and a large steamer coming suddenly close to the
landing, was announced as "the Talma of Cincinnati."

In a few minutes, I was crossing the narrow plank which led from
the steep bank to the vessel, which was actually in motion as I walked
over it, so that I was glad to find myself on deck. They told me I
must register my name at the office. . . . This conversation lasted but a
few minutes, and in as many more I was in a good berth under a mos-
quito net, listening to a huge bell tolling in the fog, to warn every
flat-boat to get out of the way, on peril of being sent instantly to the
bottom. In spite of this din, and that of the steam funnels and
machinery, I soon fell asleep for the third time. . . .

Letters from Albert Sidney Johnston

CHINA GROVE PLANTATION IN BRAZORIA COUNTY, TEXAS

*Born at Washington, Mason County, Kentucky, Albert Sidney John-
ston, youngest son of Dr. John and Abigail Harris Johnston, received
his education from private tutors and later at Transylvania University.
In 1822 he received an appointment to West Point, where he made a
fine record. The illness of his wife, Henrietta Preston, whom he had
married January 20, 1829, caused him to resign his commission in 1834.
Mrs. Johnston died August 12, 1835, and after a brief attempt at farming near St. Louis, Johnston went to Texas where he enlisted as a
private, but on January 31, 1837, he had risen to command of the in-
surgent army. Appointed Secretary of War of the Republic of Texas on*

December 22, 1838, he resigned March 1, 1840, and returned for a while to Kentucky. There he married Eliza Griffin, who was a cousin of his first wife. She had three brothers in the armed forces of the United States.

He bought China Grove Plantation in Brazoria County and, except for a brief tour of duty with the First Texas Rifle Volunteers during the Mexican War, remained there until 1849 when he accepted a commission as paymaster in the United States Army.

Living at China Grove with the Johnstons and their two babies were a Negro and his wife, two Negro boys and a girl and an Irish ditcher named John. Their nearest neighbor lived some fifteen miles away.

Despite the fact that the cultivation of sugar cane had proved successful in Texas—there were 165 sugar plantations in the state in 1850 —China Grove was a financial failure. Shortly before they gave up the plantation in 1849 Mrs. Johnston had written, "Our home is now a beautiful place, and I have become so attached to it that I shall grieve a great deal when we must leave it."

Albert Sidney Johnston rose to be brevet brigadier general in the U. S. Army. He was serving in California in command of the Department of the Pacific when the war began. After an arduous overland journey to Virginia he presented himself to President Davis, was named full general and given command of the Western Department. His brilliant service was ended by his death at Shiloh on April 3, 1862—a most grievous loss to the Confederacy.

George Hancock was the uncle of Johnston's first wife. He lived at Hayfield near Louisville, Kentucky.

Johnston's son, William Preston Johnston, was sixteen years old in 1847, the date of our first letter. He was later graduated from Yale. During the War between the States he was on Jefferson Davis' staff and was captured with him on May 10, 1865.

### TO HIS SON WILLIAM PRESTON JOHNSTON

China Grove, August 3, 1847

Dear Preston: . . . I will effect all or more than I expected in coming here, without encountering the dangers from the climate, with which the apprehensions of our friends threatened us. If by any good fortune I can obtain the capital to cultivate my plantation in sugar-cane, I feel sure that I will accumulate wealth. Like the poor, imprisoned abbé of the Castle d'If. I am sure that, in the ownership of this beautiful estate, I possess a great treasure; but I fear I shall not be able to make it manifest to any capitalist. . . .

## TO GEORGE HANCOCK

China Grove, February 28, 1847

Dear Hancock: You have long since, I fear, condemned me for neglect, and appearances are so much against me that I would not blame you; but I had a reasonable excuse in the unremitted labor I had to encounter in repairing my farm and preparing for a crop. I may say with truth that I have scarcely taken time to rest since we came here. The plantation has quite a renovated appearance, and I hope by next winter to have it in complete reparation, with a comfortable house to live in, and everything farmer-like about it. I hoped to be able to return in the autumn in time to make you a visit, but I was detained so much later than I expected that I was compelled to come here at once and go to work. This I believed to be the best course to pursue, whether I sold the place or kept it; and I have no doubt that what I have already done would make the place sell for two thousand dollars more. You would be surprised, I think, at what I have achieved in three months with my limited means. If a good opportunity to sell occurs, I will not let it pass. . . .

The successful cultivation of the cane here is no longer a problem. Everywhere it has been tried in this neighborhood it has succeeded excellently well. The yield has been great; and the quality Mr. Kenner, I understand, says equal, if not superior, to Louisiana sugar made by the most improved means. Mr. Caldwell, fifteen miles from here, on the same kind of soil as mine (peach-land), made 104 hogsheads (or thousands of pounds) of sugar, besides molasses, with sixteen hands, which is selling from eight to ten cents per pound. Sweeney has been quite as successful, and others that I have heard from.

## TO GEORGE HANCOCK

China Grove, October 21, 1847

. . . We have been blessed with excellent health since we came here, and everything has prospered with us better than we had any right to anticipate. I have cribbed 900 bushels of corn, and will send enough cotton to market to pay all of our expenses of every kind, besides considerable repairs and improvements. This, I think, is as much as could have been expected from so small a force. I esteem it also of great importance to me to have acquired some practical knowledge as a farmer; and mine has been truly so, for I have often lent a hand in the work.

My object in coming here with a force so inadequate was to repair the dilapidations which rented property always suffers, and to keep the place until I could sell it, or make such an arrangement for the cultivation of the whole of the cleared land as to enable me to pay the remainder of my debt. The latter arrangement I would prefer, as I still regard this as a splendid estate, which, if possible, I would like to hold. If I had it paid for, I would be satisfied to live here with the little force I have, with the confidence of supporting myself, but it would be a pity to let so large a place lie idle, when its cultivation in sugar-cane would, without doubt, produce abundant wealth in a few years. . . .

I promised my wife last year that, if she would patiently submit to my volunteering for six months' service, I would then, if she desired, abandon military life forever. I found her, upon my return, more obstinately bent upon my withdrawal than ever; so much so that, although I told her it might result in daily labor for my support, she said she would cheerfully encounter every trial rather than I should return. I therefore yielded up all the hopes and aspirations of a soldier, and with them has vanished all regret. I made no effort to obtain a post in the army, nor did I request any friend to do it; nor would I, after that, have accepted any offer. I have had the firmness to resist the most powerful impulse of Nature and education; and, no doubt, for the best, at least so far as my family is concerned. . . .

### TO GEORGE HANCOCK

March 22, 1848

We like our residence here, although entirely secluded from the world and from all society whatever. If we lose the pleasures and sweets of society, we are free from all the drawbacks, which themselves form a numerous catalogue. Happy contentment reigns under our humble roof. We both industriously endeavor to do our part in our own sphere, and the result of our efforts is never the subject of complaint. We have been married nearly five years and the first unkind word or look has never passed between us. If this is true—and it is so, for I have said it—have we not sufficient indemnity for the loss of society and the absence of wealth? There are those who, not comprehending the object of life, would sneer at our humble and satisfied views of it, but experience will in the end convince. . . .

We are now in the midst of spring. Everything is very beautiful around us. The grounds around our cabin are filled with China-trees in full bloom; large roses, also blooming; the Cherokee-rose hedge, its dark green spangled with large white roses; the Quasatchee, a species of acacia, "waving its yellow hair;" and the air redolent of sweets. We have fine strawberries and Irish potatoes, tomatoes in bloom, and many other vegetables. My corn all came up in February, and the stand is excellent and growing finely. I had a time of it to save it from the birds. "The price of *corn* is eternal vigilance" here.

### TO WILLIAM PRESTON JOHNSTON

China Grove, May 16, 1849

My crops are small, but since I have become a farmer I have the gratification of success in everything I have attempted; and in gardening I have succeeded as well. We have had a great abundance of strawberries; and at this time have a good variety of excellent vegetables. Our cantaloupes will soon be ripe, and in a short time we will have plenty of figs and watermelons.

The statistics of the poultry-yard and dairy are still more creditable to the industry and attention of your mother. She boasts of her flock of 100 turkeys, with prospects of as many more, besides swarms of chickens and ducks, and as many eggs as we want. All these things, with butter and milk, and a good appetite gained by some toil, enable us to live, so far as these matters are concerned, as well as rich folks; and these are the things within the reach of the industrious poor from the St. Lawrence to San Francisco. . . .

### TO EDWARD HOBBS

China Grove, June 10, 1849

. . . The life of seclusion and obscurity in which I have lived accounts for your not having heard from me. . . .

We have been away from home but about three or four times to visit a neighbor since we came here. . . .

On my return from Mexico after the campaign of Monterey, I found that all the proceeds of the Louisville property would scarcely suffice for the education of Will and his sister, and that it was necessary to go to work at once with small means for the support of my family. My own personal labor (this is no figure of speech—I don't mean head-work) was necessary in conducting my small farming operations; and I have yielded it with cheerfulness, and have thus, after three years' toil, become a rugged farmer, with good habits. . . .

## Stephen S. Perry

### PEACH POINT PLANTATION IN TEXAS

*James F. Perry and his wife, Emily Margaret Bryan, moved to Texas from Missouri, at the repeated suggestion of Mrs. Perry's brother, Stephen F. Austin. In 1832 they settled on the Brazos River, ten miles below Brazoria on a plantation which they called Peach Point. The family included six children (four of them Mrs. Perry's by her first husband)—William Joel, Moses Austin, Guy M. and Mary Bryan, and Stephen S. and Eliza Perry. They brought their slaves from Missouri.*

*Mr. Perry earned a reputation of being one of the best planters and masters in the state. Until the fifties Peach Point was primarily a cotton plantation. Then sugar cane became the leading crop and a sugar mill was installed on the plantation. Tobacco was a minor crop and enough corn and other products were raised to supply the plantation needs.*

*Stephen S. Perry, who inherited Peach Point upon his father's death in 1853, kept for many years a journal which presented in brief the work of the plantation. Here is his synopsis of the first three months of 1848.*

The months of January, February and March have been exceedingly favorable to the Planters in this Latitude. Very little rain for the last four or five years, the Winter and fall has been noted for dryness: The sun has been obscured the greater part of the months of February and March. Heavy clouds have constantly been threatening us with a deluge, the atmosphere; in consequence of this and the cool winds blowing almost constant from the north & south also the heavy dews at night with the few refreshing showers that have fallen. This keeps the earth moist & mellow & in a good condition to *moisten* the seed and bringing forth vegetation. The field is in good condition to work, all (except the prairy part which requires heavy rains) being very stiff land the soil will not undergo filtering like the [bottoms] on account of the few rains and strong winds.

The atmosphere has become impure which has produced sickness among the negroes. they complain principally of pains in the breast and sides—rumatisoms &c &c &c—The months of February and March has been practically dry. We commenced Ploughing on the ninth of February. The ground was in an excellent condition and broke up well, we had very little rain during this month not sufficient to prevent the Ploughs from runing. On the 22 of March we finished braking up the whole plantation (the middles in both cotten & corn ground) the ground was in excellent condition. Commence planting corn on the 17 day of February. Finished planting corn on the 25 Feb. Corn up on the 26. Commenced Minding birds on the 26 Febr—commenced planting cotton on the 1 of March   Commenced planting cotton in the Prairy field on the 9 of March. Finished planting cotton on the 26 March   Cotton up on the 14 of March. Commence running round the cotton with a one horse plough on the 31 of March. hoes commenced on the 2 of April.

Commenced ploughing corn on the 23 of March hoing corn on the 24, of March, Finished hoing and ploughing on the 31.

Planting potatoes on the seventh of March   finished Planting on the 10 of March. Potatoes coming up on the 26 of March.


Rutherford B. Hayes

## PEACH POINT AS SEEN BY A FAMOUS GUEST

*During the last days of December 1848, Peach Point Plantation welcomed two guests from Ohio. Rutherford B. Hayes, Kenyon College classmate of Guy M. Bryan, accompanied by his uncle, Sardis Birchard, arrived for a visit of some two months. Mrs. Perry, his hostess and mother of Guy M. Bryan, made a profound impression on young Hayes. "Mrs. Perry," he wrote to his mother, "instead of having the care of one family, is the nurse, physician, and spiritual adviser of a whole settlement of careless slaves. She feels it her duty to see to their comfort when sick or hurt, and among so many there is always some little brat with a scalded foot or a hand half cut off, and 'Missus' must always see to it or there is sure to be a whining time of it in the whole camp. Besides, to have anything done requires all time. It may be I am mistaken, but I don't think Job was ever 'tried' by a gang of genuine 'Sambos.' "*

The friendship between Hayes and Guy Bryan lasted for the rest of their lives. During the war Bryan served as volunteer aide-de-camp on the staff of General Herbert and afterwards as assistant adjutant general, with the rank of major, of the trans-Mississippi Department. Hayes rose to the rank of major general. He was wounded at South Mountain and was with Sheridan in the Shenandoah Valley in 1864. Bryan served in Congress 1857-1859, and in the State House of Representatives for many years.

*Wednesday, December 27, 1848.*—Leave Galveston for the Brazos on steamer *S. M. Williams.* Pass around Galveston Island by San Luis over a shallow bar into the Brazos about 5 p.m., at Velasco, a faded town; dilapidation and ruin. . . . About sundown pass Mrs. Jack's plantation, the only one yet seen. Wild prairie, low grassy banks, chocolate-colored water, cattle, and buzzards, the striking features of the scenery of this part of the river. Mrs. Jack's, a pretty place. . . .

About dark landed at Aycock's. Found Mr. Perry's "Sam"; took his mule myself and Uncle borrowed a horse of Aycock. Through a level, muddy country, mostly wooded, trees weeping from all their abundant foliage and gray hanging mosses, two and one-half miles to Mr. Perry's. Hitch our horses and are met by a bushy-headed fine-looking boy who resembled Stephen so much that I shook him heartily by the hand, supposing him to be my old friend Stephen, but a connection. A cordial welcome by Mr. Perry to his most hospitable home. Stephen and Guy gone to a horserace. Return early in the evening. Make the acquaintance of Mrs. Perry, Eliza (an agreeable girl of twenty-one or thereabouts), and spend the evening till midnight talking over old times. Been a wet, gloomy month; country shows to the worst advantage, we are told.

*Thursday, December 28, 1848.*—Day wet. Housed up. Discuss politics, old friends, sweethearts, etc., etc., with Guy, making the day seem short. The home is delightfully situated in the edge of the timber, looking out upon a plain on the south extending five or eight miles to the Gulf. A large and beautiful flower-garden in front, trimmed and cultivated under the guardian eye of Mrs. Perry.

*Friday, 29.*—Day spent in talking about and primping up for the party in the evening. At 2 P.M. gentlemen and ladies begin to arrive. Gentlemen and ladies on horseback, through mud and rain, ten, fifteen, or twenty miles. An exceedingly agreeable, gay, and polished company. The ladies particularly noticeable for the possession of the winning qualities. Merriment and dancing until 4:30 A.M. Sleeping arrangements for all got up in all manner of ways, but comfortable. . . .

*Saturday, 30.*—Guests breakfast from 10 till 11:30. All off by 12 M. Weather bright, warm, and spring-like. Look forward to a delightful visit, judging by what I see. Frightful stories of the cholera in several Texas towns. . . .

*Monday, January 1, 1849.*—Ride with Eliza and Guy over to Mr. Westall's to visit Miss Emily Jones, a modest, pretty Buckeye lassie of seventeen. A grand day for a gallop over the prairies. A good visit. Return home after dark.

*Tuesday, January 2, 1849.*—Start on a visit to the Misses Lewis, but learn that they are absent from home. Weather fine. Return and afternoon take a ramble with Henry after deer. Saw seven, also a wild hog. Had two shots at too great a distance to do hurt. Saw "Gus" "rope" (lasso) a wild cow. Exciting and somewhat perilous, in the eyes of the uninitiated. Home at dark and had chess with Henry until a late hour.

*Wednesday, January 3.*—Fine weather. Spent at home, writing letters, pistol firing, and playing chess.

*Thursday, January 4.*—Ride with Eliza and Guy eight miles over to Mrs. Jack's beautiful home on the east bank of the Brazos. Found there Miss B. L. Hardiman ("Teenie"), Miss "Hally," Mrs. Jack, Mrs. McKinney, and Thomas Harrison. Mrs. Jack is a large, noble-looking woman, benevolence, kindness, and humor beaming from every feature, shedding sweet influence on all around her. Miss Teenie, an agreeable girl of twenty from Tennessee; Miss "Hally," a blonde of singularly pleasing manners, graceful and handsome; Harrison a witty, sensible, educated, and *moral* young lawyer of Houston.

*Friday, January 5.*—Housed up at Mrs. Jack's. Chatty and pleasant; sleeping late and eating much.

*Saturday, 6.*—Ditto, only better acquainted and more familiar. A lovelorn swain riding with his sweetheart over one of these bald prairies, at a loss for anything else, says: "A fine hill for turkeys just here." "The Bible is a good book."

*Sunday, January 7.*—Ride home. Wet by a warm spring shower.

*Monday, January 8.*—Cold and cloudy. Hunt without much success, A.M.; P.M., afoot with Guy down to Joel's. *Get lost on Guy's home farm.* Guy "bored," of course. Little Perry, a lad of eight years old, "ropes" hogs, chickens, etc., and rides like a Pawnee. Uncle hunts wild hogs with a heavy rifle *unloaded* (which Guy retorts on him for the *last* joke) and rides a runaway chase after wild cattle. Evening at Joel's. A fine, lovely moonlight. . . .

*Tuesday, January 9.*—Clear and bright, but the coldest day of the winter in this part of Texas. Bishop Freeman with three attendant clergymen here making his visitation. Preaches in the schoolhouse church to a congregation of thirteen gentlemen, six ladies, and five children. The bishop travels his somewhat extensive diocese, to-wit, Arkansas, Texas, and the Indian Territory, in a stout cart, covered with canvas, drawn by a pair of large mules, driven by a stout negro, who cooks, etc., etc.

*Saturday, 13.*—Spent in assisting Guy to make out lists of lands belonging to the family in other counties, amounting to a square league and forty-four hundred and fifty acres. Labor one hundred and eighty. Weather pleasant. . . .

*Monday, 15.*—Start for Austin Bryan's, on Oyster Creek. Spend afternoon and night with Mrs. Jack. Story of their run-away negro; his honor in showing himself next morning according to promise and *then* running away. Swift chocolate-colored current in the Brazos.

*Tuesday, 16.*—One of the new steamboats passes down with its load of four hundred bales of cotton, pecan nuts, etc. In the rain with Mr. Harrison over to Mr. Bryan's. Ride over to a point of timber; see an abundance of deer but get no shots. A large blue crane killed flying, Guy and Harrison both shooting at once. . . .

*Thursday, 18.*—Guy and self swim horses over the bayou and home. . . .

So far I have seen few villages, no mechanics, no public improvements. Country appears very new. Many fine improved sugar plantations in this part of Texas.

*Wednesday, 24.*—Ride with Uncle and Guy over Gulf Prairie to the mouth of the Bernard, to fish and eat oysters. A glorious day. Deer, cattle, cranes, wild geese, brant, ducks, plover, prairie hens, and the Lord knows what else, often in sight at the same time. The roar of the Gulf is heard for miles, like the noise of Niagara. Staked out horses with "lariats," eat old Sailor Tom's oysters, picked up shells, fished and shot snipe until 5 P.M., then rode home through clouds of mosquitoes, thicker than the lice or locusts of Egypt—like the hair on a dog's back. Notice the eagle's nest on the lone tree in the prairie, and reach home glad to get away from the mosquitoes.

*Thursday, January 25.*— . . . These Texans are essentially *carnivorous*. Pork ribs, pigs' feet, veal, beef (grand), chickens, venison, and dried meat frequently seen on the table at once. Two little black girls for waiters pass everything possible around, and take the plates of the guests to the carvers, *never failing to get the right name. Mem.:*—All Texans famous for name memories.

*Tuesday, 30.*—Ride with Mr. Perry over to Sterling McNeal's plantation. A shrewd, intelligent, cynical old bachelor, full of "wise saws and modern instances"; very fond of telling his own experience and talking of his own affairs. Living alone he has come to think he is the "be-all and end-all" here. The haughty and imperious part of a man develops rapidly on one of these lonely sugar plantations, where the owner rarely meets with any except his slaves and minions. Sugar hogsheads vary from 1100 to 1800 lbs. White and black mechanics all work together. White men generally dissolute and intemperate. Returned, found Uncle Birchard returned from Oyster Creek, with the trophy of a successful onslaught upon a tiger cat. Glorious weather. One little shower.

*Monday, February 5.*—Cold and clear. Forenoon spent with Stephen and the ladies—music and flirting. Afternoon rode up to Major Lewis's. Three agreeable young ladies; music, singing, and dancing. . . .

*Wednesday, February 7.*—Uncle, Guy, and self left Mr. Perry's for a trip through northern and western Texas. Guy mounted on a high Mexican saddle covered with a red sheepskin on Joel's mule, a grand beast; Uncle on a stout bright bay—"Hotspur" (Guy's favorite horse), a fine animal; and I on a tall, gaunt, black, awkward, frisky piece of horseflesh bought out of one of the Kentucky regiments, sent to Mexico;—all with saddle-bags, overcoats, and ropes for lariats. . . .

## Mrs. Isaac H. Hilliard

## "SHORT CROP—SHORT JOURNEYS"

*Mrs. Isaac Hilliard, from whose diary the following selections are taken, was Miriam Brannin of New Castle, Henry County, Kentucky. She and her husband Isaac and their little son Isaac Henry lived on a cotton plantation at Grand Lake, Chicot County, Arkansas. Their house faced the Mississippi River, and steamboats—the Magnolia, the Concordia, the General Lane, the Luna and the Peytona among them —busily plied the river.*

*Many relatives and friends visited the Arkansas plantation. At Christmastime Miriam's sister-in-law, Mrs. George W. Polk, and her family came to stay. Shortly afterward Mr. and Mrs. Hilliard and little Isaac Henry were guests of Bishop Leonidas Polk at Bayou Lafourche in Louisiana.*

*Bishop Polk, born at Raleigh, North Carolina, in 1806, was educated at the University of North Carolina and at West Point. He resigned his commission in the army to enter the Virginia Theological Seminary. His wife was Frances Devereux of Raleigh. In 1841 he was made Bishop of Louisiana and shortly after he entered his diocese he bought a sugar plantation. When war came he was offered a commission in the Confederate Army by his old classmate Jefferson Davis. He was killed at Pine Mountain near Marietta, Georgia, in June 1864.*

*The "Sister Mary" with whom Mrs. Hilliard spent a month was Mrs. William Hardeman of La Vega near Jackson, Mississippi, another of Mrs. Hilliard's sisters-in-law.*

[Grand Lake, Arkansas]

*Christmas Eve, 1849*
I am frequently appealed to, in reference to the date of certain occur-

rences. On this point my memory is particularly defective;—therefore, to supply the deficiency, I will keep a journal—beginning with a brief summary of the past three months.

*Sept. 15th*—Mr. Hilliard in Tennessee. I go to Louisville worried with shopping for other people. Nevertheless, the sight & warm greeting, of so many old acquaintances renders my visit most delightful. . . . Mr. Hilliard arrives Oct. 6th, absent six weeks.

*Oct. 11th*—Carriage at the door. Bonnetted & gloved to return visits. . . . Mr. Hilliard enters in haste—boat leaving that afternoon—Party of southern friends aboard—thinks we had better take her—only half like it, but have the trunks packed; and that night . . . under way for Arkansas. Pleasant compagnons all voyage—to wit, The Keenes, Higgins; Millers & Wards. Aground in the daytime; lie by, at night. Nevertheless finally landed at home October 20th. Gloomy prospect—short crop; cotton opening slowly; five negroes in the woods; nothing in the garden; raining all summer; books, piano, furniture, silk etc. much injured by the dampness. Thanks to careful tending, & the plentiful use of assafetida, we have raised sixty (60) turkeys. Not many chickens.

Looking daily for my sister-in-law Mrs. Polk & her children. I am all impatience & eagerness to see them. Sister Mary will join us, and then we shall be truly a happy circle—do hope I shall succeed in making their visit comfortable & agreeable. My resources are few & poor; but much can be done with good cheer, a hearty welcome & considerate attention—Send for Oysters & Oranges every trip of our packet—arrange & rearrange, until we despair of their coming. Brother Abe pays us a visit—greatly disappointed he did not bring Bettie according to agreement. Proceeds to New Orleans—back to Bunch's Bend—returns here to take a boat. Gives me five minutes to write letters, fold parcels, pack boxes, send messages, say parting words, etc., etc. . . . as he expects to be off in a twinkling. At the end of three days, here still. No boats to be seen—one would think they were all ice-bound—dreadful weather—it storms without and brother Abe storms within—at length (on the third day) he descries a "Boat"—Oh, joyful sight! The sight of land was not more grateful to Columbus.

Mr. Hilliard & George started North 29 Nov.—took passage on *The Scott*—Alone—Keep a Bowie knife under my head, and Rob plays sentinel, in the adjoining chamber. Take these precautions, by advice of brother John. Mr. Raynor arrives—dines & stays all night. The long-

looked & much wished-for come at last. Steamer *America* landed Col.
Polk & family Tuesday morning Dec. 18th. Five children; pretty &
smart—much grown since I saw them last. My sister has not recovered
from the blow inflicted by her Mother's death—looks saddened & subdued. I hope change of scene & cheerful company will restore her
spirits. Mr. Hilliard lands at home about daylight 22nd Dec.

### Christmas Day

Wakened up betimes by the "Christmas gift" cries of Jim, Rufe and
Sallie. The dear merry hearted little creatures look very wise, and insist
it was not Santa Claus who filled their socks but Aunt Miriam. The
customary bowl of Egg-nogg duly prepared & drank. Mr. Raynor and
the two Mr. Paynes dined with us.

### Dec. 26th

Sister & myself alone—brother Geo. & Mr. Hilliard dine with Mr.
Payne. Mr. Raynor has a dinner party given him in Miss.

### Dec. 27th

Mr. Raynor dines with us—refused wine—suffers from the "leetle too
much" forced upon him the day before.

### Dec. 28th

Mr. Raynor, Col. Taylor, Mr. Polk & Mr. Hilliard go surveying—run
the line between us & Mr. Raynor . . . return at half past four—dinner
spoiled by waiting. . . .

### Dec. 29th

Weather bad—brother John comes up. Mr. Raynor to dinner.

### Sunday 30th

Disagreeable weather—rain & sleet. Brother John takes lunch and returns home. Mr. Hilliard dines with Mr. Raynor, who returns with him
& passes the night—always entertaining, but in a particularly happy
vein this evening.

### Monday 31st

Mr. Raynor bids good-bye—homeward bound. Commence Isaac Henry's dresses—puzzling business—dread the undertaking so much. I

want to put it off; but my sister takes the affairs in her own hands, and will admit of no delay. She is to cut & shape; Melie to do the sewing. I look on in helpless ignorance, until it comes to the braiding and drawing patterns; when I am restored to life—that is my element. Makes me uncomfortable to see my sister work for me—she with five to fit out, and I one—object—but overruled.

*New Year's Day—1850*
Egg nogg before breakfast. Disagreeable weather. Children have a candy pulling & tea party. Nothing to tempt us from our sewing, so we keep at it very industriously.

*Jan. 2nd*
Mr. Raynor got off on Yorktown No. 2—roads almost impassable.

*Jan. 3rd*
Mr. Hilliard & brother George go hunting—didn't get a shot—Mr. Moore killed a deer & sent us a hind quarter.

*Jan. 5th*
Bright morning—gentlemen sally out for a hunt—joined by Moore & Hogan—dinner waits—get hungry & impatient—just about to order it in, when they appear in sight: and glorious to behold, a fine, fat deer slung across Mr. Hilliard's horse's neck! at length, he has killed one! and bears home the trophy—a chevaree, he must have—all the niggers are called to sound a jubilee with horns, bells, tin pans, trumpets, etc., etc. but alas for the finale! Old Hogan killed the deer, and my luckless husband must still be the butt of sportsmen.

*Jan. 8th*
Clouds in the morning, but soon dispelled. Mr. Hilliard took the *Concordia* for Memphis. Slow boat. Jimmie's birthday—give him a party—Bettie Lathrop, the only child near, invited down.

*Jan 9th*
Mr. Moore sends us venison very frequently. This morning I sent to his children oranges, nuts, cakes & other nice things.

*Jan. 11th*
Brother George takes the little boys hunting. No game. I make jelly, maccaroons & plum pudding.

*Jan. 12th*
About daylight, Steamer *Concordia* rang her bell and landed Sister
Mary. Brother William detained at home by business—overjoyed to
see her—thorns must be mixed with roses—together at last, the day
would have passed so happily, but for the sudden indisposition of
sister—severe sick headache.

*Jan. 13th*
Fine morning. Col. Taylor called and insisted that we should go to
church: and in default of Mr. Shaw, let them tell us our duties. Promised to dine with him Thursday. Counts upon his daughters (Mrs.
Cable & Theo) arrival by that time. In the afternoon, we all made
the rounds of the quarter—in honor of our coming, many curiously
patterned quilts displayed.

*Jan. 14th*
Fine day. Received three letters from home. Phronie is to be married
the 22nd to Mr. Somers, a young lawyer. May the union prove a happy
& honorable one. A girl happily married is *thrice blessed,* but an in-
different husband, or even an ill assorted union, carries in its train
pangs unnumbered and griefs unspeakable. I hope her husband will
show himself devoted to her happiness, comfort & interests—and she
I trust will make him a diligent & loving wife. *Luna* landed Mr.
Hilliard at 4-½ AM . . .

*Jan. 16th*
. . . Steamboat ringing about tea-time—proved to be the *America*
for wood—tied up all night—Mr. Andrew Irwin & Col. McGavock
came ashore and sat with us until 10 o.c.

*Jan. 17th*
Raining in torrents—obliged to disappoint Col. Taylor—numerous
company invited to meet us. Perfect deluge of rain—so we betake ourselves to my Noah's Ark—alias, big cedar chest—crammed with silks,
crapes, embroideries, linens, velvets &c.—the extravagance of my girl-
hood—wish I had the contents in money. I lack system sadly—Sisters
Mary & Sallie assorted & labeled everything. . . . Am puzzled what to
do—stay at home—go with Sister Mary, or accept brother George's &
Sister's invitation to accompany them in a visit to their Brother,
Bishop Polk. I have never had any but a passing glimpse of a sugar

plantation—from its reputation, I should especially like to see this one. Then too, I have heard so much of Mrs. Polk's admirable system of housekeeping, that as I am a novice in the art, I should doubtless find it both profitable & agreeable. The *cui bono* can be satisfactorily enough answered, but I look at my boy and think I ought to count the cost. Well! I'll sleep on it tonight and abide tomorrow's decision. If I should put cotton receipts under my head, to assist me in a judgment, their response would be *"no go."* Certain sure—short crop, short journeys.

Brother John came up just after dinner—has sold his plantation to Mr. Goza—is on his way to Kentucky—hope he will arrive in time to see Phronie married. He is wearied with southern life & negro property —and is rejoiced to quit. Says the only thing he regrets is leaving me here. I tell him not to let this disturb him—that is nothing—the mouth does not always speak the language of the heart. He has made me a present of a fine saddle horse—giving me the choice of keeping or disposing of him for anything I fancy. . . .

*Jan. 18th*
Cloudy and occasional sunshine. . . . Brother John expecting *Peytona* all day—No appearance of her.

*Jan. 19th*
Early in morning, cold and prospect of clear weather—About 11 o'clock, commenced raining—increasing in violence as night came on. Brother John grew weary of waiting for *Peytona*—so he hailed the *Genl Lane*—a dead slow boat—got aboard amid a torrent of rain. I do not allow myself to think about it, but oh how much my heart yearns for home and those who love me for myself—faulty though I be. It seems strange that I should not be present at Phronie's marriage. Had a "boned chicken" and a "monkey" for our 10 oclock supper. Talking of bygone days make all so sad, they went away almost untouched—nobody inclined to eat.

*Jan. 22nd*
Sun rose gloriously. Col. Taylor called and insisted on our going out to his house to eat the turkey, duck &c. which had been killed in our behalf some days previous—ladies declined—gentlemen accepted. I will take notes of our own bill of fare, and compare notes when they return—To begin, Gumbo—a Boned Turkey & Young Rooster—Beef

Tongue—guava jelly—vegetables & pickles etc. Dessert—Plum Pudding & Syllabub.

*Jan. 23d.*
Mr. Moore sent us a hind quarter of venison. On account of the sickness of her children, Sallie has abandoned for the present, her trip to Lafourche. We all commenced packing and expected to be ready for the *Belle Key.* Greatly to our surprise & disappointment she came booming along about 3 oclock this afternoon.

*Jan. 24th*
All aboard the *Martha Washington* at ½ past 4. Uncomfortable enough, but short trip—so easily endured. Isaac Henry sick—so kept awake almost all night.

*Jan. 25th*
Landed at Vicksburg by 10 oclock. We had arranged to dine at McMakins—then take the afternoon train to sister Mary's—our plans were unexpectedly defeated—out of repair; the cars had stopped and were not expected to be in travelling order for two weeks. Sister Mary concluded she must try to force a march home so we left her in Vicksburg with brother William. After due debate, our lords came to the conclusion to take us on to New Orleans & Lafourche. Sallie voted the M.W. unendurable, so we changed to the *Magnolia,* making it like a transit from the hovel to the palace—large state rooms, excellent fare, piano etc.
Isaac Henry 10 months old today.
Mr. Hilliard brought in Genl Barros (whose wife it is said I much resembled) and introduced him—not at all entertaining. Miss Eubanks *compagnon de voyage*—pretty interesting girl. . . .

*Jan. 26th*
Delicious egg-bread for breakfast—must get the recipe. . . . Arrived at Natchez about dark—disappointed in going ashore.

*Jan. 27th*
Raining and blowing all day. Tired of the cabin, we clambered & waded up to the pilot's house—passed Baton Rouge—saw the new State House. . . . Eager to lose nothing, we run first to one guard then the other. About 40 miles above New Orleans, a tremendous crevasse—

distressing sight to see handsome houses, grounds, fields etc. under water. Landed at New Orleans at ½ past 7. . . . Mr. Hilliard & brother Geo gone up to secure rooms.

*Jan. 28th*
St. Charles full—go to the *Verandah* amid a shower of rain—rain-bound all day. All shadow, no substance at dinner—elegantly served but badly prepared. Invitation from Mr. & Mrs. Ward to attend St. Charles soiree (wish we were located there—no acquaintances here) decline—go to Placide's Varieties. Mrs. Howard is quite a pleasing actress.

*Jan. 29th*
Shopping until 4 . . . Number of calls . . . Intended to see Romeo & Juliet . . .

*Jan. 30th*
Send invitations to our soiree. Shopping until 4—dress for the soiree in my Brocade & pearls. Mr. Hamet sends me a magnificent Japonica—enjoy myself exceedingly . . . handsome supper—sip champagne compliments until my head aches.

*Jan. 31st*
Shopping until 2 oclock . . . Attend the American Theatre to see Miss Davenport in The Stranger.

*Feb. 1*
Shopping until 1—too late to return visits. Pitch everything into the trunks helter skelter. On board *Mary Foley* at ½ past four—bound for Bishop Polk's residence . . . on Lafourche. Merchant ships an imposing sight—one crowded with emigrants.

*Feb. 2d*
Late breakfast and miserable enough. Enchanted with the Bayou. A continuous line of dilapidated time-worn cottages—giving it something of the appearance of an Indian village. These are chiefly owned by the French whose ancestral pride will not induce them to sell. Back of these, as far as the eye can reach, extend magnificent plantations owned & cultivated by our own energetic Americans. . . . Arrive at Bishop Polk's ½ past 2 o.c.—company to dinner—we have dined,

so we are shown to our apartments. Mine is tastefully furnished and commands a front view—1st Creole houses opposite—then Bayou between dotted with sail boats, ships etc. Grounds very handsomely laid off—outer hedge of Cherokee roses. Dress and descend to the parlor—strangers leave—tea at 9. Family prayers—retire at 12 o.c.

## Feb. 3

Winter morning—attend church at Thibedeauxville. The Bishop keeps and pays a man $300 to preach to his negroes. In the afternoon young negroes assembled in the hall and catechized.

## Feb. 4th

Sew in the morning till 2 oclock. Then dress—dining hour 3. . . . This is not a fine house nor sumptuously furnished—comfort and convenience seem to be the object instead of pomp and show. Mrs. Polk appropriates to her own use a suite of apartments—viz—Bishop's study, bed chambers, bath-room. She has a faithful nurse (negro) to whose care she abandons her babes entirely. Only when she has a fancy to caress them does she see them. Eight children and cannot lay to their charge the loss of a single night's rest. In another department she is equally fortunate in having a housekeeper who gives out, regulates, and is everything she ought to be.

## Feb. 5th

Isaac Henry was very sick all night. Slept but little—give him syrup and laud[a]num—arranged my trunk All walk up to the sugar house. Handsome building, 290 feet long. Bishop first shows us the manner of carrying up the cane—then the engine (which is now painted for preservation) the way in which the juice runs—from thence into the immense boilers—process of dipping, skimming etc.—thence to the ware-rooms—500 hogsheads of sugar and 500 barrels of molasses. Vats below to receive the molasses which drips from the sugar. . . .

## Feb. 7th

Our "piece of perfection" kept us awake the entire night. Mr. Hilliard got terribly out of patience—vowed this breaking of his rest would kill him. Nevertheless this morning in his boots and fully adequate to eat his allowances of breakfast, take a solitary stroll over the grounds—draw off some of the designs of the frames and plates. The gardener is paid $500.00 a year. At dinner thought I should faint—dress is so tight—brocade silk, must have it altered. . . .

*Feb. 8th*

. . . Raining in torrents. Milleroy puts up each of us, a box of shrubbery
—hot house plants & roses. Bishop gives "Ike" a barrel of molasses.
Miss Steers, governess, sang for me this morning. What fine opportunities the Bishop's daughters have—such an extensive & rare library. I
could linger forever over the Books of Prints collected in Italy. We
expect to leave in the morning on the *Alvarado.*

*Feb. 9th*

Waiting all day for the boat—got off on the *Mary Foley,* at 2 o clock
in the morning.

*Sunday, Feb. 10th*

Rise at 2 o clock—doubtless would have indulged longer, but roused
by Mr. Hilliard to look at a Mardi Gras procession. Crowd on board—
all French, white & black. Get in port about 10. Determine not to go
ashore until morning.

*Monday 11th*

Returned to the *Verandah.* Shopping all day. Distracted to see Jeru-
salem, but no possible chance to get a box. . . . Madam Bourdin fits me
for a dress—can't speak English so compelled to talk French. . . .

*Tuesday 12th*

Returned visits. Before we had quite finished, commenced raining in
torrents—unfortunate for the Mardi Gras festivities. On board the
*Magnolia* at 5 oclock. Very genteel French family—invited to join
them at cards—couldn't speak a word of English.

*Feb. 13th*

Excessively cold . . . plantations & towns all overflowed. Rumors of
travelling on the railroad being again interrupted—burden train
fallen through.

*Feb. 14th*

Overflow everywhere—arrive at Vicksburg about 5 o'clock. Gentlemen
give us an Oyster supper. . . .

*Feb. 15th*

. . . Take the cars at half past 2. Mr. Hilliard finds it necessary to return to plantation. The crossing of Big Black is enough to make the stoutest heart quake. Mrs. Hardeman met us at the Depot—carriage not yet arrived—so late, sister & myself get into a hackney coach. Driver ignorant of the road. Drew up at the wrong house—lost in the woods— reach sister Mary's finally some time after dark. She has a handsome house and tastefully fitted up. . . .

*Feb. 19th*
Visited the capitol. Better looking body than our Legislature in Kentucky with its backwoodmen & mechanics . . . Gov. Quitman is not making himself at all popular. Excuses himself from entertaining and giving parties on account of his house being unfurnished, Lent and a variety of pretexts which satisfy no one but himself. . . .

*Feb. 22d*
Grand procession, followed by an oration from Mr. Tarpley in the Senate House. As it was a national celebration we expected a national theme—but not so—an eulogy on James K. Polk was the most *appropriate subject*. Bishop Polk & Freeman arrived about 9 oclock in the evening. . . .

*Feb. 23d*
Go to Church. . . . Wish I could see my dear husband or at least hear from him. . . .

*Feb. 24th*
Raining all the past night—roads wretched. Started in to Church very early. House crowded—all anxious to witness the consecration of Mr. Green . . . After dinner, write to Mr. Hilliard. I never in my life wanted to see him so much—perverse thing that I am: always appreciate him most when absent. . . .

*Feb. 26th*
Cutting out for Isaac Henry all the morning . . . Letter from Mr. Hilliard & five or six from Kentucky . . .

*Feb. 27th*
Sister Mary gives a dinner party today. . . .

*March 2d*
Went to the Capitol—no speaking . . . Long letter from Mr. Hilliard—not a word about coming. I am crazy to see him. . . .

*March 9th*
. . . Mr. D Hardeman arrived tonight—very handsome & polite. Mr. Hardeman has business to arrange with Mr. Hilliard—hope he will come on the morning train. . . .

*March 14*
Drove into town . . . thence to the mantua-maker's. Whilst listlessly sitting there waiting the return of carriage; the voice of Mr. Hilliard broke upon my ear, and the next minute, I was in his arms. . . .

Poor Col Taylor is drowned! Country overflowed . . . everywhere—yet he persisted in spite of expostulations & warnings, in going up to Mr. Johnson's horseback. If he had striking faults, he had also many noble qualities of heart & mind. Isaac Henry knew his Papa. . . .

*March 16th*
Took our departure from Sister Mary's and set down by the morning train at Vicksburg by 11 oclock. So much engaged purchasing groceries etc. that we missed our dinner & the *Peytona*; which passed up about 3 oclock . . . Bought confectionaries to make up a birthday box for Venie. . . . Aboard the *Kendall* by 10 oc that night. Julia Dean, the actress, fellow passenger.

*Sunday 17th*
. . . Reach home by 3 o'clock—all well. House in complete order (Melie having executed my orders faithfully) and garden quite flourishing. Peas almost in bloom & lettuce finally headed. About nightfall, a hailstorm & wind rose, which blew down the fences & timber all over the plantation. Levelled the peas & riddled the lettuce.

*March 18th*
Had the storeroom thoroughly cleaned and set to rights—unpacked my trunks and arranged every thing in proper places. . . .

*March 22nd*
Mr. Hilliard has fine luck fishing—two or three messes of trout. . . .

*March 23d*
Clear, cold day . . . furious wind last night. Could not sleep, so much afraid this frail old house would blow down.

*March 25th*
Made an immense Black Cake, half a bushel of Caroway and a Lady Cake. Mr. Hilliard too much engaged to come home to dinner—sent home 5 fine trout.

*March 26th*
Drizzling rain & very cold. Begin look for Mrs. Polk. . . .

*March 27th*
Brother Geo & sister, reach here this morning about 3 oclock—dark & gloomy—late breakfast—ground covered with snow—cold & windy all day.

*March 28th*
Made a Charlotte Russe & Sponge Cake. Set Melie to work at brother Geo's *robe de chambre*. In the afternoon, attempt to assist myself. Gentlemen go fishing, and send home some fine trout. . . .

*March 29*
All go fishing—poor luck. I caught one trout. At dinner had so many courses that Mr. Hilliard & Brother Geo rather rebelled—turned up their sleeve cuffs and declared, they would not eat another mouthful. Sallie is so fastidious, and so *perfect* a housekeeper, that I am on the rack all the time, for fear my "table d' hote" will not be prepared and served to please her. Mr. Hilliard has caught 25 trout in all.

*March 30th*
Mr. Payne came down to go fishing. Brother Geo sent home one weighing 3¾ lbs—4 or 5 others—have neuralgia in the face tonight.

*March 31st*
Tossing all night with pain in the face—sun shining brightly.

*April 2d*
Mr. Hilliard takes boat for Choctaw Bend, with the intention of engaging an overseer. . . .

*April 3d*
Awful storm last night—distressed about Mr. Hilliard—never slept
*until 4 oclock*. This afternoon, planned and made preparation for my
dinner tomorrow. Mr. Wright from New Orleans, bearing a letter of
introduction from Chas Allen to Mr. Hilliard, is to dine with us. I
know Mr. Hilliard would like to give him a handsome dinner, so I must
put best foot foremost; and by way of a start Rob has brought home
2 first courses—i.e., a tremendous turtle and ½ dozen magnificent
Trout.

*April 4th*
Dinner went off admirably—turtle soup & almond pudding delicious—
disappointed that Mr. Hilliard did not come. No other can talk &
amuse guests, with his ease & spirit. Write a letter to Mrs. Bishop Polk.
Mr. Wright to take charge of some grape vine roots and a Barrel of
Kentucky sugar cured hams I send her. He is waiting to take first boat.

*April 5th*
Mr. Wright hailing boats all day with no success. Rains continuously.
Made a Black Cake for Venie.

*April 6th*
Mr. Wright succeeded at last, in getting a boat before breakfast this
morning. Gave out materials for Indian pudding, jumbals, maccaroons
& pastry.

*April 7th*
About eleven oclock, all seized with a panic for fear the *America*
should come along and find no one ready. All hands get to work. . . .
Soon trunks are carried out and behold all in readiness.

*April 8th*
Looking out all morning for the *America*. In the afternoon *Winfield
Scott* woods—learn from her, the *America* had broken her engine, and
expected not to leave Orleans until Saturday. . . .

*April 9th*
*America* called about 7 oclock this evening. All gone—what dis-
mally sounding words! and how sad I feel—As the Boat receded, I
caught a glimpse of Sallie Hawkins, standing on the Guards—wonder

when I shall see her again—she is a sweet child. May this, and their journey through life, prove ever safe & prosperous.

*Apr. 10th*
Set Rob to making shrubbery frames. Mr. Hilliard comes in drenched. . . .

*April 12th*
. . . Mr. Hilliard sent home 3 trout—and this afternoon Mr. Moore sent us half a Deer—comes in the nick of time—as we are looking for Kentucky friends. . . .

Nathaniel Parker Willis

### "WE SHALL BE PROUD YET OF OUR PLANTER SCHOOL OF GENTLEMEN"

*Nathaniel Parker Willis had been associated with several magazines and newspapers, and at the time of his visit to the South in 1852 he was correspondent for the* Home Journal, *which he owned in partnership with his lifelong friend, George Pope Morris. Earlier, Willis had gone to Europe as a correspondent for the* New York Mirror *on a pittance hastily scraped together. He remained for five years and became one of the best-known and most admired Americans in Europe. He married Mary Stace, daughter of General William Stace of Woolwich, after a brief courtship.*

*The death of his loved wife in childbirth and his own poor health sent him on the Southern tour. The articles he wrote were later published under the title* A Health Trip to the Tropics.

*Success came early to Willis—a book of his poems was published the year he was graduated from Yale. His friends were as devoted as his critics were bitter. Lowell's comment on Willis' work in his* A Fable for Critics *runs, "'Tis not so deep as a river, but who'd have it deep?"*

*Willis died in 1867, and at his funeral in Boston, Longfellow, Lowell, Dana and Holmes were among the pallbearers.*

*The following sketch is a brief impression of New Orleans and the planters who gathered there.*

New Orleans, Middle of May, 1852

The Hotel St. Louis is an immense structure on the scale of the
Astor House of New York, but built around a lofty rotunda, that was
once, I believe, the City Exchange. The towering dome of this imposing architectural centre reaches to the roof, and is surrounded with
corridors and a gallery; and the hotel (an excellently kept and highly
luxurious one,) seems quite secondary to it, in its magnificent use as a
"bar-room." It is paved with marble, a marble counter extends around
one-half of its circular area, and so vast is the interior, that the half-
moon of busy bar-keepers, seen from the opposite gallery, as they stand
and manipulate behind their twinkling wilderness of decanters, looks
like a julep-orama, performed by dwarfs—the murmur of the gliding
ice and the aroma of fragrant mint betraying their occupation, but their
features quite undistinguishable in the distance. . . .

New Orleans is studded all over with these temples of drink—none
quite as architecturally imposing as the St. Louis dome, but all sumptuously splendid and costly. . . .

In the five hundred or more whom you may see walking up to "take
a drink" at any of the fashionable "bars" of New Orleans, on a warm
morning towards noon, there is, of course, a difference of class and great
variety of character. . . .

The planter "takes a drink" a dozen times in the forenoon—but he
does not *drink* it. He seldom calls for it when alone. It is with him a
matter of eitiquette. Wherever he meets friend or acquaintance, there
is a drinking saloon near by—and he would feel as much at a loss to
exchange the compliments of the day, without stepping in to do it over
a glass, as to bow to a lady without his hat, or manage an interview
without mention of health or weather. In the way he walks up, signifies
his wish to the bar-keeper, sees that his friend is properly attended to,
and disposes of his own glass—in the *manner* of all this—there is a
certain absolute ease, and a sort of cotton-bale solidity of suavity, that
form a type of politeness which borrows nothing from intoxication.
It is the Westerner at home—perfectly self-trustful, and ever ready for
emergency, but boundlessly hospitable and courteous, and, withal,
careful in his drink. The arrangements for the convenience of tobacco
chewers receive the greater part of what he takes into his mouth for
courtesy, and he modifies the mixture of his own glass with such
adroitness as not to make it a comment on the stronger drink of his
companions. I was amused at the clever manner in which this was
done, and the many instances of it that came under my observation.

So many are the strangers, that they are part of almost every coterie in a bar-room; but, whatever or whoever they were, the planter was the man of mark among them. He is a gentleman by every influence of education and climate. With a slight touch of the tetrarch in his manner, perhaps, the constant habit of authority has made it sit grace- fully upon him, and it impregnates his whole bearing with that inde- scribable air of conscious superiority which never can be assumed, but which is prized above all other traits by the high-born in Europe. We shall be proud yet of our planter school of gentlemen. The early-learnt self-possession as master, the climate's lavishness of generosity, the habituation to personal risk and chivalric promptness, and the large amounts and elegant intermediary leisure with which plantation busi- ness is transacted, are the training for a peculiar as well as a very high spirited class of men. By the members of the professions, and by those who have long resided at the West, the manners of this class are very much adopted, It is the secret of that gracefully cavalier tone pervading the upper classes of the Valley and the Southern Tier—the more valu- able because the same thing is fast dying out in the lands where it has been historical. . . .

I find it takes new eyes to be surprised at very thought-stirring scenes, sometimes; but, to give a strong instance of what people may get so used to as to give over looking at it with any particular curiosity, I will describe *what was set out upon two tables* on the opposite sides of the bar-room of my hotel. . . . It is thronged at the drinking hour, and, on the morning I speak of, I had gone down to take a lounge through the crowd, interested as always in the faces and manners of a strange city, but looking for no special novelty beyond. The day was warm and the drinkers many. I was amused with the usual contrast, as I went in, the architectural sublimities commonly reserved for places of sacred resort (a dome sustained by lofty columns, and admitting light only from the meridian sky), enclosing a throng so careless and lively. I strolled along one side, and saw the lunch-table spread out with *terrapin soup, olives, sandwiches,* etc., and then, with a chance turn, I crossed the crowded floor and came upon another table on the opposite side, set out with—what does the reader suppose?—*half a dozen nicely dressed negresses,* from eighteen to twenty-five years of age, seated in chairs upon the top of the table, and waiting to be sold presently at auction!

And, to this, nobody was giving a second look. Groups of men stood about, on the marble floor of the vast area, with hats on and glasses in

their hands, conversing gayly. The white-aproned waiters ladled out
the soup. The gracious and gentlemanly master-bar-keepers stood
braiding rainbows across their firmament of decanters as they flung
the ice and the rosy liquor back and forwards into fragrant contact
with the mint. Politics were talked loud, and business was talked
low. . . .

The negresses were perfectly natural and their amused interest in
the scene around, was sufficient to make them as gay as children at a
show. The front of the table was on a line with the circle of columns,
and it extended back across the corridor in the rear—one of the women,
who had two children at her knee, sitting back against the wall of the
dome. This last was the only one whose face expressed any seriousness
or anxiety, though all were modest in their cheerfulness. . . .

The auctioneer mounted a chair, presently, and the sale proceeded.
. . . With what I could see of it, I was exceedingly interested, though,
of the crowd around, no one else except the bidders seemed to have
the curiosity to look on. The girls seemed bashful more than anything
else, dropping their eyes as the auctioneer told their ages and qualities,
or stealing furtive glances at the low-voiced namers of the dollars they
might be worth—their vanity, doubtless, somewhat excited in watching the ladder up which their value was so reluctantly ascending.
Imagination might paint very touching pictures from this scene. It was
over before I had got out my "brushes and colours." I just remember
that the mother looked pleased with the destiny of herself and her
children. The others were gone without my having been able to designate even their prices. . . . But I looked down, from the gallery above,
upon the two bare tables, later in the day, and indulged reverie over
the contrasted disposal of the respected viands—the stomach's digestion of what had been spread upon one, and Fate's digestion of what
had been spread upon the other.

Susan Dabney Smedes

## PLAGUE AT PASS CHRISTIAN

*All winter Pass Christian, the little village on the Gulf of Mexico
midway between New Orleans and Mobile, was a quiet place, but in
summer it became a gay and lively resort. The visitors, citizens of New*

*Orleans, planters from Mississippi and Louisiana, opened their sum-*
*mer houses or stayed at the Pass Christian hotel. Many of the gentle-*
*men owned yachts and the bay was gay with white sails. Every fort-*
*night a regatta was held.*

*In the summer of 1853 our friend Thomas Dabney and his family*
*made their usual journey of a hundred and eighty miles from Burleigh*
*Plantation to Pass Christian. There were reasons for them to be espe-*
*cially eager to reach this pleasant spot—and then to be disappointed.*
*Susan Dabney Smedes tells what happened at Pass Christian and*
*on the way home.*

The summer of 1853 was an anxious one in the South, for the yellow
fever was raging in New Orleans and in other Southern cities. It had
never been known to reach Pass Christian, and the Dabneys felt safe
there. But the New Orleans daily papers, giving the mortality at two
hundred, and finally even three hundred a day, cast a gloom over all
faces. A great many New Orleans people fled for safety to the Pass.
The daily boats were crowded with refugees. Quarantine laws were
unknown then.

In September it began to be rumored that the disease had broken
out at the Pass Christian hotel, and that the victims were buried every
night, lest people might be deterred from going there.

It was all too true. But scarcely any one believed it.

Charles Dabney had come home after two years of study at the Law
School of Harvard University, having graduated there with honor. His
mother feared that his having been so long in a Northern climate made
him particularly susceptible to the fever. She urged on him this danger, and begged her husband to take the family away from the Pass.
But he did not believe it possible that the fever could spread in that
air. Charles was full of youthful spirits, and so happy to be in the home
circle once more, that he could not be made to apprehend any danger.
When the last week in September came, the fever was more deadly
than ever in New Orleans. This decided Thomas to take his whole family to Burleigh by the overland route. He and the mother and the little
ones and the servants had always gone by this way.

His wagons were commodious, and he invited a number of friends to
become his guests in this journey, and to remain at Burleigh until it
should be safe for them to return to their homes in New Orleans.
Quite a party accepted the invitation, and it was looked forward to as a
delightful and novel excursion. But different things interfered, and all

but one young lady found it impossible to accompany the family on the seven days' journey through the country.

On the afternoon of the first day's travel she got out of the wagon to take a long walk. Charles was on his riding-horse. He felt ill at the time, as he afterwards told his mother, but he could not see a young lady, his guest, walk unattended by himself. He walked two and a half miles with her, when he found himself near fainting. They had now reached the house where the travellers were to spend the night. The next morning it was decided that he was not able to continue the journey that day; but no special anxiety was felt. Yellow fever was not thought of. It had been maintained that it could not be contracted on the Mississippi coast of the Gulf of Mexico.

One of the children held back to say good-by to brother Charley, but the father said that there was no use in that; he had only a bilious attack, and would be up in a day or two. So Edward was sent forward with the charge of the children and wagons, and the rest of the household, amounting to twenty-one persons.

Thomas and Sophia, with the baby and nurse and a man-servant, remained behind with Charles. Thomas was not long in finding that the sickness that he had hoped was so slight was baffling his knowledge of disease. The symptoms were unlike any that he had seen. The situation was agonizing. Neither physician nor medicine was to be had in that country, not even a cupping-glass to relieve the throbbing temples.

Still, no thought of the yellow fever crossed the mind of any one. Even if it had, the result, under circumstances so disastrous, could hardly have been other than it was.

They were not much longer to be in doubt as to the enemy that was battling with that young life.

A gush of black vomit let them know that their boy was dying of the yellow fever. He asked his mother to hand a looking-glass to him. She held it before his face, and he was shocked to see the blood on his mouth. At once he prepared himself for the death that could be but a few hours off. "Lord, have mercy on me," his mother heard him whisper. "Tell Virginius," he said, "to set a good example to his younger brothers and sisters; much depends on him, now that he is to be the eldest. No one knows how I have felt the responsibility of being the eldest. I have tried to set a good example. I felt the responsibility." Turning to his father, he said, "Do not expect so much of your other children as you expect of me. I was injured by that. I tried too hard not to disappoint you. . . ."

He spoke lovingly of each brother and sister by name. Only that summer he had said that he would like to marry a wife like any one of his six sisters. . . .

The poor distracted father rushed from the house and into the woods. It was more than an hour before he had regained self-control and could trust himself to go back to that bedside. Death seemed slow in coming. [Charles] stretched himself straight and close to the side of the wretched room, and kept the position for more than an hour. "It is too hard," he said at last. "I cannot stand it. I tried to lie there straight, that you might not have any trouble in composing my limbs. Bury me here now, in these woods. But do not leave me here. In the winter take me up and put me by the side of my brothers."

When the sun rose on Wednesday, the 28th of September, it was all over. The father who, but a few days ago, knew that he had a son ready to take his place as the worthy head of the family, now felt that his staff had been taken from him. The mother's grief was quiet but crushing.

The poor, ignorant people in whose house they were staying were kind and sympathizing, and did all that they could to help my dear father and mother. They had a number of children, and Thomas Dabney spoke with regret to the father of the family at having brought a dangerous and contagious disease under his roof. The man answered that he was not afraid, and that even if there were danger he could not have turned a sick man from his door.

They laid their son there to rest among the pines till January. Then he was carried to Raymond, where he now sleeps beside his brothers.

## Letters to Sarah Childress Polk

### FURTHER NEWS FROM YALOBUSHA

*In the letters that George A. Bratton wrote to James K. Polk from Yalobusha back in 1839 we had a picture of the cares and duties that fell to a conscientious, if illiterate, overseer.*

*Mr. Polk died on June 15, 1849, and his charming widow, Sarah Childress Polk, became absentee mistress of the Mississippi plantation. Some of the following letters were written by her overseer, John A. Mairs, no less ingeniously phonetic and no less painfully conscientious. In 1855 he had been in charge of the plantation for a little more than ten years.*

*The other letters were written by her cotton factor, Mr. W. S.*
*Pickett, of the New Orleans firm of Perkins, Campbell and Company.*
*In the year of the letters he withdrew from this connection and estab-*
*lished his own business.*

*The plantation produced 148 bales of cotton in 1855, for which*
*Mrs. Polk received $5,981.61.*

[Okacheckina, Miss.] June 17, 1855
Mairm

i have Just Receved your leters 1 of 4th and 1 of 7th   Your woman
Jane had a child and at 2 weaks old overlyed it   the rest of your servants are all well at present   we have had some fivores for the last 3
weeks   the wether is fine at present warm with some rane   the crop
lucks well though i had to plant over 40 acres   but it groing finely   if
the seasons is good and a good fall i think we will make a good crop   I
receved a draft drone on Messrs Purkins Campbell and Co for five
hundred and fifty dollars in my favor   you wanted to know hough
much you had to pay your negros   you in ginerly pay them About 200
hundred dollars at a time   i have not collected much of the black
smith act counts   the most of them got thir coten burnt   Harry dous
not git much work to dough   the most of the planters has a black
smith and makes out with them   if you wish I will pay them some of
my oune mony. . . .

Respectfully
JOHN A. MAIRS

August 29, 1855
Mairm

inough write you a few lins about your plantation and sirvants
your sirvants are all well at present   your woman evy increased hir
family on 16th   calds hir child Henry Polk   We have had some dry
wether sens irote you   the coten opeen vary fast   the hands has picked
finely   the crop of coten has bin cut short by the bold worm   ihear
goodeal of complaint in this naberhood   idough not think we will
make a large crop nough but istill hope we will make a far crop   the
corn is made   it is good   we had a fine rane last evenig which will
help the coten and pee crop and potaters   the stock all lucks as well
as cold be expected   iwill dough my best

Respectfully
JOHN A. MAIRS

November 7, 1855

Mairm

inough write you a few lins   your servants are all well at present we hald Ten Bags of your coten to troy to day and will hall about 80 Bags before we stop   we will stop then untwel we ship some   we have had a good deal of raine and the Rivir is in good order for Boting   the steamer unicorn has bin up all the summer   will go out this rise   is asking $4 four dollars pur Bag.   i think that is rather high   coten is low   perhaps we will dough beter yet on this rise   your coten is in the care of Powell and Trummell   troy   Miss   we have a good deal of Coten to pick out yet   the negros behave themselve vary well   we are doing the best we can   write me when you git this leter

Vary Respectfully

JOHN A. MAIRS

[New Orleans] November 22, 1855

Dear Madam:

On my return *home yesterday* I found your esteemed favor of 12th Oct. It is I hope, needless to say that my long absence from home (much longer than I anticipated) has caused the delay in replying to you.

I attended promptly to your request on my arrival at Memphis several weeks ago, about the Insurance of your cotton, by taking out a policy *against fire* while in the warehouse at Troy, and as I have policies to protect it against loss by navigation on the rivers and against fire while in store in this city, there is now, no interregnum of insecurity between its leaving your gin-house, and final disposition here. You need therefore give yourself no further uneasiness about it. All shall be right. The talk about "Condemned boats," "new regulations," etc is no new thing. The board of underwriters here, *condemn* and *reinstate* boats every season for some cause or other, but I have no idea that your agents at Troy will ship your cotton in such a manner as to vitiate the insurance upon it.

Our cotton market is doing well under all the influences bearing upon it. Such cotton as you have generally sent to this market, would now command about 11 cts.

Very Respfy yr. ob. Svt

W. S. PICKETT

[New Orleans] December

Dear Madam:

. . . Your favor of 20th Ult  came duly to hand. The shipment of 52 B/Cotton in the hands of Mr. Perkins is not yet sold. The best offer had for it last week was 10 cts but I doubt if the offer will be repeated as our market has undergone a change for the worse. I see no reason however to hurry the sale, under the anticipation of much lower prices.

I shall esteem it a favor if you will order the remainder of your crop to be shipped to my new firm, and even to give me an order for the shipment now here. . . .

Very Respfy your friend
W. S. PICKETT

[Okacheckina, Miss.] December 15, 1855
. . . ilurn today that the steam bote unicorne Burnt las weak on the asue  [Yazoo]   river  She had 55 fifty Bags of your coten on bode  it Burnt oup   iam in hops you had good inshurrans on it. . . .

JOHN A. MAIRS

[New Orleans] January 3, 1856

Dear Madam:

Your esteemed favor of 18th Ulto came duly to hand and shall receive proper attention. The bill of supplies as stated by Mr. Mairs for your plantation this year, shall be forwarded in due season, when navigation is most favorable. We have so informed Mr. Mairs.

We have today received from Perkins and Co $1969.41 at your credit with us being the proceeds of your first shipment of 52 B/C as p. act sales herein. Your next shipment of 55 bales, for which a bill of lading was received here, was burned on the steamer "Unicorn" in Yazoo River, a total loss so far as has been ascertained. This is a "streak of *good luck*" as the Cotton was insured at $50 p. bale which, you will perceive, is more than the value of the first shipmt. The Insurance Office claims the usual 2 pct. discount for cash, or 60 days time after proof of loss. We shall allow *the time*, as you are not pressed for money, and 2 pct. is a heavy rate for 60 days. In the meantime, you may rely upon our attention to the adjustment of the loss. . . .

W. S. PICKETT

[Okacheckina, Miss.] January 7, 1856

Mairm

Inough writ you a few lins about your plantation and servants ireceved your letter of 15th and 18th of las month 1855 ihave sent to Memphis after Harbard and got him home Harbard is a bad boy idyed not rite you word that he had left the plas he has left wons or twis before but dyed not stay out long come in himself iwill try to ceap him at home and make him attend to his bisniss the rest of your servants is at home and all well except colds we are don picking out coten but not quite don gining ihave not shiped enny of your coten sens igot your letter last iwill ship the balans to W. S. Pickett and Co. . . . I am in hops we will have good helth and a good season and iwill try to make a good crope

Vary Respectfully
JOHN A. MAIRS

[New Orleans] January 12, 1856

Dear Madam:

Since our respects of 3d Inst we have received your favor of 3d. As your 55 Bales were consigned to Perkins & Co. and *insured under their policy*, we thought it best to use their name in the adjustment of the loss. The Insurance Company paid the money deducting only ½ pct, and we yesterday received the proceeds $2557.84 as p. statement herein. . . .

The Bill of Lading for 20 Bales is at hand transferred to us. The cotton also came to hand yesterday; but as the weather is awfully bad, and unfavorable for outdoor business, we may not be able to get it sampled and on the market for some days to come. The market is firm and there is no danger, we think, of any immediate decline.

Your affairs in this quarter are all perfectly straight, and your interest well looked after so you need give yourself, not the slightest uneasiness in regard to them. Hoping what has been done so far will meet your approbation we are

Very Respfy Your friends
W. S. PICKETT

[Okacheckina, Miss.] January 23, 1856

Mairm

inough write you a few lins about your plantation and people your servants are all well at present we ar don the crop of coten made 148

bags   isend you the nombers and wats of the bags   it is a lite crop
of coten but idon my best   we made a good crop of corn and aplenty
of Bacon to surply the plantation

ihave got Harbard home and will try to keep him At home   all of
your coten has bin shipped but the 21 Bals   iwill ship it on the first
ris if enny chance to do so and will ship it to W. S. Pickett and Co
New orleons. . . .

Respectfully<br>
JOHN A. MAIRS

Frederick Law Olmsted

## TEXAS SPRINGTIME

*We last met Frederick Law Olmsted on a tobacco plantation in Virginia in the winter of 1853. Two years later he and his brother, Dr. J. H. Olmsted, were in Texas. As usual they carried no letters of introduction to prominent and "hospitable individuals." They wanted to see for themselves and form their own opinions. Frederick said to a Southern friend: "The extension of slavery into Texas commenced, for good or evil, in our own day; and when we of the North had the power and the constitutional right to prevent it."*

*The Olmsteds' Texas travels covered the winter of 1855 and the spring of 1856. In those years the state shipped 116,078 bales of cotton. The brothers went as far west as San Antonio, passed through some of the cotton country, met planters, and, upon occasion, accepted their hospitality.*

After spending a pleasant week in Austin, we crossed the Colorado, into, distinctively, Western Texas.

The river is here too a blue green in color, and we enjoyed again the beauty of its placid surface and transparent depths, as the "flat" slowly rippled its way to the further bank. Its width is about a hundred yards. . . .

The impression as we emerged, strengthened by a warm, calm atmosphere, was very charming. The live-oaks, standing alone or in picturesque groups near and far from the clean sward, which rolled in long waves that took, on their various slopes, bright light or half shadows from the afternoon sun, contributed mainly to an effect which was very new and striking, though still natural, like a happy new melody. We stopped, and, from the trunk of a superb old tree, preserved a sketched outline of its low gnarled limbs, and of the scene beyond them.

Had we known that this was the first one of a thousand similar scenes, that were now to charm us day after day, we should have, perhaps, spared ourselves the pains. We were, in fact, just entering a vast region, of which live-oak prairies are the characteristic. It extends throughout the greater part of Western Texas, as far as the small streams near San Antonio, beyond which the dwarf mesquit and its congeners are found. The live-oak is almost the only tree away from the river bottoms, and everywhere gives the marked features to the landscape.

The live-oaks are often short, and even stunted in growth, lacking the rich vigor and full foliage of those further east. As far West as beyond the Guadalupe, they are thickly hung with the gray Spanish moss, whose weird color, and slow, pendulous motions, harmonize peculiarly with the tone of the tree itself. . . .

At the end of an afternoon's ride, mostly over bare prairies, we reached Manchac Spring. A lucky accident compelled us to stop at the house we found there, and for once we were obliged to confess that quarters within were better than any canvas we could have set up without. . . .

We found a plantation that would have done no discredit to Virginia. The house was large and well constructed, standing in a thick grove, separated from the prairie by a strong worm-fence. Adjacent, within, was the spring, which deserved its prominence of mention upon the maps. It had been tastefully grottoed with heavy limestone rocks, now water-stained and mossy, and the pure stream came gurgling up, in impetuous gallons, to pour itself in a bright current out upon the prairie. The fountains of Italy were what came to mind, and "Fontana de Manciocco" would have secured a more natural name.

Everything about the house was orderly and neat. The proprietor came out to receive us, and issued orders about the horses, which we felt, from their quiet tone, would be obeyed, without our supervision. When we were ushered into a snug supper-room and found a clean table set with wheat bread, ham, tea, and preserved fruits, waited on by tidy and ready girls, we could scarcely think we had not got beyond the bounds of Texas. We were, in fact, quit, for some time to come, of the lazy poverty of Eastern Texas.

There were two or three travelers besides ourselves. . . .

Our host was a man of accurate information in agricultural matters. He told us he was now (January 14) beginning to plough for his spring crops. Corn is planted usually in the middle of February. He planted cotton in May, and even in June, as there was no danger of its not maturing here as in the Eastern and Northern cotton states, and its growth is more rapid, if not exposed when young to checks from cold. This is much later than is customary; but the time varies with the amount and the period of rain of each season. Corn, he told us, was killed here if touched by frost after it is sprouted.

The prairie is broken by huge ploughs, drawn by six yoke of oxen, turning a sod thirty-two inches wide and four inches deep. He thought it better policy to use a smaller plough, drawn by two or three yoke of oxen, and in breaking fresh prairie to turn a shallow furrow. The old sod, when turned deep under, rots much more slowly, and remains a long time an impediment to cultivation. These great ploughs have two clumsy wheels attached, and once set in furrow need no other guidance. His own had a mould-board the hinder part of which was made of iron-rods, for lightness and strength. It acted like a coarse screen, and was said to answer well.

Leaving Manchac Spring, our road led us across a bleak open prairie, on whose rolls stood no house, and scarce a tree, for fifteen miles. At our right, to the north, was a range of distant hills, from which orchards of live-oak occasionally stretched to within a moderate distance of us.

While riding slowly, we saw some white objects on a hill before us. We could not make them out distinctly, and resorted to the spy-glass. "Sheep," said one. "Cattle," said the other. As we rode on, we slowly approached. Suddenly, one of the objects raises a long neck and head. "Llamas—or alpacas." "More like birds, I think." Then all the objects raise heads, and begin to walk away, upon two legs. "What! ostriches? Yes, ostriches, or something unknown to my eye." We were now within four or five hundred yards of them. Suddenly, they raised wings, stretched out their necks, and ran over the prairie, but presently left ground, and flew away. They were very large white birds, with black-edged wings, and very long necks and legs. They must have been a species of crane, very much magnified by a refraction of the atmosphere. . . .

We left San Antonio on the 14th of February for an excursion to the coast. The road lies, for some miles, through mesquit chapparal, which extends much farther from the town than on the Austin road. It is sparse, however, and good grass grows beneath it. . . . Rain soon began to fall, and we made a short day of it, camping in the lee of a mesquit thicket, some twelve or fourteen miles from San Antonio. . . .

Next day the rain continued falling, with occasional dashes of snow, a cutting north wind, making matters very disagreeable. We, of course, kept camp. . . .

February 16.—Rain at intervals. We rode on to the Guadalupe, and camped in the bottom. Our tent stood under a magnificent cypress, overhung with enormous vines. Fuel was abundant, and we did not spare it.

February 17.—A light rain continued. We made a stew for break-fast of such small birds as came within range of the frying-pan. A boy, attracted by our guns or by the savory odor, made his appearance on horseback, attended by a pack of hounds. He seemed somewhat taken aback on observing our comfortable arrangements, and after a tame proposal "to swop horses," took his departure. . . .

February 19.— . . . We passed Mount Capote, which is a wooded summit, terminating a long range of hills. . . . Today, the genial sun warmed the fresh moistened soil. . . . The beauty of the spring-prairies has never been and never will be expressed. It is inexpressible.

A few days sufficed now, in fact, to change the whole face of nature. A quick flush spread over all; the bosom of old Mother Earth seemed to swell with life.

In another day the elm-buds were green and bursting, and the wild plum in fragrant blossom; the dreary, burnt prairies, from repulsive black, changed at once to a vivid green, like that of young wheat. . . .

We passed, in the afternoon, a cotton field in the river bottom. The stalks were short, but much cotton remained unpicked. . . .

On the 20th February we reached Gonzales. . . .

We passed a number of old places having much the aspect of Virginia plantations, inclosed within very high zigzag fences, with gin-houses, negro women ploughing, and sometimes a small garden, and a half dozen peach-trees.

We were joined by a planter from the opposite side of the river, where there are many Tennesseans and Mississippians. He was from Tennessee; had moved first to Alabama, afterwards to Mississippi, whence he came to Eastern Texas. He didn't like it there, and pushed on. He liked the country better and better as he came further, and finally reached the lower Guadalupe, where he hired land, and was able to purchase it with the proceeds of his first crop. But he found it sickly there, and came higher up. Here he was well satisfied. They had no sickness, but a little bilious fever and very light fever and ague. The land was very fine; he made one bale to the acre always, and always grew twice as much cotton as his hands could pick. Seven bales to the hand was a common crop, and of corn forty to fifty bushels.

Land had "bounced up powerful." A tract that he could have bought, three years ago, for two dollars, had just been sold at ten dollars. . . .

February 22.—The country was much more wooded than yesterday, frequent mottes of live-oak, coppices of mesquit, and forests of post-oak, diversifying the prairie. The houses were old, and of a more comfortable sort. We saw near some of them the first peach-blossoms of the season. We passed cotton-fields again, and wagons loaded with cotton. One carrying eight bales, drawn by ten lean oxen, was from San Marcos, bound to the coast. The teamster, who was on horseback, told us his best day's work was ten miles. . . .

We went on some miles beyond Victoria, and not finding a suitable camping place, stumbled, after dark, into a large plantation upon the river bottom.

The irruption of such a train within the plantation fences caused a furious commotion among the dogs and little negroes, and it was with no little difficulty we could explain to the planter, who appeared with a candle, which was instantly blown out, upon the porch, our peaceable intentions. Finally . . . the growling and chattering circle about us was sufficiently enlarged and subdued for us to obtain a hearing, and we were hospitably received.

"Ho Sam! You Tom, here! Call your missus. Here Bill! John! some of you, why don't you help the gentleman? Bring a lantern here! Now, clear out with you, you little devils, every one of you! Is there no one in the house? Can't any of you find a lantern?" . . .

In the midst of the noise we go through the familiar motions, and land our saddles and hampers upon the gallery, then follow what appears to be the headmost negro to the stable, and then give him a hint to look well out for the horses. . . .

Here were thirty or forty slaves, but not an order could be executed

without more reiteration, and threats, and oaths, and greater trouble
to the master and mistress, than would be needed to get a squadron
under way. We heard the master threaten his negroes with flogging,
at least six times, before we went to bed. In the night a heavy rain
came up, and he rose, on hearing it, to arrange the cistern spout, cursing
again his infernal niggers, who had turned it off for some convenience
of their own. In the morning, we heard the mistress scolding her girls
for having left articles outside which had been spoiled by the wet,
after repeated orders to bring them in. On visiting the stables we
found the door fastened by a board leaned against it.

All the animals were loose, except the mule, which I had fastened
myself. The rope attached to my saddle was stolen, and a shorter one
substituted for it. The master, seeing the horses had yet had no
fodder, called to a boy to get some for them, then, countermanding his
order, told the boy to call some one else, and go himself to drive the
cows out of the garden. Then, to another boy, he said, "Go and pull
two or three bundles of fodder out of the stack and give these horses."
The boy soon came with two small bundles. "You infernal rascal,
couldn't you tote more fodder than that? Go back and bring four or
five bundles, and be quick about it or I'll lick you." The boy walked
slowly back, and returned with four bundles more.

But on entering at night we were struck with the air of comfort that
met us. We were seated in rocking-chairs in a well-furnished room,
before a blazing fire, offered water to wash, in a little lean-to bed-room,
and, though we had two hours to wait for our supper, it was most
excellent, and we passed an agreeable evening in intelligent conversation with our host.

After his curiosity about us was satisfied, we learned from him that,
though a young man, he was an old settler, and had made a comfortable fortune by his plantation. His wife gave us a picturesque account
of their wagon journey here with their people, and described the hardships, dangers, and privations they had at first to endure. Now they
were far more comfortable than they could have ever hoped to have
been in the state from which they came. They thought their farm the
best cotton land in the world. It extended across a mile of timbered
bottom land from the river, then over a mile of bottom prairie, and
included a large tract of the big prairie "for range." Their field would
produce, in favorable season, three bales to the acre; ordinarily a bale
and a half; the "bale" 400 lbs. They had always far more than their
hands could pick. It was much more free from weeds than the states,

so much so, that three hands would be needed there to cultivate the same area as two here; that is, with the same hands the crop would be one-third greater.

But so anxious is every one in Texas to give all strangers a favorable impression, that all statements as to the extreme profit and healthfulness of lands must be taken with a grain of allowance. We found it very difficult, without impertinent persistence, to obtain any unfavorable facts. Persons not interested informed us, that from one-third to one-half the cotton crop on some of these rich plantations had been cut off by the worm, on several occasions, and that negroes suffered much with dysentery and pneumonia.

It cost them very little to haul their cotton to the coast or to get supplies. They had not been more sickly than they would have been on the Mississippi. They considered that their steady sea-breeze was almost a sure preventive of such diseases as they had higher up the country.

There were several sugar-plantations near them, one above Victoria, which had done extremely well, always selling their sugar at the highest price, for the supply of the back country. . . . The land is very well adapted, and can be bought, improved, for $10 per acre. We were shown, as high as Seguin, cane, which was of unusual size, and perfectly developed.

In the garden were peach and fig-trees, and raspberries. Pears on quince-stocks have produced fine crops in the neighborhood. The banana is cultivated here, but only as a curiosity, requiring to be housed or well protected. . . .

We looked out in the morning upon a real sea of wet grass. A dead flat extended as far as the eye could reach, reeking with water. The rain fell in sheets, and the wind blew a gale from the southward. But we were anxious to reach the coast, and sheathing ourselves and our hampers in india-rubber, we put off in the face of the blast.

We had come a long way off the road in finding the plantation, and on leaving, our host gave us advice how to find it again—advice not at all unnecessary; for we might easily have lost all traces of our whereabouts on the limitless expanse before us. . . .

Our directions were as follows: "The wind is now just about south, and it will most likely stay so. Well, you keep the wind right square on your shoulder, and ride straight across the prairie, and when you've gone about a mile, you'll rise the tops of some timber. Then you go right toward that till you can see the bottoms of the trees, and when

you can see the ground where they grow, then you can bear off to the
right of them till you see the road."

Following these sailing orders as if we were really at sea, we at
length reached the road. . . .


An anonymous Englishman

### "THE EDEN OF LOUISIANA"

*We first met the nameless traveler and correspondent for Black-
wood's Edinburgh Magazine in the plantation country near Georgetown, South Carolina. And we left him groaning with indigestion and
in fear of burning on a cotton-laden steamboat bound for the Acadian
country in Louisiana.*

*He appears to have survived unscathed both the oyster stew and
the perils of steam travel, but the dangers of a long, snaky sentence still
crept up on him.*

*The year, it will be recalled, is 1856.*

. . . To reach [the Acadian country] we must cross the delta of the
Mississippi, and thread the innumerable channels, called bayous, by
which that father of waters, percolating through its own vast alluvial
deposits, finds its outlets to the sea. Some idea of the extent of this
delta may be formed from the fact, that a railway extends from New
Orleans for about seventy miles into the heart of it, passing all the way
through a flat and marshy country, where the tangled roots of lofty
trees twist themselves into the mud, and a thick underwood renders
any attempt to penetrate the gloomy recesses of the forest impossible.
Sometimes it crosses a moving prairie, impassable for passengers except
by the railway, which is supported on piles. Occasionally a deer, startled
by the scream of the engine, dashes through the thicket—an unusual
sight from the window of a railway carriage.

Few evidences of human habitation are there, nor does the time
seem ever likely to come when human enterprise will have overcome
the difficulties that nature opposes to the conversion of these swamps
into arable land. Here and there a rise of the ground has been taken
advantage of, and the neat house of the planter, embowered in orange-
trees loaded with golden fruit, and surrounded by a few acres of sugar
plantation, show that energy is not wanting to do more, were it

possible. And as the country improves, and alters slightly in character, and the bayous become more numerous and important, these plantations occur more frequently upon their banks; and then it is that we begin to discover that the same hospitality which we have already experienced on the rice-lands of South Carolina, will be cordially extended to us on the sugar plantations of Louisiana.

As we are now beyond railways, we are compelled to pay our visits by water, and explore in a boat the labyrinth of bayous by which we are encompassed. The character of the vegetation is totally different from anything to which we are accustomed; the beautiful live oak fans with its quivering leaves the glassy surface of the bayous; the waving cypress, here the most valuable tree of the forest, fringes its margin; the sweet gum and common oak, smothered in creepers and Spanish moss, raise their lofty summits, and "look like Druids of eld, with voices sad and prophetic—stand like harpers hoar, with beards that rest on their bosoms." The yellow hickory and fan-leaved palmetto and graceful cane conceal the sturdy trunks of the larger trees, which, meeting overhead, form an almost impenetrable shade as we glide beneath them; alligators in numbers bask on the banks like stranded logs; bright plumaged birds glance among the branches, and vie in their plumage with bright-coloured flowers. These were the bayous which the Acadian exiles threaded. . . .

This moss is the most striking feature of the forest scenery. It clothes the whole woods in a garment of sober grey, so that at a distance the absence of vivid colouring almost pains the eye, and gives a sombre tone to the scenery. . . .

These shores have doubtless lost much of their wild beauty, now that pleasant cottages and plantations dot their margin, and here and there a thriving village, of which one will ere long be reached by a railway; and already between them, and up many of the neighboring bayous, steamers ply, and form the great means of communication of the sugar planters.

The branch of its waters noted as the most beautiful is the Bayou Teche; as it is thickly bordered with plantations, numerous steamers pass up and down its gentle stream. We embark in one of them and observe with astonishment a succession of handsome residences situated in the midst of tastefully laid-out grounds, where the extensive collection of negro-houses, and the thousands of well-cultivated acres extending far and wide, betoken opulence of the proprietors. For more than twenty miles we follow the windings of the bayou, and upon either bank, except in the far distance where the forest skirts the horizon, we perceive not a rod of uncultivated ground.

It is a scene of comfort and advanced civilization so unexpected that we can scarcely persuade ourselves of its reality. We are almost on the borders of Texas, in a region popularly believed to be inhabited by Indians, who ride on mustangs, and are perpetually fighting with surrounding Chickasaws, Choctaws, Cherokees, or Creeks, but so far from that being the case, not an Indian is visible; and we perceive evidences of refinement, which, with every revolution of the paddle-wheels, make us more ashamed of our former ignorance and increase our wonder. Nor is that diminished when, as daylight fades, we reach the private wharf of an opulent planter, to whom we are introduced by our friend, who informs him that he has brought an Englishman to pay him a visit; and without further notice, and in the most natural way in the world, we at once become partakers of his hospitality, and capital quarters they prove to be.

The family is large, but there is plenty of room for strangers besides. We have a luxurious bedroom, with a pier glass, an elaborately arranged toilet-table, and a soft bed, with warm curtains and carpets, and a jovial fire crackling, with bubbling kettle near it; for this is the middle of winter, and though the days are warm and genial, fires are pleasant at night; and when we find ourselves shown into this apartment of luxury, a sort of Belgravian negro, well got up in a neat livery, informs us when dinner will be ready, and leaves us to dress for it, we are filled with dismay when we remember that our small black bag contains all that we could have supposed necessary for the wilds of Western Louisiana, and that in the category we never dreamt of including a black coat. However, we have travelled too much to be easily daunted; so we boldly descend, and make our appearance in a handsomely furnished drawing-room, where ten or twelve ladies and gentlemen are assembled, and where we enjoy for the rest of the evening all the amenities of society.

It is indeed late before we retire, for we have plunged deep into the Kansas question, and I have enough to do to hold my own, for my opponents are temperate, sensible, and liberal men, and southerners of that kidney are formidable in argument. It is to be regretted, for their own sakes, that the violent language of so many of their number is such as to justify [to] a great degree the popular opinion entertained of their rabid intolerance, which is not, indeed, greater than that of the North, but which, in the eyes of Englishmen, does not find that excuse which is accorded to the opposite party, from a natural sympathy with the cause which they espouse.

Our kind host, determined to lose no time in doing the honors of the neighbourhood, has already planned an expedition for the morrow, and immediately after breakfast we start in a carriage, with a good pair of horses, to visit some plantations further up the bayou. The road is excellent, enclosed by neat fences, on which huge Turkey buzzards perch themselves; now and then passing through belts of wood and pleasantly shaded, but generally between hedges of Cherokee rose in full bloom, beyond which the extensive plains of turned-up soil are dotted with negroes planting cane. Every mile or so we pass, embowered in orange groves, the house of a planter, whose character I get the negro coachman, a garrulous and willing informer, to furnish, and who is generally favorable, but who now and then inveighs with vehemence against some notorious oppressor, who, he informs you, allows his passion to triumph to such a degree over his pocket that he will give a thousand dollars for you one day and kill you "jes like snake de nex."

After we have passed through the neat and pretty little town of Franklyn, the character of the country begins to change; hitherto all the cultivated plains we have crossed were originally forest; now, however, we drive over soft turf, where the flowers form a brightly variegated carpet, or else mingle with the long waving grass. . . . We have entered the "fair Opelousa;" these are its "prairies and forests of fruit-trees, and under the feet a garden of flowers."

Far into Texas, even to the country of the wild Comanches, these prairies extend without a check. But we are near the towns of St. Maur and St. Martin; we have speedily accomplished thirty-five miles, and man and beast stand in need of refreshment. In a country of such abundance there is no difficulty in finding it, and we drive up to the door of a house, the construction of which evidences comparative antiquity; it belongs to a fine old Frenchman—a noble specimen of the old school of French noblesse—tottering and feeble in years, but every inch a gentleman. He does the honours of his house with a quiet dignity; his bustling wife, many years his junior, bestirs herself to set before us a sumptuous repast, and negroes and negresses crowd round in anxious attendance. Meantime the old man, with great gusto, having a stranger for a listener, fights the battle of New Orleans over again, in which he bore a distinguished part against the British. Declining his hospitable invitation to prolong our stay, we are once more en route, and, as the sun sets, are ferried across the Teche. The scene was one of inexpressible beauty.

We found good quarters that night at the house of a prosperous young planter, and went over his sugar-houses. His good fortune had been somewhat greater than that of others in his neighbourhood, and the process of boiling was going on briskly. Generally the season of '56 had been deplorably bad, and some of the plantations, usually largely productive, did not yield a single hogshead of sugar, so that numbers of planters, with hundreds of acres in bearing, which usually yielded a net profit of from 50 to 75 dollars an acre, found themselves not only without an income, but seriously out of pocket.

As we passed through sundry plantations on the following day, we stopped to inspect the process of grinding, as well as planting cane; in fact, the mysteries of sugar-manufacturing were fully explained; but I will give my readers credit for a fuller knowledge of the subject than I had at that time, and spare them a repetition of it. Should any one be tempted to investigate for themselves the details of Louisiana sugar-planting, and propose to explore its bayous, by all means let him have time enough at his disposal to be able to accept all the invitations he receives to stay on plantations, as, if he be a sportsman, he will find plenty of amusement. The waters teem with wild-duck, and the marshes with snipe. I only went out once into the woods, for about an hour, and got a shot at a deer, which it was my own fault I did not kill. Unfortunately, my time did not allow of my vindicating my character as a shot, and my experience was just sufficient to cause me to regret not being able to remain longer. Returning then down the waters of the Teche and Atchafalaya, I crossed from the Bayou Boeuf to the old French town of Thibodaux, on the Bayou Fourche, where, disappointed of any immediate means of conveyance, I was compelled to pass a night in a miserable public-house. . . .

The next morning a little after daylight I walked down to the bayou to embark on a steamer. . . .

Along its whole extent the shores of the bayou bear all the evidences of a long-settled, thickly-populated country. There was not the same appearance of wealth as on the Bayou Teche, but a look of great ease and comfort. Creole maidens, with twined arms, strolled beneath the orange-trees on the banks; patriarchs in summer houses, in neat gardens, smoked their pipes and gazed on us as we puffed past. Vehicles of divers sorts passed along the well-kept roads between tidy fences, while, behind all, stretched acres of cane-fields. Every few hundred yards we stopped to take in cargo, principally consisting of molasses, sugar, or Spanish moss, which, packed in bales, is sent to be manufactured into stuffing for mattresses, chairs, etc. It has been found to answer all the purposes of horse-hair, and is becoming quite an important article of commerce.

We proceeded so slowly that the sun was settling over the pretty French town of Napoleon when we reached it, and it was midnight ere we found ourselves hurried along by the broad current of the Mississippi....

Wade Hampton

## WILD WOODS PLANTATION IN MISSISSIPPI

*Wade Hampton, the third to bear that name in South Carolina, was born in Charleston in 1818. His boyhood was spent at the family home, Millwood, near Columbia. In 1836 he was graduated from South Carolina College and two years later married Margaret Preston. One son, Wade, was born March 2, 1840, and another, Thomas Preston, on November 26, 1843. Margaret Hampton died in 1851.*

*Though he had studied law, Wade Hampton elected to follow family tradition and become a planter. And well he might, for his grandfather, the first Wade Hampton, who had served in both the Revolutionary War and the War of 1812, had supplemented his original South Carolina holdings by acquiring sugar plantations in Louisiana, including Houmas. He was so successful in the management of his far-flung properties (he was the first to try cotton in Richland County, South Carolina, realizing $90,000 from his initial crop) that he was reputed to be the wealthiest planter in America when he died in 1835.*

*Wade Hampton II added to the family fame by breeding blooded race horses. The stables at Millwood were famous throughout the South. Though he seldom let himself be actively involved in state politics, his influence was very great. In his time Millwood was a brilliant social mecca, attracting to it some of the most distinguished gentlemen of the day. Wade Hampton II died in 1858.*

*Wade Hampton III wrote the following letters to his younger sister Mary Fisher—he generally called her "Mary" but occasionally*

"Fisher"—*from Wild Woods Plantation in Mississippi. In addition to Wild Woods, which covered 835 acres, he owned Bayou Place, which, when expanded into Richland, embraced 2,729 acres; Otterbourne, 1,354 acres; Walnut Ridge, 2,529 acres; and Bear Gardens, 2,962 acres. The combined 10,409 acres were worked by 900 slaves. In 1850 Wild Woods alone produced 5,000 bushels of corn and 453 bales of cotton. There were 177 slaves on the plantation.*

*Hampton and his second wife, Mary Singleton McDuffie—she is the other "Mary" referred to in these letters to his sister—whom he married January 27, 1858, paid annual visits to the Mississippi plantations. Besides supervising operations on all his properties he entertained the many guests who came to Wild Woods.*

*In Washington County, Mississippi, his brother Christopher (Kit) Hampton owned a plantation called Linden.*

*Tall, handsome, Wade Hampton III did not get back to South Carolina in time to attend the secession convention in Charleston. On the outbreak of war he raised a beautifully mounted cavalry company, and in due course became lieutenant general and chief of cavalry. At Burgess Mill on October 27, 1864, he suffered the terrible sorrow of seeing his older son Wade wounded, and his younger boy Thomas Preston killed. He had already lost his brother Frank (his wife was Sally Baxter), who was killed at Brandy Station, June 9, 1863.*

*After the war Hampton was twice elected governor of South Carolina, in 1876 and again in 1878. Shortly after his second term began he was named United States senator. He served in the Senate till 1891.*

*Wade Hampton died in Columbia, April 11, 1902.*

Wild Woods, Mississippi, Nov. 2, 1857

Your letter by Col. [A. H.] Gladden, My Dear Mary, was the only letter I rece'd last week, and the date of that was the 12th Oct. . . . I fear you all have been writing by Memphis in which case, if the letters come at all, they will spend two or three weeks on the road. . . . I never knew as much sickness thro' the country. But I hope the frosts have made the country safe now. I am the only one, I think, who has escaped an attack, and I do not know what to attribute my exemption to, except my having been wet every day since my arrival. I have been out day and night and have been quite well, which is more than I deserve. . . . The crops are turning out very well. I have out about 500 bales and I hope to get 1000 more. The weather is favorable for picking, tho' we have had rather too much rain. . . . The sickness on my place has decreased, but not ceased. There have been two deaths since my arrival: one a fine young man, and the other the youngest child of Lizzy, making in all 37 *deaths, this year*. I am greatly distressed at this mortality. The people seem cheerful now, and I hope soon to see them all well again. Give all love to all and with a kiss to Sally.

I am Yr. affectionate brother
W. HAMPTON, JR.

If the parade horse is left, you must have him put in fine order for me.

Wild Woods, Nov. 8, 1857

My Dear Mary: . . . Since the establishment of our wonderful P.O. we rarely get any letters and it often takes two or three weeks to get answers from N.O. Your letters, however, have come with regularity, and have been most acceptable to me. They gratify me to by showing how kind you have been in going to see Mary. . . . I shall rely on you to have her in Columbia when I arrive. You can make her pay her visit to Millwood at that time. Be sure to do so, and *then* I won't stop on the way. I expect to leave on the 14th which ought to take me to Millwood by the 18th or 20th but I will telegraph you en route.

Two days ago, on our return from hunting, I found here *another* Englishman, Capt. Tower of the Guards, who was in every action of the Crimea. He called to see the Duncans and not finding them, he came here as he had a letter to me. He is a very nice fellow, and seems to regret much not being able to stay here longer. But he says he will come back. Today I took them bear-hunting and we killed four. Unfortunately I could not get them in to the death, as they are not accustomed to the sport. Lord Althrop (or as Sam calls him "Lord") was with me and he literally had his clothes torn off. I had to furnish him with my *drawers*, so as to enable him to come home decently. To show them the full glory of the country, we had a severe thunder storm and came home in the hardest rain I ever saw. I fear they will all be knocked up tomorrow. They get on very well, and as Frederic is sick and has been all the time, I just let them take care of themselves. Tomorrow (Sunday) all are going except the Portmans, who stay because *he* is not very well. . . .

Wild Woods, Mar. 27, 1858

My Dear Mary: I know you would like to be here tomorrow, so as to give me a kiss upon my birth-day; but your *heart* will be with me, I am sure, my darling, and no one will offer kinder or warmer wishes for my welfare than my dear little sister. I wish you were with me, for I think you would be happier and now the weather is so exquisite that you would enjoy your rides with us. Mary has grown to like them very much and she has improved in her riding a great deal. She has entire confidence in the sobriety and gentleness of Fanny, so that they get on very well together. No one rides the little mare but herself, and she is as fat as a butterball. . . . The Duncans are up at Linden, and are to dine here today. We dined at Linden yesterday.

The country is beginning to look charmingly and the ladies all enjoy it very much. My boat has been nicely fixed, and we go out in it some times. Mary says I must not sell this place, as she likes it very much. I think she will like the country a great deal and but for the long journey out she would always come. By the last packet she rece'd a very affectionate letter from Wade, which gratified her greatly. I am very sorry to hear that you all do not wish to go to Europe. . . .

Wild Woods, Apr. 10, 1858

My Dear Fisher: The day for writing to you has come again and though I have no good news to give you, I can not omit my usual letter. I hoped, when I wrote last, to tell you in this letter, that we should leave in a very few days; but we are in great danger from the river, which is higher than it has ever been. Many of the levees are broken and Steels Bayou is rising very rapidly. I am very much afraid that we shall all be overflowed, and I must wait a little while to see what will be the result. If the river does not fall very soon, we shall have the most disastrous freshet ever known in this valley. . . . My places were in good order and I had hopes of making the best crop I ever have made; but now I fear I will have none.

The Portmans expect to leave in a day or two. They seem quite settled in their purpose of coming back here next fall to live. I have discouraged this plan, but they wish to try it, so I will do all I can to assist them. Mally Howell is here, and is very anxious to sell his place so as to settle here. He will go in a short time up the river and proposes to meet us in N.O. to go on with us to Ca.

Mary is getting on famously, and does not seem to be tired of the country. She rides a good deal, and sometimes goes out in the boat, tho' she does not like sailing. . . .

Wild Woods, Apr. 16, 1858

My Dear Mary: . . . The water has been rising ever since I wrote, and though the river has fallen, the bayou has injured us very much. I hope however, that it will be down in time for us to get some more cotton in, and though it will be too late for a good crop, still we may make some thing. I could have saved nearly all the land I have, had I not depended on the river levees. It will be a lesson to me however and I will now go on with my own levees.

Now I am at work clearing new land and preparing *another* crop and *another* plantation. I hope to get off in a week, if the river goes down, but you must not count *too* certainly on my leaving here.

We are all getting on very well and but for the water, our sojourn here would have been very pleasant. Mary has improved a great deal and looks very well. She has got on much better than I expected and seems to take a great interest in every thing. . . .

Wild Woods, Apr. 24, 1858

. . . We expected to leave tomorrow, but I was  not able to get ready so soon. The water fell some what, but we hear of another rise and I fear if that comes down now, that our prospects for a crop will be but poor. As it is we have been thrown back greatly, and could not make full crops in any event. I hope we may escape, but matters are very critical at present. We are just going to the Duncans' to dine with them and I expect to hear full accounts from the upper rivers there. The only topic now, is the high water. . . .

Wild Woods, May 1, 1858

You will, I fear my dear Mary, be quite in despair, when you see the date of my letter; but as I write to say that we will take the packet *tomorrow certainly* D.V. The river rose so much this week, that I was afraid to attempt to get a boat, so we waited for the packet. Indeed I ought not to leave here now, as the river is nearly as high as it has been and all accounts from above would make us fear that there will be a terrible overflow. But as the ladies are anxious to get off and I want to see you all very much, so I hope to have the pleasure very soon, to be once more with you all, and to take *you* to ride and drive with me. . . . I hope you will have the horses in good condition when I get there. . . .

Old Point Virginia, July 15, 1858

My Dear Mary: We reached here last evening and found such a

crowd, that *not a room* was to be had. But Mr. Segar (who owns the Hotel) brought us to his own house about a mile from the Point, and we are very comfortable, waiting for some persons to vacate. Neither my letter or despatch came. Nor are the boys here at which I am greatly disappointed. I have telegraphed to them to come on. . . . Do have the Carolinian sent to me. . . .

This is a pretty place and so far the weather is delightful. There is a great crowd here, 700 persons, but Segar promises to make us comfortable. . . .

Old Point, July 23, 1858
. . . We are quite comfortably fixed, having three rooms (one parlor) in a cottage, though the crowd is still very great. The proprietor has done all he could for us, and I never was at a place where greater attention was shown to me. The bathing is not good, nor is there good driving in the neighborhood as the people seem to think the best way to *locomote*, is by boats. The worst feature in the matter, is, that the fishing is a complete humbug; they catch only a small fish, and even these not in large numbers. So as the driving, bathing, and fishing are bad, I think our stay will be but short. I think I shall go to the sps. and spend some time there.

The boys have grown very much, and it has been a great pleasure to me, to have them here. They will go on in a day or two. . . .

White Sulphur Springs, Va., Aug. 14, 1858
. . . The place is fearfully dull, and there are but few persons here whom I know. So I think we shall not stay here much longer but will try the Sweet Springs where I think the bath will be of service to Mary.

A good many Carolinians are coming in now but I do not know many of them. . . . I hope you won't ride your horse if he is not in proper order, or dangerous. Nothing a horse can do, is as bad as stumbling, for no good riding can guard against accidents from that fault. Can't you get some other horse for the present? . . .

Wild Woods, Nov. 6, 1859
My Dear Fisher: Though I know you have written to me, yet no letters have come, but I hope to get a good supply by the packet today and to hear of the well doing of all the dear ones at home. Here we have had the most beautiful weather and this last few days have been

as bright and balmy as spring. My work is getting on slowly, but well. I will get the Levee finished, and I think it will stand. The crop will turn out somewhat better than I supposed, and I hope to make 850 Bales. But my places look desolate to the last degree and I was ashamed to show them to Capt. Hamilton. Tell Frank that he must be civil to him, as he is a nice fellow. I think Frank had better rent 1000 acres of land to the Turpentine man, if he can get 1200 pr. ann for it. Say to Frank that the dog he gave me quite comes up to his reputation and that he is one of the best bear dogs I ever saw. . . .

Wild Woods, Nov. 4, 1860
. . . I am in expectation of hearing very soon what the Legislature will do and if the Session is continued until the fourth Monday in Nov. I must go on though I shall dislike to do so. If they only remain in Session, for a few days, then there will be no necessity for me to be there.

The weather is perfect, but the crops are too far gone to improve. W.R. [Walnut Ridge Plantation] will make I think as good, if not the best crop ever made there, but on all these places the cotton is very bad. Tult is greatly dispirited about this, but says that "if his life had depended on making a good crop he could not have tried harder." All are well. Take care of yourselves and God bless you all.

Yrs affy
W.H.

A. De Puy Van Buren

## "MISSISSIPPI IS A COTTON GROWING STATE"

*A. De Puy Van Buren, a young gentleman from Battle Creek, Michigan, arrived in Yazoo County, Mississippi, in November of 1857. "I had sought the South," he explained, "not so much to win this 'pedogogic laurel,' as to find a healing balm in its mild and healthy climate for my injured health."*

*He spent two months at Ridge House Plantation as the guest of Major W. W. Wildy. He was then engaged by several planters in the neighborhood as a teacher and divided his time between H. Barksdale's Oak Valley and John S. Paul's Willow Dale. When his book describing his sojourn in the South appeared, he dedicated it to these*

*three gentlemen, "Worthy Southern Planters and Gentlemen—the
pleasure and delight of a sojourn in whose homes we shall long cherish in pleasing remembrance."*

"Dr. Y." was Doctor Young, of "Rough and Ready" Plantation.

Satartia, Yazoo county, Mississippi, is put down in my memorandum
as the terminus of my journey. That journey was commenced at 12
o'clock at night, and, after twelve days' travel, it is finished at 12 o'clock
at night. . . .

An old negro, whose hair was as silvery as the moonlight that fell
upon it, took one of my trunks, and placing it on his head, told me to
follow him and he'd take me to the tavern. . . . If we remember right,
not the scattered fancy of a dream disturbed our repose. . . .

As I had yet to go ten or twelve miles into the country, to my
friend's, Major Wildy, I asked if I could get a horse and carriage for
that purpose. There was but one carriage owned in town, and that
could not be got. The people here traveled mostly on horseback. Could
I have a horse and saddle, then? Not one to be found. . . . In this
dilemma, a young gentleman visiting here from New Orleans, informed
me that one of Mr. H.'s negroes was in town, and, as he was going to
Major Wildy's plantation, I could send a letter by him, informing
him of my arrival. A note was written and sent.

The next morning a little negro boy came on a mule bringing me a
horse and saddle. . . . I mounted my horse and followed my little guide.
My day-dream of years was here realized—to see the sunny South with
its fields of "mimic snow."

I remember the first cotton-field I ever saw. It was in Olney's old
Geography. The overseer stood with his arms folded, whip in his hand,
off a little way from the negroes hoeing in the cotton-field. The big
white blossoms hung, like snow-balls, among the green leaves, from
the little plants. . . .

But here was a picturesque scene, drawn by an "old master"—Nature. The cotton was higher; in many places over the heads of the
negroes; and they were picking instead of hoeing it; and the overseer
was on horseback, or in some fields was walking round among the
negroes. But he had the same broad-rimmed hat on, and the same
whip in his hand, and he was overseeing the same negroes. But yet how
different! The painter's best representations of the world are pleasing
things; but the world that is not painted is the most interesting to
see. . . .

After something over an hour's ride we came to Major W.'s plantation. It is in the valley. Here is the old plantation-house, in which the family formerly resided, but which is now occupied by the overseer, and here are the "quarters," the negro cabins. The family live in the uplands, some two miles from here; their home is called the "Ridge House."

Having arrived at the gate, at the foot of the sloping lawn, in front of the house, I was met by Major W.'s two oldest sons. They showed me much attention, respect and kindness. The eldest, a recent graduate from Nashville Military Academy, had just returned from a hunt; his horse yet saddled, with the bridle thrown loosely over his neck, was cropping the Bermuda grass on the side of the knoll; his hounds lay here and there, on the side of the slope, resting after the chase. The other son was acting overseer for the time being. They excused their delay in not sending a servant sooner to me at Satartia—their father was from home with the carriage, and the horses were away, and they had to wait till their return.

"But walk in, Mr. Van Buren; this rain and mist will wet you through." We walked up the sloping knoll to the house. The air was rather cool, and the house so open that I felt even chilly by their fireside. The rain had now increased, and it was deemed best that I should stay here all night. I found part of a library in the room, and an old set of college books. . . .

In the morning Master Harry W. came after me; his mother requesting me to come to the family house. A few moments' ride through the woods, and we were alighting from our horses at the gate of the Ridge House. Here I met a cordial reception from Mrs. W., a lady of true Southern frankness—of a generous and spirited nature, and whose countenance expresses much of the feeling of her heart.

A relation of her family has some celebrity as a literary writer. She is also a kin of Mrs. James K. Polk. Soon a very pretty young lady came into the room, whom she presented to me as Miss Mattie W., her daughter. The rest of the family are small. I met here a young lady from the North, Miss Bessie G., their teacher.

The family had been expecting me for some time. I had brought letters of introduction to them from my friend, Miss E.M.P., of New York, who had resided with them as a teacher.

Here I begin to see Southern life and observe Southern manners. . . .

While sojourning a few days at the Ridge House, I had taken views on horseback of much of this part of Mississippi. This, besides being cavalierish, is the only way we "peers of the realm" have of riding here; for the rains make such sad havoc with the roads that a heavy shower of three or four hours, and you find your carriage half-spoke deep in mud or clay loam. And then, the ladies claim the carriage, at all times. A planter told me that he paid six hundred dollars for his carriage in Philadelphia, and though he had had it two years he had never rode a rod in it. You often meet the fair of the South, also, upon their palfreys, galloping through the woods.

Riding out in a carriage a short time since with Mrs. W., she rallied me about my driving—holding the reins so tight. I told her we "held in" our horses. She replied they "let theirs go."

It is said that the earth is an old nurse, and that everything shows that she is decrepit and wearing out. But these valleys that have produced a rich crop of cotton, year after year, for more than half a century, are as fertile today, and yield as large a crop of cotton, without fertilizing, as they did when first cultivated.

Nothing is more beautiful than to view this long, winding valley from some high bluff of the uplands, that wall it in on both sides of the river. Far along, as far as the eye can reach, you see both up and down the stream, from a half to two miles wide, nothing but fields of "mimic snow," dotted here and there with planters' residences, set in green trees and shrubs, which, with the neat, white-washed negro cabins, ranged in rows near them, look like trim villas scattered along the vale. Much of the valley is yet open-forest land.

That beautiful and richest leafed of all trees—the magnolia—you find here, standing among the gum, the oak, and the hickory, like a rich prince among his vassals. The holly is here too. These evergreen hollies and magnolias standing among the common trees, seem like beautiful pledges of another spring, to the leafless forest. I have often rein'd my horse from the road up to these lovely trees and stood and admired them. . . .

The planters' houses are mostly alike in style of building. They are long, log, story-and-a-half structures, verandaed in front and rear, with an open hall in the middle. They are elevated from the ground for coolness in summer, and retreat back from the road. They are generally surrounded with beautiful trees and shrubbery, much of it in evergreen, making even the rudest log building look romantic.

In thus adorning their grounds about their dwellings, and in cultivating a rich variety of flowers in their gardens, the planters exhibit fine taste.

But there is one plant he cultivates, which, if it does not exhibit his taste, does his wealth; and that, in common parlance, is called the *cotton plant*. Mississippi is a cotton growing State. She stands, among the other States, unrivaled in this field. This little plant is the wealth of the Indies to her. It has many enemies among the vermin, freshet and blight. But the season is kind to it, not allowing the winds of March to visit it too roughly, nor the cold storms of December to hinder its being gathered in.

They are the whole year attending to it. One crop is scarcely secured ere enother is planted. It brings the planter about forty dollars per acre. Think of seven hundred acres—that is not a large plantation—yielding him more than Buchanan's salary. Planters make more money than Presidents. The modern adage—"Cotton is king," that one often hears in reference to the influence this little plant gives to the planter, in home and foreign trade, is, in the *richest* sense of the world, true. ....

It is said the South, like Calypso, has a smile and a charm for every one of her defects; and not only detains her guests seven years, but usually the threescore and ten.

In regard to myself, after a sojourn of some months, I like her very much. I like her warm-heartedness and hospitality. I like her beautiful climate. I like her fine country. ....

Major Wildy came home soon after my return. He is one of South Carolina's chivalrous sons; a courteous gentleman, of fine intellect, much reading, and good literary taste.

He is six feet high, though not a heavy man, has light brown hair, bluish grey eyes, and, were it not for the browning of this clime, would have a fair complexion. His plantation is in the valley. It is about midway, on the "Big Road" between Vicksburgh and Yazoo City. The house, though it is now being finished inside and out, like a frame building, is built of oak logs hewn square. It is some thirty feet wide by sixty feet long, and a story-and-a-half high, while the roof extending out, like a planter's broad rimmed hat, over its sides, and, resting on posts, forms wide porches, a cool and pleasant shade in the warm summer weather. An open hall connects these two porches.

Some thirty slaves, under command of his "field-marshal" work his large and beautiful prairie-farm; and the fruit of their labor is an "argosy" of cotton, which is annually shipped to New Orleans.

My first conversation with him, was about the panic among the Northern banks. He discoursed at some length on the banking system. He spoke of our Congress as if it were a chess-board, and he clearly understood the games that were being and had been played on it, by those men in Congress. . . .

I have noticed many traits of old English life in the South. The plantation-house, like the old English manor-house, has its broad grounds, but without the carpet of green, between its shady retreat and the road. The beauties of the landscape, about his rural seclusion, have not been violated. The planter also, may be considered a lord in possession of a large estate, and his slaves are his vassals. And, like your English gentleman of landed possessions, he loves the chase, keeps a parliament of hounds, and the requisites for the hunt. His horse is ordered at early dawn, when from his porch you can hear the winding of his horn, and instantly

"Tray, Blanch, and Sweetheart, all,"

are frolicking about him. He soon dashes off into the woods with them, and you may not see him again till nightfall. . . .

There is much provincialism in the habits and customs of the South. And finally, should an Englishman seek the hospitality of the planter's roof, he could repose on a mattress spread on an old English bed-stead, the same lofty and rich posts, and richly ornamented canopy, with curtains, that once graced the royal bed-chamber of "Good Old Queen Bess."

The planter's fare is simple, and the chase supplies his table with much of its meat. . . .

Their tables are usually long, and remain stationary in the dining-room. This is sometimes a little log building separate from the house.

The father, at meals, takes seat at one end of the table, his eldest son at his right, then the next younger, and so on, down to the "wee bairn" that can "toddle" to his seat.

The mother is seated at the other end of the table, and her eldest daughter at her right, the sister next in age succeeding, down to the youngest. The guests, if gentlemen, are seated at the planter's left hand; if ladies, at his wife's left. If the father is a member of the church, a blessing is asked. I have known those, who did not profess to be Christians, ask blessings at their tables.

The boiled ham, cooked whole always, and which, on extra occasions, is tricked off with cloves, green leaves, and various-colored dainty bits, in a tasteful manner, is placed before the planter; his wife has the tea, coffee, and the delicacies before her. By the aid of servants every one at the table is served.

The planter takes his time in eating. Leisure and ease are inmates of his roof. He takes no note of time. . . . Time here,

> "Had lost his glass and was asleep on flowers."

A clock, almanac, and a good fire, are hard things to find in a planter's house. The only chronometer he has, is the cotton-plant, and that "ticks" but once a year. The word, haste, is not in a Southron's vocabulary. . . .

This morning, ere I was up, just as the day was coming in from the East, the negro servant came into my room to build a fire, and he had scarcely opened the door, ere he shouted—"*Christmas gift*, Mr. Van Buren! *Christmas gift*, Mr. Van Buren!" and ere he had shouted twice, another came in, and yet another, till the room was filled with a joyous, merry chime, of negro voices, shouting "Christmas gifts," to me.

But it was not only in my room; I hear them shouting it to every one about the house. The cry sounded from every room,—"Christmas gift, massa!"—"Christmas gift, missus!" "Christmas gift!" to every one they met.

As soon as this greeting was over, and we had all assembled in the sitting room, servants came in with foaming cups of egg nogg, on servers. . . .

We were soon summoned to breakfast. Our repast was truly a sumptuous one. Barrels of apples, oranges, oysters, large quantities of wine, and all the cheer for the holidays had been received from New Orleans.

I can give no better idea of the manner of spending the holidays in the South, than by quoting from a writer who thus describes them in "Merry England."

In large houses are large parties, music and feasting, dancing and cards. Beautiful faces, and noble forms, the most fair and accomplished of England's sons and daughters, beautify the ample firesides of aristocratic halls. Senators and judges, lawyers and clergymen, poets and philosophers, there meet in cheerful, and even sportive ease amid the elegancies of polished life. In old-fashioned, but aristocratic country abodes, old-fashioned hilarity prevails. In all the families, hearty spirits are met, and here are dancing and feasting, too.

This is literally true of the South. Throughout the country, on every plantation, there is a merry time—a joyous leisure from all work; merry

Christmas is with them all. The negroes, whole troops of them mounted on mules, male and female, laughing and singing, go from one plantation to another; thus gathering in jolly groups they feast and frolic and dance the time away.

Dancing is not confined to the negroes alone, the planter's whole household is entirely given up to merry-making during the holidays.

The dance and festival is first held at one planter's house, and then at another's; two or three often assembling in one place, where they have what is termed a "storming."

I spent the holidays at the Ridge House. We had, beside our own family, two cousins with us, and several of the young ladies from adjacent plantations.

During the evening I was much amused with young Dr. Y., a wealthy planter's son. He had got rather merry with the dance and wine, and called upon the old negro who was fiddling for the party, to play a favorite tune of his, for *that* dance. And after it had been played for him repeatedly, he called for it again; throwing down, as usual, a half-dollar at his feet.

The old negro replied, "Why massa, I jus done play that tune, for you, five or six time."

"Play away, I tell you," cried the Dr., "there's your money," throwing down another half-dollar. This he repeated so often that we began to wish ourself in the place of the old negro, fiddling for such a shower of silver.

During the evening some of the young folk left, to attend a wedding among the negroes at the quarters. . . .

The hospitality of the Ridge House was extended to many a guest for the night. Our room was supplied with couches for several.

After the sound of revelry had ceased, the last taper been extinguished, and the revelers were all asleep, or in the realms of dream land, the loud and repeated "halloo" was heard sounding out from the gate, on the still air of night.

A servant answered it, and soon ushered in young Mr. H., a neighboring planter's son, who came with news that soon aroused the whole household.

The negroes, in the east part of the county, had banded themselves, in a fierce and furious band, against the whites, and were coming into our neighborhood, murdering every family in their approach.

Major Wildy read the letter the young man brought, containing the awful news, then calmly told his family and guests that they might get out their guns and make every necessary preparation for defense. But they would please excuse him, as he had been up late and needed rest, he would retire again. But he would thank them to let him know when they came, and he would get up—marshal all his forces and defend his "Castle."

At this, feeling safe, in the coolness with which Major Wildy treated this report, we all retired to rest again, and soon forgot the cause of our alarm. . . . The negroes never came.

New Year's morning we had for the accustomed—"I wish you a happy New Year," that which I had been used to hear—the Southern one of—"A *New Year's gift.*" The festival went on during the day, and at night we had a "storming." . . .

After a respite of the holidays, I got into the saddle once more, to make another adventure. My route was along the Yazoo valley. Major W., and Dr. Y.'s son, who resided there, assured me that I could get a good school in that region. . . .

I soon came to Mr. B.'s, one of the gentlemen to whom I had been referred, who wished a teacher. I stopped and took dinner here; mentioned my errand. I was opportune; and from the manner of the gentlemen I knew that I was dealing with one in whom I could repose confidence and trust.

After dinner Mr. B. mounted his horse, and we rode a mile and a half to his neighbor, Mr. P.'s plantation. This planter, also wishing a teacher, ordered his horse, and we three rode still another mile, to Dr. Y.'s residence, where in a very short time, these three wealthy planters secured my services as teacher, giving me a salary of five hundred dollars per year, and a home, besides allowing me all I could make out of extra scholars. After two months' search I had found the prize. . . .

In a few days I left my home at the Ridge House for one in the valley.

I had sojourned in Major W.'s family over two months, and had, during that time, not only received the kindest hospitality from him and his family, but had had a servant to wait on me, and a horse and saddle at my command. And when I asked what I had to pay for all this, he replied—"*Not one cent, sir.*"

Mr. Barksdale is a Tennessean—an intellectual, reading, energetic, reliable man. He is a true Southern gentleman; urbane, chivalrous, and dresses with taste. Were I to draw a portrait of a real Southron, I should ask him to sit for it. He is of a fine family; has himself been elected to a seat in the Mississippi Legislature; was a delegate to the Cincinnati Convention and helped nominate Mr. Buchanan. One of his brothers is the editor of the "Mississippian," the first paper in the State; and another is a member of the Lower House of Congress.

He has a fine plantation of four hundred acres of arable valley-land, worked by forty or fifty slaves. His negro quarters are a little village amid sheltering trees.

His residence is a neat and tasty edifice, embowered in a profusion of shade.

In the front ground, you see several magnificent China-trees. The orange myrtle, with its glossy green foliage, trimmed in the shape of a huge strawberry; the crepe myrtle with its top hanging thick with long cone-shaped flowers of a peach-blow color; the cape jasmine, with its rich polished foliage spangled all over with white starry blossoms; and that richest and sweetest blossom of tropical shrubs—the japonica.

There are rows of cedar trees, the trimmed arbor vitae, and other perennial shrubs, in clumps about the grounds, with the holly and that pride of Flora's—the rich glossy-leafed, and snowy-blossomed magnolia.

Adjoining the front grounds is a garden, abounding in every variety of esculent vegetables, choice fruit-trees, and luscious grapes. It is also radiant with flowers and roses.

The house is expensively furnished inside.

Mrs. B. is a very amiable lady. They have an interesting family of children, whom they intend shall have the benefit of a fine education.

My home, for the last six weeks of my sojourn on the banks of the Yazoo, was in this delightful abode at Oak Valley.

So much had been said about a Northerner's coming South, to me, last fall, that the Southrons looked upon them all with suspicion; that one must "overhaul" his politics, and leave at home all that was not convenient; and then, unless he could give the true Democratic "shiboleth," there was danger in crossing "MASON AND DIXON'S" line; that I felt, on coming here, like a Themistocles throwing myself upon the clemency of the people.

But in this I was disappointed. I found that the South that one reads and hears of, is altogether different from the one that one *sees* and becomes acquainted with.

Sir Walter Scott never met his friend Irving, at his gate, with a more friendly—"Ye are welcome," than I have received wherever I have been in this "sunny land."

And I have sat by the planter's fire-side, and conversed with him on that hateful subject, which those "boys" in Congress have quarreled about and fought over so long—talked about the Union—the North and the South—children of the same parents—till they fell out on the slavery question; and but one Southron yet has asked me my politics.

Willow Dale, so long my home on the banks of the Yazoo, and where I have spent so many happy and delightful days, is truly a noble mansion and a very pleasant home. I had a very fine room furnished with everything to make one comfortable—a servant to build my fires, black my boots and do my errands. The family was a very pleasant one. And we had in addition to it, spending the winter with us, two fair cousins.

Our evenings at Willow Dale were given to amusements. The ladies of our household read, were fond of the works of literature and romance, and among authors they were very fond of Scott. He is a favorite of the South. Of the manners and scenes of his novels one is much reminded among this people. Nowhere have I enjoyed reading him so much as in this clime. Life here has its tranquil repose, and a book in your hand is like a friend, that is entertaining and enjoying it with you. And there is no noise, nor any one to disturb you.

I have seen Willow Dale so quiet for hours that the birds would stop singing in its trees, in love of its silence. And then, when the sportive laugh or merry shout of the children playing in the yard, sounded out, or the whistle or splashing of a steamer, passing by, or the hallo of a stranger at the gate, and the hounds baying at him, you heard and listened to them with pleasure.

Besides reading, and the light work of the needle, our ladies gave their time to various pleasures—visiting and receiving visits, music, vocal and instrumental, the dance, and *tete-a-tete*. Whist is universally acknowledged a lady's game. But euchre is the game of the South, and by choice, the Southern lady's game.

The plantation proper, that part that is cultivated, is some four hundred acres. I presume Mr. P. has a thousand or two acres in all. He raises usually two or three thousand bushels of corn, and makes three hundred bales of cotton. He is supposed to be worth $100,000. A young widow, a short distance up the river from here, is worth half a million.

A man not only shows his taste but his wisdom, in his house and its surroundings. Mr. P.'s house is a capacious mansion, sixty-five feet square, two stories high, both verandaed. The grounds about it are finely laid out, and adorned with many rare trees and shrubs. Many a planter with thrice his wealth has a rough log dwelling for his home.

Planters build their houses of nearly the same style. I find they are much given to mannerism among themselves. For instance, you generally find in their houses a large high-posted, heavy-topped bedstead—some cost over a hundred dollars, and are massive and rich. One would think that such a piece of furniture was a relic of feudal days, on which once had couched the chivalrous Coeur de Leon, or William the Conqueror, or the lordly inmates of Warwick or Windsor Castle.

The family of Mr. P. consists of himself and lady, four children, and an Irish girl as their seamstress. You frequently find poor, white young ladies sewing in their families. Mr. P. is from North Carolina. His lady is from Tennessee. It is considered as honorable to be a Virginian here, as it was once to be a Roman citizen. A good story is told of the North Carolinians, who, feeling all the Virginian's pride of birth, often reply, when asked what State they are from, "From North Carolina, near the Virginia line."

Mr. P.'s slaves were divided into house-servants, carpenter and blacksmith, and field-hands. The servants about the house are well-dressed, and each has his or her respective duty to perform. Aunt Betty, the cook, is in her "sanctum," hard by the dining room, and during meals a servant is in direct communication with her and the table, who conveys the viands warm to the table, and replenishes them as soon as they get cold.

Where they do not have good mechanics among their slaves, they put out some ingenious one of them as apprentice till he has learned his trade. Nathan, Mr. P.'s carpenter, is also a preacher, and on Sundays discourses to his brethren and sisters of that better land, far away. The field-hands have their quarters near by the house, some thirty rods to the right. These consist of little frame cabins, boarded with cypress, and white-washed. They are very often log-cabins; but a planter of pride and taste has everything neat and orderly about him. They are arranged in rows, fronting the road, and shaded by a fine row of cone-shaped cotton-wood and China-trees before them. These are their homes.

They raise their own chickens, and have all the money they can make from selling them and their eggs in market. They often have a patch of corn, from which they gather sometimes five or six hundred bushels. Saturday night they take whatever they wish to carry to town, get a "pass" from Mr. P.—they have no right to sell without it—and put them into a skiff and row up to Yazoo City, six miles, and dispose of them. Besides this, they have all they can make by selling wood to the steamers. An industrious negro can make quite a sum in a year by selling wood.

His negroes have the advantage of having the word of God expounded to them. A little chapel school-house, in a tuneful grove of willow oaks, is the sanctuary for a few planters and their families. The negroes grouped together on seats near the door, the planters and their families are seated within the house. The parson—clergymen are usually called parsons here—standing near the door, so that both parties can hear. Japhet in his tent, and Ham, his servant, sitting at his door. Our parson is a Methodist, a young gentleman of fair talent.

We often had guests—ladies and gentlemen—from Yazoo city and other places, who sometimes would remain several days with us, and sometimes a planter's daughter would stay two or three weeks.

Then we had moon-light sails on the noble Yazoo. There is a charm in Southern moon-light that I never before felt, that makes the night exceedingly lovely. It was on one of these lovely nights when—

"The moon like a rick on fire had risen o'er the dale"

and the silvery Yazoo flowed murmurless between the deep, heavy foliage of willows that hung over it on each side, like a soft, undulating bank of green, that a party of us at Willow Dale stepped into the boat, with a favorite negro, an adept at the oar, for oarsman, to take a moon-light sail. We were on a serenading trip—were going to serenade Dr. Y.'s daughter at "Rough and Ready"—her home, one mile up the river.

It is beautiful to sail in a light boat "on such a night," when all nature is asleep, and, on a river itself, in a lethean tranquility when no sound is heard but the light dipping and soft splashing of the oars in the water, and the muffled sound of their working in the row-locks. And where the voice has a charmed sound that the night and the water give, and when you are fonder of talking of music, and musing, and fonder of your own existence.

Thus in love with ourselves and the scene around us, we moved up stream, repeating passages of poetry and snatches of song.

To complete the scene of our trip, a magnificent steamer, brilliantly illuminated—the Indian's "Fire Canoe," dropped down stream by us, like a thing of glorious beauty.

When we had reached a point a little above the "Castle" of our

lady-fair, we crossed the stream, and silently glided down till we were
opposite her abode; when the Misses B., one playing on the guitar,
began to serenade. Their voices sounded out on the clear moon-lit air—

> "Soft as the chant of Troubadours,
> Or the rhythm of silver bells."

Our lady and her guests came out into the porch of the mansion,
which was trellised with honeysuckle and woodbine; but we could not
see them—only caught sight of a white handkerchief waving out from
the trellis-work.

The South has much of romance. . . .

Our Academy is within a stone's-throw, by the smallest scholar,
of the Yazoo. The river rolls along in front of it. Parallel to this, in the
rear of the house, is a bayou. On this peninsular strip of land is situated
the schoolhouse. It is built of gum-logs hewn square, and instead of
being "chinked up," it is battened on the outside with cypress boards.
It has two windows, one on each side. The door is in front, facing the
river. It has a broad stone fire-place, at the opposite end, with a stick
chimney running up on the outside. The floor is of smooth cypress
boards. The one overhead is of cypress-shakes laid from joist to joist,
like battened-work. Two strips of desk are nailed against the wall, one
on each side of the window, on one side; on the other side is a movable
desk of cypress wood, for the teacher. Four chairs, with cow-hide bottoms, and one with a basket bottom, and three smaller ones for the
small children, with several blocks of wood, sawed off chair-hight, from
a gum-log, are all the seats we had. There is a mantle-piece over the
fire-place, and several pegs in the logs on the east side, to hang hats,
bonnets and shawls on.

The house stands in a beautiful grove of willow-oaks, and from their
branches Southern birds sang their roundelays to us, all winter long. . . .

My pupils were seven boys—intelligent, fine lads, three of whom
were fourteen or fifteen years old, and two tiny damoiselles, one having
a little black waiting maid, who attended her in school and out.

This was my school on commencing it; a month or two later we
had three larger scholars. Their studies embraced Latin and the higher
English branches. In history I never saw a class of scholars, of their
age, that would equal them. I believe the South is ahead of us in
giving attention to this study. Are not their Congressmen better informed in history than ours?

But to my school. At one time the boys had obtained permission to bathe in a little bayou that the high water had formed, a short distance from the school-house. This bayou was separated, by a strip of land about three rods wide, from another larger and deeper one. Two of the boys returned, after a while, and wanted permission to go and tell the overseer to come and shoot the alligators in the "big bayou" on the other side of the path from the one in which they had been swimming.

Startled at such news, I called them in; when they informed me that they did not see the alligators, till they had been bathing some time. They expressed no fear from sporting in the water near such terrible play-fellows; merely wished to go and inform the overseer, or some of the negroes, that they might enjoy the sport of seeing them shot—that's all. . . .

The advantage of teaching here, whether in the "old-field" schools—the common school South, or as tutor in a planter's family, or in the academies, is, you have a less number of scholars, and more time to devote to each study. The teacher has not got time, he cannot stop long enough by the way, North, to do anything like justice to the various branches he pretends to teach.

We think the little Southron, on the whole, an interesting student, and we must say that we have ever been pleased with the deportment of children in planters' families; and it is a pleasure to walk along the streets in a Southern town, and witness the well-behaved conduct of children. You hear no swearing—no vulgar language. You see no vagrant boys—no wicked little urchins; nothing but the lively pranks and shouts and prattle of well-dressed children. . . .

Frederick Law Olmsted

## BETWEEN WOODVILLE AND NATCHEZ

*After his Texas travels Mr. Olmsted did not return directly to New York but continued his Southern excursion through Louisiana and Mississippi. He traveled alone this time and from the trip came another book,* A Journey in the Back Country, *which was published in 1860.*

*Olmsted's observations about agriculture are of some weight, for he was himself a farmer and an amateur naturalist. His interest in landscape gardening (Andrew Jackson Downing, the famous landscape*

*gardener who introduced the Swedish novelist Fredrika Bremer to the
Poinsetts earlier in this book, was a friend of his) developed rapidly
and it was soon apparent that his genius lay in this area. When New
York wanted a great park in the middle of the city, Olmsted and Cal-
vert Vaux, an English architect and one of Downing's pupils, entered
the competition together. They won, and Central Park is the result.
Despite bitter political battles they managed to realize to a large extent
their original ideas.*

*In his field scarcely a single public project of importance was under-
taken in the United States without his advice—Belle Isle Park in
Detroit, parks in Rochester, the design for Stanford University at Palo
Alto, the Chicago World's Fair, to mention a very few—and he continued to serve private clients too.*

*Olmsted laid out parks for many Southern cities, notably for Louis-
ville. George W. Vanderbilt's Biltmore estate at Asheville, North
Carolina, was designed and built under his personal supervision.*

*During the War between the States Olmsted took leave of absence
from the Central Park project to go to Washington as General Secretary for the United States Sanitary Commission, forerunner of the
American Red Cross.*

For some miles about St. Francisville the landscape has an open,
suburban character, with residences indicative of rapidly accumulating
wealth, and advancement in luxury among the proprietors. For twenty
miles to the north of the town, there is on both sides a succession of
large sugar and cotton plantations. Much land still remains unc, cultivated, however. The roadside fences are generally hedges of roses—
Cherokee and sweet brier. These are planted first by the side of a
common rail fence, which, while they are young, supports them in the
manner of a trellis; as they grow older they fall each way, and mat
together, finally forming a confused, sprawling, slovenly thicket, often
ten feet in breadth and four to six feet high. Trumpet creepers, grape-
vines, green-briers, and in very rich soil, cane, grow up through the
mat of roses, and add to its strength. It is not as pretty as a trimmer
hedge, yet very agreeable, and the road being sometimes narrow, deep
and lane like, delightful memories of England were often brought to
mind.

There were frequent groves of magnolia grandiflora, large trees, and
every one in the glory of full blossom. The magnolia does not, however, show well in masses, and those groves, not unfrequently met, were

much finer, where the beech, elm, and liquid amber formed the body, and the magnolias stood singly out, magnificent chandeliers of fragrance.

### THE PLANTATIONS

The soil seems generally rich, though much washed off the higher ground. The cultivation is directed with some care to prevent this. Young pine trees, however, and other indications of impoverishing agriculture, are seen on many plantations.

The soil is sandy loam, so friable that the negroes, always working in large gangs, superintended by a driver with a whip, continued their hoeing in the midst of quite smart showers, and when the road had become a poaching mud. . . .

The slaves generally of this district appear uncommonly well— doubtless, chiefly, because the wealth of their owners has enabled them to select the best from the yearly exportations of Virginia and Kentucky, but also because they are systematically well fed.

The plantation residences were of a cottage class, sometimes with extensive and tasteful grounds about them.

An old gentleman, sensible, polite, and communicative, and a favorable sample of the wealthy planters, who rode a short distance with me, said that many of the proprietors were absentees—some of the plantations had dwellings only for the negroes and the overseer. He called my attention to a field of cotton which, he said, had been ruined by his overseer's laziness. The negroes had been permitted at a critical time to be too careless in their hoeing, and it was now impossible to recover the ground thus lost. Grass grows so rampantly in this black soil, that if it once got a good start ahead, you could never overtake it. That was the devil of a rainy season. Cotton could stand drouth better than it could grass.

The enclosures are not often of less area than a hundred acres. Fewer than fifty negroes are seldom found on a plantation; many muster by the hundred. In general the fields are remarkably free from weeds and well tilled. . . .

The country, for some distance north of Woodville, is the most uneven, for a non-mountainous region, I ever saw. The road seems well engineered, yet you are nearly all the time mounting or descending the sides of protuberances or basins, ribs or dikes. In one place it follows along the top of a crooked ridge, as steep-sided and regular for nearly a quarter of a mile, as a high railroad embankment. The ground being too rough here for cultivation, the dense native forest remains intact.

This ridge, a man told me, had been a famous place for robberies. It is not far from the Mississippi bottoms. . . .

Not far north of the ridge, plantations are found again, though the character of the surface changes but little. The hill-sides are so plowed that each furrow forms a narrow terrace. After the first plowing, thus scientifically directed, the lines are followed in subsequent cultivation, year in and year out, so long as enough soil remains to grow cotton with profit. On the hills recently brought into cultivation, broad, serpentine ditches, having a fall of from two to four inches in a rod, have been frequently constructed; these are intended to prevent the formation of more direct gullies, during heavy rains. Of course, these precautions are not perfectly successful, the cultivated hills in spite of them losing soil every year in a melancholy manner.

I passed during the day four or five large plantations, the hill-sides gullied like icebergs, stables and negro quarters all abandoned, and given up to decay.

The virgin soil is in its natural state as rich as possible. At first it is expected to bear a bale and a half of cotton to the acre, making eight or ten bales for each able field-hand. But from the cause described its productiveness rapidly decreases. . . .

The plantations are all large, but, except in their size and rather unusually good tillage, display few signs of wealthy proprietorship. The greater number have but small and mean residences upon them. . . .

I called in the afternoon at a house, almost the only one I had seen during the day which did not appear to be the residence of a planter or overseer, to obtain lodging. No one was at home but a negro woman and children. The woman said that her master never took in strangers; there was a man a few miles further on who did; it was the only place she knew of where I was likely to be entertained.

I found the place; probably the proprietor was the poorest white man whose house I had passed during the day, but he had several slaves; one of them, at least, a first-class man, worth $2,000.

Just before me, another traveler, a Mr. S., from beyond Natchez, had arrived. . . .

He was a middle-aged, well-dressed man, devouring tobacco prodigiously; nervous and wavering in his manner; asking questions, a dozen at a breath, and paying no heed to the answers. He owned a plantation in the bottoms, and another on the upland; the latter was getting worn out, it was too unhealthy for him to live in the bottoms, and so, as he said, he had had "a good notion to go into ranchering, just for ease and pleasure.

"Fact is, though, I've got a family, and this is no country for children to be raised in. All the children get such foolish notions. I don't want my children to be brought up here—ruins everybody; does sir, sure—spoils 'em; too bad; 'tis so, too bad; can't make any thing of children here, sir—can't sir; fact." . . .

Then he turned to our host and began to ask him about neighbors, many of whom he had known when he was a boy, and been at school with. A sorry account he got of nearly all. Generally they had run through their property; their lands had passed into new hands; their negroes had been disposed of; two were now, he thought, "strikers" for gamblers in Natchez.

"What is a striker?" I asked the landlord at the first opportunity.

"Oh! to rope in fat fellows for the gamblers; they don't do that themselves, but get somebody else. I don't know as it is so; all I know is, they don't have no business, not till late at night; they never stir out till late at night, and nobody knows how they live, and that's what I expect they do. Fellows that come into town flush, you know—sold out their cotton and are flush—they always think they must see every thing, and try their hands at every thing—these fellows bring 'em in to the gamblers, and get 'em tight for 'em you know."

"How's —— got along since his father died?" asked Mr. S.

"Well, ——'s been unfortunate. Got mad with his overseer; thought he was lazy and packed him off; then he undertook to oversee for himself, and he was unfortunate. Had two bad crops. Finally the sheriff took about half his niggers. He tried to work the plantation with the rest, but they was old, used-up hands, and he got mad that they would not work more, and tired o' seein' 'em, and 'fore the end of the year he sold 'em all."

Another young man, of whom he spoke, had had his property managed for him by a relative till he came of age, and had been sent North to college. Two years previously he returned and got it into his own hands, and the first year he ran it in debt $16,000. He had now put it back into the hands of his relative to manage, but continued to live upon it. "I see," continued our host, "every time any of their teams are coming back from town they fetch a barrel or a demijohn. There is a parcel of fellows, who, when they can't [get] liquor anywhere else, always go to him."

"But how did he manage to spend so much the first year, in gambling?"

"Well, he gambled some and he run horses." ...

"But sixteen thousand dollars is a large sum of money to be worked off even in that way in a year," I observed.

"Oh, he had plenty of other ways. He'd go into a bar-room, and get tight and commence to break things. They'd let him go on, and the next morning hand him a bill for a hundred dollars. He thinks that's a smart thing, and just laughs and pays it, and then treats all around again."

By one and the other, many stories were then told of similar follies of young men. Among the rest, this:

A certain man had, as was said to be the custom when running for office, given an order at a grocery for all to be "treated" who applied in his name. The grocer, after the election, which resulted in the defeat of the treater, presented what was thought an exorbitant bill. He refused to pay it, and a lawsuit ensued. A gentleman in the witness box being asked if he thought it possible for the whole number of people taking part in his election to have consumed the quantity of liquor alleged, answered:

"Moy Goad!" (reproachfully). "Yes, sir! Whay, I've been charged for a hundred and fifty drinks *'fore breakfast*, when I've stood treat, and I never thought o' disputin' it."

At supper, Mr. S., looking at the daughter of our host, said:

"What a pretty girl that is. My dear, do you find any schools to go to out here—eh? I reckon not. This isn't the country for schools. There'll not be a school in Mississippi 'fore long, I reckon: nothing but Institutes, eh? Ha! ha! ha! Institutes, humph! Don't believe there's a school between this and Natchez, is there?"

"No, sir."

"Of course, there isn't."

"What sort of a country is it, then, between here and Natchez?" I asked. "I should suppose it would be well settled."

"Big plantations, sir, nothing else—aristocrats; swell-heads I call them, sir, nothing but swell-heads, and you can't get a night's lodging, sir. Beyond the ferry, I'll be bound, a man might die on the road 'fore he'd get a lodging with one of them, eh, Mr. N.? so, isn't it? 'Take a stranger in, and I'll clear you out!' That's the rule. That's what they tell their overseers, eh? Yes sir; just so inhospitable as that—swell-heads! swell-heads, sir, every plantation—can't get a meal of victuals or a night's lodging from one of them, I don't suppose, not if your life depended on it. Can you, Mr. N.?"

"Well, I believe Mr. ——, his place is right on the road, and it's half way to the ferry, and I believe he tells his overseer if a man comes and wants something to eat, he must give it to him, but he must not take any pay for it, because strangers must have something to eat. They start out of Natchez, thinking it's as 'tis in other countries; that there's houses along, where they can get a meal, and so they don't provide for themselves, and when they get along about there, they are sometimes desperate hungry. Had to be something done."

"Do the planters not live themselves on their plantations?"

"Why, a good many of them had two or three plantations, but they don't often live on any of them."

"Must have ice for their wine, you see," said Mr. S., "or they'd die; and so they have to live in Natchez, or New Orleans; a good many of them live in New Orleans."

"And in summer they go up into Kentucky, do they not? I've seen country houses there which were said to belong to cotton-planters from Mississippi."

"No, sir; they go North, to New York, and Newport, and Saratoga, and Cape May, and Seneca Lake—somewhere that they can display themselves worse than they do here; Kentucky is no place for that. That's the sort of people, sir, all the way from here to Natchez, and all round Natchez, too, and in all this section of country where there's good land. Good God! I would n't have my children educated, sir, among them, not to have them as rich as Dr. ——, every one of them. You can know their children as far off as you can see them—young swell-heads! You'll take note of 'em in Natchez. Why, you can tell them by their walk; I noticed it yesterday at the Mansion House. They sort of throw out their legs as if they had n't got strength enough to lift 'em and put them down in any particular place. They do want so bad to look as if they were n't made of the same clay as the rest of God's creation. . . ."

I asked how rich the sort of men were of whom he spoke.

"Why, sir, from a hundred thousand to ten million."

"Do you mean that between here and Natchez there are none worth less than a hundred thousand dollars?"

"No, sir, not beyond the ferry. Why, any sort of a plantation is worth a hundred thousand dollars; the niggers would sell for that."

"How many negroes are there on these plantations?"

"From fifty to a hundred."

"Never over one hundred?"

"No; when they've increased to a hundred they always divide them; stock another plantation. There are sometimes three or four plantations adjoining one another, with an overseer for each, belonging to the same man; but that isn't general—in general, they have to strike off for new land."

"How many acres will a hand tend here?"

"About fifteen—ten of cotton, and five of corn; some pretend to make them tend twenty."

"And what is the usual crop?"

"A bale and a half to the acre on fresh land and in the bottom. Four to eight bales to a hand they generally get; sometimes ten and better, when they are lucky."

"A bale and a half on fresh land? How much on old?"

"Well, you can't tell—depends on how much it's worn and what the season is, so much. Old land, after a while, isn't worth bothering with."

"Do most of these large planters who live so freely, anticipate their crops as the sugar planters are said to—spend the money, I mean, before the crop is sold?"

"Yes, sir, and three and four crops ahead generally."

"Are most of them the sons of rich men? are they old estates?"

"No, sir; many of them were overseers themselves once."

"Well, have you noticed whether it is a fact that these large properties seldom continue long in the same family? Do the grandsons of wealthy planters often become poor men?"

"Generally the sons do; almost always their sons are fools, and soon go through with it."

"If they don't kill themselves before their fathers die," said the other.

"Yes; they drink hard and gamble, and of course that brings them into fights. . . ."

At breakfast, Mr. S. came rather late. He bowed his head as he took his seat, and closed his eyes for a second or two; then, withdrawing his quid of tobacco and throwing it in the fireplace, he looked round with a smile, and said:

"I always think it a good plan to thank the Lord for His mercies. I'm afraid some people'll think I'm a member of the church. I aint, and never was. Wish I was. I am a Son, though, of Temperance. Give me some water, girl; coffee first—never too soon for coffee. And never too late, I say. Wait for any thing but coffee. These swell-heads drink their coffee after they've eaten all their dinner. I want it with dinner, eh? Don't nothing taste good without coffee, I reckon."

Before he left, he invited me to visit his plantations, giving me careful directions to find them, and saying that if he should not have returned before I reached them, his wife and his overseer would give me every attention if I would tell them he told me to visit them. He said again, and in this connection, that he believed this was the most inhospitable country in the world. . . .

If they had a reputation for hospitality, he said, it could only be among their own sort. They made great swell-head parties; and when they were on their plantation places, they made it a point to have a great deal of company; they would not have any thing to do if they didn't. But they were all swell-heads, I might be sure; they'd never ask anybody but a regular swell-head to see them.

His own family, however, seemed not to be excluded from the swell-head society. . . .

From the Homochitto to the suburbs of Natchez, a good half day's ride, I found the country beautiful; fewer hills than before, the soil very rich, and the land almost all inclosed in plantations, the roadside boundaries of which are old rose-hedges. The road is well constructed; often, in passing through the hills, with high banks on each side, coped with thick and dark, but free and sportive hedges, out of which avenues of trees growing carelessly and bending angel-like over the traveler, the sentiment of the most charming Herefordshire lanes is reproduced. There are also frequent woods, of a park-like character in their openness; the trees chiefly oak, and of great height. Sometimes these have been inclosed with neat palings, and slightly and tastily thinned out, so as to form noble grounds around the residences of the planters, which are always cottages or very simple and unostentatious mansions. Near two of these are unusually good ranges of negro-houses. On many of the plantations, perhaps most, no residence is visible from the road, and the negro-quarters, when seen, are the usual comfortless cabins.

Within three miles of the town the country is entirely occupied by houses and grounds of a villa character; the grounds usually exhibiting a paltry taste, with miniature terraces, and trees and shrubs planted and trimmed with no regard to architectural and landscape considerations. There is, however, an abundance of good trees, much beautiful shrubbery, and the best hedges and screens of evergreen shrubs that I have seen in America.

I was amused to recognize specimens of the "swell-head" fraternity, as described by my nervous friend, as soon as I got into the villa district. First came two boys in a skeleton wagon, pitching along with a racking pony. . . .

Then came four indistinct beards and two old, roué-looking men, all trotting horses; the young fellows screaming, breaking up, and swearing. After them cantered a mulatto groom, white-gloved and neatly dressed, who, I noticed, bowed politely, lifting his hat and smiling to a ragged old negro with a wheelbarrow and shovel, on the foot-path.

Next came—and it was a sweltering hot afternoon—an open carriage with two ladies taking an airing. . . . On the front seat of the carriage, was a white and veritable French bonne, holding a richly-belaced baby. The ladies sat back, good-looking women enough, and prettily dressed, but marble-like in propriety, looking stealthily from the corners of their eyes without turning their heads. But the dignity of the turn-out chiefly reposed in the coachman, an obese old black man . . . set high up in the sun's face on the bed-like cushion of the box, to display a great livery topcoat, with the wonted capes and velvet, buttoned brightly and tightly to the chin, with broad band and buckle; his elbows squared, the reins and whip in his hands, and his eyes fast closed in sleep.

William Howard Russell

## "IN THE CALM OF A GLORIOUS SUMMER EVENING"

*When this our last account was written Fort Sumter had fallen and Mr. William Howard Russell of the London* Times *was visiting a new nation, the Confederate States of America. Sent by his newspaper to report on the relations between the North and the South, he spent some time in South Carolina, traveled on to Montgomery, Alabama, where he met and talked with President Jefferson Davis and his cabinet, proceeded to New Orleans, went up into Mississippi and in early June*

*was a guest of John Burnside at Houmas Plantation, some sixty miles
above New Orleans near the town of Donaldsonville.*

*Born in Belfast, Mr. Burnside had come a poor and friendless youth
to the United States to seek his fortune. He found it. In 1857 he bought
Houmas, a great sugar plantation once the property of the Hampton
family. Houmas took its strange name from an Indian tribe.*

*Mr. Duncan Kenner, with whom Russell dined, owned Ashland
Plantation in Ascension Parish. In 1864, on President Davis' personal
orders, he made a desperate dash to England to offer the abolition of
slavery in return for British recognition of the Confederacy. When he
returned to Ashland after the war he found it in ruins, but before his
death in 1887 he had more than restored it to its old prosperity.*

*Governor André Bienvenu Roman (who introduced the British
journalist to before-breakfast mint juleps) was one of the ablest ad-
ministrators Louisiana ever had. Though he opposed disunion strenu-
ously, he accepted a position on the commission appointed to negoti-
ate peaceable separation. When Federal troops occupied Louisiana he
declined to protect his property by taking the oath to the Federal
government. Ill and destitute, he died six weeks after the war ended.
Aimée Françoise Parent was his wife.*

A quarter of an hour brought our skiff from Donaldsonville to the
levee on the other side. I ascended the bank, and across the road,
directly in front, appeared a carriage gateway and wickets of wood,
painted white, in a line of park palings of the same material, which
extended up and down the road far as the eye could see, and guarded
wide-spread fields of maize and sugar-cane. An avenue lined with trees,
with branches close set, drooping and overarching a walk paved with
red brick, led to the house, the porch of which was visible at the
extremity of the lawn, with clustering flowers, rose, jessamine, and
creepers clinging to the pillars, supporting the verandah. The view
from the belvedere on the roof was one of the most striking of its kind
in the world.

If an English agriculturist could see six thousand acres of the finest
land in one field, unbroken by hedge or boundary, and covered with the
most magnificent crops of tasseling Indian corn and sprouting sugar-
cane, as level as a billiard table, he would surely doubt his senses. But
here is literally such a sight—six thousand acres. . . .

Rising up in the midst of the verdure are the white lines of the negro cottages and the plantation offices and sugar-houses, which look like large public edifices in the distance.

My host was not ostentatiously proud in telling me that, in the year 1857, he had purchased this estate for 300,000 pounds, and an adjacent property, of 8000 acres, for 150,000 pounds. . . . Six thousand acres on this one estate all covered with sugar-cane, and 16,000 acres more of Indian corn, to feed the slaves;—these were great possessions, but not less than 18,000 acres still remained, covered with brake and forest, and swampy, to be reclaimed and turned into gold. As easy to persuade the owner of such wealth that slavery is indefensible as to have convinced the Norman baron that the Saxon churl who tilled his lands ought to be his equal.

I found Mr. Ward and a few merchants from New Orleans in possession of the bachelors' house. The service was performed by slaves, and the order and regularity of the attendants were worthy of a well-regulated English mansion. . . .

The silence which struck me at Governor Roman's is not broken at Mr. Burnside's; and when the last thrill of the mocking-bird's song has died out through the grove, a stillness of Avernian profundity settles on hut, field, and river. . . .

In the evening Mr. Burnside and his guests sat out in the twilight under the magnolias in the veranda, illuminated by the flashing fireflies, talking of the war and politics. . . .

On June the sixth, aided by a wonderful chorus of riotous mockingbirds, my chattel Joe, *adscriptus mihi domino*, awoke me to a bath of Mississippi water with huge lumps of ice in it, to which he recommended a mint-julep as an adjunct.

It was not here that I was first exposed to an ordeal of mint-julep, for in the early morning a stranger in a Southern planter's house may expect the offer of a glassful of brandy, sugar, and peppermint beneath an island of ice—an obligatory panacea for all the evils of climate. After it has been disposed of, Pompey may come up again with glass number two: "Massa say fever very bad this morning—much dew." But on one occasion before breakfast the negro brought up mint-julep number three, the acceptance of which he enforced by the emphatic declaration, "Massa says, sir, you had better take dis, cause it'll be de las he make 'fo' breakfast."

Breakfast is served: there is on the table a profusion of dishes—grilled fowl, prawns, eggs and ham, fish from New Orleans, potted salmon from England, preserved meats from France, claret, iced water, coffee and tea, varieties of hominy, mush, and African vegetable preparations. Then come the newspapers, which are perused eagerly with ejaculations, "Do you hear what they are doing now—infernal villains! that Lincoln must be mad!" . . .

The more one sees of a planter's life the greater is the conviction that its charms come from a particular turn of mind, which is separated by a wide interval from modern ideas in Europe. The planter is a de-nomadised Arab; he has fixed himself with horses and slaves in a fertile spot, where he guards his women with Oriental care, exercises patri-archal sway, and is at once fierce, tender, and hospitable. The inner life of his household is exceedingly charming, because one is astonished to find the graces and acomplishments of womanhood displayed in a scene which has a certain sort of savage rudeness about it after all, and where all kinds of incongruous accidents are visible in the service of the table, in the furniture of the house, in its decorations, menials, and surrounding scenery. . . .

June 9th. A thunder-storm, which lasted all the morning and after-noon till three o'clock. When it cleared, I drove, in company with Mr. Burnside and his friends, to dinner with Mr. Duncan Kenner, who lives some ten or twelve miles above Houmas. He is one of the sporting men of the South, well known on the Charleston race-course, and keeps a large stable of race-horses and brood mares, under the management of an Englishman. The jocks were negro lads; and when we arrived, about half a dozen of them were giving the colts a run in the paddock.

The Carolinians are true sportsmen, and in the South the Charleston races create almost as much sensation as our Derby at home. . . .

*June 10th.* At last *venit summa dies et ineluctabile tempus.* I had seen as much as might be of the best phase of the great institution— less than I could desire of a most exemplary, kind-hearted, clear-headed, honest man. In the calm of a glorious summer evening we crossed the Father of Waters, waving an adieu to the good friend who stood on the shore, and turning our backs to the home we had left behind us. It was dark when the boat reached Donaldsonville on the opposite "coast."

# BIBLIOGRAPHY

Part I—*The Old Dominion and Its Neighbors*

VIRGINIA, NORTH CAROLINA, KENTUCKY

"The Heartiest Style of Southern Hospitality"
George Ticknor, *Life, Letters and Journals*, I, edited by Anna Ticknor and George S. Hilliard. Boston: James R. Osgood and Company, 1876; Houghton Mifflin Company, 1909. By permission of Houghton Mifflin Company.

"The Kentuckians Are a High-Minded People"
Timothy Flint, *Recollections of the Last Ten Years*. Boston: Cummings, Hilliard and Company, 1826.

"There Are Few Houses in Virginia"
*Memoirs and Letters of Dolley Madison, Wife of James Madison, President of the United States*, edited by her grand-niece. Boston: Houghton Mifflin Company, 1886.

Insurrection in Southampton
Reprinted by permission of the publishers from L. Minor Blackford, *Mine Eyes Have Seen the Glory; the story of a Virginia Lady, Mary Berkeley Blackford*. Cambridge, Mass.: Harvard University Press. Copyright, 1954, by The President and Fellows of Harvard College.

"You Would Delight to Visit This Region"
Henry Barnard, "The South Atlantic States in 1833, As Seen by a New Englander," edited by Bernard C. Steiner, *Maryland Historical Magazine*, XIII (December, 1918). By permission of the *Maryland Historical Magazine*.

Thomas Dabney, Virginian
Susan Dabney Smedes, *Memorials of a Southern Planter*. Baltimore: Cushings and Bailey, 1887.

A Titled Visitor to the Tidewater
Charles Augustus Murray, *Travels in North America During the Years 1834, 1835, 1836*, I. New York: Harper and Brothers, 1839.

"I Am in the Very Best of Virginia Society"
"A New Englander's View of Plantation Life: Letters of Edwin Hall to Cyrus Woodman, 1837," edited by Larra Gara, *Journal of Southern History*, XVIII (August, 1952). By permission of the *Journal of Southern History*.

A Yankee Girl in North Carolina
"Plantation Experiences of a New York Woman," edited by James C. Bonner, *The North Carolina Historical Review*, XXXIII, no. 3 (July 1956), 384-412. State Department of Archives and History, Raleigh, N. C. By permission of Dr. Bonner.

A Tobacco Plantation in Virginia
Frederick Law Olmsted, *Journey in the Seaboard Slave States*. New York: Dix and Edwards, 1856.

"The World One Vast Plantation"
Letitia M. Burwell, *A Girl's Life in Virginia Before the War*. New York: Frederick A. Stokes Company, 1895.

A Virginia Boy Sees a Slave Auction
John S. Wise, *The End of an Era*. Boston: Houghton Mifflin Company, 1900. Copyright, 1899, by John S. Wise.


Part II—*In the Rice Kingdom*

SOUTH CAROLINA, GEORGIA, FLORIDA


Tutor to the Draytons of South Carolina
John Davis, *Personal Adventures and Travels of Four Years and a Half in the United States of America*. 1817.

A Refugee on a Georgia Plantation
Matthew L. Davis, *Memoirs of Aaron Burr*, II. New York: Harper and Brothers, 1836-37.

President Monroe Visits South Carolina
The *Winyaw Intelligencer*, Georgetown, S. C., April 24, 1819.

These Hospitable Planters
Captain Basil Hall, *Travels in North America, in the Years 1827 and 1828*, III. Edinburgh, 1830.

Affairs at Fort Hill
*Correspondence of John C. Calhoun,* edited by J. Franklin Jameson. American Historical Association, Annual Report, 1899.

A New Englander in South Carolina
Henry Barnard, "The South Atlantic States in 1833, As Seen by a New Englander," edited by Bernard C. Steiner, *Maryland Historical Magazine,* XIII (December, 1918). By permission of the *Maryland Historical Magazine.*

Country Life in the South
Harriet Martineau, *Retrospect of Western Travel.* London: Saunders and Otley, 1838.

"I Am a South Carolinian"
G. W. Featherstonhaugh, *Excursion Through the Slave States . . .* II. London, 1844.

Calhoun's Country
G. W. Featherstonhaugh, *A Canoe Voyage up the Minnay Sotor.* London: Bentley, 1847.

A Georgia Plantation
Frances Anne Kemble, *Journal of a Residence on a Georgian Plantation in 1838-1839.* New York, 1863.

A Planter's Observations
Francis W. Pickens to John C. Calhoun. Calhoun Papers, Clemson College Library, South Carolina.

"Dearest Papa"
Anne Sinkler Fishburne, *Belvidere: a Plantation Memory.* Columbia, S. C.: University of South Carolina Press, 1950. By permission of the University of South Carolina Press.

A Visit to St. Marys
Lester B. Shippee, *Bishop Whipple's Southern Diary, 1843-1844.* University of Minnesota Press, 1937. By permission of the University of Minnesota Press and Oxford University Press.

Hopeton Plantation at Darien, Georgia
Sir Charles Lyell, *A Second Visit to the United States of North America.* London, 1850.

Three Plantations
Fredrika Bremer, *The Homes of the New World: Impressions of America,* translated by Mary Howitt. New York: Harper and Brothers, 1853.

"If You Doubt My Word Come and See for Yourself"
"South Carolina through New England Eyes: Almira Coffin's Visit to the Low Country in 1851," edited by J. H. Easterby, *The South Carolina Historical and Genealogical Magazine,* XLV (1944). By permission of Dr. J. H. Easterby and the *South Carolina Historical and Genealogical Magazine.*

From the Journal of a Young Plantation Mistress
Ella Gertrude Clanton Thomas, *MS Journal.* By permission of Mrs. Gertrude Clanton Threlkeld, Atlanta, Georgia.

"There Is a Pleasant Land"
"Rambles at Random Through the Southern States," *Blackwood's Magazine,* January 1860.

General James Gadsden's Rice Plantation
Charles Mackay, *Life and Liberty in America: or, Sketches of a Tour in the United States and Canada in 1857-8.* New York: Harper and Brothers, 1859.

A Memoir of Slavery
I. E. Lowery, *Life of the Old Plantation in Ante-Bellum Days.* Columbia, S. C.: The State Company, 1911. By permission of The State Company.

Point Saint Pierre on Edisto Island
I. Jenkins Mikell, *Rumbling of the Chariot Wheels.* Columbia, S. C.: The State Company, 1923. By permission of Dr. I. Jenkins Mikell and The State Company.


Part III—*Cotton!*

TENNESSEE, ALABAMA, MISSISSIPPI, LOUSIANA, TEXAS, ARKANSAS


"The Planters Are the Prominent Feature"
J. F. H. Claiborne, *Life and Correspondence of John A. Quitman,* I. New York: Harper and Brothers, 1860.

Honeymoon at the Hermitage
Henry A. Wise, *Seven Decades of the Union.* . . . Philadelphia: J. B. Lippincott and Company, 1871.

From a Cotton Planter's Journal
Dick Hardaway Eggleston, *Diary,* 1830. From the Eggleston-Roach Papers, Department of Archives, Louisiana State University, Baton Rouge, Louisiana.

"Cotton Now Becomes the Staple of the Country"
G. W. Featherstonhaugh, *Excursion Through the Slave States from Washington on the Potomac to the Frontier of Mexico, with Sketches of Popular Manners and Geological Notices,* I. London: John Murray, 1844.

"Here We Lived in This Quiet Country Home"
Victoria V. Clayton, *White and Black Under the Old Regime.* Milwaukee: The Young Churchman Co., 1899.

Burleigh Plantation
Susan Dabney Smedes, *Memorials of a Southern Planter.* Baltimore: Cushings and Bailey, 1877.

Affairs at Yalobusha
John Spencer Bassett, *The Southern Plantation Overseer: as Revealed in His Letters.* Printed for Smith College, Northampton, Massachusetts. Copyright, 1925, by John Spencer Bassett.

"Never Have Seen as Mean a Spring"
Edwin Adams Davis, *Plantation Life in the Florida Parishes of Louisiana, 1836-1846, as Reflected in the Diary of Bennet H. Barrow.* New York: Columbia University Press, 1943. By permission of Columbia University Press.

Mississippi Wedding
Varina Howell Davis, *Jefferson Davis: A Memoir by His Wife,* I. New York: The Belford Company, 1890.

"This Has Been a Busy, But Very Happy Day"
Mahala Eggleston Roach, *Diary.* From the Eggleston-Roach Papers, Department of Archives, Louisiana State University, Baton Rouge, Louisiana.

Woodlands in Alabama
Sir Charles Lyell, A Second Visit to the United States of North America. London, 1850.

China Grove Plantation in Brazoria County, Texas
William Preston Johnston, The Life of General Albert Sidney Johnston. New York: D. Appleton and Company, 1879.

Peach Point Plantation in Texas
Abigail Curlee, "The History of a Texas Slave Plantation, 1831-63," The Southwestern Historical Quarterly, XXVI (October, 1922). By permission of The Southwestern Historical Quarterly.

Peach Point as Seen by a Famous Guest
Diary and Letters of Rutherford Birchard Hayes, edited by Charles Richard Williams. Columbus, O.: The Ohio Historical Society, 1922. By permission of The Ohio Historical Society.

"Short Crop—Short Journeys"
Mrs. Isaac H. Hilliard, Diary, 1849-50. Manuscript Collection in the Department of Archives, Louisiana State University. Baton Rouge, Louisiana.

"We Shall Be Proud Yet of Our Planter School of Gentlemen"
Nathaniel Parker Willis, Health Trip to the Tropics. New York: Charles Scribner's Sons, 1853.

Plague at Pass Christian
Susan Dabney Smedes, Memorials of a Southern Planter. Baltimore: Cushings and Bailey, 1887.

Further News from Yalobusha
John Spencer Bassett, The Southern Plantation Overseer: as Revealed in His Letters. Printed for Smith College, Northampton, Massachusetts. Copyright, 1925, by John Spencer Bassett.

Texas Springtime
Frederick Law Olmsted, A Journey Through Texas. New York: Mason Brothers, 1857.

"The Eden of Louisiana"
"Rambles at Random Through the Southern States," Blackwood's Magazine, January, 1860.

Wild Woods Plantation in Mississippi
From *Family Letters of the Three Wade Hamptons, 1782-1901*, edited by Charles E. Cauthen. Columbia, S. C.: University of South Carolina Press, 1953. By permission of the University of South Carolina Press.

"Mississippi Is a Cotton Growing State"
A. De Puy Van Buren, *Jottings of a Year's Sojourn in the South; or First Impressions of the Country and Its People. . . .* Battle Creek, Mich., 1859.

Between Woodville and Natchez
Frederick Law Olmsted, *A Journey in the Back Country*. New York: Mason Brothers, 1860.

"In the Calm of a Glorious Summer Evening"
William Howard Russell, *My Diary North and South*. New York: Harper and Brothers, 1863.

*Index*

# INDEX

Adams, Dr. Horatio, 185, 187
Adams, John Quincy, 104
Adams Run, S. C., 95
Albany Female Academy, 45
Albemarle County, Va., 37, 38, 39, 44
Alston, Aaron Burr, 186
Alston, Mrs. Charles, 186, 190
Alston, Joseph, 87, 186
Alston, Theodosia Burr, 87, 186
Altamaha River, 88, 90, 91, 143, 165, 166, 171, 183
Amelia Island, 158
Amélie, Queen, 37
Ashland Plantation, 390
Ashley Plantation, 245
Astor House, 191
Athens, Tenn., 93
Augusta Springs, 44
Austin, Stephen F., 317

Bacon, Lord Francis, 5
Baker's Institute, 218
Barbour, James, 13, 14
Barbour, Philip Pendleton, 8, 13, 14
Barbour, Thomas, 13, 16
Barksdale, H., 366, 374
Barnard, Betty, 22, 23, 109
Barnard, Chauncy, 22, 109
Barnard, Henry, 21-25, 108-111
Barrow, Bennet H., 287-295
Barrow, Emily Joor, 288
Barrow, Nancy Haile, 288
Barrow, William, II, 288
Bath, S. C., 104, 105
Baxter, Sally, see Hampton, Sally
Bayou Lafourche, La., 323
Bayou Place Plantation, 361
Bear Gardens Plantation, 361
Beaufort, S. C., 108, 109, 217
Bellevue, Va., 25, 26
Belmont Plantation, 192

Berkeley Plantation, 23, 32, 33
Bienvenu Plantation, 189
*Biographical Memoir of Daniel Boone*, Flint, 9
Birchard, Sardis, 318
Blackford, Mary Berkeley Minor, 14, 17-21
Blackford, William Matthews, 18
*Blackwood's Edinburgh Magazine*, 204, 355
Bleak Hall, 228
Bluff Plantation, 96
Bonaparte, Elizabeth Patterson, 14, 15
Bonaparte, Jerome, 14
Bonaparte, Napoleon, 14
Bonaventura Plantation, 215
Botany Bay, 228
Botetourt County, Va., 55, 56
Bowdoin College, 37
Bradford, Mary, 298
Brailsford, ———, 92
Brandon Plantation, 32, 33
Brannin, Miriam, see Hilliard, Mrs. Isaac H.
Bratton, George A., 279, 280, 282, 283-287, 343
Breckinridge, Mrs. Cary, 55
Bremer, Fredrika, 171-185, 381
Brewster, Charles Royall, 185
Brewster, Sallie, 196
Brierfield Plantation, 296, 301, 302, 303
Briers, the, 296, 300
Brookgreen Plantation, 148, 186
Brunswick, Ga., 87
Brush, Col. Platt, 235, 237
Bryan, Georgia, 196
Bryan, Guy M., 317, 318-323
Bryan, Mary, 317
Bryan, Moses Austin, 317
Bryan, William Joel, 317